ANCIENT GREEK CIVILIZATION

ANCIENT GREEK CIVILIZATION

Second Edition

David Sansone

WILEY-BLACKWELL

A John Wiley & Sons, Ltd., Publication

This second edition first published 2009
© 2009 David Sansone
Edition history: Blackwell Publishing Ltd (1e, 2004)

Blackwell Publishing was acquired by John Wiley & Sons in February 2007. Blackwell's publishing program has been merged with Wiley's global Scientific, Technical, and Medical business to form Wiley-Blackwell.

Registered Office
John Wiley & Sons Ltd, The Atrium, Southern Gate, Chichester, West Sussex, PO19 8SQ, United Kingdom

Editorial Offices
350 Main Street, Malden, MA 02148-5020, USA
9600 Garsington Road, Oxford, OX4 2DQ, UK
The Atrium, Southern Gate, Chichester, West Sussex, PO19 8SQ, UK

For details of our global editorial offices, for customer services, and for information about how to apply for permission to reuse the copyright material in this book please see our website at www.wiley.com/wiley-blackwell.

Library of Congress Cataloging-in-Publication Data
Sansone, David.
 Ancient Greek civilization / David Sansone. – This 2nd ed. 1st published 2009.
  p. cm.
 Includes bibliographical references and index.
 ISBN 978-1-4051-6732-1 (pbk. : alk. paper)
 1. Greece–Civilization–To 146 B.C. I. Title.
 DF77.S18 2009
 938–dc22

                                                                    2008026765

A catalogue record for this book is available from the British Library.

Set in 10.5/13pt Minion by Graphicraft Limited, Hong Kong
Printed in Singapore by C.O.S. Printers Pte Ltd

04 2011

CONTENTS

FIGURES

MAPS

TIMELINES

FOREWORD: LOOKING BACKWARD

In his last public speech in Mississippi City, March 1888, Jefferson Davis, former President of the Confederate States of America, said, "The past is dead," very much hoping that what he was saying might happen to be true. Another Southerner, the novelist William Faulkner, issued a stern corrective when, in his *Requiem for a Nun* (1951), he put into the mouth of a citizen of the fictional city of Jefferson, Mississippi, the following comment: "The past is never dead. It's not even past." The past, it seems, will always be with us. But it will not always be the same past. Rather, the past is in a constant process of change, as the ever-changing present increasingly imposes itself on the past. It is, perhaps, difficult to accept the notion that, for example, the civilization of the ancient Greeks, a civilization that no longer exists, is now in the process of change. We are, however, quite prepared to admit that ancient Greek civilization, while it was in existence, was constantly changing, since change is an invariable feature of living civilizations. One of the important ways civilizations change is by constantly modifying their perception of the shared past that serves as the civilization's foundation. As we will see, ancient Greek civilization was involved in a constant process of reinventing itself, by adapting its own past in the light of its own ever-changing present. We, too, have been reinventing ancient Greek civilization in a similar fashion. This process of reinventing ancient Greek civilization has been going on for quite some time. Indeed, there is a venerable tradition of doing so, a tradition that stretches from the time of the ancient Greeks themselves until this morning.

Reinventing Ancient Greek Civilization

Let us begin at a point within that tradition, somewhat closer to this morning than to the time of the ancient Greeks, so that we may have a better idea of what the nature of that tradition is. Lucas Cranach the Elder, who lived in sixteenth-century Germany, was court painter to Friedrich the Wise, Elector of Saxony, and friend of Martin Luther. Among Cranach's works, which include paintings of biblical subjects and austere portraits of princes and Protestant reformers, are representations of stories from Greek myth, among them a *Judgment of Paris* now in New York's Metropolitan Museum of Art (figure 1). The artist assumes that the viewer of the painting will be familiar with the story: the Greek goddesses Aphrodite, Athena,

Figure I Lucas Cranach the Elder (1472–1553), *The Judgment of Paris*, tempera and oil on wood, 102 × 71.2 cm, ca. 1528. New York, The Metropolitan Museum of Art, Rogers Fund, 1928 (28.221).

and Hera have been escorted by the god Hermes, who holds the prize for beauty that is to be awarded by the Trojan prince Paris (also known as Alexander) to the lucky winner. The setting of this encounter, according to the myth, is Mount Ida, in what is now northwestern Turkey. The landscape depicted in Cranach's painting, however, is conspicuously northern European and, indeed, is virtually the same as the landscape that appears in some of Cranach's portraits of his German contemporaries. Further, Paris is wearing medieval armor, rather than anything resembling what an ancient Greek would actually have worn, and the goddesses Hera and Athena are shown in the nude, as they never would have been shown in ancient Greek art (figure 2). In short, despite the fact that Cranach's painting purports to provide a pictorial representation of ancient Greek myth, the terms in which the myth is portrayed are recognizably those of sixteenth-century Germany.

Figure 2 Attic black-figure tripod-jar showing Hermes (center) leading Athena, Hera, and Aphrodite to Paris (right) for judgment; height 12.5 cm, ca. 570 BC. Paris, Musée du Louvre, CA 616 C; copyright Réunion des Musées Nationaux/Art Resource, NY; photo: Chuzeville.

It is easy enough to spot the inauthentic elements in Cranach's *Judgment of Paris* (or in some more recent depictions of ancient Greece, such as the films *Troy* or *300*). It is much more difficult to say what is genuine. But what do we mean, in this context, by "genuine" or "authentic"? The story of the judgment of Paris is just that: a story. It is concerned with gods and goddesses who never existed (although they were, of course, *thought* to exist) and with human beings who may or may not have existed and who may or may not have done what the story represents them as having done. Still, stories can tell us a great deal about the people among whom the stories circulate. Surely there is an authentic (or at least a *more* authentic) version of the story of the judgment of Paris which, if we can reconstruct it, will help us recover something of ancient Greek civilization? In any case, the ancient Greeks have a *history*. Can we not discover at least some "facts" about the ancient Greeks, or at least about some of the ancient Greeks?

As we will see, the English word "history" and the English word "story" have the same origin. They both derive from the Greek word *historia*, which was used by the Greeks of the fifth and fourth centuries BC to mean "investigations" or "the account derived from one's investigations." (The ancient Greek word for "story," by the way, is *mythos*, to which the English word "myth" owes its origin.) It may seem at first sight surprising that a word, like English "story," denoting a fictional or imaginary account shares its origin with a word associated with serious scholarly investigation. But in fact stories are told and histories are written for very much the same purpose, namely in order to make sense of, or to impose structure and coherence on, events. Just as histories need constantly to be revised and scientific theories need to be adjusted in light of new evidence, so stories take on different forms or are adapted for different audiences.

"It was up to him to judge among the three goddesses, that threefold bevy. Athena's 'gift' to Alexander was leadership in war and Trojan conquest of Greece. Hera promised Asia and the realms of Europe for him to rule, if Paris should judge in her favor. But Cyprian Aphrodite told of my good looks in extravagant terms and offered me to him if she were the one to take the prize for beauty." (Euripides, *Trojan Women* 925–31, Helen speaking)

The story of the judgment of Paris illustrates all of this particularly well. Lucas Cranach is only one of literally hundreds of artists, writers, and musicians, from antiquity until our own day, who have created versions of the story. Presumably, creative artists like Cranach or, in more recent times, Frederick Ashton, who choreographed a ballet entitled *The Judgment of Paris*, or Gore Vidal, who wrote a novel of that name, or Salvador Dalí, who made a drawing of the same name, have been attracted to the story because of its mythical resonance or its archetypal status, or simply because it is a "good story" and is familiar to the artist's audience. According to the myth, when the gods were celebrating the marriage of Peleus and Thetis, the goddess Eris, who cannot help stirring up trouble since her very name means "conflict," provoked a beauty contest involving the goddesses Aphrodite, Athena, and Hera. At the suggestion of Zeus, the three goddesses were led to Troy so that Paris could decide which of the three was the most beautiful. Aphrodite, the goddess of sexual attractiveness, bribed Paris with the promise of marriage to the attractive Helen. The bribe proved irresistible and Paris accordingly awarded the prize to Aphrodite. Marriage to Helen, however, was not without its difficulties, as Helen was already the wife of Menelaus, the king of Sparta. Nevertheless, Paris sailed across the Aegean Sea to Sparta, abducted Helen and brought her back to Troy. Understandably angry at the loss of his wife, Menelaus assembled a substantial military force and attacked the city of Troy. This was the beginning of the legendary Trojan War, a conflict that was to last for 10 years and was to provide material for poetry and song for thousands of years. Given the prominence of sex and violence, power and intrigue, moral issues and raw emotion, it is hardly surprising that this story has been told and retold through countless generations. But where does the myth originate and what does it really mean? Or is this even a meaningful question?

The earliest evidence we have for the story of the judgment of Paris is in works of Greek art that were created in the seventh century BC; that is, some time between 700 and 600 BC. The artists of these works are representing the story that appeared in verbal form in the epic poem called the *Cypria*, which perhaps dates from some time around 700 BC. Unfortunately, the poem itself has not survived, but a synopsis exists, and it is from this synopsis that the account given above has been drawn. (It is not at all unusual for our evidence for ancient Greek civilization to come to us in a form that requires amplification, supplementation, and reconstruction, not to mention outright invention.) There is no way of knowing for certain whether the poet of the *Cypria* invented the story of the judgment or was recounting a traditional story that had been told and retold through many centuries before 700 BC. Regardless of when the story originated, we can be confident that, even in its original form, it was concerned to relate events that had occurred in the distant past. For stories that introduce gods and mortals interacting on a familiar basis are naturally looking back to a remote time when, supposedly, it was common for gods to take a direct personal interest in human affairs. In other words, the Greeks of the seventh century BC were doing more or less what Lucas Cranach was doing over two thousand years later, conveying a story about the remote past in terms intelligible to an audience of contemporaries.

It is interesting to consider why artists and writers have always been so fond of setting their work in remote times and places. One reason, surely, is that it enables them to explore issues that could not be so easily addressed, or could not be addressed at all, in poems or paintings that depict the creator's own time and place. For Lucas Cranach, painting a scene from Greek myth offered the only opportunity to a serious artist of his strait-laced day of representing a figure in the nude. In similar

> "I don't for a minute believe that Hera and the virgin goddess Athena were so far deranged that the one would offer to deal the city of Argos to the barbarians and Pallas Athena would ever sell Athens into slavery to the Trojans, or that they went to Mount Ida because of frivolous pretensions over their good looks. Why in the world would the divine Hera have conceived such a desire for a beauty prize? So that she could snare a husband more worthy than Zeus? Was Athena on the prowl for marriage with one of the gods?"
> (Euripides, *Trojan Women* 971–9, Hecuba speaking)

fashion, we find ancient Greek artists and poets making use of the distant past to create in their works elements that their contemporaries would not accept if they had been set in their own day. In the fifth century BC, for example, the Athenian dramatist Euripides wrote a tragedy entitled *The Trojan Women*, which takes place immediately after the capture of Troy by Menelaus and the Greek forces. Both the Greek soldiers and the captive Trojan women are in agreement that Helen should be put to death for having caused so destructive a war. But they are willing to allow Helen to defend herself in a public debate, something that would have been unthinkable for a woman in fifth-century Athens but that could be imagined to be possible in the legendary past. Helen takes advantage of this opportunity to defend herself by placing the blame for causing the war on everyone but herself: the goddesses who bribed Paris to judge them most beautiful, Paris' parents who ignored a dream that foretold the doom that Paris would bring upon Troy, Menelaus for failing to prevent her abduction by Paris. In response to Helen's speech, Paris' mother Hecuba, the queen of Troy, argues that the whole story of the judgment of Paris is a pack of lies and that Helen is merely using it as a means of exculpating herself. What Euripides is doing, then, is to exploit the mythical past as a setting for a debate that could not have occurred in his own time, an intellectually sophisticated debate between two formidable women. But at the same time he is, through that debate, working out various ways in which that mythical past can be manipulated, constructed, even dismantled. And the participants in the debate use up-to-date rhetorical techniques and forms of argumentation that first came into existence centuries after the supposed date of the Trojan War. Thus there is a sense in which ancient Greek civilization was no more easily recoverable for the ancient Greeks themselves than it was for Lucas Cranach in the sixteenth century or is for us today.

Ancient Greece in Perspective: Time

Already, in only a few pages, reference has been made to a number of geographical locations (Troy, Sparta, the Aegean Sea) and a wide range of dates and periods, including 700 BC and the sixteenth century after Christ. We will encounter these and many other times and places as we learn about ancient Greek civilization, and it will be useful to ensure at this point that we are properly oriented both chronologically and geographically. The ancient Greeks were by no means isolated from other civilizations, and their interactions, both friendly and hostile, resulted in influences that enriched both the culture of the Greeks and the cultures of those peoples with whom they came in contact. Therefore, it will be necessary to take a brief look here at the broader Mediterranean setting in which the ancient Greeks and their neighbors lived. Also, since the Greeks were influenced by older, more advanced civilizations, and since their own influence extended, as we have seen, even into our own day, we need to view the culture of the ancient Greeks in the proper chronological perspective.

"According to the Egyptians, the reign of King Cheops lasted fifty years. After he died he was succeeded as king by his brother Chephren, who followed his brother's example in many respects. In particular, he too built a pyramid, but it did not measure up to the earlier one – I know this from having calculated the dimensions of both pyramids myself – nor did it have underground chambers or a moat supplied, like the other one, with water flowing into it from the Nile." (Herodotus, *The Histories* 2.127.1, on the Great Pyramid of Giza)

The most brilliant and most prominent manifestations of ancient Greek culture – the poems of Homer, the tragedies of Sophocles, the Parthenon in Athens, the philosophy of Plato, the career of Alexander the Great, the mathematical works of Archimedes – are in fact the products of a relatively brief period within the large span of Greek civilization. They all fall within the periods known as Archaic, Classical, and Hellenistic (see Timeline 1). Ancient Greek civilization itself is only a part of the great sweep of Mediterranean history that stretches back from today to the time of the earliest cultures for which we have reasonably detailed records. The Greeks seem to have been relative newcomers to the Mediterranean region, arriving at a time when other, more advanced, cultures had already established themselves. By the time the Greeks began to occupy the land that we know today as Greece, Egyptian civilization had been flourishing for several centuries; the great pyramid of Giza, one of the seven wonders of the ancient world, was already a venerable monument. In the Near East, the earliest versions of the Sumerian *Epic of Gilgamesh* were coming into being and the Akkadian Empire, founded by Sargon of Akkad, was being supplanted by the Babylonians, whose King Hammurabi was responsible for creating one of history's first attempts at a written codification of law.

In the course of time, the Greeks came into contact with the Egyptians and the Babylonians and, later, with other peoples, such as the Persians and the Phoenicians, whose presence affected the cultural landscape of the Mediterranean world.

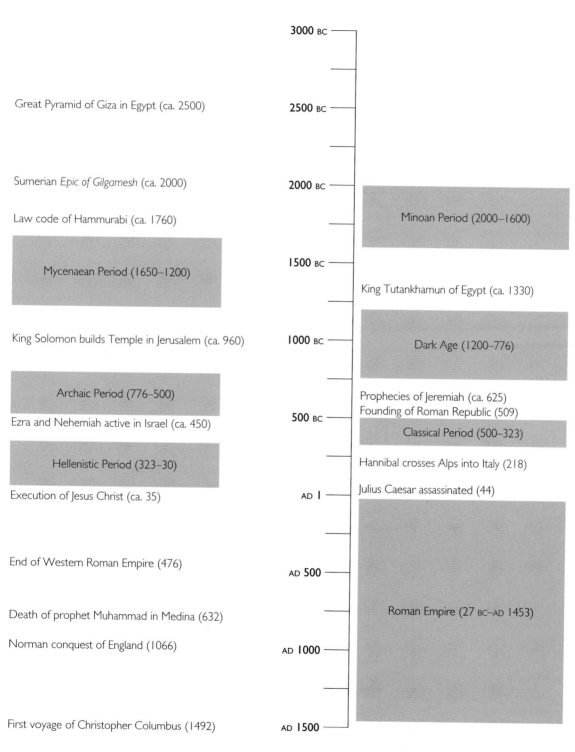

Great Pyramid of Giza in Egypt (ca. 2500)

3000 BC

2500 BC

Sumerian *Epic of Gilgamesh* (ca. 2000)

2000 BC

Law code of Hammurabi (ca. 1760)

Minoan Period (2000–1600)

Mycenaean Period (1650–1200)

1500 BC

King Tutankhamun of Egypt (ca. 1330)

King Solomon builds Temple in Jerusalem (ca. 960)

1000 BC

Dark Age (1200–776)

Archaic Period (776–500)

Prophecies of Jeremiah (ca. 625)

Ezra and Nehemiah active in Israel (ca. 450)

500 BC

Founding of Roman Republic (509)

Classical Period (500–323)

Hellenistic Period (323–30)

Hannibal crosses Alps into Italy (218)

Execution of Jesus Christ (ca. 35)

AD 1

Julius Caesar assassinated (44)

End of Western Roman Empire (476)

AD 500

Death of prophet Muhammad in Medina (632)

Roman Empire (27 BC–AD 1453)

Norman conquest of England (1066)

AD 1000

First voyage of Christopher Columbus (1492)

AD 1500

Timeline 1   Overview of ancient Greek civilization.

Eventually, the Greeks themselves were to assert themselves, both culturally and polit-ically, exerting a noticeable influence on their neighbors in the Mediterranean and beyond. In particular, the Roman Empire emerged in a context in which Greek cul-tural influence was pervasive and in which the Greek language was the recognized instrument of international communication. It was, for example, only to be expected that a Roman political figure of the stature of Julius Caesar should be bilingual and, according to the account of the ancient biographer Suetonius, Caesar's dying words, addressed to his (Roman!) assassin Brutus, were spoken in Greek. In the following century, the disciples of Jesus of Nazareth, wanting the message of their master to receive the widest possible circulation, wrote their accounts of the life and teaching of Jesus, not in their native Aramaic but in Greek, because at that time Israel belonged to a part of the Roman Empire that had long been dominated by Greek cultural influence.

The assassination of Julius Caesar occurred on March 15, 44 BC, the crucifixion of Jesus at the time of the Passover in some year around AD 35. These two events are, of course, of great historical significance, but they are also of interest to us as we try to orient ourselves chronologically in the ancient world. To begin with, one of these events is precisely dated to a particular day in a particular year; the other can only be assigned an approximate location in time. The reason for this is that our written sources chose to record the exact day and year of one event, but not of the other. As we will see, some events from antiquity can be precisely dated, but most cannot. The calendar that we use today is the calendar that the ancient Romans used; in fact, it was Julius Caesar himself who was responsible for an impor-tant reform of the calendar that took effect shortly before his death. That is, the number of months in our year and the number of days in each month, all of which is, of course, entirely arbitrary, is derived from the Roman calendar (along with the names of the months; July, for example, being named for Julius Caesar). The num-bering of the years, however, has to do instead with the Christian conviction that the birth of Jesus represents the beginning of a new era, so that the supposed year of Christ's birth is conventionally assigned the number 1, sometimes designated, as in this book, "AD 1" (an abbreviation for the Latin *anno domini* or "year of the lord"), sometimes "1 CE" (for "common" or "Christian era"). This is convenient, but it has the awkward consequence of requiring us to number the years before the birth of Christ (= "BC") in a descending order, so that a year with a larger number is *earlier* than a year with a smaller number. Similarly, the centuries are numbered in descending order, with the fifth century BC (that is, the years between 500 and 400 BC) coming before the fourth.

How, then, did the ancient Greeks and other people living before the birth of Christ, most of whom did not care and none of whom knew for a fact when the messiah was going to be born, number the years? Before we answer that question we need to understand the assumption underlying the question. We take it for granted that there is need of a consecutive numbering of years. The reason for this need, and the reason for the assumption, is that different peoples have entirely different methods of reckoning time and, when cultures come into contact with one another, it sometimes becomes necessary for them to find a means of coordinating their dates. A Roman, for example, would have referred to the year in which Julius

Caesar was assassinated as "the year in which Julius Caesar and Marc Antony were consuls," as each year was named after the two men who held the annual consulship in Rome. A Greek living in Egypt, on the other hand, might have referred to that year as "the eighth year of the reign of Queen Cleopatra." By the time of the assassination of Caesar, most Greeks were living under the rule either of the Roman Empire or of an eastern monarch. But at earlier periods in Greek history, in, say, the Classical Period, the Greeks lived in independent

> "The thirty-year truce that came into effect after the capture of Euboea lasted for fourteen years. But in the following year, at the time when Chrysis had been serving as priestess at Argos for forty-eight years, when Aenesias was ephor in Sparta, and when Pythodorus still had two months left in his term as archon of the Athenians, at the beginning of spring, six months after the battle of Potidaea, an armed band of a little over three hundred Thebans, shortly after nightfall, forced an entry into the Boeotian city of Plataea, which was then an ally of the Athenians." (Thucydides, *The Peloponnesian War* 2.2.1, describing an event in the year 431 BC)

city-states, each with its own calendar. One city might refer to a given year as the year in which so-and-so held an annual magistracy; another might use the office of a particular priesthood as a point of reference. Given the fact that a citizen of Thebes might not know when Chrysis was priestess of Hera at Argos or how long she had served – not to mention the lack of agreement among cities regarding the day on which the "year" was thought to begin – it eventually became clear to the Greeks and others that some standardized system of reckoning was desirable. One thing that all Greeks held in common was the worship of Olympian Zeus, in whose honor the Olympic Games, traditionally founded in 776 BC, were held every fourth year. This made possible a universal system of dating, and so any Greek could make sense of a reference to the assassination of Julius Caesar as having occurred "in the fourth year of the 183rd Olympiad." Other peoples also have chosen a fixed point in reference to which all later events could be dated. The Muslim calendar begins with the Hijra, the withdrawal of Muhammad to Medina in AD 622, while the Hebrew calendar eliminates the problem of dating events that occurred before "year one" by starting with the creation of the world, which is supposed to have occurred some 3717 years before the assassination of Julius Caesar.

Ancient Greece in Perspective: Space

Surprisingly, orienting ourselves in space is less straightforward than orienting ourselves chronologically. For, as it happens, it is easier to mark off the even flow of time into uniform segments than to draw stable boundaries on the seemingly solid surface of the earth. Today, Greece is a nation with more or less fixed borders and a secure place on the map (map 1). That has not always been the case. Indeed, the modern nation of Greece dates only from 1829, when the Greeks secured independence, following a lengthy insurgency, from the Ottoman Empire. At that time, however, the nation's borders were not identical with those of modern-day Greece, which are a product of the tumultuous history of the twentieth century. (To

Map 1 Modern Greece and its neighbors.

provide a sense of scale, let us note that, in area, the modern country of Greece is almost exactly the same size as England in the United Kingdom or the state of New York in the United States.) When we use the term "Greece" in reference to an earlier period, we are using the word not so much in a geographical sense as a shorthand expression meaning "the area inhabited by Greek-speaking people." For the past 4,000 years that area has included the land now occupied by the modern Greek state, but at various times it has encompassed a great deal of additional territory.

For this reason, the land shown in map 2 has no boundaries marked. That is, it is not what is called a "political map" like map 1. Rather, it is a "physical map" showing the most prominent topographical features of the lands bordering the Mediterranean Sea, with terrain at higher levels represented by correspondingly darker shades. The Aegean Sea separates two land masses, that to the east being occupied today by the country of Turkey and that to the west by the modern country of Greece. In addition, there is a large number of islands strewn over the Aegean Sea, most of which are now part of Greece, as they have been since ancient times. It is this region, consisting of the southern tip of the Balkan Peninsula and the Aegean islands,

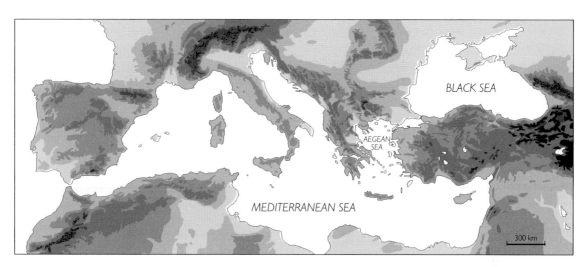

Map 2   Physical map of the Mediterranean region.

along with a narrow strip of land along the western coast of what is now Turkey, that represents what the Greeks considered to be their homeland throughout antiquity. It is important to understand the character of that homeland because the geography and climate of Greece and the Aegean represent the one constant in Greek civilization. It is also clear that the physical characteristics of the land in which the Greeks lived have to some extent influenced the way in which their civilization developed.

The most notable feature of the Greek landscape is the degree to which it is fragmented. The mainland is broken up by a series of mountain ridges that divide much of Greece into a number of relatively small pockets of habitable territory. And the islands, of which there are dozens in the Aegean Sea and a few more in the Ionian Sea to the west of mainland Greece, are merely a continuation of this series of ridges, so that, in geological terms, the only difference between the mainland and the islands is that the lowest points of the former are not under water. In fact, the sea poses less of a barrier than many of the irregularities of the terrain. For this reason, it is the islands and the areas of the mainland nearest the coast that have been the most active in cultural, social, and economic terms throughout much of Greek history. The abundance of good harbors along the Aegean coast and among the Aegean islands meant that there were frequent contacts between the Greeks and their Mediterranean neighbors, especially those in North Africa and western Asia. As we will see, these features of topography had two important effects on the way in which Greek civilization developed. In the first place, relatively easy access to the (generally more advanced) cultures of Asia and Egypt resulted in an openness to foreign influence, and the adoption and transformation of the artistic and technological advances of non-Greek peoples were to become characteristic of Greek civilization. In the second place, the fragmentation of the Greek landscape encouraged the development of numerous discrete and autonomous communities, in contrast to the more cen-tralized administrations of Egypt and the Near East.

This fragmentation is not restricted to the division of Greece by physical barriers into isolated communities. Even within a narrowly defined geographical area, differences in terrain and climate can be surprisingly diverse. The success of agriculture depends upon such factors as the quality and depth of the soil and the amount and timing of rainfall. Since these determinants can vary greatly not only between neighboring communities but even within communities, we find a quite uneven distribution of wealth both between and within communities. It should be understood that this uneven distribution existed within a rather narrow range. Greece is not well endowed with natural resources, and so a king of Sparta could tell the Persian King Xerxes, in an account by the historian Herodotus, "Greece and Poverty have always had to share the same rations." But the more scarce the resources, the greater the competition for them. So we will see that ancient Greek civilization developed as it did in part out of a need to minimize the ruinous effects of this competition and to maximize the benefits of the limited resources. Those resources include land variously suitable for the cultivation of grapevines, olives, and some grains (wheat and, more widely, barley), pasture land (for sheep, goats, swine, donkeys, mules, and, in a few locations, cattle and horses), and very widely scattered mineral deposits (iron and copper for tools and weapons, limestone and marble for building and sculpture, clay for ceramics, and silver for display). Greece is not, however, well supplied with spacious, fertile plains or large, hardwood forests. For this reason, whenever the population of Greece expanded beyond a certain point, it became necessary either for some Greeks to migrate to other areas within the Mediterranean region or for increasing numbers of goods to be imported into Greece. In either case, the most attractive areas were the same: the region around the Black Sea, whose forests supplied timber for shipbuilding and whose rich agricultural lands provided grain, and the coasts of Italy, Sicily, France, Spain, and, sporadically, North Africa. All these places, because of their easy access by sea and their availability of fertile land, became destinations for Greek traders and settlers.

> "I am aged Euphro, with no large holdings in many-furrowed land or vineyards gushing with wine. My plow etches a groove in scanty soil and my drink is a trickle from a handful of grapes. With meager means I can only give meager, though grateful, return; grant me more, divine spirit, and more will be your share." (Apollonides, *The Greek Anthology* 6.238)

Recommended for Further Reading

Braudel, F. *Memory and the Mediterranean* (New York 2001): the great sweep of ancient Mediterranean history by the man described in Oswyn Murray's introduc-tion as "the greatest historian of the twentieth century" (also published in London as *The Mediterranean in the Ancient World*).

Holford-Strevens, L. *The History of Time: A Very Short Introduction* (Oxford 2005): a fascinating account of how time has been measured throughout history, by a classicist who reads forty languages and writes engagingly in plain English.

Osborne, R. *Classical Landscape with Figures: The Ancient Greek City and its Countryside* (London 1987): an authoritative account of the landscape of Greece and its influence on the development of Greek civilization.

Pomeroy, S. B., Burstein, S. M., Donlan, W., and Roberts, J. T. *Ancient Greece: A Political, Social, and Cultural History*, 2nd edition (New York and Oxford 2008): a detailed, reliable, and up-to-date history of Greece from the earliest times until the Hellenistic Period.

THE GREEKS AND THE BRONZE AGE

1

The Bronze Age (ca. 3000 to 1200 BC) marks for us the beginning of Greek civilization. This chapter presents the arrival, in about 2000 BC, of Greek-speakers into the area now known as Greece and their encounter with the two non-Greek cultures that they found on their arrival, the civilizations known as Cycladic and Minoan. Cycladic civilization is notable for fine craftsmanship, especially its elegantly carved marble sculptures. The people of the Minoan civilization developed large-scale administrative centers based in grand palaces and introduced writing to the Aegean region. These and other features of Minoan civilization influenced greatly the form taken by Greek civilization in its earliest phase, the Mycenaean Period (ca. 1650 to 1200 BC). Unlike Cycladic and Minoan civilizations, which were based on the islands in the Aegean Sea, Greek civilization of the Mycenaean Period had its center in mainland Greece, where heavily fortified palaces were built. These palaces have provided archaeologists with abundant evidence of a warlike society ruled by powerful kings. Also surviving from the Mycenaean Period are the earliest occurrences of writing in the Greek language, in the form of clay tablets using the script known as "Linear B." This script, along with Mycenaean civilization as a whole, came to an end around 1200 BC for reasons that are not at all clear to historians.

Of all human activities language is the most misleading. We have already noted that the words "story" and "history" are in origin the same word, in spite of our desire to believe that the one is, in some sense, truth and the other fiction. This belief is encouraged by the practice of ancient historians, who distinguish between the "historical" and "prehistoric" periods of a given culture on the basis of the existence of written records, as though direct access to a people's words provides truthful – or more truthful – evidence of their lives. The fact is that humans have always communicated with one another, using either transitory means (the spoken word and signing) or, more recently, recorded forms (writing, recorded sound, and so on). It is only for the historian, looking to the past, that the presence or absence of recorded language marks a decisive distinction. Not only does access to the written word induce the historian into feeling a specious kinship with the more "articulate" people of historical periods, in contrast to the "silent" totality of their prehistoric ancestors, but it enables the historian to distinguish between the speakers of one language and those of another. So, the historian can speak of "the ancient Egyptians" or "the Hittites" because the people who spoke those languages left behind written records. But for the prehistoric period we find ourselves using designations like "Hopewell culture" to refer to a particular native people of North America or "Magdalenian culture" in connection with the inhabitants of the Dordogne region of France during the Upper Paleolithic. There is no way of knowing what language was spoken by the people of the Magdalenian culture or whether all the people of the Hopewell culture spoke the same language.

In the absence of written records, historians and archaeologists must use other features of a people's culture to distinguish one group from another, features such as the style of their ceramic ware or the method by which they dispose of their dead. If, therefore, we place the beginning of Greek "history" at the point at which we begin to find written records left by Greek-speakers, we are in effect defining Greek history in terms of our own concerns over access to a particular form of evidence. As it happens, of all languages Greek is the one for which there exists the longest continuous record, extending from the fourteenth century BC until the latest edition of this morning's Athenian newspaper. But the Greek people existed before that time and they spoke to one another using a form of the Greek language. It is our problem, not theirs, that they are more difficult to trace in the period before they began to write, the period that we refer to as their "prehistory." That problem extends even to the questions of when the Greeks began to occupy the land around the Aegean Sea and where they lived before that. Many scholars are now convinced that the Greeks first migrated into the Aegean region at some time shortly before 2000 BC and that they came there from the area of the steppes to the north of the Black Sea. Interestingly, while the evidence for the date is largely of an archaeological nature, the evidence for the place is primarily linguistic.

Greek is a member of the Indo-European family of languages, a family that comprises a number of languages spoken by peoples who have inhabited Europe and Asia. The Celtic, Germanic, Baltic, and Slavic languages are examples of European

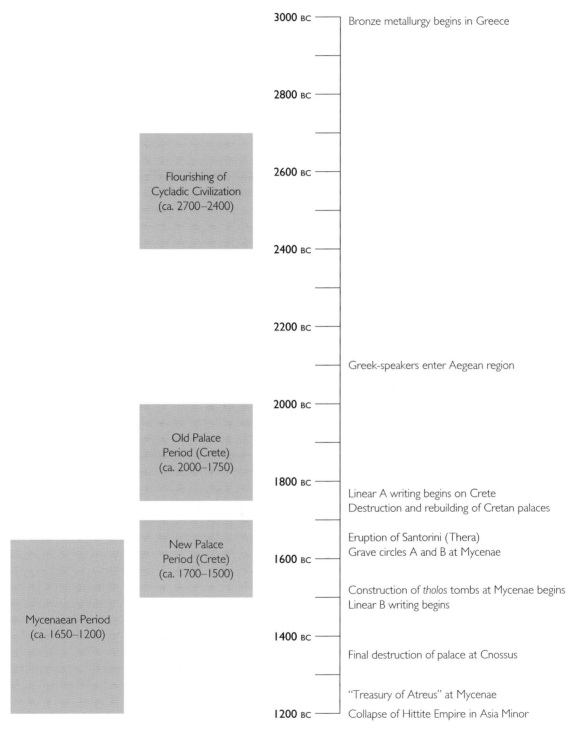

	3000 BC — Bronze metallurgy begins in Greece
	2800 BC
Flourishing of Cycladic Civilization (ca. 2700–2400)	2600 BC
	2400 BC
	2200 BC
	— Greek-speakers enter Aegean region
Old Palace Period (Crete) (ca. 2000–1750)	2000 BC
	1800 BC — Linear A writing begins on Crete / Destruction and rebuilding of Cretan palaces
New Palace Period (Crete) (ca. 1700–1500)	Eruption of Santorini (Thera) / Grave circles A and B at Mycenae
	1600 BC
	Construction of *tholos* tombs at Mycenae begins / Linear B writing begins
Mycenaean Period (ca. 1650–1200)	1400 BC — Final destruction of palace at Cnossus
	"Treasury of Atreus" at Mycenae
	1200 BC — Collapse of Hittite Empire in Asia Minor

Timeline 2   The Bronze Age.

Indo-European		Non-Indo-European	
Greek	NYX	Arabic	LEL
Danish	NAT	Basque	GAU
German	NACHT	Chinese	HĒIYÈ
Hittite	NEKUZ	Finnish	YÖ
Latin	NOX	Hungarian	ÉJ
Lithuanian	NAKTIS	Indonesian	MALAM
Old Norse	NŌTT	Shoshoni	DUGAANI
Polish	NOC	Swahili	USIKU
Sanskrit	NAKTAM	Turkish	GECE
Spanish	NOCHE	Xhosa	UBUSUKU
Welsh	NOS		

Figure 3   The word for "night" in some Indo-European and non-Indo-European languages.

branches of the Indo-European family, while Sanskrit, Persian, and Hittite are Indo-European languages spoken in Asia. (When we speak of a "family" of languages we are using the word in the sense of a group of languages that are descended from a common ancestor, which in this case is a language that is no longer spoken but which can be hypothetically reconstructed on the basis of its descendants' common features; see figure 3.) There is evidence of considerable movement of peoples who spoke Indo-European languages in the period around 2000 BC, and it is widely believed that it was in connection with this movement that Greek-speakers migrated into mainland Greece at roughly this time. Archaeological evidence exists that seems to be consistent with the appearance in Greece of a new group, or of new groups, of people in the centuries just before about 2000 BC, but the evidence is difficult to interpret and not all scholars are convinced that it necessarily points to a large-scale movement of people. The character of the artifacts that archaeologists have uncovered in mainland Greece from this period exhibits significant differences from the immediately preceding period, and several sites on the mainland have revealed evidence of destruction at this time. But the destruction is not universal, nor does it follow a neat pattern that might suggest the gradual progress of a new, belligerent population. If this is the period in which the Greeks first made their home in mainland Greece, it appears that we should think not so much in terms of a hostile invasion as a steady infiltration that resulted, here and there, in localized outbreaks of violence.

Clearly, then, the Aegean region was not unoccupied when the people we know as the Greeks appeared on the scene. Whom did the Greeks encounter when they arrived and what happened to the earlier populations of Greece and the islands when the Greek-speakers entered the region? Unfortunately, because we are dealing with a period from which no written records survive, we are not in a position to know very much about who these people were or how long they had occupied the land that they were now forced to share with the Greek newcomers. For the evidence suggests that they did not simply disappear, their place being taken by a new group of inhabitants. As we will see, we do have written records for a slightly later period from the large island of Crete, records that show that the non-Greek language of Crete continued in use until around 1500 BC. If the Greeks had driven out the earlier inhabitants or killed them off (for which, in any event, we have no evidence in the archaeological record), the language would have disappeared as well. In fact, communities of people who spoke a non-Greek language are said to have existed on Crete well into the first millennium BC. So it seems inevitable that Greek-speakers and non-Greek-speakers co-existed for an extended period of time. Eventually, the Greek language prevailed over the other language or languages, but recognition of that fact does not help us to know what happened to these non-Greek-speakers. Presumably, they and their descendants learned Greek and became themselves Greek-speakers. Also, presumably, they intermarried with the newly arrived Greek-speakers, so that the later population of Greece was a mixture, with any given individual increasingly likely, in the passage of time, to have among his or her ancestors members of both groups.

The pre-Greek population of the Aegean region included two groups of people who left behind evidence of remarkable cultural achievements. While we cannot be certain of the details regarding the extent and duration of the Greeks' interactions with these people, there can be no doubt that they left an enduring imprint on the later development of Greek culture. These people lived on the islands in and around the Aegean Sea, but their contacts with and influence upon the inhabitants of the Greek mainland are apparent. The first group flourished on the cluster of about two dozen islands east of the Peloponnese known as the Cyclades (map 3). For this reason, and because we do not know what these people called themselves, modern scholars have given the name "Cycladic" to this culture. The second group was located on the large island of Crete, but their culture, which we refer to as "Minoan" civilization, eventually imposed itself on much of the southern Aegean basin. Evidence for the existence of both these peoples was lost for thousands of years, emerging only as a result of archaeological exploration in the late nineteenth and early twentieth centuries.

Cycladic Civilization

Cycladic civilization arose around 3200 BC; that is, at about the time of the transition from the Neolithic Period (the "New Stone Age") to the Bronze Age. Its most impressive achievements date to the period from approximately 2700 to approximately 2400 BC and represent a stunning advance in terms of their artistic sophistication. The most striking creations that have survived from Cycladic civilization are a large number of marble figures (figure 4). It had been a widespread practice in Neolithic communities, both in Greece and elsewhere, to create representations of nude females in clay or stone, often referred to as "fertility figures" or "mother goddesses." These figures are generally crudely executed, and it is not known for

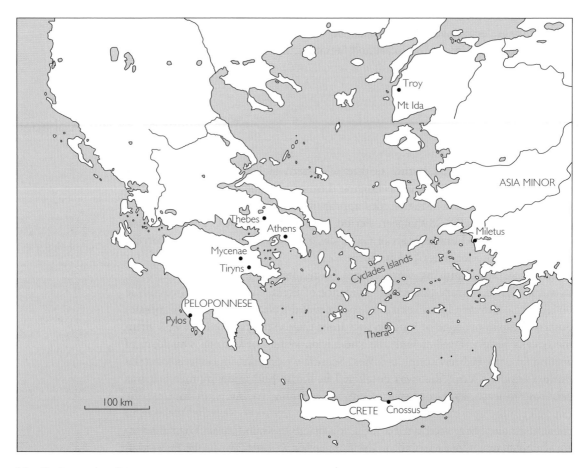

Map 3   Bronze Age Greece.

what purpose they were made. Such figures were created by the Neolithic inhabitants of the Cyclades as well. By the middle of the third millennium BC, however, Cycladic culture had evolved, apparently by a process of internal development and not from outside influences, to the point of creating remarkably refined and elegant marble sculptures. The majority of them, like the one illustrated here, represent nude females. The materials used to create these objects were all available in (and presumably all came from) the Cyclades: fine marble for the figures themselves, emery and obsidian for carving and incising, pumice for smoothing by abrasion.

We tend to think of these figures as "works of art," but the concept of a "work of art" that is created for solely aesthetic enjoyment seems not yet to have existed. These figures were made to serve a particular *function*, but we happen not to know what that function was. Nearly all of the figures that archaeologists have recovered had been buried in tombs along with the remains of the deceased, but this does not mean that the figures were necessarily *created* to serve as burial goods. They may have served some ritual function for some period before they were buried with

Figure 4 Marble Cycladic sculpture, front and side views; height 39.1 cm, ca. 2400 BC. Athens, Museum of Cycladic and Ancient Greek Art, no. 206; copyright N. P. Goulandris Foundation – Museum of Cycladic Art, Athens.

their owner or with someone else, perhaps someone of particular status. Regardless of the purpose or purposes for which they were made, these Cycladic sculptures are notable in a number of respects. Like the earlier Neolithic sculpture, these figures continue to represent females in the nude, a practice that was generally abandoned elsewhere during the Bronze Age. On the other hand, Cycladic civilization shares a feature that appears elsewhere at this period only in the urban civilizations of Egypt and Mesopotamia, namely the practice of creating large-scale sculpture. Some of the Cycladic works are life-sized or nearly life-sized, yet there is no evidence of contact between the people of the Cyclades and the people of those other civilizations.

The figures are characterized by a strict adherence to a canon of proportions that appears to have been developed locally and without influence from elsewhere. Cycladic sculptors apparently approached the creation of their works by marking off the block of marble with a compass, dividing it into segments according to strict formulas. The most significant feature of Cycladic sculpture is its two-dimensionality: it seems almost to abandon volume in order to concentrate on form and contour as apprehended by the visual sense. This abstract, almost rationalizing, character of Cycladic art sets it apart from the art of other contemporary civilizations. Nor did Cycladic art exercise an influence beyond a very limited geographical area. We find Cycladic sculptures imported only into the island of Crete and parts of the mainland of Greece.

Minoan Civilization

"According to oral tradition Minos is the first person to have established a naval power, and he held sway over much of the Aegean Sea. He controlled the Cyclades Islands and was the first to found colonies on most of them, first driving out the Carians and then appointing his own sons as governors. Naturally, he did his best to eliminate piracy from the Aegean in order to maximize the flow of revenues that came to him." (Thucydides, *The Peloponnesian War* 1.4)

After about 2000 BC, however, the Cyclades fell under the influence of a civilization that developed on the island of Crete and that came to dominate the Aegean area generally and much of southern mainland Greece. We refer to this new force in the Aegean world as the "Minoan" civilization, although we do not know what the people of this civilization called themselves. The term "Minoan" is a modern creation used by the archaeologists who first investigated the remains of this culture and wished to give it a name that indicated its distinct character. The name was chosen under the influence of myths that survive from the later, historical period of Greece. These myths tell of a powerful king, Minos, who ruled the prominent city of Cnossus on the north coast of Crete and who exercised considerable naval power in the Aegean. The myths clearly represent Minos as a Greek king, but the civilization of Minoan Crete turns out not, in fact, to have been Greek at all. We can see, then, in the naming of Minoan civilization after King Minos another illustration of the influence of stories on the construction of the past and we may recognize our own willing collusion with the ancient Greeks in the invention of their history.

"And then I saw Minos, the glorious son of Zeus, holding a scepter made of gold and dispensing justice among the dead. While he was seated in majesty they would ask him to render judgment for them, some seated and some standing, there in the house of Hades with its massive gates." (Homer, *Odyssey* 11.568–71, Odysseus describing his visit to the Underworld)

Our knowledge of Minoan civilization dates only from the late nineteenth century, since which time excavations have been carried out at Cnossus and at some other locations on Crete. Those excavations have given us very extensive and detailed evidence of a remarkable culture very different in character from the Cycladic civilization that it overshadowed. The most striking difference is that, while the people of the Cycladic civilization lived scattered over the surface of the islands in small settlements, Minoan civilization is characterized by the construction of vast, complex structures that archaeologists refer to as "palaces." These palaces were the focus of large, centralized communities. The island of Crete was divided up into a small number of regions and each of these regions was administered from the palace and its immediately surrounding community. By 2000 BC these palaces were already extensive and impressive structures, but in the period from about 2000 to about 1500 they were expanded and developed, even being rebuilt on a grander scale following devastating earthquakes that occurred around 1700.

The palace at Cnossus (figure 5) is the largest and most impressive, but it is similar in plan to the other Minoan palaces, with a large rectangular central court surrounded by very many smaller rooms, hallways, stairways, and storage areas. These palaces were built in open areas that allowed them to grow by accretion over time. They were complex, sophisticated structures built on more than one level, with lightwells providing air and illumination to lower levels and with advanced drainage facilities for sanitation. The palaces were the center of what has come to be known as a "redistributive economy," similar to the palace economies known from contemporary societies in western Asia. The extensive storage areas of the palace

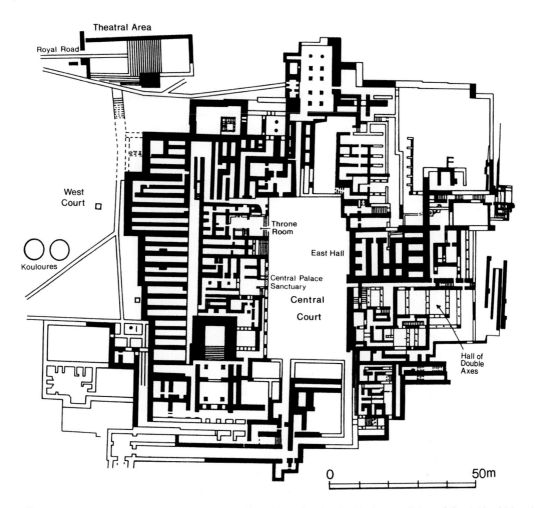

Figure 5 Plan of the Minoan palace at Cnossus, ca. 1600–1500 BC. Reprinted with the permission of Cambridge University Press from O. Dickinson, *The Aegean Bronze Age* (Cambridge 1994), fig. 5.26.

served as a central location where produce and raw materials, presumably paid to the ruler or rulers in the form of taxes, could be kept, inventoried, and used in the production of manufactured goods. These "taxes" (perhaps "protection money" paid to racketeers is a more appropriate modern analogue) could then be redistributed to the populace at the will of the ruler(s) or used as a medium of trade both within and outside Crete. And indeed there is evidence of lively economic activity between Minoan Crete and the Aegean islands, mainland Greece, Egypt, and western Asia.

The level of administration required to maintain an economy of this nature and to monitor inventory on hand may have provided the incentive behind the development of a system of writing, which is found in Europe for the first time during the Minoan Period. While the idea of using graphic symbols to represent spoken language seems to have been taken over by the people of Minoan Crete from elsewhere, the specific form of the script that developed on Crete, apparently in the eighteenth century BC, has no known connection with other ancient systems of writing. The Minoan script, which archaeologists refer to as "Linear A," came to be widely used in Crete, particularly in the eastern half of the island, and in some Aegean islands. It is found engraved on gemstones, which were used as seals, and written on tablets of moist clay, which were used as records of inventory. Both engraved seal stones and inscribed clay tablets are also found in earlier and contemporary Near Eastern civilizations, and it is presumably from them that the Minoans adopted this practice.

The appearance of Minoan writing elsewhere in the Aegean is one of several indications of the expansion of Minoan civilization beyond the island of Crete. On the Cycladic island of Thera, for example, archaeologists are discovering extensive evidence of Minoan cultural influence, both in the form of goods imported from Crete and goods created locally that imitate, sometimes quite closely, Minoan artistic style. As it happens, we are unusually well informed regarding the material culture of Minoan Thera. Today known as Santorini, the island of Thera is in fact the top of a volcano, which erupted with such violence that scientists have been able to detect evidence of volcanic ash from the eruption as far away as Greenland (figure 6). Through a combination of ice-core analysis, radiocarbon dating, and examination of tree-ring sequences, it has been possible to assign a date to the eruption of Santorini with some confidence to within a few years of 1625 BC. Fortunately for the inhabitants, there was apparently enough warning of the eruption that they were able to escape the island, taking with them (unfortunately for us) many of their valuable and portable belongings. Still, the excavations that have been carried out on Thera since the 1960s, along with those on Crete and elsewhere, have sufficed to reveal the existence of a vibrant and animated civilization characterized by an exuberant artistic temperament that presents a marked contrast to the restrained elegance of Cycladic art (see FRESCO in figure 7). It is perhaps not too fanciful to view the remainder of the long tradition of Greek self-expression in the visual arts as an attempt to balance these two conflicting and complementary tendencies.

FRESCO Painting in watercolor on a wall or ceiling whose mortar or plaster is still fresh and moist, so that the colors sink in and become more durable (figures 7 and 74).

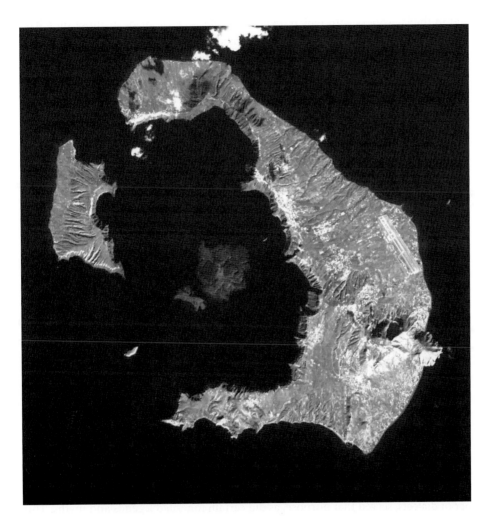

Figure 6 ASTER image of Santorini (Thera) taken on November 21, 2000 from NASA's Terra spacecraft. Image courtesy NASA and The Visible Earth (http://visibleearth.nasa.gov).

The Greeks Speak Up

Historians refer to the period that immediately succeeded the Minoan as the "Mycenaean Period" or the period in which "Mycenaean" civilization was dominant in mainland Greece and the Aegean. We saw above that the term "Minoan civilization" is a modern confection created with ingredients deriving from ancient Greek myth. The same is true of the name of Mycenaean

"And Agamemnon placed his helmet upon his head, a helmet made of four sheets of metal, with two horns and a horsehair crest that nodded menacingly over all. He took up a pair of sturdy spears fitted with sharp points of bronze, and the gleam of the bronze shone forth from him into the far-off heavens. And about him Athena and Hera made the thunder ring out, paying tribute to the lord of Mycenae, rich in gold." (Homer, *Iliad* 11.41–6)

Figure 7 Detail of fresco from Akrotiri, Thera (Santorini); height of figure 78.4 cm, ca. 1700 BC. Photograph by Jürgen Liepe, reproduced by courtesy of The Thera Foundation from Ch. Doumas, *The Wall Paintings of Thera*, Idryma Theras-Petros M. Nomikos (Athens 1992), p. 154, no. 118.

civilization, which is derived from the name of the city of Mycenae. Archaeological excavation at the site of Mycenae, on mainland Greece, has revealed that it possessed considerable wealth and power in the period beginning in about 1700 BC. But the same can be said of some other mainland Greek cities at this time. The reason Mycenae has been singled out to provide a name for this period of prosperity is that Agamemnon, the mythical king of Mycenae, was supposed to have been the leader of the Greek forces in the Trojan War. According to the poet Homer, Mycenae sent a larger contingent of troops to fight at Troy than any other Greek city. Accordingly, we now refer to this earliest period of Greek civilization as "Mycenaean."

It is legitimate to refer to this as a period of *Greek* civilization because, as we will see, the people who lived in Mycenae and other cities of mainland Greece at this time were indeed Greek-speakers. Mycenaean civilization, then, was the earliest expression of Greek culture for which we have any evidence, and it was located primarily in the settlements of mainland Greece, in contrast to the Cycladic and Minoan civilizations, which were non-Greek or pre-Greek civilizations of the Aegean islands. No written records remain from Cycladic civilization, but the people of Minoan Crete used the form of writing known as Linear A. The Linear A tablets record the language of administration in Minoan Crete, and that language was apparently not Greek. There is evidence, however, that by the fourteenth century BC the language of administration at Cnossus either had become or was well on the way to becoming Greek. It is possible to account for this change in a number of different ways, but the most attractive explanation is that control of the palace at Cnossus (and of the palaces elsewhere on Crete) had begun to pass into the hands of a different group of people, people from the mainland who spoke Greek.

Along with the Linear A tablets, archaeologists also uncovered over five thousand tablets written in a script that is later than and different from Linear A. This script, called "Linear B," is clearly derived from Linear A and is, therefore, its lineal descendant, so to speak. Tablets in the Linear B script have been found on Crete and in a few locations on the mainland, dating from the end of the fourteenth to the beginning of the twelfth century BC. While the Linear A tablets record a language that is almost certainly not Greek, the Linear B tablets represent the earliest evidence in written form of the Greek language. We know this as a result of a brilliant feat of decipherment by the British architect and amateur linguist Michael Ventris. In 1952, the 30-year-old Ventris showed that the Linear B tablets are a record of an early form of Greek. Linear B is a syllabary, a system of writing in which each symbol represents a syllable, like *do re mi*. Some languages, like modern Japanese, are well suited to representation by a syllabary; some, like English, are not. So, for example, the Japanese syllabary requires three symbols to represent the monosyllabic English word "golf": *go-ru-fu*. Greek is like English in this regard, and the Linear B script rather awkwardly represents the Greek language. This is understandable since Linear B is derived from Linear A, which was designed to represent a language unrelated to Greek. We can see this in the Linear B tablet shown in figure 8, which gives an inventory of vessels and other household items of various sorts. The first word in line 2, for example, is a form of the Greek word KRATER, a "mixing bowl" (the origin of the English word "crater"), in the Linear B script, here represented by the four syllabic signs having the value *ka-ra-te-ra*. Line 4 records the fact that eight TRIPODS are on hand, giving a form of the Greek word *tripodiskos* as *ti-ri-po-di-ko*. (Words printed in small capitals, like KRATER and TRIPOD above, can be found in the Glossary at the back of this book.) It should be noted that all forms of writing are merely approximations of a spoken language. We will see later that the Greeks eventually came to use a more satisfactory system of writing than Linear B, but the system they came to use was not (and is not) identical with the Roman alphabet used in this book. For this reason, Greek words and Greek names will appear in this book according to a conventional, but by no means universal, system of transliteration. So, for example, the names that have appeared above in the forms "Cnossus," "Menelaus," and "Athena" may be found in other books

KRATER A large, deep bowl for mixing wine with water (figure 52).

TRIPOD A pot or cauldron resting on three legs, often presented as a prize or as a votive offering (figure 18).

Figure 8   Linear B tablet Ue 611 from Mycenae, ca. 1200 BC. The four lines of text read (from left to right):

ku-pe-ra 4 *a-po-re-we* 2 *pe-ri-ke* 3
ka-ra-te-ra 1 *po-ro-ko-wo* 4 *a-ta-ra* 10
pa-ke-te-re 30 *ka-na-to* 5 *qe-ti-ja* 10
qe-to 2 *ti-ri-po-di-ko* 8 *ka-ra-ti-ri-jo* 7

Drawing reproduced with the permission of the Istituto di studi sulle Civiltà dell'Egeo e del Vicino Oriente (CNR) from A. Sacconi, *Corpus delle iscrizioni in lineare B di Micene*, Incunabula Graeca 58 (Rome 1974), p. 60.

written in English according to a different (and perfectly acceptable) system as "Knossos," "Menelaos," and "Athene."

The Emergence of Mycenaean Civilization

Mycenaean civilization developed within the context of, and shows the pervasive influence of, the Minoan civilization that it supplanted. Still, there are prominent differences in the character of the two civilizations. The point of transition, however, between the two periods is not at all well defined. It seems that the replacement of Minoan culture by Mycenaean was the result of a gradual transformation rather than a sudden overthrow. That is not to say that the transition was peaceful and without incident. In fact, there is evidence in the archaeological record of varying degrees of destruction among the Minoan palaces of Crete in the years around 1500 BC. Mycenaean control of locations on the mainland began before that time, and we may date the Mycenaean Period as beginning around 1650 BC and lasting until roughly 1200 BC.

The Minoan civilization that the Greek-speaking newcomers encountered was well organized and relatively prosperous. The large palaces on Crete represented the centers of administration, trade, and perhaps religious activity as well. This manner of centralized authority, located in a substantial palace, was adopted by the Greek-speaking Mycenaeans, although there were some very important differences. While Minoan palaces were unfortified and were built in an open area that allowed for expansion, the mainland palaces constructed by Mycenaean Greeks were heavily fortified and occupied high ground overlooking a plain. Most impressive is the palace at Tiryns, which occupies the crest of a low outcropping of rock in the middle of a plain. The fortifications, made of massive blocks of stone, are in some places as much as eight meters in thickness (figure 9). This kind of fortified palace was common on the mainland, at places like Mycenae and Argos, located near Tiryns in the Peloponnese, and Athens and Thebes, located to the north. The heavy fortification of the palaces has given rise to much speculation regarding the identity of the enemy against whom these walls were intended to protect the inhabitants. It is usually assumed either that the Mycenaean cities were constantly at war with one another or that they were fearful of invasion by outsiders. There is, however, yet another possibility, namely that these massive fortifications were constructed for display, as a conspicuous assertion of power, rather than for any practical strategic purposes. This may seem implausible, but the construction of such fortifications would seem to require a protracted period of freedom from outside interference. The Cold War of the late twentieth century illustrates the fact that nations can persuade themselves to expend vast resources on "defense" even in the absence of any verifiable threat of attack from outside.

The suggestion that Mycenaean fortifications were intended as much for show as for protection may be incorrect (and may be contradicted by considerations to be presented below), but the Mycenaean Greeks' fondness for impressive display is paralleled by another aspect of their culture, one which again serves to distinguish them from their Minoan predecessors. The people of Crete, during the Minoan Period and even during the Mycenaean Period, buried their dead in rather undistinguished communal graves. These graves took a variety of forms, but the deceased were generally buried in simple fashion, sometimes in a container and sometimes just laid on the floor of the tomb, with few grave goods or, in many instances, with none at all. The contrast presented by Mycenaean burial practice is great, and begins quite early in the Mycenaean Period. Dating to the period between about 1650 and 1600 BC are two circular burial plots at Mycenae. One, which was excavated in the 1950s, contains 24 graves, while the other contains only six graves, but the spectacularly lavish manner in which the deceased, undoubtedly members of the Mycenaean royal family, were buried made this the richest find of grave goods in the Greek world.

This burial plot, known as "Grave Circle A," was discovered in 1876 by the pioneering figure in the archaeology of prehistoric Greece, Heinrich Schliemann. In fact, the site of Mycenae was the first in Greece to be subjected to modern archaeological excavation. Schliemann was encouraged to explore the site of Mycenae by his success a few years previously, when he excavated the remains of Troy. He had been impressed by the vividness of Homer's descriptions of the landscape and topography of Troy, which convinced him that Homer was accurately describing a real location. His conviction seemed to be confirmed when he uncovered the remains

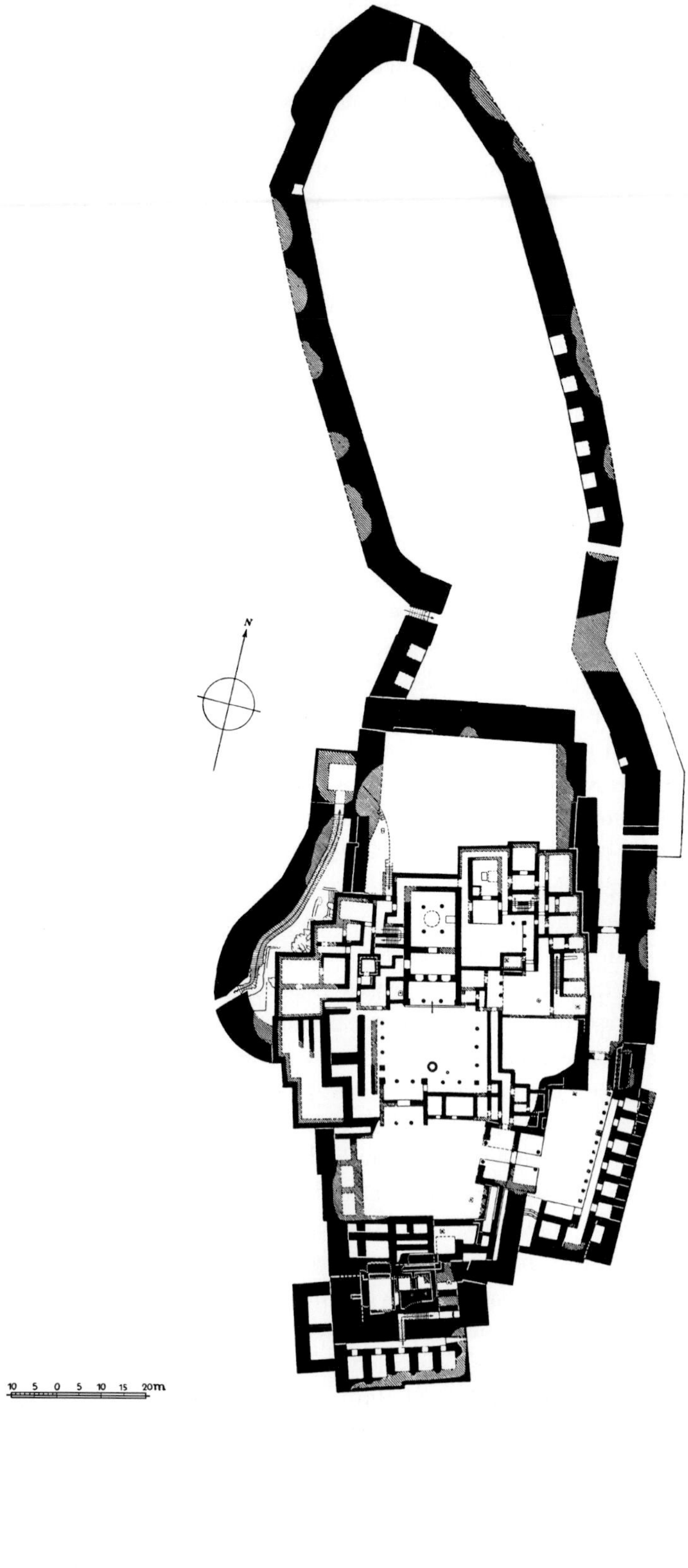

Figure 9 Plan, drawn by Heinrich Sulze, of the Mycenaean palace at Tiryns, thirteenth century BC. Reproduced from K. Müller, *Tiryns: Die Ergebnisse der Ausgrabungen des Instituts* III (Augsburg 1930), Tafel 4.

of a prosperous prehistoric city. That the city revealed unmistakable evidence of having been overrun by attackers and destroyed by fire at one point in its history proved to Schliemann that Homer's account of events was as reliable as his descriptions of locations. For Schliemann, this was the destruction inflicted on Troy by the victorious Greek forces at the conclusion of the Trojan War, whose historicity could no longer be doubted. Inspired by this apparent confirmation of his faith in Homer's trustworthiness, Schliemann began digging at Mycenae, the home of King Agamemnon, which Homer describes as "rich in gold." What Schliemann discovered in his excavation of Mycenae satisfied both his exalted opinion of Homer's historical accuracy and his craving for valuable treasures. Among the objects unearthed in Grave Circle A was a series of gold death masks, one of which Schliemann proclaimed "the death mask of Agamemnon." As it happens, the burials in Grave Circle A date to a time some hundreds of years before the traditional time of the Trojan War, in which Agamemnon is supposed to have participated.

Schliemann's discoveries, therefore, do not provide exactly the sort of confirmation that he had hoped to find (and thought that he *had* found), but they do reveal the considerable power and prosperity that Mycenae and its rulers enjoyed in the middle of the second millennium BC. In addition to the death masks of gold foil that were found placed over the faces of some of

> "Two tripod cauldrons with goat decorations, of Cretan workmanship; one single-handled tripod cauldron with one foot; one tripod cauldron of Cretan workmanship with the legs burnt away (useless); three wine jugs; one large four-handled goblet; two large three-handled goblets; one small four-handled goblet; one small three-handled goblet; one small goblet without a handle." (Linear B tablet Ta 641 from Pylos)

the men (but none of the women) buried in the grave circles, other valuable objects in large quantities were placed in the tombs. These objects include elaborately decorated drinking vessels of gold, silver, and bronze, ceramic and stoneware vases, jewelry, and weapons of war. These burial goods are impressive (and were intended to impress) not only by reason of their quantity and their value, but because they represent the extent of these Mycenaean rulers' connections outside mainland Greece. The jewelry in these tombs, for example, includes quantities of amber beads, which can only have found their way to Mycenae as a result of trade with the inhabitants of northern Europe. Some of the stoneware and ceramic vessels are of Cretan origin; others are from the Cyclades. The metalwork is so strongly reminiscent of Minoan craftsmanship that much of it was likely imported from Minoan Crete.

Some of the grave goods – particularly the large number of weapons, elaborately inlaid in gold, silver, and lapis lazuli (see figure 10) – are likely to have been made to order for the Mycenaean rulers by craftsmen brought in from elsewhere, namely from Crete or even

> "When Menelaus, the war-god's devotee, noticed him striding out in front of the ranks he felt the kind of elation that a ravenous lion feels when he comes across a hulking carcass, finding the body of a stag with great horns or a wild goat. For even if the swift hounds and the vigorous huntsmen rush at him he gluts himself all the same. That is how elated Menelaus was when his eyes lit upon godlike Alexander, for he was determined to take vengeance on his wife's abductor." (Homer, *Iliad* 3.21–8)

Figure 10 Bronze dagger blade with lion hunt inlaid in gold, silver, and niello from Grave Circle A at Mycenae, now in the National Archaeological Museum, Athens; length 22.9 cm, 1650–1600 BC. Nimatallah / Art Resource, NY.

from the Near East. The reason for this assumption – that skilled workers were brought in from outside to create luxury items for the Mycenaean rulers – is that, while the craftsmanship of these items is paralleled elsewhere, the nature of the decoration is often specifically designed for Mycenaean tastes. And those tastes run very largely in the direction of scenes of warfare and hunting (figure 11). This fact, along with the presence of large numbers of weapons in the early Mycenaean burials and the imposing fortifications by which Mycenae, Tiryns, and other mainland cities were protected, gives the strong impression that warfare and wild-beast hunts dominated the life of the Mycenaean Greeks. This impression is further strengthened by the contrast with the apparently peaceable character of Minoan art. For, while scenes of conflict, both human and animal, do appear in the art of the Minoan Period, Minoan art is overwhelmingly concerned to depict what appear to be scenes of religious ritual, lively representations of marine life (figure 12), and athletic activity, including the ubiquitous bull-leaping scenes, with acrobatic young men gracefully somersaulting over the backs of charging bulls.

This contrast between peace-loving Minoans and warlike Mycenaeans appears to be confirmed by the fact that, by the middle of the fifteenth century BC, the Greek-speaking Mycenaeans came to be in control of the Cretan palaces, as is proved by the replacement of Minoan Linear A by Linear B for administrative purposes. The picture that we want to construct from all this evidence is one of violent overthrow of Minoan society by less-civilized invading Greek-speakers, who assumed control of the Cretan palace society and were in turn strongly influenced by the culturally and artistically advanced civilization that they had come to rule. This is a satisfying picture, and is consistent with most of the evidence that we have. It is, therefore, likely to be a reasonably accurate picture.

Yet it is interesting to note (and fruitful to think about) how we form these pictures. As we have seen, the incentive to excavate at sites like Mycenae and Troy was provided by the desire to find tangible evidence that might validate an already existing account, namely the Homeric poems. Since that time, archaeologists have made great advances, not only in the basic techniques of their discipline, such as

Figure 11
Limestone STELE
(grave marker) from
Grave Circle A at
Mycenae, with scene
of warfare or
hunting; height
1.33 m, 1650–
1600 BC. Athens,
National
Archaeological
Museum, 1428.

developing more sophisticated and accurate methods of dating, but in their con-
ception of the role of the discipline. It is no longer felt, as it was in Schliemann's
day, that the archaeologist's agenda is set by the narrative provided by the more
well-established literary and historical approaches that dominated the study of ancient
Greece in the nineteenth century. Rather, the archaeologist makes use of the
available physical evidence to construct an account that is often more detailed and

STELE   An upright
stone slab, often
carved in RELIEF
and/or painted for
use as a grave
marker (figure 11).

Figure 12 Middle Minoan ceramic jar from Phaistos; height 50 cm, seventeenth or eighteenth century BC. Archaeological Museum of Herakleion, Crete, Hellenic Ministry of Culture, IAP service.

complex than the narrative preferred by others. And archaeologists have exercised considerable ingenuity both in interpreting the available evidence and in making new evidence available even in the most unpromising situations. For example, virtually all perishable items have, understandably, perished, so that many of the most commonly used objects of everyday life, like food and fabrics and wooden furniture, have not survived for us to consider. But it is sometimes possible to detect impressions made by fabric on ceramics before they were fired, or the shape of wooden structural elements can sometimes be inferred from the indentations they have left in plastered walls. Even the presence of fruits and other plants can be deduced from the painstaking analysis of the remains of seeds and pollen.

Still, the evidence available to us is necessarily partial, and often it is the specific cultural practices of a particular ancient society that help determine what evidence, and what types of evidence, are likely to survive. Mention was made above of the survival of great quantities of grave goods, particularly metal items, in the grave circles of seventeenth-century Mycenae. One of the reasons these items survived for Schliemann and other, later researchers to find was precisely the fact that they were buried along with the deceased. Metal in the ancient world is of great value, both for its decorative qualities and for its practical usefulness. Objects of metal that were not buried could be used and reused in antiquity. Sometimes this reuse took the form of melting down an object in order to create a new object of an entirely different nature or of beating swords into plowshares (or vice versa), thus obscuring for us the nature of the original object. Therefore, a culture that, like the Mycenaean, adheres to the practice of placing lavish grave goods in its burials will ensure that those goods survive for archaeologists (or tomb-robbers) to retrieve, while a culture like the Minoan, which engages in more modest burial practices, will allow chance to play a much greater role in determining what is likely to survive.

The Character of Mycenaean Civilization

The Mycenaean Greeks were determined to leave little to chance, at least when it came to the burial of their rulers. Toward the end of the sixteenth century BC, the rulers of Mycenae began to be buried in a new style of tomb that allowed them to display their power and influence even more impressively than had been the case with the earlier grave circles. At this time, both at Mycenae and elsewhere in Mycenaean Greece, a tomb shaped like a beehive came to be used. This type of tomb is referred to by archaeologists as a *tholos* tomb, from the Greek word for "dome" or "vault." Like the grave circles, these *tholos* tombs were intended to serve as repositories for the dead along with exceptionally lavish burial goods. At the same time, the size and appearance of the *tholos* tombs alone were enough to make a statement of over-whelming power and magnificence. Constructed, like the fortification walls of the citadel, of massive blocks of stone, these *tholos* tombs represent the largest space enclosed by a single span before the Pantheon was built by the Romans in the second century after Christ. The largest of the *tholos* tombs, the so-called Treasury of Atreus at Mycenae, dating probably from the thirteenth century BC, is nearly 15 meters in diameter and about the same size in height (figure 13). The tomb had a magnificent façade and was approached by a long and impressive passageway. The entire structure was built into the side of a hill (figure 14), so that the monument to this deceased king of Mycenae gives the impression of being at the same time a part of the natural world and an awesome display of one individual's authority.

But at whom is this display directed? Who is expected to feel awe at the sight of so impressive a monument? In the case of the massive fortifications of Mycenae and other mainland cities it is easy to imagine that the inhabitants intended to impress outsiders and to discourage, if not actually to thwart, their attempts at attack. Such an explanation is not so readily available in the case of lavish and monumental burials (which, on the contrary, only invite and entice tomb-robbers), and it seems more likely that these splendid tombs were designed to inspire awe among the local inhabitants. One of the features of Mycenaean society, which is most clearly visible in its burial customs, is the competitive, almost obsessive, display of wealth in the form of material goods, especially metal objects. These goods are clearly a mark of status, and even the meanest burials among the Mycenaean Greeks are provided

Figure 13 Interior of *tholos* tomb at Mycenae, called the "Treasury of Atreus," thirteenth century BC. Photo: Hirmer Fotoarchiv (Archiv-Nr. 592.0226).

with some grave goods, if only a small ceramic vessel or two. But no one was able to compete with those who were buried in the largest and most magnificent of the *tholos* tombs. That, in fact, would seem to be the point. These tombs, and perhaps the citadel-like palaces as well, are conspicuous markers of social and economic superiority within Mycenaean society. This insistence upon the clear demarcation of levels of status is one of the features that serves to distinguish Mycenaean from Minoan civilization. That is not to say that Minoan society was somehow more egalitarian than Mycenaean, or that material resources were more evenly distributed. In fact, we have very little evidence for the nature of Minoan society. Nevertheless, it is clear from the burial practices of the Mycenaean Greeks that those at the upper levels of Mycenaean society went to extraordinary lengths to distinguish themselves from the rest.

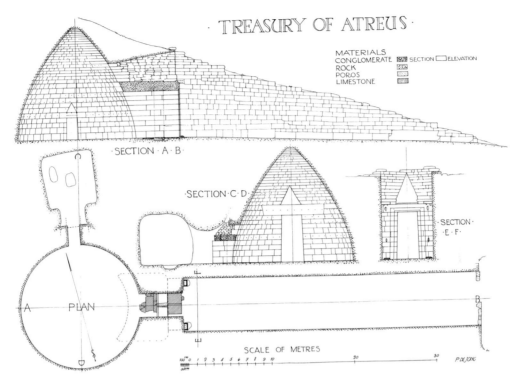

Figure 14 "Treasury of Atreus," plan and sections, drawn by Piet de Jong. Reproduced from A. J. B. Wace, *Mycenae: An Archaeological History and Guide* (Princeton 1949), ill. 5.

Thanks to the evidence of the Mycenaean Linear B tablets, we are even in a position to identify some of the terminology used to distinguish various levels of Mycenaean administration. It

> "Amphiphoetes: female slaves 32; older girls 5; younger girls 15; younger boys 4." (Linear B tablet Ak 824 from Cnossus)

should be remembered, however, that since the tablets do not provide any kind of narrative, we are very much in the dark as to the details of the relationships among the various holders of these titles. The individual most to be envied, apparently, in the hierarchy of Mycenaean society is the person identified in the tablets from Cnossus and Pylos as *wa-na-ka*, a title corresponding to the word *anax* (originally *wanax*) in Classical Greek. *Anax* is a word meaning "lord," and is applied in Homer, for example, to kings and gods; it is also a common element used in forming Greek men's names, like Anaximander and Astyanax. Mycenaean *wa-na-ka* is found in the tablets as a title, without the name of the person to whom the title is applied, and presumably refers to the king. There is one king at Pylos and one king at Cnossus, and each of the Mycenaean palaces appears to have been ruled by its own king. Another title that is attested in the Linear B tablets, in this case at Thebes as well as at Pylos and Cnossus, is *qa-si-re-u*, which corresponds to later Greek

BASILEUS. Those designated as *qa-si-re-u* are named, and there is more than one such person in each location. This implies that they are of lesser status than the *wa-na-ka*, and this is confirmed by the number of material goods that the tablets record for them. Other titles or designations appear in the tablets, including those of the lowest status, namely those designated *do-e-ro* or, in the feminine form, *do-e-ra*, "slave." These slaves (the later Greek word is *doulos*, feminine *doule*) are sometimes the personal property of other members of the Mycenaean society and sometimes the property of one or another of the Mycenaean deities, whose names also are recorded in the Linear B tablets. Among the gods and goddesses whose names appear on the tablets are some of those whom we have already met in connection with the judgment of Paris, namely Athena, Hera, Hermes, and Zeus (but not Aphrodite).

What we see, then, in the civilization of Mycenaean Greece is a culture that shares a number of features (social, linguistic, and religious) with that of Classical Greece but which is also heavily influenced by the non-Greek civilization of Minoan Crete. Mycenaean Greeks moved into an area that already had a flourishing and advanced culture. They absorbed that culture and, eventually, superseded it. Power in Minoan Greece had been concentrated on the island of Crete, but as Mycenaean influence increased, the focus of power and wealth gradually shifted to the cities of the mainland. In the area of the visual arts it is very clear that the Mycenaeans were the borrowers, and the story of Mycenaean art is one of gradual but fairly steady decline, from a high point that was reached quite early, under Minoan influence. The one exception to that picture of steady decline is in the area of architecture, in which Mycenaean civilization developed quite independently of Minoan and, as we have seen, in the direction of monumental construction. The powerful fortresses of the Mycenaean kings were products of the remarkable increase in prosperity that characterized mainland Greece during the Mycenaean Period. This increase in prosperity was accompanied by substantial population growth, and Greece in the thirteenth century seems to have been more heavily populated than at any previous time. But, for reasons that are not at all clear, with the beginning of the twelfth century a period of decline in both population and prosperity sets in that is so severe that historians generally refer to the period that begins around 1200 BC as the "Dark Age."

The End of Mycenaean Civilization

It is reasonable to consider the time around 1200 BC as the end of the Mycenaean Period, but there is no way of knowing why the Mycenaean civilization came to an end. There is evidence of physical destruction and fire at many of the centers of Mycenaean life at about this time, including Mycenae, Tiryns, and Pylos. Archaeologists have also found evidence that the inhabitants of Mycenae, Tiryns, and Athens were engaged in strengthening their fortifications and improving the means of supplying their citadels with fresh water, as though they were expecting an invasion and were preparing for a siege. And the Linear B tablets from Pylos (which survive because they were baked in the fire that destroyed the palace) talk about "the watchers guarding the coast" and appear to name locations on the coast at which guards are to be posted. The widespread instances of destruction, then, seem to have been foreseen. But who were the invaders? Were they non-Greeks or were they Greeks from other Mycenaean cities? Or were they, indeed, *non-Mycenaean* Greeks, that is, a new group of Greek-speaking people who were entering Greece for the first time? We simply do not know the answer to these questions. We do know, however, that some of the Mycenaean palaces were immediately reoccupied after the destruction and some rebuilding was undertaken, although the level of activity and prosperity was very much lower than before. Some of the palaces, like that at Pylos, were not rebuilt at all.

Still, historians are fascinated with the question of why civilizations decline and, as in the case of the decline of the Roman Empire and the setting of the sun on the British Empire, a large number of theories has been developed to account for the darkness that fell upon the Mycenaean Greeks. These theories are based variously on social, technological, economic, and climatological causes. It is becoming increasingly clear that no one factor can be singled out as being "the cause" of the end of Mycenaean civilization.

> "There was a time when countless tribes of mortals oppressed the lands with their weight, as they wandered over the broad surface of the earth. When Zeus noticed this he took pity and within his intricate mind he devised a means of unburdening the earth that nourishes all. He stirred up the great conflict of the Trojan War in order to reduce the mass of mankind and in Troy the great heroes perished, fulfilling the plan of Zeus." (Stasinus (?), *Cypria*, fragment 1)

Almost certainly, it was a combination of factors that brought Mycenaean society to an end, as it was a combination of factors that caused Mycenaean civilization to come into existence in the first place. A single, identifiable cause of an event is acceptable in a fictional narrative – the Trojan War, for example, could be attributed to the abduction of Helen by Paris or to an even more outlandish cause – but historical occurrences are the result of more complex circumstances. Whatever the causes of the decline of Mycenaean civilization, other civilizations as well in the Mediterranean region suffered a similar fate at about the same time. The Hittite Empire, which controlled much of Asia Minor and had diplomatic relations with the kings of Troy, was invaded and its central power destroyed shortly after 1200 BC, just at the time when records of the Egyptian New Kingdom speak of threatening inroads by the otherwise unidentified "sea peoples," whose attacks coincided with an irreversible decline in the prestige and power of the Egyptian kingdom.

It is possible that the Mycenaean Greeks were among these "sea peoples." In any event, the character of Greek civilization was transformed in the period following the start of the twelfth century BC. It does not appear that Mycenaean Greece was invaded by people who introduced a new culture; rather, we find a continuation of Mycenaean cultural forms, but in a greatly attenuated state. For example, the

"If some enemy arises for you, I will not abandon you, just as I have not now abandoned you, and I will kill the enemy on your behalf. If your brother or someone of your family withdraws political support from you, Alaksandu . . . and they seek the kingship of the land of Wilusa, I, my Majesty, will certainly not depose you." (Treaty between the Hittite King Muwatalli II and Alaksandu of Wilusa [= Alexander of Ilios, or Troy], ca. 1280 BC)

tradition of decorating ceramic vessels with human and animal figures, and of creating figurines in human and animal form, virtually disappears from the Greek world after about 1200 BC. An exception to this is the island of Crete, where human figurines continue to be made, but this very isolation of Crete is also characteristic of the period in question. During the Minoan and Mycenaean Periods the very frequent contact among various areas of Greece and the Aegean meant that there was relatively little stylistic variation between one area and another; in the following period, however, there is an increasing tendency toward the development of isolated regional styles. This would seem to indicate a severe reduction in the frequency of trade and commerce between parts of the Greek world, and the reduction in the amount of imported bronze and other metals found by archaeologists suggests a decline in trade with the wider world. Since trade in those metals had been in the hands of the Mycenaean rulers, it appears that the central administration of the palaces was now lacking. There was no longer a driving force behind the construction of palaces or of any buildings on a large scale. The practice of ostentatiously burying warriors with their weapons and armor is not attested during the hundred and fifty years following 1200 BC.

"And after they had satisfied their desire for food and drink Telemachus spoke to the son of Nestor, holding his head close to his so that the others could not hear: 'Look, son of Nestor, delight of my heart! Look at the glitter of bronze throughout the spacious halls, and of gold and electrum and silver and ivory! This, I suppose, is what the court of Olympian Zeus must be like on the inside, so unspeakably great is the luxury of it all. I am struck with awe as I look upon it.'" (Homer, *Odyssey* 4.68–75, on the palace of Menelaus at Sparta)

Even the knowledge of writing disappears after the collapse of Mycenaean society: the Linear B tablets cease being produced and, from the beginning of the twelfth century until the early eighth century BC, there is no evidence at all of literacy in Greece and the Aegean. When literacy resumes in the eighth century, the form of writing employed is based upon foreign models and owes nothing to Mycenaean script. It should not be thought, however, that this loss of the ability to write was responsible for the substantial discontinuity between the Mycenaean Period and the period that follows the "Dark Age." The discontinuity was brought about by the disappearance of institutions and by the break in certain technological and conceptual traditions. Other traditions, the narrative and musical traditions of story and song, which had never depended upon writing for their perpetuation, certainly did persevere. We know this because of the large body of legends and myths, preserved in the Archaic and Classical Periods, that represented the distant past as a glorious Golden Age, an age of heroes and warriors securely located precisely in those Mycenaean palaces that recent archaeological discoveries have revealed to be every bit as powerful and prosperous as the myths and legends suggest. Of course, the impressive remains of the Mycenaean citadels at Mycenae, Tiryns, and other locations continued to be visible, and the later Greeks referred to their massive fortifications as "Cyclopean," as though they must have been constructed by a race of giant Cyclopes. It would have been easy for legends to spring up regarding the ancient inhabitants of these abandoned landmarks, but legends also persisted concerning the might and wealth of Pylos, Sparta, and other Mycenaean sites of which no Cyclopean remains were visible. The focus of many of these legends was a mighty conflict, the Trojan War, in which forces from Mycenae, Pylos, Cnossus, and many other Mycenaean Greek cities banded together to attack and ultimately destroy the non-Mycenaean city of Troy. Excavations at the site of the city that Schliemann and others have identified as the city of Troy have indeed revealed evidence of widespread destruction there, like that which afflicted the Mycenaean cities themselves, in the period around 1200 BC. Whatever the connections between the later legends and the reality, these legends constructed the past against which all later Greek culture defined itself. In other words, the Greeks' stories about the Mycenaean Period became what the later Greeks regarded as their history.

Recommended for Further Reading

Chadwick, J. *The Decipherment of Linear B*, 2nd edition (Cambridge 1967): the fascinating story of the decipherment, told by Ventris's friend and collaborator.

Dickinson, O. *The Aegean Bronze Age* (Cambridge 1994): a balanced and scholarly introduction to the archaeology of Bronze Age Greece, organized by topics (arts and crafts, burial customs, trade, etc.).

Drews, R. *The End of the Bronze Age: Changes in Warfare and the Catastrophe ca. 1200 BC* (Princeton 1993): a survey of the various theories concerning the end of Bronze Age civilization, with a new (military) explanation.

Fitton, J. L. *The Discovery of the Greek Bronze Age* (Cambridge, MA 1996): the story of the recovery of the Bronze Age civilizations of Greece (Cycladic, Minoan, and Mycenaean) by archaeologists over the past 125 years.

Higgins, R. *Minoan and Mycenaean Art*, new revised edition (London 1997): a well-illustrated survey of Minoan, Mycenaean, and Cycladic art.

Latacz, J. *Troy and Homer: Towards a Solution of an Old Mystery* (Oxford 2004): a masterful survey of the archaeological and linguistic evidence from Greece and the Near East in the Mycenaean Period, presenting a compelling case for the historical reality of the Trojan War.

Renfrew, C. *The Cycladic Spirit: Masterpieces from the Nicholas P. Goulandris Collection* (New York 1991): a brilliant essay on the nature of Cycladic art, stunningly illustrated.

Taylour, Lord William. *The Mycenaeans*, revised edition (New York 1983): a clear introduction to Mycenaean civilization, part of the series "Ancient Peoples and Places," written by the former director of the British School's excavations at Mycenae.

Willetts, R. F. *The Civilization of Ancient Crete* (Berkeley and Los Angeles 1977): a history of Crete from the Minoan Period to the beginning of the Classical Age, with an especially good account of the Minoan palace economy.

IRON AGE GREECE

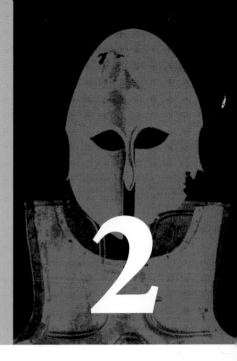

2

The collapse of Mycenaean civilization was followed by a slow period of recovery during what is known as the "Dark Age" (ca. 1200 to the eighth century BC). This recovery can be traced most reliably through an examination of the copious remains of ceramic pottery, which provides evidence of improving technology and artistic skill. In addition, the locations in which Greek pottery is found allow us to trace its distribution and circulation, which by the eighth century BC extended throughout the Mediterranean world. Contact through trade led the Greeks to adopt and adapt a number of practices from other cultures; most significantly, the Greeks' invention of the alphabet resulted from their exposure to the Phoenician system of syllabic writing. Increasing prosperity and expanding commerce within the Mediterranean gave rise to a period of overseas colonization, beginning in the eighth century BC, which saw the establishment of permanent Greek communities along the coast of the Mediterranean Sea and the Black Sea, from the Ukraine to Spain. These communities took the characteristic form that developed among the Greeks during the "Dark Age," namely the polis, a self-governing territory consisting of an urban center with a surrounding agricultural area. The diffusion of Greek culture throughout the Mediterranean area encouraged those Greeks who found themselves widely separated from their traditional homeland to define themselves conspicuously in terms of their shared culture. One prominent feature of this shared culture was the worship of a common pantheon of gods, headed by Olympian Zeus, whose festival, the Olympic Games, at the mainland site of Olympia became a focus and a hallmark of Greek identity, since participation in the Games was restricted to citizens of Greek poleis.

Dark Age Ceramic Ware

The Invention of the Alphabet

The Age of Colonization

The Polis

The Olympic Games

The Dark Age that followed the collapse of the Mycenaean administrative structure presented the Greeks with an opportunity, indeed, the necessity, to reinvent themselves. We know much less than we would like concerning the details of life during the Greek Dark Age, but we do know that this period, from the twelfth until the eighth century BC, was somehow decisive for the formation of Archaic and Classical Greek culture. The sharp decrease in population in this period throughout mainland Greece and the Aegean islands resulted in a population that lived in generally small, isolated settlements. This is in marked contrast to the thriving, palace-based communities that were the focus of a vigorous economy and an extensive network of trade during the Minoan and Mycenaean Periods. One of the results of decreased prosperity and diminished trade was a reduction in the supply of tin, a metal not found in the Aegean area. Tin is an essential component of bronze, an alloy whose main ingredient, copper, is available in Greece. Bronze was widely used during the Mycenaean Period for tools and weapons. As a result of the diminished supply of tin, the skill of Greek metalworkers was considerably attenuated during the early part of the Dark Age. Still, contacts with other areas of the Mediterranean were reduced rather than eliminated entirely, and the technology of smelting iron was gradually introduced from the island of Cyprus to mainland Greece. Iron is much more plentiful in Greece than is copper, but its potential could not be exploited until the inhabitants of Greece learned how to temper iron. Once tempered, iron is harder than bronze and is a more satisfactory material for making tools and weapons. This new technology, combined with the availability of iron in Greece, contributed to the gradual recovery that eventually enabled the Greeks to emerge from the depths of the Dark Age.

"I wish I could have had nothing to do with this fifth generation of men, but instead had either died beforehand or been born at a later time. For now it is the age of iron, nor will there ever be an end to toils and suffering, and distress will be constant both day and night. For the gods will cause brutal heartache." (Hesiod, *Works and Days* 174–8)

One of the effects of this recovery would be the re-establishment of contacts, in the form of trade and commerce, between Greece and the wider world, allowing Greek metalworkers access once again to supplies of the raw materials for making bronze. Iron did not replace bronze, which continued in widespread use for a variety of purposes. But iron was now the preferred material for making weapons, and its associations with death and destruction, combined with its dark appearance (particularly in contrast to gleaming bronze), inspired the seventh-century poet Hesiod to make iron the emblem of the age in which he lived. In his myth of the ages of humankind, Hesiod depicts a steady degeneration from an original age of gold, through ages of silver and bronze, to the present age of iron, characterized by warfare, injustice, and miserable living conditions. Influenced by this mythological schema, nineteenth-century scholars, who by no means shared Hesiod's pessimistic view of human development, divided European prehistory after the Stone Age into a "Bronze Age" and a subsequent "Iron Age." These names have continued in use as convenient, if not accurately descriptive, terms, and

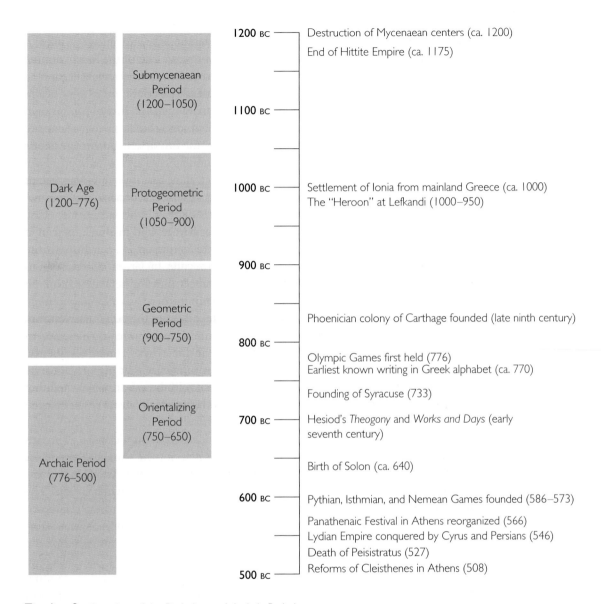

Timeline 3   Overview of the Dark Age and Archaic Period.

it is conventional to regard the eleventh century BC as the end of the Bronze Age and the start of the Iron Age in Greece and the Aegean.

Dark Age Ceramic Ware

The introduction of iron technology altered the character of Greek civilization, but in order to chart the development of that civilization, historians and archaeologists need to rely on artifacts that are available in greater numbers than the occasional iron implement. The most common artifacts found in Iron Age burials – indeed, one of the most common items to have survived from antiquity – are ceramic vessels. In Athens, for example, during the early years of the Iron Age, it was customary to deposit the cremated remains of the deceased in a ceramic vessel, which was then buried along with other ceramic vessels and metal objects of some value, while a stone and yet another ceramic vessel were placed at the surface to mark the tomb. Similar practices existed elsewhere in Greece. This pottery is of tremendous value to historians, art historians, and archaeologists because it is virtually inde-structible and because its painted decoration was generally applied before firing, which fused it to the surface of the pottery and inhibited fading. While ceramic pots can be broken – and most of them have been broken at one time or another – the fragments remain unchanged for thousands of years and can be reassembled by patient curators equipped with modern adhesives. The availability of large numbers of ceramic vessels enables us to chart changes in funerary practice, fluctuations in population, and variations over time in artistic and technological expertise.

In addition, pottery is the single most valuable resource for determining chro-nology. Since it is so common and since stylistic fashions tend to evolve fairly uniformly within a given tradition, it is possible to arrive at a reasonably reliable relative chronology based upon the analysis of the decoration of painted pottery. Once this relative chronology has been established – and for some periods of Greek civilization the evidence is so abundant and the skill of the experts so refined that a chronology can be devised that is accurate to within about a decade – it can be correlated with other types of objects that are associated stratigraphically with various points in the series. (Stratigraphy is that aspect of archaeology that is concerned with the sequence in which successive layers, or strata, of soil have built up over a given site. The excavations at Troy undertaken in the 1930s, for example, identified nearly 50 layers, or phases, of habitation over the centuries, with the earliest layer naturally being the lowest.) The combination of the analysis of pottery styles and the study of stratigraphy, along with other types of evidence, can sometimes make it possible to anchor the relative chronology at some fixed points, providing a reasonably accurate absolute chronology.

The analysis of pottery enables us to follow cultural and economic changes through the Dark Age, which is itself often divided by archaeologists into identifiable periods associated with particular styles of ceramic decoration. The earliest period of the Dark Age, down to about the middle of the eleventh century BC, is referred to as the Submycenaean Period, characterized by the repetition of a limited number of vase shapes dependent upon Mycenaean models, but executed at a much lower level of artistic and technical competence. This period also sees the abandonment of figural scenes, with the decoration consisting merely of bands of color or other simple shapes. It is also characterized by a number of local or regional styles, in contrast to the relative uniformity of technique in evidence throughout the Mycenaean world. This proliferation of regional styles provides part of the evidence for the increased isolation characteristic of the years immediately following the

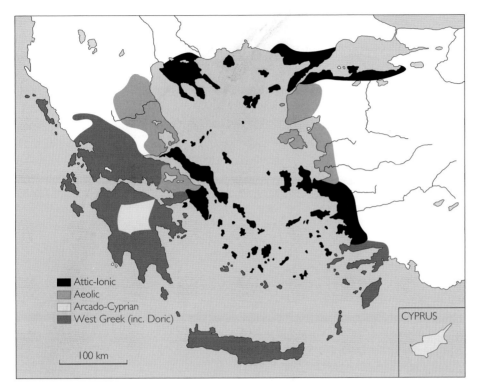

Map 4
Distribution of
Greek dialects
in the early
Classical Period.

Mycenaean Period. With the collapse of the palace-based central organization of the Mycenaean Period there was a reduction in the circulation of skilled artisans and of prestige goods, whose movement depended upon the connections established among powerful and wealthy individuals in various regions of Greece. Consequently, the isolated communities of Submycenaean Greece were exposed to a lesser degree of stylistic influence from other Greek communities. This does not mean, however, that the Greeks were immobile. There is, in fact, evidence of movement of people in the Greek world during the twelfth and eleventh centuries. That is, it appears that a number of individuals or families or perhaps even whole communities changed their place of residence, moving generally eastwards, across the Aegean Sea to the west coast of Asia Minor and the island of Cyprus. It was presumably at this time that the distribution of Greek dialects that we find in the Archaic and Classical Periods took place (map 4), a distribution that reflects this eastward movement from the mainland across the Aegean.

The end of the Submycenaean Period coincides approximately with the transition in Greece from the Bronze Age to the Iron Age, and this transition accompanies the beginnings of a protracted period of recovery for the Greek mainland and the Aegean islands. Contact with Cyprus inspired this technological change in the Greek world, and it is possible that contact with Cyprus inspired a change to a new style of pottery decoration as well. This style is known as "Protogeometric"

Figure 15
Protogeometric amphora from the Kerameikos cemetery in Athens; height 39.9 cm, ca. 975 BC. Athens, Kerameikos, Inv. 1073; photo by H. Wagner, DAI negative no. KER 4245.

since it serves as a precursor to the "Geometric" style, the justification for whose name will become immediately apparent. Pottery of the Protogeometric Period (roughly 1050 to 900 BC) is characterized by the use of a faster potter's wheel in its fabrication and by the practice of using a compass and multiple brushes connected to one another at equal intervals so that the vessel can be decorated with concentric circles or arcs (figure 15). But it is not only the style of decoration that differentiates Protogeometric from Submycenaean pottery. Potters and painters (if, indeed, these were different individuals) in the tenth century also began to take much greater care in the preparation of the clay, in the modeling of the vessels, and in the integration of painted decoration and shape of vase. Ceramic ware of the Protogeometric Period shows a notable improvement in terms of the symmetry of the vessels and in the technical details of the work both in the clay and in the glaze. The potters of the tenth century also began to experiment with a much greater variety of shapes.

These tendencies, namely a desire to experiment and an improvement in technical assurance, are taken a step farther in the period known as the Geometric, from approximately 900 to 750 BC. It is especially in Attica, the region in which the city of Athens is located, that we see the flourishing of Geometric pottery. We saw in the pottery of the Submycenaean and Protogeometric Periods the limited,

Figure 16 Late Geometric amphora from the Dipylon cemetery in Athens; height 1.55 m, ca. 750 BC. Athens, National Archaeological Museum, Inv. 804; photo by G. Hellner, DAI negative no. NM 5944.

and tentative, use of geometric shapes to serve as painted decoration; in the Geometric Period the use of abstract geometric shapes runs wild, completely covering the surface of the vessel with, sometimes, dozens of bands of small triangles, lozenges, angular meander patterns, and other regular devices, in a restless but controlled obsession to reduce the exterior of the vase to a labyrinthine organization of chaos. The surfaces of these vessels are sometimes imposingly large. The AMPHORA illustrated here (figure 16), like many of the vases created in Geometric Athens, served as the marker for a tomb. It comes from the very end of the Geometric Period and is impressive not only for its detailed and meticulous pattern of decorations but for its sheer size; at over one and a half meters in height, it is likely to have been nearly as tall as the woman whose grave it marked. A vessel of this size signifies considerable technical skill and great self-assurance on the part of the Athenian potter who made it, as well as a degree of prosperity on the part of the family of the deceased, who commissioned the vessel for the very purpose of advertising that prosperity and asserting its own importance.

AMPHORA A large, two-handled jar for storage of wine, olive oil or other liquids (figures 15, 16, 29–31, 33, and 42).

Self-assurance and prosperity were becoming increasingly common features of the Greek world in the eighth century BC, as a result of developments that took place during the Geometric Period and that brought about the end of the Dark Age. We have already mentioned the technological advance that enabled the Greeks to exploit their supply of iron ore to make more effective tools and weapons. At about the same time this technology was introduced, the population of Greece began, slowly, to rebound from the devastating decline that had occurred in the aftermath of the collapse of Mycenaean civilization. Increasing population is often accompanied by increasing prosperity, at least as long as the level of population does not exceed the level that the resources of the land can sustain. We do, in fact, find increasing material prosperity in the eighth century, as demonstrated by the magnificence of burials in Athens and elsewhere and by the extent of Greek trade, both with the people of the Near East and with the inhabitants of the western Mediterranean. The evidence for that trade consists, in large measure, of precisely the Geometric pottery that has just been mentioned. By the end of the ninth century BC, we have abundant evidence of Greek pottery at Al Mina in Syria and at other locations in what is now Jordan, Israel, and Syria. By the first half of the eighth century BC, we find evidence of Greek pottery in Etruria in Italy, and by the middle of the eighth century in the vicinity of Rome. An Attic vase from this period has even been found as far afield as the Atlantic coast of Spain.

> "I remained in Egypt for seven years, accumulating many possessions in my dealings with the men there, since they were all very generous. But when finally the eighth year came around a Phoenician man who preys on others arrived, a man well versed in deception, who had already caused much harm among men. With his clever talk he persuaded me to come to Phoenicia, where he had his estates and his merchandise. For a full year I stayed there with him, but when the days and the months reached their end and the seasons returned with the year circling back on itself he put me on board his seagoing ship bound for Libya, falsely leading me to believe that I was joining him in a business venture. But his aim was to sell me into slavery and make a huge profit."
> (Homer, *Odyssey* 14.285–97, Odysseus pretending to be a Cretan returning from the Trojan War)

The distribution of these pottery finds gives an indication of the spread of Greek trade during the Geometric Period. To facilitate that trade, the Greeks began to establish trading posts in various places in the Mediterranean, particularly in locations that would enable them to satisfy their growing demand for metals and other luxury goods. In doing this, they came into increasing contact, and to some degree competition, with the Phoenicians, a Semitic people who lived in a number of independent communities, including the important cities of Tyre and Sidon, along the coast of what is now Lebanon and Syria. Beginning in the ninth century BC, the expanding power of the Assyrian Empire required these Phoenician cities to pay increasing amounts of tribute and put pressure on them to engage in ever more active trade throughout the Mediterranean. By the eighth century, the Phoenicians had established themselves as the most vigorous traders in the Mediterranean world, with trading posts and even full-scale colonies along the north coast of Africa, on the coast of what is now Spain, and on the islands of Sicily, Sardinia, and Cyprus. They were responsible for facilitating the contacts at this time between the Greeks and other inhabitants of the Mediterranean, particularly with the civilizations of Egypt and the Near East, whose traditions of figurative art and whose venerable literary heritage would decisively influence the development of Greek culture at the end of the Dark Age. Indeed, the period from the middle of the eighth to the middle of the seventh century BC is sometimes referred to as the "Orientalizing Period" of Greek civilization because of the pervasiveness of motifs in art and literature that can be traced to Hittite or Assyrian or Egyptian origins.

The Invention of the Alphabet

The most profound and lasting feature of eastern civilization that the Greeks adopted in the eighth century was borrowed from the Phoenicians themselves. As we have seen in the case of the Greeks' appropriation of many elements of Minoan civilization during the Mycenaean Period, and as we will see repeatedly later, among the salient characteristics of Greek civilization are an openness to foreign influence and the tendency to transform elements of that influence in subtle yet fundamental and enduring ways. It will be recalled that from about 1200 BC until the eighth century there is no evidence of literacy among the Greeks. The Phoenicians, however, like several of the peoples of the Near East during this period, possessed the knowledge of writing, and from their extensive contacts with them the Greeks became familiar with the Phoenician system of writing. This form of writing, like the Hebrew script, is a West Semitic writing system derived from the Proto-Canaanite script that was developed in the second millennium BC. It was very easy to learn, as it consisted of only 22 separate characters, in contrast, for example, to the approximately 90 characters of the Linear B syllabary. And it is, in effect, itself an abbreviated syllabary. So, for example, while Linear B had a different symbol to represent each of the following syllables: *da, de, di, do, du*, the Phoenician script used only one symbol to represent any one of them. That symbol was a triangular-shaped character that seems to have originated as a pictogram for the Phoenician word for "door," *d*l*t*, with the asterisks marking the place of the vowels, which were not represented in the Phoenician script. Compare the Hebrew word for "door," *daleth*. (We know the nature of the vowels in the Hebrew form of the word, which was written using a system of writing almost identical with the Phoenician, because marks were introduced at a later time that indicated the vocalization of Hebrew texts.) That symbol was adopted by the Greeks and is the origin of the triangular-shaped Greek letter delta, whose name also betrays its Semitic origin. The other letters of the Greek alphabet were adopted in the same way.

The Greek language, however, is not well suited to being represented by a system of writing that is fundamentally syllabic in nature, and so the Greek borrowers made some slight alterations to the system that they adopted. These changes, however, transformed the system into something that was no longer syllabic in nature, and with the Greek script we are justified in speaking for the first time of a truly alphabetic system of writing (figure 17). It may seem paradoxical to refer to the Greek system of writing as the first alphabet, particularly since the very name "alphabet" encodes the debt that the Greek alphabet owes to the Semitic system of

PHOENICIAN		GREEK		
Name	*ca. 900 BC*	*800–600*	*Attic (400)*	*Name*
ʾālef	K K ⅄	△ △ A	A	alpha
bēt	2 ⺇	℞ ℞ B	B	bēta
gīmel	⼂ ⼂	Γ ⼂ C	Γ	gamma
dālet	△ ⊿ △	▷ △ D	△	delta
hē	⅃ ⅃	⅁ ⅁ E	E	epsilon
wāw	Y Y ⅄	F F ⼕		(digamma)
zajin	I ⊥ I	I ⊥ I	I	zēta
ḥēt	日 日 日	日 ⼞ H	H	ēta
ṭēt	⊗ ⊕	⊗ ⊕ ⊙	⊖	thēta
yōd	Z 2 ⼖	⟨ ⼕ I	I	iōta
kaf	⼕ ⼕ ⅄	K K k	K	kappa
lāmed	L L L	L ⼕ ∧	∧	labda
mēm	⼕ ⼕ ⼕	⼕ ⼕ M	M	mu
nūn	⼕ ⼕ ⼕	⼕ ⼕ N	N	nu
sāmek	⼕	⼕ ⼕ ☰	Ξ	ksi
ʿayin	O	O	O	omikron
pē	⼕ ⼕	⼕ Γ	Γ	pi
ṣādē	⼕ ⼕	M		(san)
qōf	⼕ ⼕ ⼕	⼕ ⼕		(qoppa)
rēš	⼕ ⼕	P D ⼕	P	rhō
śin/šin	W	⼕ ⼕ ⼕	⼕	sigma
tāw	✛ X	T	T	tau
		⼕ Y V	Y	upsilon
		Φ Φ ⼕	Φ	phi
		X ✛	X	chi
		⼕ V	Ψ	psi
		Ω Ω Ω	Ω	ōmega

Figure 17 The development of the Greek alphabet from Phoenician script. Reproduced from P. T. Daniels and W. Bright (eds.), *The World's Writing Systems* (New York and Oxford 1996), Table 21.1, p. 262.

writing, the first two characters of which are (in their Hebrew form) "aleph" and "bet." What is more, it looks as though the first of those characters, the original of the Greek letter alpha, is itself a vowel. In fact, the first character of the Semitic signary is not a vowel; it is a glottal stop, the sound that an inhabitant of, for example, Glasgow makes to separate the two syllables of the word "little," which he or she pronounces without any *t*-sound. The ancient Greek language had no glottal stop and so, when the Greeks adopted the first character of the Phoenician script, they seem to have ignored the

> "Those Phoenicians who arrived with Cadmus, when they settled in this country, brought with them into Greece a number of skills, the most significant of which was literacy, which did not exist previously among the Greeks, as far as I can tell. At first the Greeks adopted the same characters that the Phoenicians in general use, but in the course of time, as the sound of the language changed, so did the shape of the letters. At that time it was primarily Ionian Greeks who lived in the region near the Phoenicians, and it was the Ionians who learned writing from them. Although they made some alterations to the shape of the letters they still called the letters that they used 'Phoenician letters' – justifiably, since it was the Phoenicians who had introduced them into Greece." (Herodotus 5.58)

initial sound and took the sound which it represented to be the *a*-sound, which follows the glottal stop in the name of the character. Similar adjustments were made in the case of a few other characters that the Phoenicians used to represent sounds that happened either not to exist or not to be at all prominent in the Greek language. The result of this is that there is a fundamental conceptual difference between the Greek alphabet and the West Semitic writing system from which it is derived. The fourth character in the Phoenician signary, for example, can represent any one of the syllables *da*, *de*, *di*, *do*, or *du*, whereas the fourth character of the Greek (and English) alphabet represents *that which the syllables* da, de, di, do, *and* du *have in common*. In other words, the Greek letter delta stands for something that cannot be pronounced independently and can only be defined in abstract terms. The Greek alphabet is analytical, in a way that Linear B and the Phoenician script are not, in the sense that it reduces the sounds of the spoken language to its elements, beyond which it cannot be further reduced. In fact, "elements" (*stoicheia*) is the word the Greeks used to refer to the letters of the alphabet, the same word they used to refer to the material elements of the physical world. (The English word "element" derives from a Latin word whose etymology is obscure, but some scholars contend that it originates from the names of the letters *l*, *m*, *n*.)

The Age of Colonization

The time at which the Greeks began to use these Phoenician characters to represent their own language appears to have been early in the eighth century. The earliest known piece of Greek alphabetic writing, discovered only recently, consists of a few letters that were scratched on a clay pot some time before about 770 BC. This pot was found not in Greece but in Italy, east of Rome, providing further evidence of the movement of Greeks and their goods at this time. Mention has been made of outposts that the Greeks established in order to facilitate trade throughout the Mediterranean. Beginning in the eighth century BC, however, they embarked on a period of expansion that saw the establishment not only of trading posts but of new, and sometimes quite substantial, communities of Greeks living in areas that were not formerly inhabited by Greeks. This period lasts from the beginning of the eighth century and extends into the fifth century BC and represents the most significant expansion of the Greek world before the time of Alexander the Great. During this time the Greeks established settlements, or "colonies," in various places on the coast of the Mediterranean, including Italy, Sicily, and North Africa, as well as on the coast of the Black Sea (map 5). Well over a hundred new Greek cities were founded during this period of colonization, some of which became populous and powerful communities that went on to play significant roles in later times. Some are thriving cities still today, like Catania, Istanbul, Marseilles, Naples, Nice, and Syracuse. The population of Greece had grown considerably in the course of the Geometric Period and that increase in population was surely one of the causes of this colonization movement, but almost certainly it was not the only cause. Those Greek communities that had been most active in pursuing trade during the Geometric Period were also the ones that were in the forefront of the colonizing movement, so that the prospects of economic improvement may have been as effective a motive as overcrowding at home. In some cases, also, it appears that members of unsuccessful political factions were either encouraged or forced to emigrate. Founding a colony was preferable to living as an outsider in some already existing alien community, especially since one's chances of becoming a member of the "ruling faction" of a colony were considerably enhanced if one had participated in its founding.

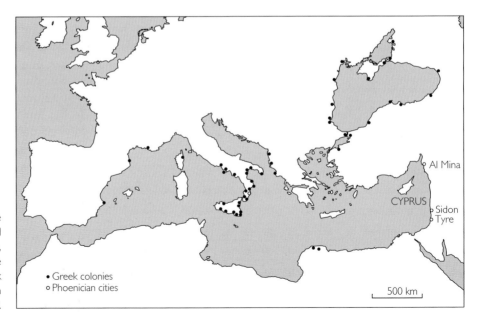

Map 5 The Mediterranean and Black Sea region, showing the extent of Greek colonization, eighth to fifth centuries BC.

Not only did the motives for the founding of different colonies vary; surely individuals participated in the founding of the same colony for a variety of reasons. Unfortunately, we know very little about the details of the founding of any of the colonies that were created before the fifth century because the very sparse written records are of little help and the later accounts that exist are overlaid with embellishment and legend. Archaeology can at least tell us whether the site of a given colony was previously inhabited and occasionally it can tell us by whom. It is clear that, in some instances, Greek settlers simply moved into an uninhabited area and built a new Greek community. In many, perhaps most, cases an earlier, non-Greek population was displaced, either forcibly or by being gradually outnumbered or assimilated. Whatever the circumstances, the new colony became a Greek community, inhabited by Greeks, and it was considered to be part of "Greece," whether it was located in what is now Spain or Libya or Bulgaria or the Ukraine. Rather, it was considered to be part of "Hellas," which is the name the Greeks used (and still use) to refer to their land, the land of the "Hellenes," or Greeks (map 6).

> "Zancle was originally settled by marauders who arrived from the Chalcidian city of Cyme in Oscan territory, but later large numbers of people came from Chalcis and the rest of Euboea and joined in the settlement. The leaders were Perieres of Cyme and Crataemenes of Chalcis. The original name was Zancle, given to it by the native Sicilians, because the place resembles a sickle in shape, the Sicilian word for which is *zanklon*. Later, however, the Sicilians were driven off by Samians and some other Ionian Greeks who put in at Sicily as they were trying to escape from the Persians. But before long the Samians were driven off by Anaxilas, the ruler of Rhegium, who settled into the city himself with a population of men drawn from various places and he changed the name to Messana after his own original homeland." (Thucydides, *The Peloponnesian War* 6.4.5–6)

The Polis

We saw earlier that, during the Submycenaean Period as well, there was a kind of colonization movement, as Greeks migrated eastward across the Aegean Sea to settle on the west coast of Asia Minor. But there is a very great difference between these two periods of migration. That earlier period was an especially unsettled time, and Greece was beset by destitution and a precipitous decline in population. The period that begins with the eighth century, by contrast, is characterized by rapidly increasing prosperity and expanding population. Perhaps of even greater importance, the nature of community organization had changed radically between the beginning and the end of the Dark Age. It is not at all clear what kind of political organization existed in Greece after the collapse of Mycenaean society, or even if there was any recognizable political organization at all. The impression given by the archaeological remains from the twelfth and eleventh centuries is that individuals and their families functioned outside of any larger social or political framework. By the eighth century BC, however, the characteristic unit of Greek social, political, and religious organization had come into being. This unit is the polis. "Polis"

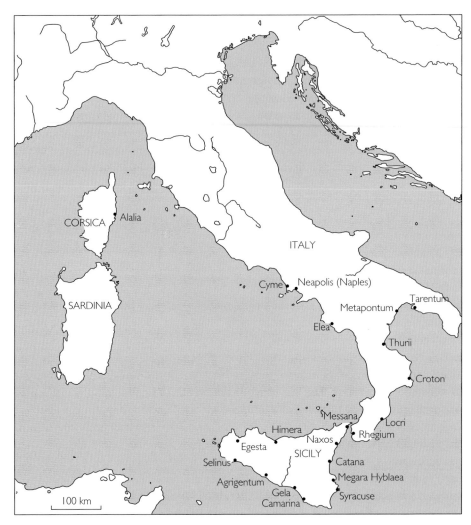

Map 6 Some Greek colonies in Italy and Sicily.

is simply the Greek word for "city" but, as we will see, the nature of the ancient Greek polis is so different from that of the cities that we are familiar with in modern nation-states that it will be less confusing if we employ the Greek word polis and its plural form, poleis.

The typical Greek polis, as we know it from its manifestation in the Archaic and Classical Periods, is a self-governing territory consisting of an urban center with a surrounding agricultural area, generally of a size such that one can walk from one end of it to the other in the course of a day. The urban center contains an open area, called an AGORA, where members of the polis can interact to conduct trade and to carry out the business of government, and a place for the cult that is shared by the members of the polis. One or more additional places for the cult, sometimes including a major sanctuary, are located in the surrounding area, often at or near

AGORA A centrally located open area of a polis where people could gather for political functions or for social and commercial purposes.

the border of the polis' territory. The details of the development of the polis as the political and social entity around which Greek life would be structured throughout the Archaic and Classical Periods are not clear. But the religious connection would seem to be fundamental, and the presence of one or more sanctuaries is as essential to the nature of the polis as the territory itself or the people who inhabit it. The polis seems to have crystallized during the eighth century BC around the sanctuary, which is marked off as a space sacred to a god or goddess, contains an altar for making animal sacrifice in the form of burnt offerings, and usually features a temple that houses the god's cult statue. All these elements, the sacred precinct, the large altar, the cult statue, and the temple building, emerge in the Greek world during the Geometric Period under oriental influence.

Thus, paradoxically, the characteristically Greek polis develops around features that the Greeks imported from the Near East. In many cases, the gods themselves, as we have seen, had been worshipped by the Greeks as early as the Mycenaean Period. The forms of worship, on the other hand, and the environment in which that worship took place bear so many "oriental" features that foreign influence can safely be assumed. That is not to say that the Greeks did not import oriental deities as well. It will be recalled that Aphrodite, whom the Asiatic Paris judged to be the most

> "She went to Cyprus and entered the fragrant sanctuary in Paphos. There is where she has her precinct and her fragrant altar. There she entered and shut the shining doors; there the Graces bathed her and anointed her with heavenly olive oil, the kind of oil that gives luster to the skin of the immortal gods, heavenly, seductive oil that had been made fragrant for her. She clothed her body magnificently with all her finery and, after she had arrayed herself with golden adornments, Aphrodite the smile-arouser rushed off to Troy, leaving fragrant Cyprus behind and making her way effortlessly high up among the clouds." (*Homeric Hymn to Aphrodite* 58–67)

beautiful goddess, was the only divine figure involved in the judgment of Paris of whom there is no mention in the Linear B tablets. The Greeks considered Aphrodite's place of birth to have been Cyprus, and it was there that the Greeks came into frequent contact with the Phoenicians, who worshipped a Semitic goddess, variously named Ashtorith, Astarte, or Ishtar, who shares numerous characteristics with Aphrodite. Everything points to the conclusion that the Greeks either adopted the worship of Aphrodite as a new goddess at some time during the Geometric Period or added so many Semitic features to the worship of an existing goddess that her original nature was wholly obscured.

At any rate, Aphrodite became a regular member of the Greek pantheon and many Greek poleis erected altars for sacrifices to her and temples to house her cult images. What is of particular significance is the communal effort that these structures and the tendance of these and other cults required. This communal effort both grew out of the newly developed structure of the polis and served to define that structure, by identifying the cult as the concern of the entire community and by proclaiming the investment of the polis' attention and resources in the maintenance of the cult. In the eighth century BC, at the same time that the polis develops its characteristic structure, we see a remarkable increase in the number of cult sites and in the lavishness with which dedicatory offerings are made at those sites. The kinds of valuable objects that previously had been buried as grave goods begin to be redirected and are dedicated in large numbers in communal sanctuaries. This redirection of resources from the grave to the communal sanctuary represents a significant shift in Greek society, as the polis begins to encroach upon the family as the focus of an individual's identity. For, while the grave is the concern solely of the descendants of the deceased, the sanctuary concerns the community as a whole.

The Olympic Games

Greece, then, in the eighth century BC consists of hundreds of separate poleis, whose inhabitants identify themselves as members of a polis on the basis of their common adherence to a cluster of cults. All Greeks recognize and worship the same pantheon of divinities, but the particular emphasis upon a limited group of those divinities, the specific character of certain festivals, and a peculiar calendar according to which those festivals were celebrated marked one Greek polis as distinct from another. As new poleis came into being with the establishment of Greek colonies along the coast of the Mediterranean Sea and Black Sea, the establishment of sanctuaries and cults served to mark the identity of the new polis and to differentiate it not only from the non-Greek communities in the surrounding area but from other Greek poleis, including the polis from which the colony had originated (called in Greek the *metropolis* or "mother-city"). This increasing contact with non-Greek populations and this differentiation of one polis from another presented the Greeks with the need to define themselves not only as members of a particular polis but as Greeks, as Hellenes. Their common Greek language, although divided into a number of dialects, served that purpose, as did certain inherited legends and myths. This purpose was also served by the development of a small number of religious festivals that attained a PANHELLENIC status; that is, festivals that were not confined to the members of a single polis but could be observed by all the Hellenes.

The most prominent, and apparently the oldest, of these Panhellenic festivals was the Olympic festival, celebrated at the sanctuary of Olympian Zeus, located in the northwestern Peloponnese, on the border of the territory of the Eleans and their neighbors to the south (map 7). The Greeks must have worshipped Zeus even before they entered Greece during the Mycenaean Period, as his name is Indo-European (compare Latin Jupiter, from the same root as Zeus + *pater*, "father," and Sanskrit *dyaus*, "sky, day"). The festival celebrated at Olympia followed an eight-year cycle of Babylonian origin, with the festival being held at the beginning and mid-point of the cycle. There is evidence of cult activity at the site of Olympia as early as the end of the tenth century BC, but the importance of the sanctuary increased in the course of the Geometric Period to the point that, by the seventh century, thousands of dedicatory offerings had been made there in the form of TERRACOTTA

PANHELLENIC
Literally "referring to all (pan-) the Greeks (Hellenes)," often used in connection with the Panhellenic Festivals and Games, which were open to all Greeks and only to Greeks, or with reference to Panhellenism, the idea that what distinguishes Greeks from BARBARIANS outweighs what divides Greeks from one another.

TERRACOTTA
Lightly fired, unglazed ceramic clay used for decorative tiles, architectural decorations, statuary, vases, and so on (figure 51).

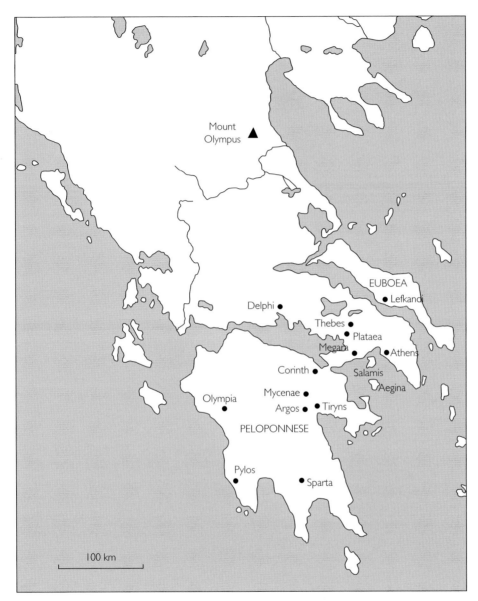

Map 7 Mainland Greece.

and bronze figurines, arms and armor, and valuable bronze cauldrons and TRIPODS (figure 18), from various Greek poleis and even from Italy and the Near East. These dedications are likely to have been made in connection with the festival which, like ancient Greek festivals generally, included large-scale animal sacrifices that took place at the altar within the sanctuary of Zeus.

This festival was particularly noted for the athletic contests that were held at the site of the sanctuary. The ancient Greeks had a tradition according to which these contests, the Olympic Games, began in the year we number 776 BC. While the

TRIPOD A pot or cauldron resting on three legs, often presented as a prize or as a votive offering (figure 18).

Figure 18 Modern reconstruction of bronze tripod "with ears" of the eighth century BC; height 1.54 m. Olympia, Archaeological Museum; photo by G. Hellner, DAI negative no. 1974/1115.

"The Spartans instituted the practice of exercising in the nude and, with their bodies exposed to public view, to anoint themselves with olive oil as they exercised. In earlier times athletes even at the Olympic Games used to compete wearing a loincloth about their genitals, and it is not many years since that practice came to an end. It is still the case among many foreigners today, especially in Asia, that when contests in boxing and wrestling are held, they engage in these activities wearing loincloths. This is one of many instances in which one can see similarities between the Greeks of old and foreigners of today." (Thucydides, *The Peloponnesian War* 1.6.5–6)

HELLENODIKAI Literally "assayers of Greeks," the title of the judges or umpires who were responsible for the organization and operation of the Olympic Games.

archaeological evidence suggests that this date might be a bit early, there seems to be little doubt that the games do in fact date from some time in the eighth century BC. A fondness for athletic contests, something on which the ancient Greeks prided themselves, was not at all an unusual feature of their festivals in honor of the gods, and the Greeks felt that this practice, and especially the habit of male participants competing in a state of total nudity, distinguished them from non-Greeks. And it was only freeborn Greeks who were eligible to participate in the Olympic Games. How the officials of the games determined whether a given competitor was in reality a citizen of a Greek polis is not known, but that it was their responsibility to determine the Hellenic identity of competitors (as well as to ensure that the rules of the contests were observed) is clear from their name, HELLENODIKAI, or "assayers of Greeks." We see, then, that in the face of increasing contact with foreigners at the end of the Geometric Period the Greeks were making an attempt at self-definition. That self-definition focused, in the case of the Olympic Games, on religious observance and on the naked display of athletic excellence. In the following chapter, we will see another form of self-definition with the development of what might be called a "national" literature, but for the fact that there was no "nation" of the Greeks.

Recommended for Further Reading

Boardman, J. *The Greeks Overseas: Their Early Colonies and Trade*, fourth edition (London 1999): a reliable and well-illustrated account of Greek colonization and trade to the end of the Archaic Period, with a valuable "Epilogue" describing recent finds and new approaches.

Bruit Zaidman, L. and Schmitt Pantel, P. *Religion in the Ancient Greek City*, English translation (Cambridge 1992): less comprehensive than Burkert's book (see below), but a concise and lively study, with full bibliography.

Burkert, W. *Greek Religion*, English translation (Cambridge, MA 1985): the standard work by the leading authority on the subject.

Burkert, W. *The Orientalizing Revolution: Near Eastern Influence on Greek Culture in the Early Archaic Age*, English translation (Cambridge, MA and London 1992): a revolutionary work that reveals the significant degree to which Greek religion and literature were influenced by eastern models.

Coldstream, J. N. *Geometric Greece 900–700 BC*, 2nd edition (London and New York 2003): a detailed treatment of the period from about 900 to about 700 BC, primarily from an archaeological point of view.

Hall, J. M. *A History of the Archaic Greek World ca. 1200–479 BCE* (Malden, MA 2007): a challenging and stimulating – and exceptionally well written – examination of the evidence for early Greek history and the way in which that evidence is treated; a splendid addition to the Blackwell "History of the Ancient World" series.

Hampe, R. and Simon, E. *The Birth of Greek Art: From the Mycenaean to the Archaic Period* (New York 1981): an authoritative and magnificently illustrated account of the continuity in Greek art from the Mycenaean Period to the Archaic.

Kyle, D. G. *Sport and Spectacle in the Ancient World* (Malden, MA 2007): a thoughtful and up-to-date account of the Panhellenic games and of the important status of sport in Greek (and Roman) culture.

de Polignac, F. *Cults, Territory, and the Origins of the Greek City-state*, English translation (Chicago 1995): an influential study of the role of religious cult as a decisive element in the formation of the Greek polis.

Powell, B. B. *Homer and the Origin of the Greek Alphabet* (Cambridge 1991): Powell's controversial thesis, that the Greek alphabet was invented by a single individual specifically to record the poems of Homer, need not be accepted in order to appreciate his excellent account of how the Phoenician script was transformed into the Greek alphabet.

Snodgrass, A. M. *The Dark Age of Greece: An Archaeological Survey of the Eleventh to the Eighth Centuries* BC (Edinburgh 1971): still the best survey of the archaeology of the Dark Age.

THE POEMS OF HESIOD AND HOMER

3

The earliest works of Greek literature, the poetry of Hesiod and Homer, are explored in this chapter. In his *Theogony* (ca. 700 BC), Hesiod tries to account in poetic form for the origin of the universe and the generations of the gods, culminating in the just and equitable reign of Zeus in Hesiod's own day. Later, Hesiod composed the *Works and Days*, which uses the mythical accounts of Prometheus and Pandora to explain the condition of Hesiod's contemporaries on the human level: the need to work hard for a living, the role of animal sacrifice in maintaining relations between men and gods, and the justice meted out by earthly kings as an imperfect reflection of the justice of Zeus, the king of the gods. Intermediate between men and gods are "heroes," mortals who become objects of cult following their death. The cult of heroes originates in Greece during the "Dark Age," and a fascinating archaeological discovery near the modern town of Lefkandi has provided us with what appears to be early evidence for the development of hero cult. Stories about the gods and about the men and women who were to become objects of hero cult had circulated for hundreds of years in the form of orally composed poetic accounts. The culmination of this tradition, which stretches back to the Mycenaean Period, can be found in the epic poems of Homer, the *Iliad* and the *Odyssey*, which recount events supposedly connected with the Trojan War, a legendary occurrence that the Greeks imagined to have taken place at the end of what we would call the Mycenaean Period. These poems are regarded today as being among the greatest masterpieces of Western literature; they were felt by the ancient Greeks to be not only literary creations of the first magnitude but embodiments of Greek culture, history, and identity.

In chapter 2, we saw a number of features that characterized the development of Greek civilization in the eighth century BC. These included the introduction of alphabetic writing, the willing adoption of elements of oriental influence, the beginnings of a period of Greek colonization throughout the Mediterranean region, the arousal of a Panhellenic sentiment in response to the expansion of the Greek world, the development of the polis as the basis for Greek social and political life, and the importance of communal cult as a catalyst of that development. All of these features can be illustrated from a reading of the poetry of Hesiod, who was himself born in the second half of the eighth century (probably between about 750 and 720 BC). His writings are among the earliest works of Greek literature that are available to us. We will consider in this chapter the surviving works of Hesiod, as well as the great epic poems of Homer, the *Iliad* and the *Odyssey*.

The Poems of Hesiod

"This is what the goddesses first said to me, the Olympian Muses, daughters of AEGIS-wielding Zeus: 'Shepherds who live in the wild, wretched disgraces, mere bellies, we have the skill to recount many falsehoods in the guise of truth, but we can also tell the truth when such is our wish.' So spoke the smooth-tongued daughters of mighty Zeus, and they gave me the branch of an evergreen laurel tree that they had picked out to be my staff, a magnificent one. And they breathed into me a superhuman power of song, so that I might tell of what was to come and what happened in the past, and they directed me to sing about the race of the blessed gods who live forever." (Hesiod, *Theogony* 24–33)

AEGIS A divine attribute, usually worn by Athena on her chest (figure 64), represented as a Gorgon's head surrounded by scales or a fringe, which confers special powers on the wearer.

Two poems survive that are unquestionably the work of Hesiod, the *Theogony* (about 1,000 lines long) and the *Works and Days* (about 800 lines). In the *Theogony*, Hesiod tells us his name and in both poems he speaks in the first person, giving us a number of biographical details. He lives, he tells us, in the Boeotian town of Ascra, not far from Thebes. Once, when he was pasturing his flocks near Mount Helicon, the Muses appeared to him and "breathed into" him the capacity for producing divine song. This epiphany was to have long-lasting effects on the course of Western civilization: for centuries, poets have spoken of themselves as "inspired." The song that the Muses have inspired in Hesiod is an account, from the beginning, of the generation of the gods (which is essentially what the title *Theogony* means). The first divinity to be generated is Chaos, "yawning void," whose name is neither masculine nor feminine, but neuter. Then female Gaia ("Earth") comes into being and generates male Uranus ("Heaven"). Between the two of them (more or less literally) a new generation of gods is created, the youngest of whom is Cronus, who eventually overthrows his father Uranus after having castrated him with a sickle. This is only one of a large number of elements in the *Theogony* that have close parallels in earlier mythological accounts from the Near East. In the Hittite myth concerning the god Kumarbi, Kumarbi overthrows his predecessor and bites off his predecessor's genitals, which he swallows; he then generates the Hittite weather god. In Hesiod, Cronus' sickle is described as having jagged "teeth" like a saw; after castrating Uranus, Cronus sires Zeus, who is responsible for the weather.

Zeus, in turn, overthrows his father Cronus, but this act is represented not as yet another act in an ongoing series of crimes but as a restoration of justice. Cronus is punished not only for his violence against his father but for his treatment of his children, whom he swallows as soon as they are born to prevent them from usurping his rule. He is, however, deceived into swallowing a stone in place of his son Zeus, who is thus spared and allowed to grow to full strength without Cronus knowing of his survival. Zeus later rescues his brothers and sisters from the belly of Cronus and begins his enlightened rule over men and gods. The whole of Hesiod's story in the *Theogony* is of a steady progression in the divine realm from (literal) chaos to order and justice, of which Zeus is the guarantor. In the human realm, the guarantors of order and justice are the basileis, the plural form of basileus, which we saw in chapter 1 was the title of the Mycenaean official just under the king. The basileis are thus the earthly counterparts of Zeus: just as the Muses sing the praises of Zeus and the other gods, so poets like Hesiod are expected to sing the praises of the earthly basileis (along, of course, with praising the gods). But, unlike Zeus, the basileus of the gods, the human basileis are in need of instruction, which Hesiod is prepared to supply. Hesiod's poetry is designed both to flatter and to teach the basileis, who are expected to put up with being lectured by a poet who is their social inferior. This is because the song of a poet confers prestige on the basileus and is the most effective instrument of what today would be thought of as "public relations."

In the *Theogony*, Hesiod's lessons for the basileis are subtle and implicit. In the *Works and Days*, which was composed later than the *Theogony*, Hesiod speaks directly to the basileis. He also addresses his brother Perses who, we are told, had bribed the basileis to judge in Perses' favor when a dispute between Perses and Hesiod arose concerning their inheritance. Having received more of the inheritance than he deserved, Perses proceeded to squander it and, impoverished, came begging to Hesiod. The lesson to be learned from this, which Hesiod does not hesitate to propound, is that injustice is invariably punished by Zeus. Justice, on the other hand, leads to prosperity, benefiting not only the individual but the polis as well. Prosperity, Hesiod tells us, is the result of being industrious and frugal, and the *Works and Days* is filled with very specific advice on the details of household management, farming, husbandry, and so on, in many instances with close parallels in the "wisdom literature" of the Near East.

As we saw in the case of the *Theogony*, Hesiod is especially concerned with origins and explanations, even going back to the very beginning of the cosmos. The same is true of the *Works and Days*, and in it the poet informs us (along with Perses and the basileis) exactly why it is necessary to work and why life for mortals is so hard. The explanation takes the form of the myth of Prometheus, part of which was also recounted in the *Theogony*. There was a time, it seems, when men did not have to work and when men feasted in the company of the gods. At one of these

"Immediately the renowned Hephaestus followed the wishes of Zeus, the son of Cronus, and molded a figure out of earth in the shape of a demure maiden. The steely-eyed goddess Athena dressed and adorned her; the divine Graces and mistress Persuasion placed golden jewelry about her body; and the fair-tressed Hours garlanded her with springtime flowers. In her heart Hermes the facilitator, the slayer of Argus, fashioned falsehoods and seductive chatter and a devious nature, all through the wishes of loud-thundering Zeus. And the spokesman of the gods gave her a voice, and he named this woman Pandora, because of her endowment by all the gods who dwell on Olympus, a disaster for bread-eating men." (Hesiod, *Works and Days* 70–82)

feasts Prometheus tried to deceive Zeus, by unevenly dividing the remains of a slaughtered ox in such a way that the inedible portion looked more attractive. Zeus chose the inedible portion, although Hesiod assures us that Zeus saw through the trick and only chose as he did so that he could punish Prometheus for injustice. Zeus also punished men, who secured the edible portion of the ox as a result of his choice, by withholding fire from them. At this point, Prometheus, again challenging Zeus' authority, stole fire from the gods and gave it back to men. To counterbalance the blessing of fire, Zeus inflicted upon mankind what Hesiod and his contemporaries appear to have regarded as the worst evil imaginable, womankind. Like the inedible portion of the ox, the first woman is superficially attractive, and so mankind is seduced into accepting this "gift" from the gods. Hesiod in fact considers the name of this woman, Pandora, to mean "the gift of all" the gods to men.

Hesiod's account of Prometheus and Pandora is a myth of a sort that has particular significance for the Greeks. A myth that is concerned, as this one is, with causes or origins is referred to as an *aition*, using a Greek word that means "responsible (for a particular outcome)." An *aition* is a story, and the fundamental characteristic of a story is that its outcome results in an intelligible fashion from the logic of the narrative. Because it is a story, it gives the impression that the outcome has been satisfactorily accounted for. In this case, Hesiod's *aition* accounts for the fact that men and gods no longer feast together as resulting from Prometheus' trick and Zeus' punishment of him (figure 19). Not only do men no longer enjoy a life of ease, dining with the gods, but men now have an extra mouth to feed. Life is especially hard now because of the presence of woman who, according to Hesiod, is a drain on man's resources but is an evil necessary for the production of an heir to keep those meager resources within the family. In addition, the myth accounts for why animal sacrifice takes the curious form it does, with humans consuming the edible portion of the victim and burning the bones and the intestines on an altar, supposedly as a gift to the gods. The ritual of sacrifice memorializes Prometheus' injustice and his theft of fire. At the same time, the gift to the gods that sacrifice represents both compensates for Prometheus' injustice and appeases the gods in hopes of avoiding future punishment.

This *aition* is complemented by another myth that Hesiod recounts in the *Works and Days*, the story of the generations of humans. According to this myth, which has numerous parallels in oriental tales and is presumably of Near Eastern origin, the earliest human generation was a golden race of men who did not need to work.

Figure 19 Interior of black-figure Laconian cup by the Arkesilas Painter, showing Atlas (left) and the punishment of Prometheus; diameter of cup 20.2 cm, ca. 565–550 BC. Vatican Museums, Museo Gregoriano Etrusco, Inv. 16592; photo: Scala/Art Resource, NY.

In contrast to the generations of the gods, which became progressively more righteous and blessed, the generations of humans degenerated through ages of silver, then bronze, then (anomalously) an age of heroes, and then finally the iron age in which Hesiod considers himself to be living. Humans have become increasingly vicious and, as punishment from the gods, conditions have become increasingly difficult. We mortals have to make the most of a very bad lot and the best we can do, Hesiod seems to be telling us, is to listen carefully to the lessons contained in the *Theogony* and the *Works and Days* in hopes that further degeneration can be minimized.

"First the immortals who dwell on Olympus created a generation of mortal men that was golden. They lived at the time of Cronus, when he ruled as king in the heavens. Their existence was like that of the gods; their hearts were free of cares and they lived without pain and toil. Nor were they afflicted with the feebleness of old age, but their limbs remained always unchanged and they took their joy in feasting, removed from all troubles. When they died it was as though they were succumbing to sleep. All good things were theirs; the fruitful furrows of the fields bore bounteous produce of their own accord." (Hesiod, *Works and Days* 109–18)

Hesiod's poetry is of considerable importance to us, not only because now, finally, we have a representative of ancient Greek civilization who can actually talk to us, but also because what he has to say illustrates so well what we have seen to be characteristic of the developments of the eighth century, the century in which Hesiod was born. His works survive as a result of the new technology of writing, and we have noticed a few of the many instances in his work of orientalizing influence. Further, the community in which he lives has an administrative and ritual focus typical of the polis that was just beginning to emerge in Greece, as we can see from Hesiod's concern with the political power of the basileis and with the details of myth and cult.

The terms in which Hesiod tells his story of the progress of the gods and deterioration of humankind seem somewhat naïve, but we can also see hints of a more abstract, even scientific mentality that will come to fruition in the following centuries. Hesiod speaks primarily in terms of biological procreation: birth and organic growth are for Hesiod the process by which development of any sort occurs. The progression from night to day, for example, is represented in Hesiod's construction of the cosmos as the goddess Night "giving birth to" the goddess Day after mating with her "brother" Darkness. Similarly Ares, the god of war, "sires" divinities named Terror and Fear. To what extent are these "mere metaphors," like the use of the word "metropolis" to refer to the "parent" city of a colony, and to what extent does Hesiod expect his audience to understand these "literally"? The difficulty of answering this seemingly straightforward question becomes apparent when we direct the same question to a modern scientist, who constructs sophisticated "models" of the brain, say, or global warming. The scientist will be unlikely to admit that these models are "mere metaphors"; rather, they are "cognitive instruments." The same is true of Hesiod's use of generation as a "metaphor" for the process of development and for what we regard as more "abstract" relationships. So poets and musicians are "descended from" Apollo and the Muses, as basileis are "descended from" Zeus, and women are "descended from" Pandora. All women are literally descended from Pandora, but so are all men; the predominately metaphorical sense here is fortified by the literal, making this an especially effective cognitive instrument, one that convincingly explains existing reality in terms accessible to Hesiod's contemporaries.

Some of the divinities whose generation Hesiod recounts are gods and goddesses familiar to Hesiod's audience from contemporary cult and ritual. Some, however, have no existence in Greek cult and may rather be the product of pure invention on the part of the poet. It is a curious feature of ancient Greek civilization that poets are generally felt to possess the authority to mold myths and to explain the origins of ritual practice, thereby in some instances actually transforming ritual practice or even generating new rituals. We have seen that communal cults are intimately connected with the development of the polis in the period in which Hesiod lived. There is nothing in

"My father and yours, Perses, great fool that you are, used to sail on shipboard in need of a decent livelihood. At some time he came here, making his way across the vast sea, departing from Aeolian Cyme in a black ship. It wasn't riches or wealth and prosperity that he was running away from but dire poverty, which Zeus bestows on men. He settled down near Mount Helicon in a miserable village, Ascra, bad in winter, unbearable in summer, never good." (Hesiod, *Works and Days* 633–40)

Hesiod's work that suggests that it is concerned specifically with the local cults of his own polis of Ascra. Rather, he is addressing a Panhellenic audience and his concern is with the wider Greek world. This is also clear from the form of Hesiod's language. We saw in chapter 2 that the Greeks were divided into regional groups of speakers of different dialects of Greek. Hesiod tells us that his father came from the city of Cyme on the coast of Asia Minor, a city where the Aeolic dialect was spoken, and migrated to the town of Ascra, where a related, Boeotian dialect was spoken. Yet Hesiod's poems are not in the Aeolic or the Boeotian dialect. In fact, they cannot be said to belong to any one dialect. Hesiod composes his poetry in an artificial dialect that combines features from a number of regions of Greece. By far the largest number of elements of this artificial, poetic idiom are derived not from the Boeotian or Aeolic dialects but from Ionic. But Hesiod's poetic dialect is essentially Panhellenic in nature, so that he could travel to various Greek communities and perform the *Theogony* and the *Works and Days* in the expectation that they would be readily understood and appreciated.

The Development of Hero Cult

In fact, Hesiod tells us briefly in the *Works and Days* about one of those occasions on which he performed in a neighboring community. He traveled, he says, to the city of Chalcis on the island of Euboea to compete in a contest associated with the funeral rites for a prominent leader of Chalcis. There he performed, perhaps reciting his *Theogony*, and was awarded a prize of a valuable tripod "with ears," a standard type of prize offered for victory in athletic or musical contests (see figure 18). This practice of holding elaborate funeral rites, including the participation of Greeks from other poleis, is a standard feature of the developing polis. We noted in chapter 2 that the polis seems to have crystallized during the eighth century BC around the sanctuary, but this was only part of the story. Also instrumental in the creation of the polis was a change, or a series of changes, in funerary practice.

As we have seen, during the Mycenaean Period prominent individuals were buried in lavish style, a practice that continued in the Dark Age, although generally on a much smaller scale because of severely reduced prosperity. A chance discovery, however, has revealed that, on occasion, even during the Dark Age some individual was able to rise to a level of prosperity that allowed him to emulate his Mycenaean predecessors. In 1980, a citizen of the town of Lefkandi on the island of Euboea, less than 10 kilometers from Chalcis, while using a bulldozer to clear some land, uncovered and partially destroyed the remains of a large structure dating to the first half of the tenth century BC. The name of the town looks different from the names of the other locations in Greece that we have been considering. The reason for this is that the other locations we have encountered have been places whose ancient names we know because they are referred to in texts from antiquity. Lefkandi is a modern Greek name; we do not know what the name of the community was in ancient times. The structure that was discovered at Lefkandi, and which has subsequently been subjected to expert archaeological investigation, is remarkable in a number of respects. To begin with, it is unusually large for a building of this date, being some 10 meters wide and over 45 meters in length (figure 20). The walls were made of mud brick, plastered on the inside, on a stone foundation. An overhanging thatch roof, which protected the walls from the elements, was supported by series of wooden posts, both inside and outside the building. This feature makes this structure the distant ancestor of the familiar Classical Greek temple which, as we will see, takes the form of a rectangular building surrounded by stone columns supporting an overhanging roof.

The tenth-century building at Lefkandi, however, was not a temple. In fact, it is not known for certain what the function of the building was. The most surprising feature of the building is that, underneath the floor in the center of the building, archaeologists discovered a burial site more or less contemporary with the building

Figure 20
Axonometric drawing of the "Heroon" at Lefkandi as reconstructed, 1000–950 BC. Reproduced with permission of the British School at Athens from *Lefkandi* II: *The Protogeometric Building at Toumba*, Part 2 (Athens 1993), Plate 28.

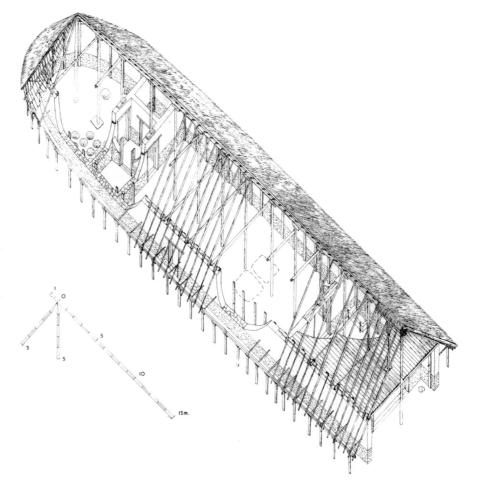

itself, consisting of two graves. One of the graves contained the bones of four horses, apparently the victims of some form of sacrificial ritual. The other grave held the remains of a man and a woman, whose bodies received very different treatment. The man had been cremated and his ashes, wrapped in a linen cloth, were placed in a twelfth-century bronze amphora that was decorated with scenes of hunting. Around the amphora were a whetstone and an iron sword and spear. The woman, however, had not been cremated. She was buried, with an ivory-handled iron knife beside

> "With much lamentation Achilles quickly added four proud-necked horses to the pyre. There were also nine dogs who accompanied their master at table and he slit the throats of two of them and added them to the pyre, along with twelve well-born sons of the valorous Trojans, whom he slaughtered with his bronze weapon... In tears they gathered up the white bones of their sweet companion, enclosing them in two layers of fat inside a golden urn, which they covered over with fine linen and placed in his tent. Then they encircled the grave by setting foundation stones about the pyre and immediately heaped up the earth over it." (Homer, *Iliad* 23.171–6 and 252–6, describing the funeral for Patroclus)

her head, in a posture that is suggestive of the possibility that she had been sacrificed, perhaps like the horses, in connection with the funeral of the man. Her body was lavishly decorated with gold ornaments. It would seem, then, that this was the burial of a very powerful and wealthy individual. Ownership of horses is restricted to only the most affluent of the ancient Greeks and the expense of the structure and the grave goods can only have been borne by a handful of families in Greece at this time. But what was the function of the building? In fact, not long after it was constructed, portions of the building were torn down and the whole structure was covered over with a great mound of earth.

All of these unusual circumstances have puzzled archaeologists and historians, who can only hypothesize over the meaning of this extraordinary building. The archaeologists who were responsible for the original excavation of the site proposed that the building was a *heroon*, or a shrine in honor of a hero, namely the unnamed man, presumably a warrior, whose ashes were buried along with his horses, his wife or concubine, and other personal effects. What is especially puzzling about the building at Lefkandi is its isolation in both time and space. Nothing remotely like it from the Dark Age has been discovered by archaeologists, and the community in which the building was constructed appears to have been too small to produce either the manpower or the resources necessary for such an undertaking. Nor is it clear what the source of the dead man's wealth might have been. Perhaps he was a mercenary soldier who sold his services as a warrior or perhaps a trafficker in human beings, a slave-dealer who sold other people's services. Despite all the questions that surround the tomb at Lefkandi, it appears that it somehow supplies a precious piece of evidence, still requiring a great deal of interpretative ingenuity, that points to some degree of continuity between practices of the Mycenaean Period and developments that were to occur at the end of the Dark Age.

It is not clear whether it was the community as a whole or just the relatives of the (obviously quite wealthy) deceased who were responsible for constructing this tomb. At any rate, during the Dark Age it was generally the family of the deceased who were concerned with the arrangements of burial and the maintenance of the grave. By the eighth century BC, families had begun to reduce their expenditure of resources on expensive goods to be buried with the deceased and concentrated instead on calling attention to the location of the burial with conspicuous markers like the Geometric amphora shown in figure 16. That is to say, families appear to have begun to consider burial more as a form of display among the living, so that funerary rituals, like the one depicted in the figured scene on the amphora, are likely to have become more lavish, while less emphasis was placed on the magnificence of the objects hidden away in the earth with the dead. This conspicuous display in honor of deceased family members may have turned into a sort of competition, as wealthy families sought to outdo one another in the extravagance with which they commemorated their own. But this type of rivalry was inimical to the communal spirit required by the developing polis.

Somehow – and the details of this process are subject to vigorous scholarly debate – the polis found a way to channel that eagerness for funerary display into a new type of communal funerary commemoration with the introduction of hero cults in the second half of the eighth century. The Greeks were aware, because of the perpetuation in legend of heroic stories and because of the visible evidence of Mycenaean ruins, that at some point in the distant past their poleis had been more prosperous and more powerful than in the immediately preceding Dark Age. There is evidence that in some places rituals were occasionally carried out during the Dark Age at the site of ancient Mycenaean tombs, satisfying a desire to connect with the distant past by ritual means. These rituals had the effect of incorporating the supposed glories of the past directly into the life of the present, thereby redefining the past through a process of selective appropriation. We do not know whether the participants in these rituals considered themselves to be direct descendants of those whom they venerated, nor do we know, in most instances, exactly whom they thought they were venerating. Beginning around the end of the eighth century, there is a good deal of evidence for regular ritual observance at locations that were thought to be the graves of specific individuals considered to be prominent warriors or members of royal families from the distant past. These individuals were called by the Greek word *heros*, "hero," that is, a deceased mortal who became the object of ritual observance by the polis and whose rituals it would be dangerous for the polis to omit. Gradually, the accounts of who these heroes and heroines were and what they had done while alive were subject to elaboration and embellishment, not to mention outright invention. And, just as it is the poets who were expected to mold the myths and ritual practices relating to the gods, so the poets had the authority to explain who the heroes were whom the polis revered and what they had done.

We have seen that Hesiod inserted an age of heroes into his myth of the generations of humans, interrupting the otherwise steady degeneration represented by increasingly base (and increasingly destructive) metals. Hesiod tells us that these heroes, whose generation occurred between the violent bronze age and the depraved iron age in which Hesiod himself lives, included those who died "fighting for the sake of Oedipus' flocks at Thebes of the seven portals" and those who went by sea to fight at Troy "for the sake of Helen of the lovely tresses." Hesiod knew, and obviously expected his audience to know, at least in outline, the stories of these epic battles. These stories were recounted in epic poems belonging to an oral tradition that was in existence for some centuries before Hesiod's own time. As it happens, some descendants of that oral tradition were written down and were copied and recopied often enough that hundreds of copies still survive today. Two of those descendants, the *Iliad* and the *Odyssey*, which the ancient Greeks considered to be the work of a poet named Homer, are among the greatest and most influential works of poetry in Greek or in any language.

The Poems of Homer

The *Iliad*, a poem of nearly sixteen thousand verses, takes place during the Trojan War and is concerned with the quarrel between the Greek basileis Achilles and Agamemnon and the disastrous consequences of that quarrel. The *Odyssey*, about twelve thousand lines long, recounts the adventures of Odysseus, another Greek basileus, and the difficulties he encounters as he attempts to return home after the end of the Trojan War. Among the many striking features of these poems – their inexhaustible literary merit being the most notable – is how remarkably similar in language, meter, and dialect they are both to each other and to the poems of Hesiod. Their consistency with each other is not surprising if they are, in fact, the work of a single poet, but their similarity to the works of Hesiod requires some other explanation. Straightforward influence by one poet on the other is, of course, a possibility. For example, the phrases quoted above from Hesiod, "Thebes of the seven portals" and "Helen of the lovely tresses," both occur in Homer as well, and one poet may have appropriated them from the other. Yet the similarity is so much more extensive than the sharing of a few, or even a great many, specific expressions that it will be necessary to understand the peculiar nature of poetic composition in Greece of the Geometric Period before we can begin to understand the relationship between Hesiod and Homer.

Mention was made above of the artificial dialect that Homer and Hesiod share. This purely literary, or "artistic," dialect contains not only elements that derive from different regions of the Greek world but also elements that belong to discrete periods of the development of the Greek language. But what is the point of such an artificial language? A satisfactory explanation was not forthcoming until the work in the 1920s and 1930s of a brilliant American scholar named Milman Parry accounted for the eclectic character of Homeric language as deriving from a tradition of orally composed poems. What Parry studied were those pervasive expressions, such as "Thebes of the seven portals" and "Helen of the lovely tresses," that consist of a name and an EPITHET. He did not examine these specific expressions,

EPITHET An adjective or descriptive phrase indicating some quality or attribute which the speaker or writer regards as characteristic of the person or thing described, for example, "swift-footed" in the expression "swift-footed Achilles."

which occur only a couple of times each in the Homeric poems, but rather certain combinations of noun plus epithet that occur dozens of times each in the *Iliad* and *Odyssey*, like "the steely-eyed goddess Athena" or "swift-footed Achilles." What Parry discovered was that Homer normally does not use more than one such combination *having the same metrical value* for any one character in his poems. There are several different combinations that Homer uses when he refers, for example, to the main character of the *Iliad*: he may call him "Peleus' son Achilles" or "swift Achilles" or "noble Achilles," in addition to "swift-footed Achilles," but *none of them is metrically equivalent to any of the others.*

Parry referred to this system as an "economy of epithets," and he concluded that so elaborate a system can have arisen only by evolving over a lengthy period of time for the purpose of facilitating oral composition; that is, composition in the course of oral performance. Homeric (and Hesiodic) poetry is composed using a metrical form known as the DACTYLIC HEXAMETER, a verse form consisting of 12 to 17 syllables that follow a standard pattern of short and long syllables. If in the course of his performance the poet reaches a particular point in the hexameter line and wishes to fill out the rest of that line with an expression meaning "Achilles," the poet normally has one and only one expression in his repertoire that will fit into the remaining space in the line. The advantage of this system is that it releases the poet from the need to choose between competing and metrically equivalent expressions so that he can concentrate more upon what he is about to say than upon what specific words he is going to use to say it. It is not in fact individual words that are the elements of the oral poet's repertoire, but regularly recurring groups of words that Parry referred to as "formulaic expressions" or "formulae." In addition to these regularly recurring verbal patterns, Parry and other scholars came to recognize the presence in the Homeric poems of repeated narrative patterns or "typical scenes." Frequently in the *Iliad* and the *Odyssey* the poet describes a sacrifice or the arrival of a messenger or the arming of a warrior. The sequence of events in these scenes usually follows a regular pattern, sometimes including verbal formulae that are repeated in other, similar scenes. These "typical scenes" are not repeated word for word from one occurrence to the next, but are shaped and modified to suit the specific requirements of the narrative. It should not be thought that this adherence to patterns or formulae deprives the poet of the opportunity for originality. These merely represent the essential framework within which composition can take place, whether that composition is banal or brilliant, oldfangled or novel.

Parry had the opportunity, rare among researchers in the humanities, to subject his hypothesis of oral composition to empirical testing. In the 1930s, in the country then known as Yugoslavia there existed a tradition of bards who were mostly illiterate who performed original poems which they composed in the course of performance. Parry was able to study and record the performances of these Serbo-Croatian bards and he found that many of the same features present in the Homeric poems – repeated verbal formulae, "typical scenes," the co-existence of old and new, a thriftiness comparable to the Homeric "economy of epithets," subject-matter concerned with glorious military accomplishments of the distant past

DACTYLIC HEXAMETER A metrical form in which each line of verse is made up of six (Greek *hex*) dactyls (a unit consisting of one long syllable followed by one or two further syllables), a meter appropriate to epic poetry, prophecies given by the Delphic oracle, and other poetry of a serious or philosophical character (for example, the poems of Hesiod).

– were present in the Yugoslav tradition as well. (This Yugoslav oral tradition has since fallen victim to the spread of literacy, but it has been artificially preserved for the benefit of tourists.) The work of Parry and his followers has shown conclusively that the *Iliad* and *Odyssey* derive from a tradition of orally composed verse, and Parry was himself convinced that these poems were in fact themselves orally composed. But, as we have seen, the language, style, and dialect of Homer and Hesiod are nearly identical, and there is every reason to believe that the works of Hesiod were originally composed in written form. The similarity between the works of these two poets can readily be explained by the fact that their language, style, and dialect are the products of a tradition of orally composed poems, even if the poems themselves were composed by literate poets with the aid of writing. The formulae, the typical scenes, the stories themselves may have been transmitted orally by a tradition that preserved and transformed all these elements over a period of hundreds of years, but the poems in the form in which we now possess them are likely to be the product of a literate age which, as we have seen, began in Greece in the eighth century BC.

The poems of Hesiod seem to have originated in the period close to 700 BC, at the end of the eighth century or the beginning of the seventh. What about the *Iliad* and the *Odyssey*? And what about Homer, the man who is supposed to have composed them? Unfortunately, despite the enormous amount of research that has been undertaken, there is nothing even approaching a scholarly consensus regarding the questions of when these poems were composed, whether the same poet was responsible for the composition of both poems, or what the nature of that act of composition was. The reason for the difficulty is precisely the traditional nature of the Homeric poems, which include elements of language and references to artifacts that can be dated to various times ranging from the Mycenaean Period down to the sixth century BC. It might be possible to take the date of the latest element represented as giving an indication of the time of composition, with earlier elements having been preserved because of the inherently conservative nature of the tradition. On the other hand, it is equally possible that individual passages containing those isolated "late" elements were subsequently added to an already "complete" text. It does seem very likely, however, that by the sixth century BC the *Iliad* and the *Odyssey* attained essentially the written form in which we currently have them. But there is no agreement regarding what the poems looked like before the sixth century, whether they differed from the sixth-century text only slightly, or were substantially different, or even differed so radically that they would not be recognizable to us as the *Iliad* and the *Odyssey*.

What does seem reasonably clear, however, is that these two poems reached their present form during the period from the middle of the eighth to the middle of the sixth century (approximately 750–550 BC), the period of the development of the polis, the creation of hero cults, Greek colonization, and the rise of Panhellenic sentiment. The oral tradition of which the *Iliad* and the *Odyssey* are the culmination was engaged during this period in inventing a heroic, Panhellenic tradition that rooted itself in a dimly remembered Mycenaean heritage. We have seen a reflection of this in Hesiod's myth, in the *Works and Days*, of the generations of humans, with its age of heroes. Since Hesiod's poem belongs to the tradition of wisdom literature, the age of heroes is described briefly, in only a few lines of verse. The *Iliad* and the *Odyssey*, however, belong to an epic tradition of large-scale heroic poetry and they aim to tell a coherent story of the heroic past, thereby providing the present with a "history." The present, that is the period from approximately 750–550 BC, was the time when the polis was in the process of formation out of the unstructured communities of the Dark Age. We can only speculate regarding the character of that process but, given the pervasive competitiveness of the ancient Greeks, it is natural to assume that the polis took the form that it did as a result of the necessity to balance the conflicting ambitions of the wealthier and more powerful individuals and families of the region. This conflict, along with its eventual unstable resolution, may have provided the pattern for the largely fictitious world of the past, with its volatile and ambitious heroic characters.

The Homeric poems create an entire society in which these heroes can function, a society that contrasts markedly with (although it cannot help including elements of) the more egalitarian world of the polis. This society consists of individuals whose power resides not in any kind of organized political structure but in their military effectiveness and their "prestige," an intangible but very real capacity for being acknowledged as a leader. This prestige can, of course, be bolstered by tangible tokens, which

> "The son of Peleus then laid out other prizes, prizes for swiftness of foot. First was a well-wrought silver krater. Its capacity was only six measures, but for beauty it was easily the finest in all the lands, since expert artisans from Sidon had worked it skillfully. Phoenician men had brought it over the frothy sea and, when they landed in the harbor, they presented it to Thoas as a gift. Euneus, the son of Jason, gave it to the warrior Patroclus to serve as the ransom price for Lycaon, the son of Priam. This krater Achilles laid out as a prize in honor of his companion." (Homer, *Iliad* 23.740–8)

Homer often describes in lavish detail. Such tokens can include valuable items that have been won as prizes in contests, like the tripod won by Hesiod. Homeric warriors, however, win their prizes in athletic contests or chariot races rather than in musical contests. Other heroes, who display their own entitlement to honor by giving gifts of great value, are another source of prestige goods, like golden vessels or horses and chariots. This gift exchange is an important means by which Homeric heroes establish, maintain, and reconfigure social relationships among themselves. These gifts are objects of value not merely because they are made of expensive materials or are the products of fine craftsmanship. They are accompanied by a story that attests to the owner's standing and his connections with other influential basileis. For example, in the *Odyssey* there is a 30-line account of the history of Odysseus' bow, which was given to Odysseus by the hero Iphitus, who inherited it from his father, the great archer Eurytus, and who was himself later killed by Heracles. Finally, another way in which Homeric heroes can acquire valuable items is on the battlefield, by slaying a notable warrior in single combat and then stripping the armor from his body. This armor can then be displayed (and the story of its acquisition told) as visible proof of the victor's prowess.

Homeric heroes sometimes strike modern readers as being excessively acquisitive, but the material objects that the hero values so highly are unique marks of his identity and his standing in the community. If he is deprived of one or more of them his honor is seriously diminished and his capacity for being acknowledged as a leader may be jeopardized. This is the situation that sets in motion the plot of the *Iliad*. During the 10 years of the Trojan War, the Greeks supplied themselves by attacking and plundering smaller cities in the region of Troy. In one of these raids, Agamemnon, Menelaus' brother and the acknowledged leader of the Greek forces, acquired as his personal property the young woman "Chryseis of the lovely cheeks," daughter of a priest of Apollo. The *Iliad* opens with her father entreating Agamemnon to return her to him, but Agamemnon refuses, despite the general sentiment among the Greek troops that the priest's request is reasonable. Chryseis' father then prays to Apollo, who afflicts the Greek army with a plague, which can only be ended by Agamemnon's restoration of Chryseis to her father. Agamemnon reluctantly sends her back to her father and her function in the *Iliad* is complete (although she will live on as Criseyde in Chaucer and as Cressida in Shakespeare). Agamemnon's honor has been diminished and he demands recompense. Achilles suggests that Agamemnon wait until Troy has been taken, at which time the Greeks will more than compensate Agamemnon for his loss. Agamemnon is angered by this suggestion and, after both men have exchanged insults, Agamemnon appropriates "Briseis of the lovely cheeks" – Briseis and Chryseis are metrically equivalent names – whom Achilles had acquired on an earlier raid. This in turn provokes the anger of Achilles, which lasts throughout most of the lengthy epic.

"Anger," in fact, is the first word of the poem, which begins, "Sing, goddess, of the anger of Peleus' son Achilles." In his anger Achilles refuses any longer to fight, and he threatens that he and his troops will return home to Greece, where his aged father longs to see him. There is no point in his risking his life if he is not going to be accorded the respect and the honor to which his military accomplishments entitle him. Eventually respect and honor become irrelevant, as Achilles returns to the fighting, not because of the insistent pleas of Agamemnon and the other Greeks, but in order to avenge the death of his closest friend Patroclus, who is killed in battle by the foremost Trojan warrior Hector. Even after he has killed Hector, Achilles' anger does not abate and, contrary to the normal standards of the society which the Homeric poems purport to represent, Achilles is unwilling to grant burial to

"Priam spoke, and in doing so aroused in Achilles a tearful longing for his own father. Taking hold of the old man by the hand he pushed him gently away from himself, and the two of them began to reminisce; the one, huddled before the feet of Achilles, wept copious tears for Hector the slayer of heroes while Achilles lamented now his own father, now Patroclus. Their wailing penetrated throughout Achilles' quarters. But when godlike Achilles had fully indulged his grief and the longing for tears had vanished from his heart and body, then he rose up from his seat and he lifted up the old man by the hand, out of pity at the white hair and the white beard. Addressing him he spoke in pointed words: 'Poor man! Really you have taken upon yourself many sorrows. How did you bring yourself to come alone to the ships of the Achaeans, into the very presence of the man who slaughtered many of your fine sons?'" (Homer, *Iliad* 24.507–21)

Hector's corpse. In the last of the 24 books of the poem, however, Hector's father Priam, the king of Troy, comes under cover of darkness to the tent of Achilles to entreat Achilles to return to him the body of his son. In one of the most sublime passages in all of literature, Achilles and Priam together come to a recognition of the essence of human existence, that it is limited and, therefore, defined by death. Achilles knows, because he has been told by his divine mother Thetis, that his own death is soon to follow upon that of Hector. Priam knows that, in the absence of the mighty warrior Hector, the city of Troy is doomed to destruction at the hands of the Greeks.

As we have seen, the Homeric poems arose out of an oral tradition that of necessity uses traditional forms of expression that conceal, because they appropriate selectively, marks of individual poetic creativity. At the same time, these poems celebrate the glorious accomplishments of heroes who insist on their own personal worth and their individual identity. This situation is analogous to the circumstances surrounding the creation of hero cults in Greek poleis. A hero was a singular individual with a unique story that set him (or her) apart from all other members of the community, and yet the cult of the hero was a collective enterprise that was conducive to the solidarity of all members of the polis. This tension, between the claims of the individual and those of the community, are reflected in the *Iliad* and the *Odyssey*. Achilles is admirable, in the eyes of Homer's audience, both because of his excellence and because of his insistence that his excellence be appropriately recognized. At the same time, his withdrawal from the fighting endangers the community of Greek warriors and results in the death of his beloved Patroclus.

The *Odyssey* is in many ways a more sophisticated and subtle work. (For this reason, many scholars have been convinced that it is not the work of the poet of the *Iliad*, but given the oral and traditional background to both poems it is impossible to tell how much of either poem can be ascribed to an individual poet.) The hero of the poem is himself an unusually subtle and sophisticated character. Odysseus was one of the prominent Greek warriors who fought in the war at Troy, and the story of the *Odyssey* is the story of his 10-year attempt to overcome the obstacles to his return home to the remote island of Ithaca and the challenges to his re-establishing his position as husband, father, and basileus. His standing and his personal identity, therefore, are central concerns of the poem. Indeed, Odysseus, no less than Achilles, insists upon recognition of his accomplishments, even when such insistence endangers himself and those who depend on him. So, for example, when Odysseus and the crew of his ship are rowing furiously in their flight from the blinded Cyclops and his men urge Odysseus to keep quiet, Odysseus insists upon shouting out and telling the Cyclops that the man who blinded him was "Odysseus, son of Laertes, who lives on Ithaca," giving as complete an identification as possible. Yet part of the reason Odysseus was able to deprive the giant Cyclops of his single eye and escape from his cave was his willingness to withhold his identity until this point. In fact, he had deviously told the Cyclops earlier that his name was Nobody, so that when the Cyclops' neighbors responded to his calls for help by asking if somebody was trying to kill him, he replied by saying, "Nobody is trying to kill me."

Odysseus repeatedly conceals his identity by disguising himself and by fabricating accounts of who he is and where he comes from. These actions, which give a most unheroic impression, are undertaken in the service of enabling Odysseus to return to his home and his family. By the end of the poem, as a result of extraordinary personal exertions, Odysseus is finally and fully reintegrated into the community from which he had been separated for 20 years. This community bears little resemblance to the polis, the type of community in which the *Odyssey* and the *Iliad* reached their final form but which is not explicitly seen in the Homeric poems. Rather, the Homeric poems create a fictionalized type of community that can be used to explore the tensions inherent in the polis, which imagines itself to be grounded in a heroic past but which requires the individual to be subordinated to the interests of the community. The character of Odysseus seems to be ideally suited to serve as the symbol of this tension and its desired resolution.

Recommended for Further Reading

Athanassakis, A. N. (trans.) *Hesiod: Theogony, Works and Days, Shield* (Baltimore and London 1983): a lively and readable translation, including a brief commentary that emphasizes the continuities in rural Greek life from Hesiod's day to the twentieth century.

Fowler, R. L. (ed.) *The Cambridge Companion to Homer* (Cambridge 2004): an excellent and up-to-date guide to all aspects of the Homeric poems, written by an international team of experts.

Griffin, J. *Homer on Life and Death* (Oxford 1980): an old-fashioned, but sensitive work of literary criticism that examines the centrality of life and death and the opposition between gods and mortals in the Homeric poems.

Lamberton, R. *Hesiod* (New Haven and London 1988): an excellent introduction to all aspects of Hesiod and his poems.

Lattimore, R. (trans.) *The Iliad of Homer* (Chicago 1951): the English translation that comes closest to the feel of Homer's Greek.

Lattimore, R. (trans.) *The Odyssey of Homer* (New York 1967): not as successful as Lattimore's *Iliad*, but one should read the same translator's *Iliad* and *Odyssey* to avoid an exaggerated impression of the differences between the two poems.

Lord, A. B. *The Singer of Tales*, second edition (Cambridge, MA 2000): the classic study, by Parry's student and friend, of the nature of oral technique in a new edition with an audio and video CD documenting Slavic oral performances recorded by Parry.

Seaford, R. *Reciprocity and Ritual: Homer and Tragedy in the Developing City-state* (Oxford 1994): an important but controversial book that synthesizes a great deal of recent work on Homer and on the importance of rituals in the development of the polis.

Vernant, J-P. *Myth and Thought among the Greeks*, English translation (London 1983): a collection of essays by one of the most brilliant students of Greek culture, including revelatory studies of Hesiod's myths of human degeneration and Prometheus.

POETRY AND SCULPTURE OF THE ARCHAIC PERIOD

4

The Archaic Period (eighth through sixth centuries BC) is the time when many of the defining features of Greek civilization began to take shape. This chapter will concentrate on two of those features, the centrality of the human figure in the visual arts and the emphasis on personal self-expression in the lyric poetry of the period. Archaic sculpture is characterized by the development of life-size stone statues representing young men and women, which were used either as dedicatory offerings or as grave markers. The pose of the male statues, or kouroi, and the techniques used in their creation were adopted from the Egyptians. But, in contrast to the Egyptian statues, which are intended as representations of specific individuals, Greek kouroi depict young men in the nude, with no defining attributes. Similarly, statues of young women, or korai, represent unidentified women of considerable means, as is indicated by their opulent clothing and costly jewelry. These are, then, idealized depictions of beautiful young men and women who represent the model citizen of the Archaic polis. In contrast, the small-scale lyric poetry of the Archaic Period, which survives often in only a fragmentary state, allows the poet to express (or affect to express) his — or her — own individual personality and to sing of specific, named members of his or her own community. Archaic poets may sing of their love for this or that young man or woman, revile their personal enemies by name, or urge their fellow citizens on to acts of bravery in the new, communal style of warfare that developed in the eighth century BC, replacing the individualized, "heroic" combat celebrated in the Homeric epics.

The Human Figure in Archaic Art

Lyric Poetry of Archaic Greece

The tensions we have seen in chapter 3 between the conflicting claims of individuality and uniformity can be seen working themselves out also in the visual arts of the Archaic Period. This is the name conventionally given to the period from the middle of the eighth to the beginning of the fifth century BC. It is a particularly unfortunate name, as it gives the impression that the Greeks of the time were in some sort of holding pattern awaiting the full flowering of their civilization in an age that we call the "Classical" Period, using a word derived from a Latin root. Nor are the limits of this "Archaic" Period particularly well chosen or well defined. It used to be the case that the Archaic Period was felt to begin precisely with the year 776 BC, the traditional date of the first Olympic Games and, supposedly, the earliest securely dated event in Greek history. We are no longer as confident as we once were that the ancient Greeks had reliable grounds for dating the start of the Olympic Games to 776 BC, but it is legitimate to regard the eighth century BC in general as a period in which notable changes occurred in the Greek world. There is somewhat better reason for regarding the beginning of the fifth century BC as marking a decisive turning-point for Greek civilization, namely because of the overwhelming effects of the Persian Wars, which occurred at just that time. In any event, the name and the concept of the Archaic Period are so well established that it would be perverse to abandon them. In this chapter, we will consider some aspects of the sculpture and poetry of the period, which we will continue to call by its traditional name.

The Human Figure in Archaic Art

One of the most dramatic developments during the Archaic Period of Greek civilization is the sudden appearance and rapid refinement of the ability of Greek artists to represent the human figure. It will be remembered that after the end of the Mycenaean Period representation of human and animal figures in Greek art disappeared almost entirely. It is only toward the end of the ninth century BC that figurative art begins to reappear. In most instances, figures of animals are used by vase painters of the Geometric Period sparingly and almost as just another geometric pattern that can be repeated indefinitely around the circumference of the vessel. We can see this in the eighth-century amphora illustrated in figure 16, where two of the bands on the neck of the vase are decorated with repeated figures, one with grazing deer and one with recumbent goats. That same vase is decorated with another figured scene. This scene is much more prominent both because of its size and its location, between the vessel's handles and just above the point of greatest circumference, and also because it is much less schematic than the animal-FRIEZES. This scene shows a number of human mourners lamenting the death of the central figure, shown lying on a funeral bier. The amphora itself stood as the marker of a grave, so that there is an intimate connection between the decoration and the function of the vase. But the human figures are no less schematically portrayed

FRIEZE A horizontal band of decoration, usually either painted or sculpted in RELIEF (figures 46–8 and 63–5).

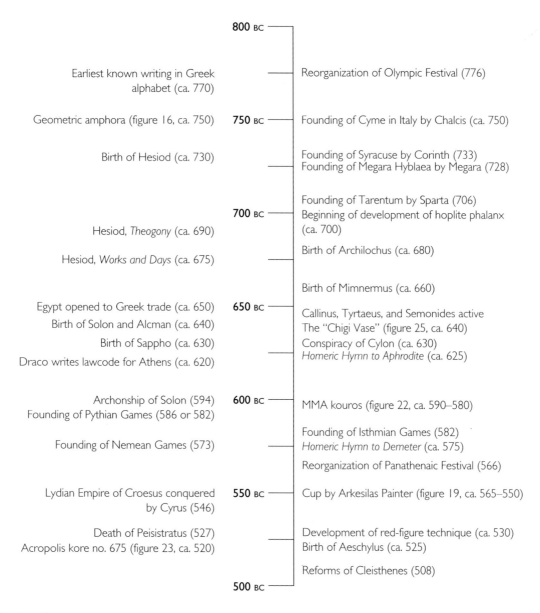

Earliest known writing in Greek alphabet (ca. 770)

800 BC

Reorganization of Olympic Festival (776)

Geometric amphora (figure 16, ca. 750)   750 BC   Founding of Cyme in Italy by Chalcis (ca. 750)

Birth of Hesiod (ca. 730)

Founding of Syracuse by Corinth (733)
Founding of Megara Hyblaea by Megara (728)

Founding of Tarentum by Sparta (706)
700 BC   Beginning of development of hoplite phalanx (ca. 700)

Hesiod, *Theogony* (ca. 690)

Hesiod, *Works and Days* (ca. 675)

Birth of Archilochus (ca. 680)

Birth of Mimnermus (ca. 660)

Egypt opened to Greek trade (ca. 650)   650 BC
Birth of Solon and Alcman (ca. 640)
Birth of Sappho (ca. 630)
Draco writes lawcode for Athens (ca. 620)

Callinus, Tyrtaeus, and Semonides active
The "Chigi Vase" (figure 25, ca. 640)
Conspiracy of Cylon (ca. 630)
Homeric Hymn to Aphrodite (ca. 625)

Archonship of Solon (594)   600 BC
Founding of Pythian Games (586 or 582)

MMA kouros (figure 22, ca. 590–580)

Founding of Nemean Games (573)

Founding of Isthmian Games (582)
Homeric Hymn to Demeter (ca. 575)
Reorganization of Panathenaic Festival (566)

Lydian Empire of Croesus conquered   550 BC
by Cyrus (546)

Cup by Arkesilas Painter (figure 19, ca. 565–550)

Death of Peisistratus (527)
Acropolis kore no. 675 (figure 23, ca. 520)

Development of red-figure technique (ca. 530)
Birth of Aeschylus (ca. 525)

Reforms of Cleisthenes (508)

500 BC

Timeline 4   The Archaic Period.

than the repeated deer and goats on the neck of the vase. They are in nearly identical poses, with their hands to their heads in conventionalized attitudes of mourning, either beating their heads or tearing their hair, and they are identically represented with triangular torsos and circular blobs for heads. The artist has made no effort to differentiate the mourners in the interests of creating a more varied composition; on the contrary, he seems to have gone out of his way to keep them uniform.

One might be inclined to attribute this uniformity to a lack of imagination or a want of skill on the part of the painter. That, however, would be to impose today's values on the art of Archaic Greece. In fact, it appears that artists of the Archaic Period, even after they had become much more adept at portraying the human figure, were quite comfortable with the idea that figures serving the same function ought to be uniform in appearance. We can see this particularly clearly in the case of a series of large-scale sculptures representing young men, a series that begins around the end of the seventh century and lasts until the start of the fifth century BC. The inspiration behind this series of statues can undoubtedly be traced to the Greeks' increasing contact with Egypt in the middle of the seventh century. The Egyptians, unlike the Greeks, had a tradition of creating monumental stone sculptures, a tradition that had been in existence for many centuries and that resulted in the creation of a standardized set of proportions and poses. Those proportions and one of those poses are reproduced by Greek sculptors who adopted Egyptian techniques and conventions for use in a Greek context. The Egyptian king from the mid-third millennium shown here (figure 21) is striding forward with his hands held stiffly at his sides. Nearly 2,000 years later Egyptian sculptors were still depicting their kings in the same posture, a posture that is reproduced by the Greek sculptor of the young man in figure 22. This is one of many similar sculptures, mostly life-sized, created by Greek artists during the Archaic Period and now referred to by art historians as KOUROI.

KOUROS (PLURAL: **KOUROI**) An Archaic statue of a naked young man in a standing pose (figure 22).

Figure 21 Stone statue of Egyptian King Menkaure (Mycerinus) and his queen; height 1.422 m, 2490–2472 BC. Boston, Museum of Fine Arts, Harvard University – Museum of Fine Arts Expedition, 11.1738; copyright 2002 Museum of Fine Arts, Boston.

Figure 22 Attic marble statue of a young man ("kouros"); height 1.927 m, ca. 590–580 BC. New York, Metropolitan Museum of Art, Fletcher Fund, 1932 (32.11.1).

"Kouroi" is simply the plural form of the ancient Greek word *kouros*, which means nothing more than "young man." The fact that art historians use this term indicates that they, and we, simply do not know whom these statues are intended to represent. In the case of Egyptian statues there is usually no doubt. The figure is shown, for example, with the unmistakable attributes of the pharaoh or, in many cases, is specifically identified by an inscription that names the individual whose likeness is portrayed. Greek kouroi, too, are sometimes accompanied by an inscription, usually on the base on which the kouros stands, but the inscription cannot be interpreted as saying, in effect, "This statue is a representation of so-and-so." Rather, the inscription gives the name of the god to whom the statue is dedicated or the name of the person making the dedication or the name of the person over whose tomb the statue stands. For, like works of sculpture generally in the Archaic Period, kouroi can serve one of two functions, either as a grave marker or as a dedicatory offering to a god. The only other function that large-scale Archaic sculpture fulfills is that of cult statue of a god or goddess, in which case there can be no uncertainty regarding the identity of the subject of the statue: the cult statue is a representation of Apollo, say, or Athena, as is clear from the statue's placement in the god's temple, or from the fact that the figure is represented with the attributes of the deity, Apollo with his bow, Athena with her aegis.

But the young man has no attributes. Or, rather, he has no attributes that mark him as an individual. His attributes – his youthful appearance, his powerful build, his conspicuous nakedness – mark him as the abstract representation of virility, vitality, and vigor. There is a curious paradox here: Greek civilization, particularly in the Archaic Period, has often been thought of as the birthplace of the Western concept of the individual, and yet the Archaic kouros is far less individualized than the representations of specific Egyptian pharaohs that inspired its creation. What seems to underlie this paradox is the difference between the types of society that form the context for the Egyptian and the Greek sculptures. The statue of an Egyptian king proclaims to his subjects the king's identity – there is, after all, only one king – and his authority. In the context of the Greek polis, however, to proclaim one's individuality in so direct and conspicuous a manner would (probably rightly) be regarded as dangerous and as threatening to the stability of the community. So the individual who sets up a dedicatory offering to a deity or who wishes to mark the grave of a deceased relative commissions a statue that is neither a portrait of himself nor of the deceased. It is not a portrait at all, but rather a representation of a generic citizen, in the same way that the figures on the eighth-century funerary amphora (figure 16) represent generic mourners.

"As far as the art of sculpture is concerned, Daedalus was so far superior to all others that the story was later told of him that the statues that he created were just like living creatures. For they could see and walk about and, in short, they reproduced the state of the body in its entirety, so that his creations were indistinguishable from human beings. Since he was the first to furnish statues with eyes and to separate their legs, and the first to give them outstretched arms, it is hardly surprising that people were in awe of him. For in earlier times artisans used to make their statues with closed eyes and with hands hanging down and attached to their sides." (Diodorus of Sicily, *The Library of World History* 4.76.2–3)

There is one other signal that the kouros sends: it proclaims – paradoxically, for a piece of stone – that it is alive. This vitality is conveyed by the figure's youthfulness, by its uninhibited display of its organs of procreation, and by its slightly advanced left leg, which is intended to give the impression that the figure is in motion, walking toward the viewer. It is characteristic of all sculptural traditions (at least until the twentieth century AD) that sculpture is concerned to represent animate figures, whether human or bestial or monstrous, in contrast to decorations on ceramics or on fabrics, which often allow non-representational patterns, like those on Greek vases of the Geometric Period. This animate quality of sculpture is reflected in two Greek myths, both of which are connected with the regions of Greece that have the closest connections with Egypt and the Near East, from which the Greeks adopted the practice of creating large-scale sculpture and the tradition of figurative representation. The myth of Pygmalion, recycled in George Bernard Shaw's play of the same name, concerns a king of Cyprus who fell in love with a statue of a beautiful woman. In response to Pygmalion's prayers to the goddess Aphrodite, the statue came to life and became Pygmalion's wife. The other myth concerns Daedalus (after whom the hero of James Joyce's *A Portrait of the Artist as a Young Man* is named), who was himself a sculptor of such skill that, according to Plato, his statues had to be tied down to prevent them from walking away. Although Daedalus was an Athenian, most of the myths concerning him are connected with Crete, where he is supposed to have built a labyrinth for King Minos (presumably a reminiscence of the labyrinthine Minoan palace at Cnossus: figure 5).

These myths suggest that it is reasonable to see the kouroi that we have been considering as, among other things, powerful assertions of vitality. It may require a stretch of the imagination for us to think of these rather stiff, stone statues in this way but, in fact, we are today not seeing them as they were intended to be seen. Not only is our vision clouded by over two thousand years of what we regard as progress in the representation of the human figure, but also the kouroi as they now exist are literally not the same as when they were created. Very faint traces of pigment on some of the kouroi indicate that they, like apparently all ancient Greek sculptures, were originally painted. We have to imagine – and this *does* require a considerable stretch of the imagination – the skin of the kouros painted a realistic flesh color, the whites and the irises of the eyes painted in the appropriate colors, the hair dyed black or brown or blond, the lips and nipples reddish, and the fillet in the young man's hair perhaps a deep purple. Even more colorful will have been the sculptures representing young women. For, corresponding to the series of kouroi, Greek sculptors of the Archaic Period created scores of figures of young women, which we now refer to as "korai," the plural form of the ancient Greek word KORE, which means "young woman." Unlike the kouroi, korai were represented as fully clothed, since the Greeks considered it shameful for women, but not for men, to be seen in the nude. The kore shown in figure 23 still has noticeable traces of paint, but much of the original paint on her clothes, face, and hair has disappeared. Like many korai, in her original state she was probably further decorated with gold jewelry, which has naturally been looted in the course of time.

KORE (PLURAL: **korai**) An Archaic statue of a clothed young woman in a standing pose (figure 23).

We are not used to seeing stone sculpture brightly painted, just as we are not used to thinking of Greek temples as constructed of anything other than gleaming white marble. But ancient Greek buildings and statues were regularly elaborately colored. Almost all the marble sculpture and marble architecture, however, that survives from antiquity has been stripped of its original paint by the action of sun and moisture and time. This accident of history has distorted our perception of Greek art and architecture to the point that we find aesthetically acceptable ancient sculpture and ancient buildings that are the pure and natural color of naked stone. Artists and architects of more recent times who work in a classicizing tradition – Bernini, say, or Rodin or the designers of countless public buildings and monuments in Washington, DC and Paris – have created "classical" masterpieces of pure white marble. This, in turn, confirms our perception and encourages us to condemn as gaudy those historically accurate reconstructions that restore the bright colors with which ancient Greek statues and buildings were originally painted. In fact, we have already been guilty of a similar distortion in our presentation of Cycladic art. We characterized Cycladic sculpture with the aesthetically judgmental terms "refined and elegant" and illustrated a Cycladic figurine (figure 4) in the pristine white state in which it is exhibited today in the Museum of Cycladic and Ancient Greek Art

Figure 23   Marble statue of a young woman ("kore"); height 0.55 m, ca. 520 BC. Athens, Acropolis Museum, no. 675.

in Athens. When Cycladic art first came to light in the nineteenth century it was considered rude and primitive, but Western perceptions changed rapidly under the influence of the growing appreciation of traditional African, Polynesian, and aboriginal art by such molders of perception as Paul Gauguin, Constantin Brancusi, and Pablo Picasso, aided no doubt by the already existing prejudice in favor of white marble statues from the Classical Period of Greece. But in fact traces of paint on surviving Cycladic sculpture indicate that it, too, was regularly decorated in bright, even garish, colors. Our historical awareness urges us to restore these colors but our aesthetic sense inhibits us.

"To you, Artemis, Phileratis made this dedication; accept her gift, goddess, and be her salvation." (Callimachus, Epigram 33)

The colors with which Archaic kouroi and korai were originally decorated undoubtedly served to enhance their life-like appearance and will have contributed to their function as, virtually, an abstract representation of vitality. For this reason, they were appropriately used as grave markers, as an indication, not of who the deceased was or what he or she looked like, but of the vitality that the deceased now lacked. Alternatively, kouroi and korai were set up in the sanctuary of a deity as a dedicatory offering. Again, the statue does not particularize the dedicator, although an inscription may specify who dedicated the statue.

In fact, the inscription in some instances makes it clear that a given kore was dedicated by a man, so that the statue cannot be seen as being a representation of the dedicator. Nor can it be a representation of the deity to whom it is dedicated. For, although korai are generally dedicated to female deities and kouroi generally to male, just as goddesses are generally served by female priests and gods by male, there are enough exceptions that this cannot be taken as an absolute rule. In any event, the kouroi and korai are lacking the attributes that would identify them with a particular deity. The one attribute that korai, but not kouroi, have is the dedicatory offering that they hold out to the deity in their right hand. In most instances, as in figure 23, the extended right forearm of the kore has been broken off; in the few cases where the offering survives it is a piece of fruit, usually a pomegranate, or a small animal, either a bird or a hare. In fact, the statue is itself a dedicatory offering, so that a kore is a life-like representation of a mortal making an offering to a god and it is itself an offering by a mortal to a god. Its permanence marks a contrast with the ephemeral character of the mortal dedicator and of the object offered to the deity by the kore. Therefore, whether the statue is used as a grave marker or as a votive offering, its (fictive) vitality marks a contrast either with the lifeless state of the deceased or with the everlasting life of the deity.

We have spent so much time discussing kouroi and korai both because of their importance in the history of Western art and because they relate particularly well to a number of the features that we have seen to be characteristic of the Archaic Period. The polis form of society that was taking shape in the

> "Stop and grieve at the monument for Croesus, now departed. He died in the front ranks of battle, slain by furious Ares." (Inscription from the base of a kouros in the National Archaeological Museum, Athens, ca. 530 BC)

Archaic Period encouraged public expression but necessitated a tempering of individual ambition. These statues of generic yet highly attractive and youthful citizens allowed families to memorialize their loved ones in conspicuous fashion and allowed individuals to display their pious devotion to the god without erecting portrait statues that might vie with the cult statues of the gods for individuality. Further, these statues were erected either in communal cemeteries or in communal sanctuaries, both of which arose in conjunction with the development of the polis. And, like the oriental influences seen in the poetry of Hesiod and the adoption of the Phoenician writing system, these sculptures represent characteristically Greek modifications of imports from non-Greek cultures, in this case the appropriation and transformation of iconography derived from Egypt. Part of that transformation took the form of removing the (minimal) clothing worn by the pharaoh and exposing the kouros in a state of total nudity, which, as we have seen, is the state in which men trained for and competed in the athletic contests in the Panhellenic games, another product of the Archaic Period.

The Greek acceptance of (male) nudity in public statuary and at the public games has been the subject of a good deal of scholarly debate, and it cannot be said that the reasons for this acceptance are fully understood today. This phenomenon, which dates to the period of the development of the polis, seems to have arisen out of the same tension that we have seen at work in some of the other phenomena that also date to this period, namely the tension between individuality and uniformity. Public nudity is, in one sense, the ultimate form of self-expression, but at the same time, by stripping away the external accouterments of wealth and privilege, it sets everyone on the same level. The naked man is at once vulnerable and supremely self-assertive, so that nudity is an appropriate symbolic garment for the citizen of a Greek polis, which arose by both curbing and exploiting the impulses of men who saw themselves as cast in the same mold as Achilles. (Women were not regarded as citizens of the polis – they are rather appendages, first of their citizen father and then of their citizen husband – so that the causes that inspired male nudity did not affect women.)

Lyric Poetry of Archaic Greece

Just as the kouros can be seen as an instance of exhibitionism confined within the safe limits of standardization, so the developments in literature during the Archaic Period feature the baring of the poet's soul, but only in a conventionalized frame-work. In chapter 3 we discussed the large-scale poetic works of Hesiod and Homer, works composed in the meter known as the dactylic hexameter and using an artificial literary dialect that had evolved in the course of several centuries of oral tradition. That meter and that dialect continued to be used by Greek poets for well over a thousand years, for composing epic poems in the tradition of the *Iliad* and the *Odyssey* and didactic poetry in the tradition of Hesiod. This poetic idiom was also used for hymns in honor of the gods, a collection of which has survived. These hymns, some of which are only five or six lines long, some of which are a few hundred lines, were attributed in antiquity to Homer and so are known today as the "Homeric Hymns." None of them, however, was composed by the same person who was respons-ible for the *Iliad* or the *Odyssey*, and in fact a number of them date from long after the sixth century. But the longer hymns, those to Demeter, Apollo, Hermes, and Aphrodite, are early and belong to the period between the middle of the seventh and the middle of the fifth century BC. The reason for the similarity in meter and dialect between these hymns and the poems of Hesiod and Homer is that hymns to the gods were conventionally used to open a recitation of poems like those of Homer and Hesiod, and when these hymns are referred to by ancient Greek authors they are often called "preludes." Indeed, Hesiod's *Theogony* and *Works and Days* open with brief hymns to, respectively, the Muses and Zeus.

The Homeric Hymns glorify the deity to whom they are addressed by recount-ing myths that illustrate the deity's power and influence. They open with a con-ventional "I begin my song with . . ." or "Tell me, Muse, of . . ." but they tell us nothing further about the "I" who is responsible for the song. This is characteristic of the authors of hexameter poetry, whose individuality is submerged under an impersonal tradition. Even Hesiod, who tells us his name and some further auto-biographical details, speaks either as the inspired mouthpiece of the Muses (in the *Theogony*) or in the standard persona of the purveyor of wisdom literature (in the *Works and Days*). The autobiographical details serve to enhance his authority and his credibility; he is not interested in providing his audience with revelations concerning the state of his psyche. There are, however, poetic traditions active in the Archaic Period in which the poet reveals (or, at least, claims to be revealing) his or her innermost feelings. These traditions are connected with poetry on a smaller scale than the hexameter poems of Hesiod and Homer. The poetry we are concerned with is sometimes referred to as "lyric" poetry because "lyric" is a word with an appropriately Greek etymology (meaning "accompanied by the lyre") and because today "lyric poetry" means poetry characterized by an outpouring of the poet's own thoughts and feelings. Despite our use of the word "lyric" to refer to them, many of the small-scale, non-hexameter poems of the Archaic Period were accompanied not by a lyre but by an oboe-like reed instrument called an AULOS, and the thoughts and feelings poured out by the poet may have been just as conventional and contrived as the elaborate metrical conventions in which they were expressed.

This is not to say that the poetry of the Archaic Period was somehow lacking in "sincerity" or "authenticity," merely that the metrical and musical form in which it was composed dictated what kinds of thoughts and feelings were expressed, in the same way that, in more recent times, blues or hip hop can be expected to embrace certain types of content and to exclude others. One type of poetry, for example, is that known as IAMBIC, which was composed in iambic (and related) meters and is often satiric in nature and direct, even coarse, in expression. It is conventional for the iambic poet to express strong personal feelings and to use his verse to attack those whom he portrays as his enemies. The greatest exponent of iambic verse was the poet Archilochus, who lived in the middle of the seventh century BC. He was revered in antiquity as a poet whose skill was on a level with that of Hesiod and Homer. Unfortunately, we do not have the opportunity to assess that judgment because all that survives of Archilochus' works are scraps and fragments, lines here and there quoted by much later Greek authors or bits of PAPYRUS that have been preserved by chance in the sands of Egypt. Some of those brief fragments give us a taste of the pugnacious character for which his iambic verse was famous. For example, Athenaeus, writing in about AD 200 quotes Archilochus as saying in one of his poems, "the way someone thirsts for a drink, that's how I crave a fight with you." That is the extent of the quotation, nor do we know whom Archilochus was addressing. In another fragment, found in Theophilus of Antioch, a Christian contemporary of Athenaeus, Archilochus boasts (in Martin West's translation)

> I do have one good skill,
> that's to repay whoever hurts me with a corresponding ill.

In this way, Archilochus assimilates himself to the prickly hedgehog, of whom he elsewhere says, "while the fox has many, the hedgehog has one good skill."

AULOS An oboe-like reed instrument, used as an accompaniment for sacrificial ritual, certain athletic activities, ELEGIAC poetry, and the advance of HOPLITES into battle (figures 25 and 26).

IAMBIC Referring to a metrical form that was considered to approximate to the rhythm of ordinary speech, generally used in the Archaic Period for invective and satire, but later also used for epigram and other serious purposes, including the dialogue of drama.

PAPYRUS A marsh plant native to Egypt; also, the sheets used as a writing surface made by laying thin strips of the stem of the papyrus plant side by side, with another layer of similar strips crossing them, and usually a third layer again parallel to the first, the whole being then soaked in water, pressed together, and dried (figure 24).

Another writer of iambic verse is Archilochus' near-contemporary, Semonides. He appears to have been a more bland and less interesting poet than Archilochus, but at least we have a continuous quotation of respectable length from one of his iambic poems. The quotation is over one hundred lines long and may, in fact, constitute a complete, or nearly complete, poem. In it, Semonides classifies womankind according to a variety of types, all of which (with one exception) are vile. This is the same attitude toward women that we have seen in Hesiod. Semonides shares with Hesiod also a fondness for using the language of generation as a metaphor for the process of development. For Zeus created women, according to Semonides, "from" a variety of different animals, and these animals (the slovenly sow, the devious vixen, the wanton bitch, and so on) are spoken of as the "parents" of the various types. So, for example,

> One type is sprung from a long-maned, high-strung mare.
> She finds chores a bore and scorns hard work:
> She won't touch a handmill, won't lift a sieve,
> won't cart the dung outside . . .

The only type of woman that a man is lucky to get for his wife – and it is clear that Semonides is addressing a male audience – is the type "descended" from the industrious bee. Like Hesiod, Semonides considers women only in their domestic capacity and, like Hesiod, he is convinced that they are merely a drain on the resources of the household. But his tone is much more down to earth and his language less elevated than the formal and formulaic "epic" diction of Hesiod.

It is characteristic of iambic verse that it is the poetic form most like everyday conversation, both in its manner of expression and its subject matter, and we have seen that both Archilochus and Semonides deal with ordinary human emotions and are not above making comparisons with commonplace members of the animal kingdom. (Homer, by contrast, often compares his characters with the more "heroic" lion.) These two iambic poets have other things in common as well. They were both born on Aegean islands in that area of Greece that is home to speakers of the Ionic dialect, Archilochus on Paros and Semonides on Samos (map 8), but both of them left their place of birth and settled on yet other Aegean islands as colonists sent out by their native poleis. Further, both of them write in a vivid manner about the uncertainty of human existence. This may result in each instance from personal experience of their own uprootedness. It may equally well derive from the standard persona of the iambic poet, whose satiric character requires that the poet pose as an outsider in order to distance himself from the objects of his invective.

The invective that is characteristic of iambic poetry appears to have a ritual

"For a long time Demeter sat upon the chair, grieving in silence, nor did she engage with anyone either with words or actions. Instead she sat, without smiling, without tasting food or drink, wearing herself out with longing for her richly girdled daughter, until, that is, keen-witted Iambe, with mockery and much jesting diverted the mind of the august goddess, causing her to smile and laugh and raising her spirits." (*Homeric Hymn to Demeter* 198–204)

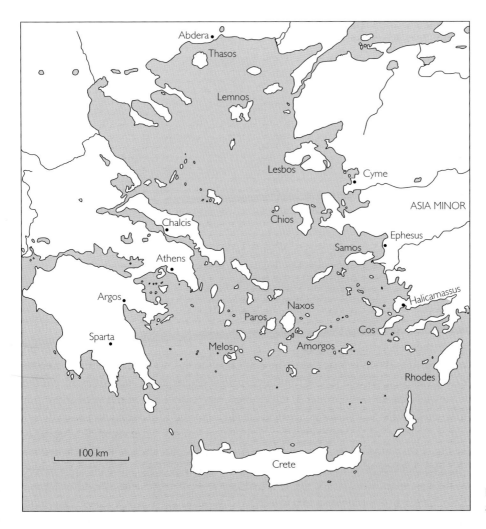

Map 8 Greece and the Aegean.

origin, and the Greeks considered the word "iambic" to derive from the name of a mythical character Iambe, a woman who relieved the sorrow of the goddess Demeter by telling indecent jokes when Demeter was searching for her abducted daughter. Other forms of Archaic poetry also have ritual origins, particularly those that involve singing, either by a chorus or by an individual performer, at weddings or at communal festivals. Again, our appreciation and understanding of this poetry is limited by the fact that it survives only in fragments, but we are fortunate to possess, along with a number of smaller fragments, a fairly lengthy portion of a song composed by the Spartan poet Alcman, born in the seventh century BC. This poem, composed in the local Doric dialect, was written for performance by a chorus of 10 Spartan girls who sang and danced to instrumental accompaniment at a festival in honor of one of the deities worshiped at Sparta. The ritual with which the poem is connected appears to have been one of a number of festivals of an initiatory character that prepared young people for their future roles within the polis, girls as wives, boys as citizens and soldiers. In Alcman's poem, attention is called to the musical skill and especially the physical attractiveness of the members of the chorus, and two girls in particular are singled out as challenging each other for recognition as most beautiful and desirable. The rivalry among the members of the chorus is, however, necessarily subordinated to the requirement that these young girls perform in harmony, as they sing and dance together to the words and music that Alcman composed to highlight the girls' attractiveness. Interestingly, the girls' charm is conveyed by Alcman's comparing them to fleet horses. Here the comparison does not serve a satiric purpose, as it does in Semonides. Rather, Alcman's choristers are sleek racehorses, competing for the esteem and admiration of the onlookers:

> For Hagesichora outshines the rest,
> like a filly in a flock of sheep,
> a sturdy, prize-winning filly with hammering hooves,
> the sort that soars aloft in one's dreams.

The members of Alcman's chorus are obviously drawn from the leading Spartan families of the day, for only girls from such families would have had the leisure and the opportunity for the kind of training in music and dance that Alcman's poetry demands. It is, in fact, primarily as a vehicle for socialization and education that these choruses, and the songs written for them, existed. In the absence of formal schools, the role of preparing boys and girls, particularly those of the leading families, to take their place as adults in the polis fell to less formal circles, led by mature men and women of refined taste and literary cultivation. One such, apparently, was the poet Sappho, who was a contemporary of Alcman's but who spent her life on the other side of the Aegean Sea, on the island of Lesbos. The philosopher Plato, who had the opportunity to read much more of her poetry than survives to us and who himself had an exceptional literary sense, suggested that the traditional number of the Muses should be increased so as to include Sappho. What little of her poetry does survive is dazzling beyond description and amply justifies Plato's enthusiasm. Like Alcman, she writes in her own local dialect, but in Sappho's case this is the Aeolic dialect, and she composes in a variety of meters that are characteristically Aeolic. The most frequent subject of her passionate verse is the expression of erotic desire, often her own and often directed toward other women or girls. (It is from these expressions in Sappho's verse that in English the word "lesbian" has come to have its present meaning.) In one tantalizing fragment, Sappho compares the radiance of a girl to that of

> the quince-apple at the end of the branch, the one
> right at the very end, the one the fruit-pickers missed.
> No! They can't have missed it – they just couldn't reach it.

It is difficult to tell whether the female objects of Sappho's passion are women of Sappho's own age or are unmarried girls who perhaps sang and danced in the choruses that performed some of Sappho's songs. Indeed, it is difficult, if not impossible, to tell in most instances whether a given song of Sappho's was performed, or was intended for performance, by a chorus or by a single performer, presumably Sappho herself.

In the case of the song of Alcman's discussed above there can be no doubt that it was composed for performance by a chorus because the girls who performed it are individually named in the text of the poem, and the same is likely to be true of some or even many of Sappho's songs. In Alcman's song the girls of the chorus direct expressions of erotic feeling toward one another and toward the female leaders of the chorus. What we are dealing with, then, is poetry composed within a loosely organized social and educational context, the socialization and the education taking the form of learning and publicly performing song and dance designed to promote cohesion of the group and to instill the values of the polis. Those values include a recognition of the importance of physical attractiveness, grace in movement, and musical and literary accomplishment, all of which makes the girl the object of desire and, therefore, sought after as a potential bride. A similar situation will have existed in the case of choruses of young boys (with, naturally, the "values" slightly modified to accord with the role that the boys are expected to adopt when they reach adulthood), but very little happens to survive of the poetry written for such a context. What is of particular interest, however, in the poetry of Sappho and Alcman is the intensity of personal emotion expressed in what appears to be poetry composed for public performance by a collective body of performers. Again, it seems that individual and personal expression is countenanced so long as it is either defused by appearing within a conventionalized context or diffused among a number of voices. In this way, these collective choruses of boys and girls on the verge of adulthood, whose training confers credit on a named and individualized adult, are the literary equivalent of the anonymous kouroi and korai, likewise on the verge of adulthood, whose inscriptions name the individual adult by whom or in whose memory they are dedicated.

One of the preoccupations of Sappho, and, indeed, of Greek poets in general, is the transitory character of human attractiveness and of human life. The very verse in which Sappho, Alcman, and others celebrate the fleeting loveliness of youth is subject to the same ravages of time and decay. As we have seen, most of Archaic poetry has not survived, but on occasion we are lucky enough to witness the recovery of a

> "Pursue the fair gifts of the Muses, girls, the Muses whose breasts are fragrant as flowers; pursue the limpid song of the lyre. My own body, which once was lithe, is now the victim of age, and my hair is gray, once black. My spirit has become so heavy that my knees won't bear me up, though once they were frisky as fawns and eager for the dance. This is cause for constant complaint, but what can I do? To be human and ageless, that cannot be. Once, they say, Tithonus aroused the passion of Dawn of the rosy arms, and she carried him off to the ends of the earth. Young he was and handsome; but still, with time, he was seized by gray age, though his wife was forever young." (Sappho, P. Köln 21351 + 21376)

Figure 24

Fragment of papyrus from Egypt with a poem by Sappho copied on it, later used as wrapping for a mummy; text first published in 2004; early third century BC. Institut für Altertumskunde der Universität zu Köln, Papyrussammlung Inv. 21351 + 21376 recto.

precious remnant of that tradition. In 2004, a recently discovered papyrus fragment (figure 24) was published that contained a nearly complete poem by Sappho. The text was written in the early third century BC and thus preserves the earliest manuscript evidence for Sappho's work. As was often the case with texts written on papyrus, after the text had outlived its usefulness, it was used as cartonnage for a mummy in Egypt. It is for this reason that it was preserved until today, since the dry conditions of the Egyptian sands inhibit the deterioration that would occur in most European locations. Appropriately, the poem laments Sappho's own deterioration as she ages and is no longer able to participate in the dance. Even the mythical Tithonus, she says, was overtaken by the decay that comes with old age, referring to the story of the lovely goddess of the Dawn, who fell in love with a mortal and requested that he be made immortal, but forgot to ask that he be exempt from aging. With characteristic subtlety, by associating herself with the fate of Tithonus, Sappho gracefully compliments the young girls to whom the poem is addressed, who are implicitly likened to the radiant and immortal Dawn.

One last type of Archaic poetry needs to be mentioned here. ELEGIAC verse was recited by a single performer to the accompaniment of an aulos and was composed in elegiac couplets. The first verse of the couplet is a dactylic hexameter, the verse of Hesiod and Homer, and the second is a shorter variant of the hexameter. Elegiac poetry is related to epic not only metrically but in dialect as well, since elegy is regularly written in the Ionic dialect, the predominant element in the language of Hesiod and Homer. This is the case even when the poet is a native of an area of Greece that is not Ionic-speaking. Two of the earliest elegiac poets, both of whom were active in the middle of the seventh century BC, are Callinus from Ionic Ephesus and Tyrtaeus from Doric Sparta, and yet their surviving works are scarcely distinguishable either in language or in subject-matter. Both poets use their elegiac verse to inspire and encourage their fellow citizens to pursue glory on the battlefield. And, in keeping with the "epic" character of elegiac verse, the language of both poets is overwhelmingly "Homeric." But the battlefield that Callinus and Tyrtaeus describe is very different from that found in the *Iliad*, where individual warriors fight each other in single combat. That sort of combat is what Homer and his audience imagine (perhaps correctly) to have prevailed in the heroic world of the distant past. But the style of warfare and the equipment appropriate to it in the time of Callinus and Tyrtaeus were a recent development, from the time around 700 BC.

Warfare in the Greek poleis of the seventh century and later took the form of encounters between masses of similarly equipped soldiers known as HOPLITES. The hoplite took his name from his characteristic piece of equipment, the circular shield (*hoplon*) that he carried on his left arm, and the whole of his equipment, his "panoply," included bronze helmet, corselet and greaves, and a thrusting-spear that he held in his right hand (figure 25). It was necessary for these hoplites to maintain a tight formation and to advance into battle side by side, in order that each man could protect the exposed right side of the hoplite to his immediate left. As Tyrtaeus puts it (in West's translation):

> You know that those who bravely hold the line
>   and press toward engagement at the front
> die in less numbers, with the ranks behind
>   protected; those who run, lose all esteem.

Thus, the success of this mass formation, known as the "hoplite PHALANX," depended upon the coordination of the individual hoplites' movements, no less than upon the strength, courage, and sheer number of the men included in the phalanx. For this reason, the hoplite's early training included singing and dancing in a boy's chorus, so that he might become accustomed from an early age to moving in rhythm with his fellows. For this reason, also, the phalanx was accompanied, as we can see, by a musician playing an aulos, the same instrument that accompanied the inspiring elegies of Callinus and Tyrtaeus (and whose sound was undoubtedly as stirring and arresting as that of the bagpipe). The bravery and fortitude of the individual hoplites were, naturally, of great value to the polis, but the nature of the phalanx

ELEGIAC Referring to a metrical form consisting of couplets, the first line of which is a DACTYLIC HEXAMETER and the second is a shorter variant of the hexameter, used for funerary epigrams and for other small-scale poems, often composed for performance in the SYMPOSIUM.

HOPLITE A heavily armed foot soldier, equipped with helmet, shield, spear, and body armor covering his torso and shins (figures 25 and 33).

PHALANX A formation of heavily armed infantrymen (HOPLITES) drawn up in close order and carrying spears and overlapping shields (figure 25).

Figure 25 Detail of Protocorinthian pitcher (the "Chigi Vase"); height of figured band 5 cm, ca. 640 BC. Rome, Museo Nazionale di Villa Giulia, no. 22679; copyright Scala / Art Resource, NY.

ensured that those individual qualities contributed to the security of the polis only if they were confined within a standard pattern, even to the extent of requiring hoplites who were naturally left-handed to fight using their right hand.

The success of the polis was both promoted and threatened by the rivalry of its leading citizens, whose ambition was to fashion themselves into figures of the sort sung about by Homer. But the seventh-century polis was not like Agamemnon's Mycenae, nor did the battlefield of the Archaic Period resemble the plain of Troy. These changed circumstances are reflected in the art and literature of the Archaic Period. The kouros and the kore glorify the grace and beauty of the aristocratic body without representing an identifiable individual. By contrast, much of the poetry of the Archaic Period celebrates the individuality of the poet or of the poet's acquaintances, but it does so by safely situating that individuality within a range of roles acceptable to the polis. That is to say, the art and literature of the Archaic Period, indeed every aspect of the period's culture, encouraged the illusion of continuity with the "heroic" past and at the same time encoded the new values of the present in a pleasing and harmonious format.

Recommended for Further Reading

Campbell, D. A. *The Golden Lyre: The Themes of the Greek Lyric Poets* (London 1983): contains chapters on love, wine, athletics, and so on, in the iambic, elegiac, and lyric poets of the Archaic Period.

Easterling, P. E. and Knox, B. M. W. (eds.) *Early Greek Poetry* (Cambridge 1989): the section of the *Cambridge History of Classical Literature* dealing with Archaic poetry, written by experts and including extensive bibliography.

Hanson, V. D. (ed.) *Hoplites: The Classical Greek Battle Experience* (London and New York 1991): a collection of essays by experts on every aspect of hoplite warfare, edited by the influential and controversial Senior Fellow of the Hoover Institution.

Hurwit, J. M. *The Art and Culture of Early Greece, 1100–480 BC* (Ithaca 1985): an unusually well-written and perceptive discussion of the development of Archaic art within its cultural and intellectual environment.

Osborne, R. *Archaic and Classical Greek Art* (Oxford and New York 1998): a stimulating and well-illustrated account of Greek art from ca. 800 BC to the end of the Classical Period.

West, M. L. (trans.) *Greek Lyric Poetry* (Oxford 1993): clear and accurate translations of nearly all the poems and fragments of the Archaic iambic, elegiac, and lyric poets.

West, M. L. (ed. and trans.) *Homeric Hymns, Homeric Apocrypha, Lives of Homer* (Cambridge, MA and London 2003): accurate and readable translations of all the "Homeric" hymns by the world's leading expert on Greek poetry.

Whitley, J. *The Archaeology of Ancient Greece* (Cambridge 2001): an excellent introduction to Greek archaeology, with an up-to-date synthesis of current research on the material culture of Greece, particularly strong on the Archaic Period.

SYMPOSIA, SEALS, AND CERAMICS IN THE ARCHAIC PERIOD

5

This chapter examines further features that characterize Greek culture of the Archaic Period. The symposium was a ritualized feast accompanied and followed by consumption of wine, which provided affluent male citizens with an opportunity to display to a small company of their peers the social and intellectual skills that both individualized them and enabled them to blend in to this exclusive community. Such men could be expected to possess an engraved gemstone, which was a unique mark of its owner's identity that could be used to seal documents, storerooms, and so on. Paradoxically, for all the uniqueness and individuality of each engraved stone, the repeated marks it left were uniform and indistinguishable from one another. The social and political pressure both to "fit in" to the Archaic polis and to display one's fitness precisely by excelling led to the rise, in many poleis, of an individual known as a "tyrant" who wrested political power for himself. Tyrants often sought to secure their authority by encouraging public works projects and supporting the expansion of religious festivals that served to enhance their popularity with the citizen body as a whole. In Athens, for example, the sixth-century tyrant Peisistratus is connected with the development of the Panathenaic festival, which included prestigious competitions in athletic and equestrian contests. Prizes at these contests included impressively decorated ceramic vessels. Athens was at this time the leading producer of fine pottery in the Greek world, and the survival of large numbers of black-figure and, later, red-figure ceramics allows us to follow in great detail the developing skill and creativity of Athenian artists, several of whom proclaim themselves by putting their names to their work.

The Symposium

Seals

Tyranny

Ceramics

Poetry in the elegiac meter, with which we closed our discussion in chapter 4, was written not only to inspire martial courage. Toward the end of the Archaic Period it became common practice to use elegiac meter to compose epitaphs for inscription on tombstones – the Greeks thought that the word *elegos* originally referred to a song of lamentation – and during the Classical and Hellenistic periods epigrams on all manner of subjects were regularly composed in elegiac couplets. In the Archaic Period as well the elegiac meter was used for a great variety of purposes, including the expression of intense erotic and political feelings. In fact, these feelings were not unrelated. The Greeks were well aware that the lust for power is essentially erotic in nature, and one of the standard perils (or advantages, depending on one's per-spective) of absolute power, according to Greek authors, is the ability to impose oneself sexually on whomever one wished as often as one wished. The context in which sexual and political matters were frequently discussed, and the context in which elegiac poetry on both these topics was frequently performed, was the SYMPOSIUM, an institution that attained considerable importance for privileged Greek males in the Archaic Period. In this chapter, we will look at some of the ways in which the symposium reflects the literary, political, and social concerns of the Archaic Period. It must be understood, however, that these reflections are cast by a distorting mirror, as it is really only the concerns of privileged Greek males that are reflected.

SYMPOSIUM

Literally a "drinking together," a ritualized gathering of privileged males who, after dining together, drank wine mixed with water and entertained themselves with poetry, music, games, and sexual activity (figure 26).

The Symposium

The word "symposium" simply names the practice of "drinking together" that was its characteristic feature, although it was by no means merely an unstructured drink-ing party. The symposium had developed during the Archaic Period into a more or less ritualized institution, beginning with the adoption, apparently from the Near East in the eighth or seventh century, of the practice of reclining on couches when eating and drinking. Symposiasts reclined on their left elbow so that they could take their food and drink with their right hand, right-handedness being as much a requirement in the symposium as on the battlefield. This reclining posture lim-ited the number of couches, and hence the number of symposiasts, that could be accommodated in the normally small rooms of ancient Greek houses, and generally a symposium was attended by no more than one or two dozen men. It was restricted to a select group of men from the upper stratum of Greek society who used the symposium as a means of solidifying and perpetuating their own outlook on the world. Some of the features of the symposium echoed the more polis-oriented practice of public sacrifice, but its exclusive character gave it the appearance, surely inten-tionally cultivated, of constituting an alternative polis or even the *real* polis at the heart of the polis. The communal sacrifice featured libations and was normally accom-panied by music of the aulos; the participants wore wreaths and were given equal shares of the sacrificial meat. The aulos also featured prominently in the symposium as

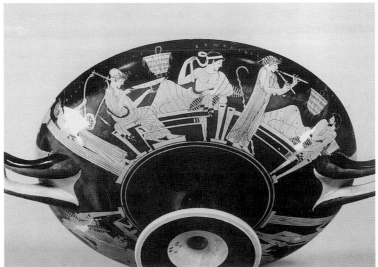

Figure 26 Exterior of red-figure cup, attributed to the Brygos Painter, showing wreathed symposiasts accompanied by female entertainers, two playing the aulos and one holding a wine cup similar in shape to the one on which the scene is painted; diameter of cup 32 cm, ca. 490–480 BC. London, British Museum, GR 1848.6–19.7 (Vases E 68).

an accompaniment to the songs sung by the symposiasts, who were subject to elaborate rules that ensured equal distribution of the food and wine (figure 26).

The symposium took place in a room called the *andron* or "the gentlemen's quarters." The women of the household were excluded; they ate and drank separately, with the children, sitting on chairs rather than reclining. The couches in the *andron* were arranged along the walls of the generally square room, so that there was no hierarchy of position and so that all the guests could participate equally in the conversation and other entertainment. The evening began with a dinner, followed by the drinking of wine, mixed with water in a ceramic krater or mixing bowl. The entertainment that accompanied the drinking was often provided by the symposiasts themselves, in the form of reciting poetry or singing songs that they knew by heart, or improvising songs or speeches, or playing a variety of games that required them to demonstrate their physical coordination and clear-headedness despite the influence of the wine. Alternatively, the entertainment could be provided by professionals hired by the host. "Professionals" should be understood in this context to mean people of lower social standing than the symposiasts themselves, who would have regarded it as demeaning in the extreme to be in the employ of another person, as that would constitute allowing someone else to exercise authority over them. The symposiasts were, rather, landowning gentlemen, and the entertainers will have included female slaves, whom the symposiasts referred to as "companions," who were accomplished in the arts of dance and music and who were also available to fulfill the symposiasts' sexual needs. The ceramic vases and cups used for the consumption of the wine were often decorated with scenes from the symposium, including some scenes of immoderate, and sometimes violent, group sex.

We are led to believe, however, that part of the point of the symposium was to demonstrate one's strength of character by exercising restraint and displaying one's mental acuity in the face of challenges posed both by large quantities of wine and by the availability of attractive young sexual partners of both genders. For the symposiasts generally included both younger and older men, distinguished on the vases by the absence or presence of a beard. The symposium, like the boys' choruses mentioned in the previous chapter, will have served to educate and socialize young citizens, with the choruses forging bonds that united boys under the age of about 18 to one another and the symposium encouraging associations between mature men and those boys who had recently reached their majority. One of the marks of reaching one's majority was the opportunity to be invited to join the symposium, where the young man would be provided with examples of restraint and proper behavior, but at the same time his character would be put to the test by being subjected to attempts at seduction by older men. Thus the symposium, like the boys' choruses, served to a certain degree an initiatory function and may have originated in institutions, like those attested for a number of other societies, in which the initiation of young men was overseen by mature men with whom they were expected to have some form of sexual engagement. It is very difficult to say to what degree these sexual encounters in the symposium, whether between men or between men and women, were expected actually to occur or were rather an instrument of scrutiny. That is to say, the graphic sexual scenes painted on the vases, rather than illustrating normal symposium behavior, may have been part of the test as well, like the wine that they contained.

"Wine and truth" is a proverbial expression that appears as early as the poetry of Alcaeus, a contemporary of

"We are concerned only with quality, Cyrnus, when we breed sheep and mules and horses, and everyone wants to breed them from good stock. But a man of quality, if someone offers him a fortune, has no scruples about taking a worthless wife from a worthless family. Nor does a woman refuse to be the wife of a man who's worthless – and rich, choosing wealth over worth. It's riches they value. Men of quality get their wives from worthless stock and worthless men from the upper class. Money debases the race." (Theognis 183–90)

Sappho's who, like Sappho, comes from the island of Lesbos and whose lyric verses are largely connected with the symposium. The same sentiment is found in a poem by another Archaic poet, who says:

> Fire is used by experts when it comes to testing silver and gold,
>   but it's wine that brings to light the temper of a man.

These lines come from a collection of verses in elegiac meter that are attributed to the poet Theognis. This collection is of interest both because its contents reflect many of the concerns of the symposium – indeed, the symposium seems to have been the context for which these verses were composed and in which they were performed – and because it well illustrates the tensions that we have noted earlier between the claims of individuality and uniformity. The collection consists of a large number of brief elegiac poems run together in a continuous sequence of nearly 1,400 verses. The poems, of which it is difficult to tell where one ends and another begins, concern themselves with conveying sage advice, reflect on the mutability of fortune, and rail against the nouveaux riches who threaten to debase the stock of the well-bred. (In this connection, Charles Darwin in his *The Descent of Man* quotes a poem from the collection as recognizing the importance of "selection" in the breeding of humans.) There was a poet Theognis, who seems to have lived around 600 BC in the mainland polis of Megara, and he names himself in one of the poems of the collection. Some of the poems in the collection, however, demonstrably date from the fifth century, and some are clearly the work of other poets, including Tyrtaeus, so that the collection we have is apparently an anthology of elegiac verse that grew by accretion around a core of genuine work by Theognis.

Seals

Interestingly, Theognis seems to have anticipated that his work would suffer just this fate. In the elegy in which he names himself, Theognis addresses his young friend Cyrnus, saying, "let a seal be placed on these verses that I am crafting and no one will ever get away with stealing them . . . Everyone will say that these are the verses of Theognis of Megara." By using this image of a seal, Theognis is suggesting that in addressing his poetry to Cyrnus he is giving his friend a valuable gift, one that Cyrnus should treasure and guard in the same way valuables are protected with a seal. In fact, we know a good deal about the use of seals in ancient Greece, and the seal seems to be an ideal metaphor for the kind of poetry composed in the Archaic Greek polis, poetry that, as we have seen, proclaims its individuality at the same time as it adheres to traditional forms and themes. For the seal is a unique mark of personal identity that can be, and is intended to be, repeatedly and exactly replicated.

"Let us suppose, hypothetically, that there is in our mind a chunk of wax, and that one person has a larger and one person a smaller chunk, one person a clearer and one a less pure, in some cases a harder chunk and in some a more moist, while some have a chunk of just the right consistency. Let us say, further, that this is a present from Mnemosyne, the mother of the Muses, and that, whenever we want to remember something that we have seen or heard or thought of ourselves, we make an impression in this wax, subjecting it to our thoughts and perceptions, in the same way we make an imprint of our seal rings. We remember and have in our mind whatever is impressed in the wax, so long as the impression remains, but we forget and are unaware of any impressions that do not take or have been wiped away."
(Plato, *Theaetetus* 191c–d)

INTAGLIO A figure or design carved into the flat surface of metal, stone, or other hard material, as opposed to carving in RELIEF.

The use of seals was widespread in the ancient civilizations of Egypt and the Near East as early as the fourth millennium BC. The practice of using and producing seal stones was adopted by the inhabitants of Minoan Crete and became common throughout Mycenaean and later Greek civilization. Today, thousands of Greek and Minoan seal stones exist, many of exquisite beauty and refined craftsmanship. Seals were sometimes made by carving in ivory or soft stones, but most commonly they were made of harder gemstones. The artist would engrave an image in INTAGLIO; that is, he would carve into a flat surface of the gem a design in the shape of a lion, say, or, as here (figure 27), of two dolphins swimming. Then, either a small hole would be drilled through the stone so that it could be worn on a string around the

Figure 27 Minoan green jasper seal stone from Crete and plaster impression of the same (top), showing two dolphins swimming; diameter 15 mm, early second millennium BC. Oxford, Ashmolean Museum, University of Oxford, 1941.91.

Figure 28
Obverse of silver
coin, perhaps from
the island of Thera,
showing two
dolphins swimming;
diameter 21 mm, ca.
550–525 BC. Photo:
Hirmer Fotoarchiv
(Archiv-Nr.
13.0528 V).

wrist or neck, or the gem could be set into a metal ring and worn on the finger.
The purpose of the seal was to make an impression in wax or clay, the design in
the impression appearing in RELIEF; that is, the lion or the dolphins would stand
out from the flat surface of the background, like the figures on today's coins. (Indeed,
the invention of coinage, probably in Lydia in the seventh or sixth century BC, owes
its inspiration to the techniques of seal engraving. Coinage was enthusiastically adopted
by many Greek poleis already in the sixth century BC, and some of the same devices
that had long been popular on seals were engraved as well on the iron dies that
were used to create gold and silver Greek coins: figure 28.) In this way the wax or
clay impression was used to "seal" a written document or jar or storeroom. This
could not, of course, prevent an unauthorized person from reading the document
or taking the contents of the jar or storeroom; the purpose of the seal was, rather,
to give assurance that no tampering had in fact taken place or, in the event the seal
was broken, to provide evidence of trespass. In the latter case, the person, generally a slave, who had been entrusted with the sealed object could be appropriately
punished. The seal, then, is a unique mark of ownership and serves as an assertion
of authority and authenticity. Authority, of course, is the province of the wealthier
and more powerful members of society, the very ones who can afford the services
of skilled craftsmen to engrave the seals and who can afford to own the gems on
which the seals are carved. Further, they are the people who own property and who
use documents requiring a seal. They are also the participants in the symposium.

This, then, is the context for which Theognis composed his elegies and in which
he used the image of a seal on his verses so that "no one will ever get away with
stealing them." The seal cannot prevent others from appropriating Theognis' work
but, however he imagines the metaphorical seal to operate, it can apparently
ensure that any unauthorized appropriation will be detected. This is the same principle that lies behind other methods of asserting ownership, like branding horses,
mules, or cattle, a practice with which the ancient Greeks were familiar. The Greeks
also on occasion employed tattooing to mark runaway slaves or prisoners of war.
("Tattoo" is a Polynesian word introduced into English by Captain Cook in the

RELIEF Sculpture
created in such a
way that the figures
project toward the
viewer from a flat
background (figure
46), as on most
modern coins, in
contrast to carving
in INTAGLIO.

eighteenth century; the Greek word for tattoo is *stigma* which, along with its plural *stigmata*, has developed a somewhat different meaning in English.) All of these practices, the use of seals, brands, and tattoos, are means used by property owners to assert their ownership and their authority over objects and over animate creatures treated as objects. Generally, they operate within a small, closed, aristocratic circle, and it is necessary for the owner to "recognize" his mark because the marks are usually arbitrary, in the sense that there is no necessary connection between the form of the mark and the person of the owner. Although someone might recognize an impression as that of a friend's seal, the only way to prove conclusively one's ownership is in person, by producing the seal and demonstrating that it matches the impression. For this reason, the seal can take on very great significance, virtually assuming the identity of the individual to whom it belongs.

This is illustrated by an extraordinary story told by the historian Herodotus. The story is outright invention, but it concerns a very real historical character, Polycrates of Samos. Polycrates lived in the second half of the sixth century BC, about a century after Semonides, who was also a native of Samos. According to Herodotus, Polycrates was phenomenally successful in everything he attempted – so successful, in fact, that his good friend King Amasis of Egypt became concerned that the gods, out of jealousy over Polycrates' good fortune, might cause Polycrates to come to a bad end. So Amasis wrote Polycrates a letter (sealed, no doubt, with the royal seal in the form of a scarab) advising him to thwart the gods' resentment by, in effect, making a sacrifice. Amasis recommended that Polycrates should choose his most valuable possession, the one thing which it would be most painful for him to lose, and throw it away. Recognizing the soundness of Amasis' advice, Polycrates thought long and hard before choosing, as his most valued possession, the seal that he regularly wore. Polycrates disposed of the seal, apparently irrecoverably, by throwing it from a ship when he was in the middle of the sea. Some time later, however, Polycrates was given a gift of a large fish which, when cut open, was found to have his seal in its stomach. When Polycrates told his friend Amasis about this remarkable occurrence, Amasis immediately severed all relations with Polycrates, convinced that the gods had indeed marked him out for disaster. (Amasis was right: Polycrates was later killed by the Persians in a manner so horrible that Herodotus cannot bring himself to describe it.)

The point of Herodotus' story relies upon our understanding of the convention whereby the seal serves as a substitute for the person, virtually embodying the identity of the seal's owner. Polycrates sought to avert the ill will of the gods by putting himself, in the form of his seal, out of harm's way. But the gods' purpose cannot be deflected – this is standard Greek thinking and is a recurrent theme of Herodotus' *Histories* – and seal and owner are miraculously reunited before the gods' punishment of Polycrates for his earlier misdeeds can be carried out. Herodotus' story is very detailed, and he tells us nearly everything there is to know about Polycrates' seal: it is made of green jasper set in gold. He even tells us the name of the craftsman who created the seal, where he came from, and what his father's name was: Theodorus of Samos, the son of Telecles. The one thing Herodotus does not tell us is the nature of the device on Polycrates' seal. It might have been a horse or a ship or a SATYR or any one of the hundreds of other devices that we find engraved on Archaic gems. But Herodotus does not tell us, either because he does not know or because it is of no particular importance. That is because there is no necessary connection, not even a symbolic one, between device and owner. This lack of any explicit connection between the device and the owner actually enhances the potency of the seal; if it were easy to predict what a person might choose as a device, it would also be easy to create successful forgeries and the very arbitrariness of the device makes its ability to stand for the person of the owner seem almost magical. The fact that the nature of Polycrates' device was not known to later Greeks made it possible for further invention to take place: in a newly discovered epigram, first published in 2001, the third-century poet Posidippus claims that the device on Polycrates' seal was a poet's lyre, suggesting that the emblem of Posidippus' own craft marked the most highly prized possession of a famous ruler from the distant past.

SATYR An imaginary creature appearing for the most part like a man but with some animal features (the tail, ears, or legs of a goat or a horse), who inhabits the wilds and has limitless appetites for wine and sex (figure 40).

Tyranny

Herodotus' story is obviously fictional, but the part about Polycrates being the friend of the king of Egypt is, in fact, historical. For Polycrates was no ordinary individual. He was the ruler of the island of Samos, which was, largely because of Polycrates' determination, in the sixth century BC the most prosperous and influential Greek state in the Aegean region. Samos and Egypt were allies, sharing a common apprehension of the resolute expansion of the Persian Empire. This apprehension was perfectly justified and both Egypt and Samos were eventually subjected to Persian control, but not until after the death of Amasis and the assassination of Polycrates. Amasis – this is the Greek form of the name of the Egyptian King Ahmose II – had become king of Egypt as the result of a coup that overthrew the previous king. Polycrates became the ruler of Samos as the result of a coup as well, but Samos, unlike Egypt, was not a monarchy. Rather, Polycrates appropriated for himself power that previously had belonged to an aristocracy, of which Polycrates was himself a member. What happened on Samos, when Polycrates became ruler of the island in about 535 BC, is not at all untypical of what happened in any number of Greek poleis in the period beginning in the early seventh century BC. The government of nearly all Greek poleis in the period immediately following the Dark Age was in the hands of a local aristocracy consisting of a small number of influential landowning families. The members of these families were generally thought to be, and certainly thought of themselves as, "the best" people in their respective poleis, and they were regularly referred to by the Greek word that means "the best," ARISTOI. The English word "aristocracy" comes from the Greek word that means "rule by the *aristoi*."

The form that the polis had taken during the Archaic Period required a certain degree of cooperation among the *aristoi* in order for the polis to function

ARISTOI Literally "the best (men)," used to refer to the members of the leading landowning families of a polis and serving as the first element of the words "aristocrat" and "aristocracy."

successfully. Still, there was, naturally, a great deal of competition and friction among these individuals, and the social and economic changes of the seventh and sixth centuries provided the tinder that, in a number of instances, was ignited by this friction. Specifically, overseas trade, which was facilitated by colonization, and the general increase in material prosperity in the Greek world enabled some individuals who did not belong to the traditional group of *aristoi* to amass considerable wealth. (We saw earlier that Theognis complained bitterly about the effect these *nouveaux riches* had on the supposed purity of the aristocratic stock.) At the same time, the development of the hoplite phalanx required the *aristoi* and these *nouveaux riches* to stand literally side by side on the field of battle and to take equal responsibility for the security of the polis. Equal responsibility, combined with equal danger but without equal power, can lead to an inflammatory situation, and in a number of poleis in the seventh and sixth centuries an ambitious member of the *aristoi*, with backing from some of the hoplites, took over control of the government of the polis and ruled in his own name. The Greek word for a person who seizes power for himself in this manner is *tyrannos*, the ancestor of the English word TYRANT (and of the name of the dinosaur Tyrannosaurus rex). Actually, the Greeks borrowed the word from the speakers of a non-Greek language of Anatolia, but made it their own and applied the newly adopted foreign term to this new figure who appeared on the scene beginning in the seventh century BC.

TYRANT One of a number of usurpers who, beginning in the middle of the seventh century BC, seized autocratic power in a polis and established (or attempted to establish) a hereditary monarchy.

Polycrates of Samos was only one of the many tyrants who seized power at some point during the Archaic Period. According to Herodotus, Polycrates overthrew the government aided by his two brothers and some 15 hoplites, and ruled the island until he himself was overthrown by the Persians in 522 BC. Herodotus paints a rather brutal picture of Polycrates, telling us that he killed one of his brothers and exiled the other so that he could enjoy unchallenged supremacy on the island. Once he had consolidated his rule on Samos, he began attacking and plundering all the neighboring poleis indiscriminately because, as Herodotus tells us, he claimed to be able to win friends and influence people by first seizing their property and then giving it back to them. This is in fact typical of the stories that circulated about tyrants, stories that often were fabricated by those who opposed the rule of the tyrant and sought to justify his overthrow. Yet the rule of many of the Greek tyrants was beneficial, or at least was not oppressive, and the Greek word *tyrannos* did not have the necessarily negative connotation that the word "tyrant" has in English. Indeed, the "tyranny" of Polycrates is associated with a considerable improvement in the standing of Samos, not only militarily but materially and culturally as well. For, like many of the Archaic Greek tyrants, Polycrates sponsored a lavish program of public works. The reason for this promotion of public works by the tyrants was primarily, of course, in order to claim personal credit for benefiting the citizens of the polis (a practice that is annoyingly common among today's politicians, facilitated by the eager collusion of the news media), but also in order to focus on the public and communal aspects of the polis in contrast to the more limited, elitist concerns of the *aristoi*, such as the exclusive symposium with which we began this chapter. Consequently, during the tyranny of Polycrates, Samos was provided with an impressive man-made harbor that accommodated Polycrates' fleet of one hundred warships, perhaps the most substantial Greek navy until that time. Also, a new temple of the goddess Hera, the patron deity of Samos, was begun, a temple that Herodotus calls "the largest of all temples that we know of." And a tunnel of about a kilometer in length, parts of which can still be seen today, was constructed to ensure the fresh water supply of the city of Samos. (When this tunnel was dug, excavation began at both ends simultaneously; that there was only a very slight misalignment when the two shafts met is testimony to the level of accomplishment in geometry among Polycrates' engineers.) In addition, Polycrates attracted two of the leading lyric poets of the day to his court, Ibycus from Rhegium in southern Italy and Anacreon from Abdera on the north coast of the Aegean Sea.

While there is no such thing as a "typical" Greek tyrant, Polycrates has a great deal in common with several of the tyrants of other poleis about whom we know. So, for example, after Polycrates lost his power and his life, the poet Anacreon, along with other leading poets, was welcomed to Athens by Hipparchus, the brother of the reigning tyrant of Athens and the son of his predecessor. Nor was the character of Polycrates' "friendship" with the king of Egypt at all unusual. Today, we would think of this type of relationship in more political terms, and we would speak of an "alliance" between Samos and Egypt rather than a "friendship" between Polycrates and Amasis. But alliances between states that are ruled by autocrats, no matter how "political" their motivation, are conducted in purely personal terms, and there is evidence for several Greek tyrants who maintained personal relationships with non-Greek kings and with tyrants in other Greek poleis. For example, Periander, who became tyrant of Corinth in about 627 BC (and was the patron of the almost legendary lyric poet Arion), sent a lavish gift to King Alyattes of Lydia. The gift consisted of three hundred young boys, the sons of the leading families of a Greek polis that was responsible for putting Periander's son to death; the boys were to be castrated and put into the service of Alyattes as eunuchs. Periander seems to have cultivated relations with the king of Egypt as well; his nephew was named Psammetichus, which is the Greek form of the name of Psamtek, the pharaoh of Egypt at the time Periander became tyrant. Periander also maintained friendships with tyrants of other Greek poleis, like Thrasybulus of Miletus on the coast of Asia Minor; this "alliance" between the two poleis considerably benefited Corinth's capacity for trade in the east and Miletus' in the west. Sometimes these personal relationships between tyrants were formalized by marriage. Periander, for example, was the son-in-law of the tyrant of the neighboring polis of Epidaurus, which polis he eventually invaded and annexed, taking his father-in-law prisoner.

In this adherence to a personal mode of diplomacy and statesmanship the Archaic tyrants were continuing an aristocratic tradition that is in evidence also among the basileis in the Homeric poems, for whom the exchange of valuable gifts is a ratification of the reciprocal ties of friendship and mutual obligation between noblemen living in different parts of the Greek world. The Greek warriors who participate in the Trojan War are represented as being bound by personal ties to Menelaus and his brother Agamemnon, who are themselves married to

"I am referring to your fellow citizen and mine, Hipparchus son of Peisistratus, from the family of the Philaedae. He was the oldest and most sensible of Peisistratus' sons and, to name but a few of the many shining examples of his good sense, he was the first to introduce the Homeric poems into this land, requiring the rhapsodes at the Panathenaea to recite them from start to finish, taking turns as they still do today. He also dispatched a ship from his navy to transport Anacreon of Teos to our city, and he kept Simonides of Ceos always in attendance, inducing him to stay with lavish payments and gifts. He did this out of a desire to educate the citizens, so that he would have the best possible subjects to rule." (Plato, *Hipparchus* 228 b–c)

two daughters of the Spartan basileus Tyndareus. In some instances, tyrants could lay claim to a more direct Homeric connection. The sixth-century tyrant of Athens, Peisistratus, claimed to be directly descended from Nestor, the basileus of Pylos who appears in both the Homeric poems. In fact, Peisistratus is the name of Nestor's youngest son in the *Odyssey*. This is rather suspicious. It is all the more suspicious when we consider the fact that Peisistratus' son Hipparchus, whom we mentioned above as a patron of poetry, introduced the Homeric epics into Athens and instituted formal recitations of the *Iliad* and the *Odyssey* at the festival of the Panathenaea, a festival that was expanded on a grand scale by Hipparchus' father, the tyrant Peisistratus. It seems all but certain that we are dealing here with outright invention on the part of Peisistratus and his family. That is, the name and the role of Peisistratus, the son of Nestor, were fabricated and included in Homer's *Odyssey* in sixth-century Athens in order to provide an ancestry for the tyrant of Athens (and his son) that could be represented as connecting him with a Homeric character especially known for his wisdom and sound advice.

Another feature of the Athenian festival of the Panathenaea, the festival especially promoted by the tyrant Peisistratus, was the inclusion of athletic and equestrian contests which attracted the finest contestants from all over the Greek world. In addition to patronage of the arts and substantial public works projects, Greek tyrants typically involved themselves, either as participants or as sponsors, in major sporting events. Myron, the tyrant of Sicyon, was a winner in the chariot race at the Olympic Games in 648 BC, as was his descendant, the tyrant Cleisthenes, about 70 years later. In 640 BC, the victor in one of the foot races at Olympia was the Athenian Cylon, son-in-law of Theagenes, the tyrant of Megara, who tried but failed to make himself tyrant of Athens. Earlier in the seventh century, Pheidon, the tyrant of Argos, marched with his army to Olympia and took control of the games, presiding over them himself as Hitler was to do in Berlin in 1936. The Olympic Games were the oldest, and for nearly two centuries the only, Panhellenic Games. They afforded tyrants and other members of the *aristoi* an opportunity to display their individual accomplishments in the manner of Homeric heroes. For Greek athletic contests, such as wrestling, boxing, foot races, and chariot races, are exclusively individual affairs, in which one person attempts to assert superiority over all other contestants; there are no serious "team sports" in ancient Greece. After the development of the hoplite phalanx and the virtual disappearance of the Homeric style of warfare, in which the individual warrior sought to secure fame by distinguishing himself in single combat, success in athletic contests became an especially desirable method of displaying one's individual worth. For this reason, in the sixth century BC, a need was felt to increase the number of venues in which such displays could take place. In rapid succession, between 586 and 573 BC, three additional Panhellenic Games were founded, the Pythian Games at Delphi, the Isthmian Games near Corinth, and the Nemean Games near Argos. Shortly afterwards, in 566 BC, the festival of the Panathenaea at Athens was reorganized and began to include athletic and equestrian events. Peisistratus himself may have been responsible for this reorganization, as the tyrant Cleisthenes of Sicyon seems to have had a hand in the founding of the Pythian Games.

The Panathenaic Games were not Panhellenic. They were, rather, a series of contests, in musical performance and dancing as well as in equestrian and athletic events, for citizens of Athens, of the sort that very many ancient Greek communities held for their own citizens.

> "For the team of two colts: 40 amphoras of oil; second place: 8. For the team of two horses: 140 amphoras of oil; second place: 40." (*IG* II² 2311, listing prizes for the Panathenaic Games in the fourth century BC)

The Panathenaic Games also included several events that were open to competitors from elsewhere in Greece as well, and the great value of the prizes – in contrast to the Panhellenic Games, which offered prizes of no monetary value – ensured that highly qualified competitors from all over the Greek world could be counted on to participate. These prizes included golden crowns, substantial amounts of gold and silver, and, specific to the Panathenaic Games, quantities of large ceramic vessels containing great amounts of fine Athenian olive oil. These "Panathenaic amphoras" were of a standard shape and size, with a capacity of just under 40 liters, and were decorated in uniform fashion: one side of each vase was painted with a representation of the goddess Athena, the patron of the games and of the city of Athens, while the other side depicted the event for which the vase served as a prize. The amphora illustrated here (figures 29 and 30) was decorated by one of the leading Athenian vase painters of the early fifth century BC, to serve as part of the prize for the wrestling contest. Every four years the authorities of the Panathenaic Games, a group of Athenian citizens chosen by the governing body of the polis, would commission hundreds of these vases. For, as we know from a fourth-century inscription, first prize in the wrestling contest in the boy's category at that time was thirty amphoras of olive oil and second prize was six amphoras. Since the prizes for men were regularly double those for boys – there was also a third age category, between the men and the boys – we can be confident that the winner in the men's category received sixty amphoras, containing nearly 2,400 liters of olive oil.

Ceramics

At the time the Panathenaic Games were reorganized in 566 BC, during the tyranny of Peisistratus, Athens was just replacing Corinth as the leading Greek center for

Figure 29
Obverse of Panathenaic prize amphora attributed to the Berlin Painter, showing Athena and inscribed "[one] of the prizes from Athens"; height 62.2 cm, ca. 480–470 BC. Hood Museum of Art, Dartmouth College, Hanover, NH, C.959.53. Gift of Mr. and Mrs. Ray Winfield Smith, Class of 1918. As supplied by the museum.

the production of painted pottery with figured decoration. For the remainder of the sixth and throughout the fifth century BC, painted Athenian ceramic ware was a desired commodity and was widely exported throughout the Greek world and beyond. Vases from Athens turn up in large numbers in Italy, for example, in Etruscan tombs. Athenian ceramic ware in the sixth century BC was regularly decorated in a style now known as the "black-figure" technique, in which men, horses, or other figures were painted in black on the reddish-orange background of the local clay and the vase was then fired in such a way as to give the paint a lustrous black gloss. Interior details, like the lines for the muscles, facial features, and drapery in figure 30, were produced by drawing lines with a graver, which scraped the paint, allowing the color of the natural clay to show through. By convention, women were painted with white skin, reflecting the fact that Athenian women – and their divine counterparts (figure 29) – were expected to spend their time indoors, whereas the more public life of men left them sunburned and dark. The scenes depicted on Athenian black-figure vases include numerous representations of contemporary life, like the symposium of which the ceramic ware was itself an integral part, as well as incidents from myth and the life of the gods. These scenes provide us with a unique source of plentiful evidence for the way Greeks in the sixth century BC saw their world. For the details of everyday life, which are often conveyed on the vases in a seemingly spontaneous fashion, are generally ignored in the more conventionalized

Figure 30 Reverse of figure 29, showing two wrestlers and an umpire. Hood Museum of Art, Dartmouth College, Hanover, NH, C.959.53. Gift of Mr. and Mrs. Ray Winfield Smith, Class of 1918. As supplied by the museum.

epic and lyric poetry of the same period. And the myths, which have taken on an almost canonical form in the literary sources because of the authority and ubiquity of Homer and Hesiod, appear in the visual arts to be largely independent of the literary tradition as it has come down to us.

This independence from the literary tradition has nothing to do with the question of whether the vase painters were literate or not: "literature" in sixth-century Greece was assimilated more commonly by hearing it recited than by reading texts. We know that some, at least, of the vase painters were literate because they sometimes label the figures in the mythical scenes with names painted next to the figures. (By the same token, there are many vases with random strings of letters, presumably intended to enhance the prestige value of the object in the same way that unintelligible runs of English words are applied to articles of clothing manufactured today in parts of eastern Asia.) In addition, some of the artists, beginning in about the 570s BC, sign their work. This is a conspicuous mark of self-promotion and self-assurance, and is reminiscent of the way in which Theognis, at approximately the same time, names himself when he "seals" his poems. Sixth-century Athenian vase painters had every reason to promote themselves and to feel self-assured. Their technical competence and their artistic and narrative sensitivity had reached an unprecedented level of accomplishment. No better example of this can be found than the amphora painted by Exekias (figure 31), showing on one side two heroes

Figure 31   Attic black-figure amphora signed, "Exekias made and painted me," showing Ajax and Achilles (both labeled) playing dice; height 61.1 cm, ca. 540–530 BC. Vatican Museums, Museo Gregoriano Etrusco, Inv. 16757; photo: Vatican Museums.

of the Trojan War, Ajax and Achilles, who are relaxing by playing a game of dice. The intense concentration of the figures is matched by the artist's elimination of everything except what is necessary to convey the essence of the narrative. The two figures are labeled, so that we know immediately who they are and what the setting is. Achilles, on the left, is the dominant figure, with the plume of his helmet looming above Ajax's head. That he is winning the game is confirmed by the labels "three" and "four" next to the two figures, revealing each man's throw in the game. This reflects the general rank of the two men, since Homer tells us that Ajax was the best looking and most accomplished of the Greek warriors at Troy, with the exception of Achilles. Both men, as Exekias and his customers would have known, were destined to die at Troy and, in fact, Exekias elsewhere painted scenes involving the death of both men: the dead body of Achilles and his armor being carried off the battlefield by Ajax and Ajax committing suicide because the armor of Achilles was awarded to Odysseus rather than to him. Thus, this apparently simple scene has profound and complex undertones, as is characteristic of the art of Exekias.

Shortly after this vase was created, Athenian artists began to experiment with a new technique of vase painting, the technique now known as "red-figure," which gives the appearance of being merely the converse of the black-figure technique. Around 530 BC, instead of painting the figures in black and incising the interior details, painters tried painting the figures in outline and then filling in the background with paint, so that the figures remained in the reddish color of the natural clay while the background became black when the vase was fired. There were two prominent advantages to this technique over the black-figure, one from the point of view of the painter and one from that of the viewer. From the perspective of the viewer, the figures in red-figure scenes produce a more convincing illusion of three-dimensionality, in part because, in general, a light-colored figure stands out more sharply from, and appears closer to the viewer on, a dark-colored background. The illusion of three-dimensionality is further enhanced because now it is much easier to paint figures that overlap with one another (figure 32), in

Figure 32 Interior of Attic red-figure cup by the Epidromos Painter, showing two men about to sacrifice a pig; diameter of cup 19.8 cm, ca. 510–500 BC. Paris, Musée du Louvre, G 112; photo: Erich Lessing/Art Resource, NY.

contrast to the often isolated characters in black-figure scenes. In addition, the figures in red-figure scenes were no longer painted in the uniform, flat black of their black-figure counterparts, and the interior details of the figures, which are darker than their surroundings in red-figure but lighter in black-figure, correspond to the places where shadows appear in three-dimensional figures. From the perspective of the creator of the scene, the artist was now painting, rather than incising, those interior details, which could now be produced with a freer, more fluid motion. Further, those details could be better differentiated from one another by the use of a more or less diluted pigment. This new red-figure technique superseded the black-figure within the span of a generation and was the preferred medium for nearly all the great Athenian vase painters from the end of the sixth century through the end of the Classical Period. A prominent exception to this, however, were the Panathenaic amphoras mentioned above, which continued to be decorated consistently in the old-fashioned black-figure technique even in the fourth century BC. There were, it seems, limitations to the tolerance of innovation, especially when the artist's patron was an arm of government.

Recommended for Further Reading

Andrewes, A. *The Greek Tyrants* (London 1956): a brief, lucid, and valuable study of the Greek tyrants from the seventh through the fifth centuries and of the various factors that brought them to power.

Boardman, J. *Greek Gems and Finger Rings: Early Bronze Age to Late Classical*, new expanded edition (London and New York 2001): a sumptuously illustrated and authoritatively written account with photographs of over a thousand seals by engravers whose skill is in some instances almost superhuman.

Boardman, J. *The History of Greek Vases: Potters, Painters and Pictures* (London 2001): a learned yet lively history of Greek vases and how they were made, decorated, used, and sold.

Lissarrague, F. *The Aesthetics of the Greek Banquet: Images of Wine and Ritual*, English translation (Princeton 1990): a sophisticated study of the often sophisticated images painted on the vases and cups used in the symposium.

Murray, O. (ed.) *Sympotica: A Symposium on the Symposion* (Oxford 1990): a learned collection of articles that examine all aspects of the Greek symposium, including its later adoption by the Etruscans and Romans.

Seaford, R. *Money and the Early Greek Mind: Homer, Philosophy, Tragedy* (Cambridge 2004): an absolutely brilliant and original work that examines the way in which the invention of coinage affected every area of Greek life, including even the development of philosophical thinking and the origins of drama.

THE BIRTH OF PHILOSOPHY AND THE PERSIAN WARS

6

The Greeks' contact with their neighbors to the east was both beneficial and dangerous. Familiarity with the science and thought of the Babylonians, Persians, and other flourishing civilizations contributed to the intellectual ferment that produced the earliest philosophers in the sixth century BC in the eastern Greek city of Miletus. These philosophers were concerned to answer fundamental questions about the origin and the organization of the universe for the first time without recourse to mythical or supernatural entities. While they may have been prompted to undertake their enquiries because of contact with the advanced civilizations of their non-Greek neighbors, it was the open environment of the Ionian Greek poleis that allowed them to challenge the assumptions of their predecessors and of each other. That same open environment encouraged the development of the earliest forms of democratic government, just at the time when the cities of Ionian Greece had become subjected to rule by the expanding Persian Empire. The remainder of the chapter traces the course of the series of conflicts between the Greeks and the Persians in the early fifth century BC, beginning with the unsuccessful Ionian Revolt, continuing with the spectacular Athenian victory over Persian forces at Marathon, and concluding with the final defeat of the Persians at sea at the battle of Salamis and on land at the battle of Plataea.

We have seen in previous chapters that a number of the most characteristic features of Greek civilization emerged as a direct result of Greek contact with non-Greek neighbors in the Near East and Egypt: the alphabet developing from the West Semitic writing system, the pose of Archaic kouroi from that of Egyptian statuary, the symposium from the oriental practice of reclining on couches, coinage from the technology of the Lydians. In this chapter, we will examine some further results of that contact: the invention of philosophy in sixth-century Ionia and the military conflict in the early fifth century that we refer to, because of our dependence primarily upon Greek sources, as the "Persian Wars."

Miletus and the Beginnings of Philosophy

In the seventh and sixth centuries BC, the city of Miletus was among the most prosperous and powerful of Greek poleis. It was located on a peninsula that afforded the Milesians excellent harbors, at the mouth of the Maeander River, which winds its wayward course down from the interior of Asia Minor (map 9). The site of Miletus therefore favored contact by sea with the rest of the Greek world and by both land and sea with the non-Greek inhabitants of Asia and North Africa. The Milesians were Ionian Greeks and considered themselves to have migrated to the coast of Asia Minor from the mainland of Greece by way of Athens. Linguistic, archaeological, and other evidence indicates that this tradition may reflect historical reality and that Ionian Greeks indeed settled Miletus from the mainland in the eleventh century BC. At the end of the Dark Age, as the Greek world began to prosper and expand, the Milesians began to engage energetically in trade and colonization, establishing numerous settlements on the coast of the Black Sea and along the Hellespont, the waterway that connects the Aegean with the Black Sea. Miletus' success and its overseas connections attracted the attention of the Lydians, whose territory lay just inland, and whose affluent empire extended over most of western Asia Minor in the first half of the sixth century BC.

The Lydians had incorporated a number of the Ionian Greek cities into their empire by military conquest, but Miletus successfully resisted Lydian aggression and maintained open and relatively friendly relations with Lydia and its kings Alyattes and Croesus (ca. 610–546 BC). In fact, according to the historian Herodotus, a Milesian citizen named Thales, serving as an engineer, accompanied the army of King Croesus on his campaign against the Persians in eastern Asia Minor. What little we know about Thales indicates that he lived in the first half of the sixth century BC and that he concerned himself with geometry and with scientific inquiry. He is said, for example, to have devised a procedure for determining the distance to a ship visible from shore and to have predicted the occurrence of a solar eclipse (presumably that of May 28, 585 BC). If these accounts are accurate, they point to a familiarity

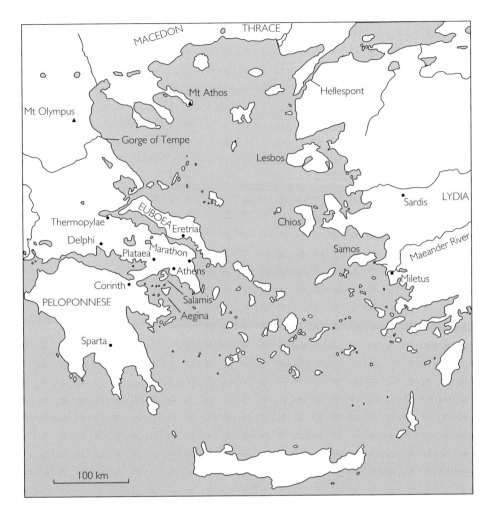

Map 9 Greece and the Persian Wars.

on Thales' part both with Egyptian surveying techniques and with Babylonian records of celestial phenomena.

Thales' most impressive accomplishment, however, was in the field of philosophy, of which he may be said to be the founder. None of Thales' writings has survived; nor do we even know for sure that he put any of his ideas into written form. We are told, however, that he claimed that the earth is supported by water, like a floating piece of wood, and that, indeed, water is the ultimate and original substance of everything that exists. These claims bear some similarity to earlier Egyptian, Babylonian, and Hebrew accounts of the origin of the universe (compare "and darkness was upon the face of the deep" from the opening of the book of Genesis). But, in these essentially mythical accounts, either the primordial waters are personified as deities, as when Homer refers to "Ocean, the source of the gods,"

"When Croesus reached the Halys River, what happened next, as far as I can tell, is that he got his army across the river using the already existing bridges. According to the prevailing account among the Greeks, however, it was Thales of Miletus who managed to get his army across for him. For they say that, when Croesus was unable to figure out a way for his army to cross the river (since, supposedly, the aforementioned bridges did not yet exist at that time), Thales, who was in the camp with the army, got the river to flow to the right of his army as well as in its regular course to the left. This is how he did it: beginning at a point upriver of the camp he had a deep trench dug, directing that it curve around so as to flow behind the place where they had pitched camp. In this way he used the trench to divert the river from its old course and then, when it passed around the camp, to return to its original bed, so that the river became fordable in both places as soon as it was divided in two." (Herodotus 1.75.3–5)

or they are part of the raw material from which a creator-god crafts the world as it is now. Thales seems to have divested his own propositions of any mythical elements. Now this, of itself, is not necessarily either a philosophical or a scientific development, but its consequence is both. For, while different, and even incompatible, mythical accounts often happily co-exist, an assertion like that of Thales can only either be accepted as a valid explanation or challenged and replaced by a more satisfactory account.

Thales' assertion did not have to wait long to be challenged. In fact, it was another Milesian, Thales' younger contemporary Anaximander, who propounded a rival theory. According to Anaximander, it is not water that is the basic element of the universe; rather, it is something that Anaximander called "the indefinite" or "the infinite." Anaximander even attempted to account (in the one brief fragment of his actual wording that we possess) for the perpetual process of change that the universe undergoes, in terms of the "compulsory penalty" that entities pay for wrongfully encroaching upon one another. Anaximander's theory was itself subjected to encroachment by yet another Milesian, a younger contemporary named Anaximenes, who proposed that the fundamental substance of the universe was neither water nor "the indefinite" but air. Anaximenes, too, attempted to explain change in the universe by appealing to the processes of condensation and rarefaction, by which air can become water and fire and, indeed, everything that is found in the universe.

It is perhaps not surprising that Miletus was the birthplace of philosophy and of scientific inquiry as we know it. Like other Ionian cities on the coast of Asia Minor, Miletus prospered during the seventh and sixth centuries and its citizens had relatively easy access to the sophisticated civilizations of Egypt and the Near East. Unlike the other Greek cities on the coast, however, Miletus had managed to maintain its independence from its Lydian and, later, its Persian neighbors. In 546 BC the Lydian Empire of King Croesus came to an end, defeated in battle by, and incorporated into the Persian Empire of, Cyrus the Great. This was the unintended result of the campaign mentioned above, on which Thales accompanied Croesus, who was hoping to forestall the expanding power of Cyrus and the Persians. Before the battle in which Cyrus overthrew Croesus and the Lydians, Cyrus had sent messages to the Greek cities that were tributaries to the Lydians, requesting that they revolt from Croesus. Since they had refused to do so, they now became tributaries to Cyrus and the Persians, on terms harsher than those that they had enjoyed under

Croesus. Miletus had been independent, and so Cyrus renewed the treaty that had been in effect between the Milesians and Croesus. Cyrus seems to have done this in part to encourage disunity among the Greek cities.

The Agora

The Greek cities were, indeed, disturbed by this new development because it was not at all clear what further ambitions for expansion Cyrus and the Persians might have. Accordingly, the Spartans, who possessed the most potent military force among the Greeks of the mainland, sent an ambassador to the newly victorious King Cyrus with a proclamation to the effect that the Spartans would not tolerate any aggression on Cyrus' part against any Greek city. After learning from an adviser who exactly these Spartans were, Cyrus replied, according to Herodotus, that he "had never been intimidated by the sort of men who have an open space in the middle of their city in which they gather together for the purpose of deceiving one another." Herodotus explains that Cyrus intended a reference to the agora, a characteristically Greek institution quite foreign to Persian practice. Among other things, the agora served as the marketplace at the heart of every Greek polis, and as such it could symbolize the open market economy of the Greeks in contrast to the old-fashioned, centralized economy of the Persian kingdom, which was similar to (although on a much vaster scale) what the Greeks had been familiar with during the Mycenaean Period. But the Greek agora served not only as a marketplace for the exchange of goods; it was also the location where the public business of the polis was carried out and was regarded by the Greeks as an indispensable feature of any polis worth the name. This, too, was indicative of the difference that the Greeks perceived between themselves and the Persians: the Greeks considered that their own institutions were public and that the policies of the polis were the product of communal deliberation, whereas the Persian king was an authoritarian despot.

The freedom and the public nature of Greek society extended not only to political and civic matters. The challenges to which the ideas of the earliest Milesian philosophers were subjected were equally a product of this open, and open-air, mentality. For the agora was an intellectual and cultural institution as well. It was often the place where athletic and equestrian contests were held in conjunction with the many festivals that enlivened the calendar of most Greek cities. Public performances by bards and musicians, themselves often in the form of competitions as well, will also have taken place in the agora. For this reason, when, for example, a colony was founded, the plan of the new city always included an open space set aside for public meetings and for the other gatherings that were an essential feature of Greek life. What is particularly interesting about this openness is that it is a feature of the Archaic Greek polis regardless of the type of government. During the seventh and sixth centuries, Miletus, like many Greek cities during the same period, alternated

OLIGARCHY
Literally "rule by the few," it denotes a type of government that, unlike democracy, excludes the majority of citizens from participation, generally restricting political power to a small number of wealthier citizens.

between an OLIGARCHIC form of government and government by a tyrant. These alternations, which were accompanied by bitter and often brutal outbreaks of civil strife, seem to have had no inhibiting effect on such things as the open development of science and philosophy. This is in contrast to, for example, the nature of scientific inquiry in ancient Babylon, which attained a remarkable level of accomplishment in the field of astronomy, but which was subsidized by the royal court and existed largely for the purpose of alerting the Babylonian king to potential dangers allegedly foretold by the observed celestial phenomena. In Miletus, however, and in other Ionian cities, scientists and thinkers could expect their theories to be subjected to radical challenges that questioned not only their validity but even the underlying premises on which their theories were based.

Ionia in the sixth century BC was the birthplace not only of philosophy and of a kind of scientific inquiry with which we today are familiar. There are hints that, had the Ionian poleis been allowed to develop without interference from outside, they might also have introduced democracy to the world, an accomplishment that is, instead, generally credited to fifth-century Athens. For example, there survives a fragmentary inscription from Chios, an Ionian island just off the western coast of Asia Minor. The inscription dates from the first half of the sixth century BC and refers to the existence on Chios of a "public council," consisting of 50 members elected from each of the tribes (probably six in number) and having the authority to overturn decisions of the highest magistrates in cases of appeal. It is only a matter of chance that this inscription has survived, and experts are not in agreement over the extent to which the inscription provides evidence of genuinely democratic institutions. In any event, there are striking similarities between the institutions reflected in the inscription and those of Athens, about which we are much better informed, in roughly the same period. It is usually assumed that democracy originated in Athens, but it is perhaps equally possible that the idea of some form of democratic government was something that was "in the air" in Athens and in other Greek cities in the sixth century BC. We have ample evidence that, in Athens, this idea was allowed to take hold in practice; for the Ionian cities of Asia Minor the evidence is meager and, in any case, the cities of Ionia were not free to develop as they wished.

The Ionian Revolt (499–494 BC)

What prevented the Ionians from developing as the Athenians were able to do was, precisely, the proximity of those foreigners, contact with whom influenced the intellectual and cultural development of Ionia. This proximity resulted in various parts of Ionia, at various times, coming under the power, first of the Lydians and later of the Persians. As we have seen, most of the Ionian cities (and most of the other Greek cities on the Aegean coast of Asia Minor) were required to pay tribute to the Lydians by the middle of the sixth century BC. After the conquest of Lydia in 546 BC by Cyrus and the Persians, those Greek cities became absorbed into the Persian

Empire and now paid tribute to the SATRAP, or governor, who administered for the Persian king the province that had previously been the Lydian Empire. The Greeks had been in awe of the wealth and power of King Croesus, and one wealthy Athenian father even named his son after the Lydian king (see p. 75); now Lydia was merely a small part of an empire the magnitude of which the Greeks could scarcely comprehend. Considering its vast extent, the Persian Empire was administered with remarkable efficiency. Its territory was divided into administrative districts, or satrapies, each overseen by a satrap whose responsibility it was to exact revenues and transmit them to the king. The satrap owed his position and his allegiance to the king, and he was allowed considerable latitude in how he governed the non-Persian population of his satrapy, provided that peace was maintained and the tribute collected. For the most part, the satrap permitted the native population a good deal of self-governance but, understandably, he preferred dealing with individual rulers rather than with councils or assemblies. Therefore, the satrap was generally in the habit of establishing tyrants in the Greek poleis under his jurisdiction.

We saw in chapter 5 that tyrannies arose in many Greek poleis in the course of the seventh and sixth centuries. In many instances, the tyrants were welcomed by a substantial portion of the population and they came to power as a result of social and political developments within the polis. On the other hand, the tyrants in the cities under Persian domination, although they were Greeks and natives of the cities that they ruled, were imposed by an outside power. They owed their authority and their loyalty to the satrap, who was not even Greek: the satrap was a Persian and his court was located in the Lydian city of Sardis, which had formerly been the capital of Croesus' empire. These newly installed tyrants, since they could rely on the support of the satrap, with his seemingly limitless power and resources, felt no need to moderate their rule. Many of them became autocratic and oppressive rulers of the sort that gave the word "tyrant" the meaning that it has today. So, since their authority rested upon that of the Persian satrap and the Persian king, their Greek subjects projected these tyrants' behavior onto their Persian overlords, and the image arose in the minds of the Greeks of the Persian king as despotic and "tyrannical." The contrast between their own oppression and the relative freedom of the Greek poleis of the Aegean islands, the mainland, and the west cannot have escaped the attention of the Ionian Greeks. By the end of the sixth century, the Ionian cities were ready to revolt from their local tyrants and from the Persians who had imposed them.

At this time, the Persian king was Darius I, who ruled from 521 until his death in 486 and who oversaw the expansion of the Persian Empire to its point of greatest extent. Under Darius, the Persian Empire stretched from the shores of the Mediterranean Sea to the banks of the Indus River and included Egypt and a small portion of Europe

> **SATRAP** The title used to refer to the governor of a formal territorial subdivision (satrapy) of the Persian Empire.

> "Darius the King says, 'These are the lands that are subject to me, lands of which I became king by the grace of Ahura Mazda: Persia, Sousiana, Babylon, Assyria, Arabia, Egypt, the lands by the sea, Lydia, Ionia, Media, Armenia, Cappadocia, Parthia, Drangiana, Areia, Chorasmia, Bactria, Sogdiana, Gandara, Scythia, Sattagydia, Arachosia, and Maka, a total of twenty-three.'" (Persian inscription commissioned by Darius I found in Bisotun, Iran)

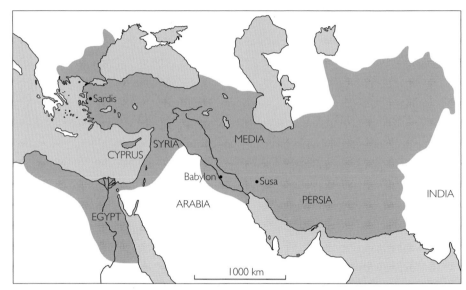

Map 10 The Persian Empire at its greatest extent under Darius I (ca. 500 BC).

between the Aegean and Black Seas (map 10). The contrast between the power and size of the Persian Empire and the insignificance of the Ionian cities on the coast could not have been greater. The Ionians, in particular, were in a position to comprehend the magnitude of that contrast because one of them, the Milesian philosopher Anaximander, had earlier in the sixth century created the first map of the world. Another Milesian, Aristagoras, was the instigator of the Ionian Revolt, which began in 499 BC. Aristagoras was himself tyrant of Miletus, but he stepped down in that year and encouraged the other Ionian cities to rid themselves of their tyrants. Aristagoras knew that he was inciting rebellion against the most massive empire on the face of the earth, and he sought support for his efforts from some of the Greek cities on the mainland, especially Sparta and Athens. At this time, these were the two most powerful Greek poleis. Sparta was never comfortable committing its soldiers to serve very far from home and declined to provide any support. Athens, however, was willing to contribute a small fleet of 20 ships, and the Euboean city of Eretria sent an additional five. The Athenians and the Eretrians were themselves Ionian Greeks, and they seem to have been motivated in part by a special feeling of kinship with the Ionians on the other side of the Aegean Sea.

The Athenian and Eretrian forces sailed to Miletus, where they joined up with the troops of the Ionian cities that were prepared to revolt from Persia. The Greeks then marched on Sardis, which they were able to capture with relative ease. They could not, however, seize the citadel at the heart of the city, which was defended by the troops of the Persian satrap. Before the Greeks could mount an assault on the citadel, a fire broke out in the city; whether the fire was deliberately set by the Greek invaders is not known. At any rate, because of the type of construction used in Sardis at the time, the fire spread quickly and soon engulfed the entire city. The Greeks retreated hastily and returned to the coast, pursued by the satrap and his army, which was soon joined by other Persian troops from the nearby satrapies. After a battle in which the Persian forces inflicted heavy casualties on the rebellious Greeks, the Athenians sailed back home, leaving their Ionian kinsmen to a fate which, by this point, must have been abundantly clear. It took some years, however, before the Persians were able finally to put down the Ionian Revolt. In 494 BC, a naval battle took place just off Miletus in which the Ionian fleet was resoundingly defeated by a navy that consisted largely of ships provided by the Phoenicians, who were loyal subjects of the Persian Empire. After the battle, the Persians captured and destroyed the city of Miletus, enslaving those of its inhabitants that they did not put to death.

The Persian Wars: Marathon

The end of the Ionian Revolt did not mean the end of conflict between the Persians and the Greeks. Indeed, it was only the beginning. Darius was determined to punish Athens and Eretria for their role in aiding the Ionians in their revolt. According to Herodotus, Darius ordered one of his slaves to remind him daily of his obligation to exact vengeance by repeating three times, "Master, remember the Athenians!" Darius also sought to avenge himself on the other Greek poleis that had contributed military assistance during the course of the Ionian Revolt. These latter included cities on the islands of Samos, Chios, and Lesbos that lay just off the coast of Asia Minor. These islands were soon annexed to the Persian Empire, which was now in a position to continue expanding westward across the Aegean Sea. In 492 BC, Darius sent his son-in-law Mardonius with a fleet and an army to invade mainland Greece, but the army suffered substantial losses, even before it reached Greece, at the hands of BARBARIAN tribes in Thrace, and the navy came to grief in the northern Aegean as a result of a severe storm that arose as the fleet rounded the promontory of Mount Athos. After this abortive attempt, Darius dispatched another fleet and another army in 490 BC. The aim was to reduce Athens and Eretria to slavery and to restore to power the aged Athenian tyrant Hippias, the son of Peisistratus, who had been deposed and exiled 20 years before. This time the Persian fleet avoided the northern route and sailed straight across the Aegean, with Hippias on board one of the ships. The Persians first attacked Eretria, which was easily overcome, especially after the city was betrayed from inside the walls by some Persian sympathizers; or, rather, by some Eretrians who recognized that Persian victory was inevitable and who could profit from appearing to be Persian sympathizers. The surviving population of Eretria was enslaved and transported to Asia for settlement at a site near the Euphrates River in what is today Iraq; the city's sanctuaries were burned down in retaliation for the sanctuaries of Sardis that had been destroyed by fire during the Ionian Revolt.

The Persians then crossed over the channel that separates the island of Euboea from the mainland of Greece and, following the advice of the Athenian Hippias, set up camp in the territory of Athens on the plain of Marathon. There were in

BARBARIAN The term used by the Greeks to refer to any non-Greek, whose unintelligible speech was thought to resemble the nonsense syllables "bar-bar" from which the word was derived.

Athens, as there had been in Eretria, those who could profit from appearing to be Persian sympathizers and there were certainly those who, for political reasons, would have been happy to see the tyrant Hippias restored to power. It was perhaps only a matter of time before Athens, too, was betrayed to the invaders. Further, the Athenian forces were heavily outnumbered by the Persians and the only neighbors who sent help were the Plataeans, whose entire army numbered only in the hundreds. The Athenians sent a messenger in great haste to the Spartans to ask them to send help immediately. Because of the rugged terrain of much of Greece, runners rather than horsemen were often used to transmit messages from one city to another. The distance from Athens to Sparta is slightly over two hundred kilometers, and the Athenian runner made the journey in two days. Remarkable though his accomplishment seems, it is even more remarkable that the Spartan army, in full battle gear, covered the same distance in three days. But the Spartans could not commit their troops immediately; a ritual requirement would not allow them to send an army into the field until the moon was full, which would not be the case for another six days. When the Spartan army did finally arrive on the scene, it was too late to be of any assistance to the Athenians. The battle of Marathon had already been fought and lost – by the Persians.

"This is grain-bearing Gela's memorial to Aeschylus the Athenian, late son of Euphorion. The hallowed ground of Marathon could tell of his glorious valor, as could the long-haired Persian, who knows all too well." (*Epigrammata Graeca* 454–7 Page, epitaph for the tragic poet Aeschylus)

The defeat of the Persian forces by the Athenians and Plataeans at Marathon in the late summer of 490 BC was the last thing anyone could have expected. The Athenians were convinced that they had been successful because they were a free people fighting against a horde of servile barbarians whose will was ener-vated by their subservience to a despotic master. They were further convinced that the gods that they worshiped played a significant role in securing their victory. (It is worth noting that in all of human history a vanquished army has never taken its defeat to be evidence of the inefficacy of its gods.) Modern scholars prefer to explain the outcome of the battle of Marathon in terms of the Greeks' superiority to the Persians in discipline and equipment. Over the previous 200 years, the Greeks had become accustomed to the discipline and coordination required by the tactics of hoplite warfare. For this reason, Greek mercenaries were recruited in the seventh and sixth centuries to serve in the Babylonian and the Egyptian armies. Hoplite tactics had led to the development of bronze protective armor and long thrusting-spears that turned out to be more than a match for the less substantial equipment of the Persians (figure 33), who were accustomed to relying on their superior numbers to overwhelm their opponents. Of course, the Greeks would not have considered their own explanation and that of modern scholars as mutually exclusive alternatives: the Greeks' superior discipline was undoubtedly the outcome of self-determination, just as the Persians' lack of self-control resulted from their subjection to an absolute ruler, and Greek armorers were undoubtedly more pious, and therefore more successful, than their Persian counterparts.

Figure 33 Detail of Attic red-figure amphora, showing a hoplite spearing a Persian warrior who holds a bow and a sword; height of figured scene 11.6 cm, ca. 480–470 BC. New York, Metropolitan Museum of Art, Rogers Fund, 1906 (06.1021.117).

Whatever the reasons for their victory at Marathon, the Athenians and Plataeans had no time to savor it. The Persian fleet, which was still intact, set sail immediately and headed around the promontory of Attica for the port of Athens itself. By the time the Persians arrived, the victorious Athenian troops were already there, having marched the roughly 40 kilometers as quickly as they possibly could. The Persians had expected to find the city undefended; when they saw the Athenian army ready to repel any attack, they turned around and sailed back to Asia, taking the disappointed Hippias with them. As if the reality of the event was not fabulous enough, a number of legends arose in its wake, the most enduring of which concerned the messenger who had run from Athens to Sparta. A later, fictitious account has him then running back to Marathon to participate in the battle, after which he rushes to report the victory to the Athenians with his dying breath. The marathon race that commemorates this last (and least impressive) feat is a purely modern invention and dates only from the first modern Olympic Games, held in Athens in 1896. At that time a race was held from Marathon to the stadium in Athens, a distance of 42 kilometers. (By contrast, the longest foot race at the ancient Olympic Games covered a distance of only about five kilometers, if that.) The marathon race is now a standard feature of the Olympic Games and is a popular event in other contexts as well. That it is derived from a fictionalized embellishment of an historical event serves as a pointed reminder that "history" is merely what posterity makes of its past.

The Persian Wars: Thermopylae, Salamis, and Plataea

While the battle of Marathon was to become the stuff of legend among the Greeks, it was an affront to the dignity and might of the Persian king. Darius set about making preparations for an invasion of Greece on an even larger scale, but he died in 486 BC before those preparations could be completed. Darius was succeeded by his son Xerxes, who inherited, along with the Persian throne, a rebellion in Egypt and a commitment to punish the Athenians for the burning of Sardis and, now, for defeating the king's forces at Marathon. Xerxes attended first to the Egyptian revolt, which he quelled in short order, and then began massive preparations for an invasion of Greece. The Persian king and his advisers had learned from the setbacks suffered by their navy in the northern Aegean in 492 and by their army at Marathon in 490, and they were determined to leave nothing to chance. Fully four years were taken up with raising the forces that would invade Greece by both land and sea and with making such arrangements that would ensure the success of the invasion. These arrangements included the storage of vast quantities of provisions along the route to be followed by the army and navy, the cutting of a canal through the peninsula of Mount Athos, and the construction of two pontoon bridges, each over a kilometer in length, across the Hellespont. And so the ruler of the world's lone superpower, convinced that his mission had divine support, prepared to complete a job that he considered his father to have left unfinished 10 years before, by leading a vast and heavily equipped multi-ethnic invasion of a land on another continent that posed no threat to the security of his mighty empire.

The Greeks were well aware of these preparations and of their magnitude, and it must have been obvious to all that the Persians would readily succeed in overcoming any opposition. Indeed, the conspicuous measures that the Persians were taking seem to have been designed in part to ensure that there would be no opposition. Consequently, by the time the Persian forces were ready to cross over into Europe in the spring of 480, most of the Greek cities were prepared to come to terms with the invaders. After all, it was felt that the Persian attack was primarily directed at Athens and Sparta, the two cities that had refused to give "earth and water" to the ambassadors of King Darius, who had gone around to the Greek cities in the late 490s to demand these traditional tokens of submission to Persian authority. If any of the cities was in some doubt as to what should be done in the face of the imminent invasion, the Delphic oracle could be consulted and could be counted on to give sound advice fortified by divine sanction: in every instance that we know of, the oracle of Apollo advised either accommodation with the Persians or wholesale emigration. So, for example, when the Athenians sent ambassadors to

Delphi in the hope of receiving some encouragement from the oracle, the god instructed the Athenians to abandon their homes and to "flee to the ends of the earth," as there was no hope that Athens could be saved. When pressed to provide a somewhat less discouraging response, the god suggested that the only thing that would not be ravaged by the invaders was "a wooden wall," which would give some help to the Athenians. The wooden wall was pretty clearly intended as a reference to the ships of the Athenian navy which, the oracle seemed to be indicating, could be used to transport the population of Athens to a new and distant home. There were those in Athens, however, who interpreted the words of the god to mean that the Persians could be defeated in a naval engagement.

The leader of this group of seriously deluded optimists was an Athenian named Themistocles, who had a vested interest in promoting the merits of the Athenian navy. For Themistocles was himself largely responsible for the fact that, in 480 BC, the Athenian fleet was the largest in Greece. Not long before that time Athens was engaged in a war with its neighbor and rival, the island of Aegina, with neither the Athenian nor the Aeginetan navy asserting clear dominance. In 483, the Athenians experienced a stroke of good luck – or, as the Athenians would have seen it, a reward from the gods – that would improve their position in their rivalry with Aegina and would, eventually, affect considerably their odds of withstanding the Persian invasion. At the state-owned mine in southern Attica a new vein was discovered that yielded some 2,600 kilograms of silver in the first year alone.

Some Athenian politicians, whose descendants are easily recognizable today, proposed that this windfall be divided up and distributed equally among the citizens of Athens. Themistocles, however, managed to persuade the Athenian assembly to invest these new resources in the construction of a new fleet of TRIREMES (warships with three banks of oars). Triremes were the state-of-the-art naval weapon, superior in speed and maneuverability to the old-fashioned warships with two banks of oarsmen that were rapidly being superseded (figure 34). Speed and maneuverability were at this time the decisive factors in naval engagements, which involved

TRIREME The standard warship of the Greeks during the Classical Period, which used sail for long passages but was rowed into battle by oarsmen arranged in three rows, one above the other (figure 35).

Figure 34 Attic black-figure cup, showing warship with two banks of oars (right) about to ram a merchant vessel; height of cup 8.4 cm, late sixth century BC. London, British Museum, Vases B 436.

Figure 35 The *Olympias*, a full-scale reconstruction of an ancient trireme, built in 1985–7 to test the properties of such a vessel under actual sailing conditions; photograph courtesy of the Hellenic Navy.

the need for ships to turn quickly and disable enemy vessels by ramming them at the waterline with a bronze-clad wooden ram that projected from the ship's prow (figure 35). In the three-year period that preceded the Persian invasion, the Athenians constructed 200 triremes, financed by the revenues provided by the newly discovered lode of silver. Ostensibly, these ships were intended for use against the Athenians' Greek neighbors in Aegina, but they would prove invaluable at the battle of Salamis against the Persians. In addition, as we will see in chapter 7, the Athenians' commitment to the development of their naval power was to have a decisive effect on the character of Athenian political life throughout the fifth century.

During the spring and summer of 480 BC, Xerxes and his considerable army and navy made their deliberate way along the north coast of the Aegean, accepting the surrender of the various Thracian, Macedonian, and Greek peoples along the way. Only a small number of mainland Greek poleis were determined to stand up to the invaders, including Sparta, Athens, Corinth, and about 30 other cities, many quite insignificant in size and power, most of them located in the Peloponnese and under the influence of Sparta. Because of this influence, and because the Spartan army was the most experienced and effective military force in Greece, the Spartans assumed and were granted general command of the resistance to Persia. The Greek poleis had had very little experience cooperating with one another and coordinating their efforts, which made the planning of strategy against an already formidable opponent all the more difficult. Greek strategy in 480 BC was, in fact, neither consistent nor unanimously endorsed by the various contingents. Originally, the Greek forces moved as far north as the area around Mount Olympus, intending to hold the narrow pass at the Gorge of Tempe near the coast, but that position had to be abandoned even before the Persian army approached. The next place at which it seemed practicable to forestall the enemy army was about 100 kilometers to the south, at Thermopylae, where there was only a narrow path between the mountains and the sea. This position had the further advantage of being near the northern entrance to the channel separating the island of Euboea from the mainland, a position at which the Greek naval forces were not at too great a disadvantage against the larger Persian fleet.

As it happened, the pass at Thermopylae was held for about four days by a contingent of a mere 300 Spartans and some of their allies, under the leadership of the Spartan King Leonidas. At about the same time, a sudden storm arose, which drove a number of the Persian vessels against the rocky coast, wrecking several of them. Although the Persian fleet still maintained numerical superiority over the Greek, this fortuitous occurrence – or reward from the gods, as the Greeks would have considered it – served to make the numbers somewhat more even. Leonidas and his Spartan troops, however, were not able to prevent the Persian army from forcing the pass at Thermopylae, particularly after a local Greek guide showed the Persians a mountain path by which they could outflank the Spartan position. The Spartans fought and died with a determination that immediately became legendary. After all, in a case like this, where there are no survivors, a legendary account is the only one available. Leonidas and his 299 companions were memorialized in a contemporary epitaph that contributed to the legend:

> Take a message to the Spartans, passer-by:
> We followed their orders, and here we lie.

The report of the heroic stand of the Spartans at Thermopylae seems to have inspired the remaining Greeks with a conviction that resistance to the Persians could still hold rewards, even if the rewards consisted only in the assurance of a glorious death. There was, however, no other place where the terrain afforded a suitable location for resistance to the Persian army except at the isthmus that joins the Peloponnese to central Greece. This meant that Athens would have to be abandoned, and so, before the invading army reached Attica, the Athenian non-combatants were ferried to safety in

"You may be sure that the ships of the Persians would have been victorious if it had simply been a matter of numbers. For the total number of ships on the Greek side amounted to three hundred, including an elite squadron of ten. But under Xerxes' command – I know this well – were a thousand ships, with a total of two hundred and seven especially distinguished for speed. Such is the count. In this respect we were at no disadvantage in the battle, don't you think? But it was some divine spirit that brought this destruction upon our fleet, by loading one side of the balance with an unequal fate. The gods were the salvation of the goddess Athena's city." (Aeschylus, *The Persians* 337–47, a Persian messenger reports on the battle of Salamis)

ACROPOLIS
Literally "the highest point of the city," a rocky eminence sometimes used as the site of a citadel during Mycenaean times and later serving as the religious focal point of the polis from the Archaic Period onward; often used specifically to refer to the acropolis of Athens (figure 43).

the northern Peloponnese. When the Persians took possession of the city they occupied the **ACROPOLIS**, burning the temples and throwing down all the statues and other dedicatory offerings. The burning of Sardis during the Ionian Revolt had now been avenged, but Greece had not yet been conquered. The Greek fleet was drawn up in the channel between the coast of Attica and the island of Salamis. The Peloponnesian contingent would have preferred to retreat and defend the coast of the Peloponnese, but Themistocles, who was in command of the Athenian navy, manipulated the situation so as to force an engagement in the waters off Salamis. This was a considerable help to the Greeks, as the Persians could not take full advantage of their numerical superiority in the narrow channel, and the Greek fleet won a resounding victory.

Xerxes, who had witnessed the battle in person from a position on the coast of Attica, ordered what remained of his fleet to return at once to Asia, and he himself set out for home, leaving behind a portion of his army, under the command of Mardonius, for the purposes of subduing the remaining Greek land forces. It was now the end of September, and by convention ancient armies fought one another only during the summer months. Mardonius spent the winter with his army in northern Greece, which was, after all, still under Persian control, and he spent his time trying to create dissension among those cities that were determined to hold out against the Persians. When those

> "It is reported that, while watching the battle, Xerxes became aware of her ramming the other ship and someone who was present said, 'Lord, do you see how brilliantly Artemisia is performing? She has sunk an enemy ship!' Xerxes asked his staff whether it was indeed Artemisia who was responsible and they confirmed it, since they could clearly recognize the device on the ship as hers ... When he was told this Xerxes is reported to have said, 'My men have turned out to be women and my women men!'" (Herodotus, 8.88.2–3, on Queen Artemisia of Caria, who commanded five ships at the battle of Salamis)

attempts failed him, Mardonius marched in the spring of 479 BC and occupied Athens once again. The Greek forces mobilized and encountered Mardonius and the Persians in a decisive battle at Plataea, near the border that separates Athenian from Theban territory. During the course of the battle, Mardonius himself was killed, the Persian battle lines were broken, and the Greeks were victorious on land, as they had been in the battle of Salamis at sea. Not long after the battle of Plataea was fought, the poet Simonides composed an extended elegiac poem to commemorate the event, portions of which have only recently come to light in a fragmentary papyrus first published in 1992. In the poem, Simonides invests this victory with epic significance, associating it explicitly with the legendary Greek expedition into Asia to conquer Troy (and associating himself implicitly with the poet of the *Iliad*). As we have seen, Homer was looking back to an event that took place – if, indeed, it ever did take place – hundreds of years before his own time, so that the tendency to elaborate and magnify could hardly be resisted. In the case of the defense of Greece against Xerxes and the Persians, the event itself was already of such magnitude that it could only be conceived of in the mythic terms that Homer had established.

Recommended for Further Reading

Green, P. *The Greco-Persian Wars* (Berkeley 1996): a lively and engaging account of the Persian Wars that reads like a novel, yet is fundamentally sound in terms of historical and scholarly accuracy.

Harrison, T. (ed.) *Greeks and Barbarians* (New York 2002): a stimulating collection of essays and excerpts from larger works by prominent scholars concerning the Greek construction of foreigners and, by extension, of themselves.

McKirahan, R. D., Jr. *Philosophy before Socrates: An Introduction with Texts and Commentary* (Indianapolis 1994): a collection of virtually all the fragments of the Greek philosophers who lived before the end of the fifth century BC, with very helpful discussions that place these fragments in their intellectual and cultural context.

Miller, M. C. *Athens and Persia in the Fifth Century BC: A Study in Cultural Receptivity* (Cambridge 1997): a well-illustrated study of the (rather surprisingly) large influence "the enemy" had on the cultural life of Athens in the wake of the Persian Wars.

Morrison, J. S., Coates, J. F., and Rankov, N. B. *The Athenian Trireme: The History and Reconstruction of an Ancient Greek Warship*, 2nd edition (Cambridge 2000): a detailed study of every aspect of ancient Greek naval construction, sailing, and warfare, along with the story of the successful design and launching of the full-scale modern replica of a trireme seen in figure 35.

Strauss, B. *The Battle of Salamis: The Naval Encounter that Saved Greece – and Western Civilization* (New York 2004): an exciting specimen of military history that attempts to convey not only what happened at Salamis in 480 BC but how the battle and its outcome affected the development of Western democracy.

SETTING THE STAGE FOR DEMOCRACY

7

The two Greek poleis that had played the most significant role in the defeat of Persia were Athens and Sparta. This chapter will concern itself with these two cities and their very different characters, Athens being a progressive, democratic city with the largest navy in the Greek world, and Sparta being a conservative, even reactionary, oligarchy whose infantry was regarded as invincible. The special character of Spartan society arose in part because of its earlier conquest of the territory of its Greek neighbors, whom it reduced to the status of state slaves. The Spartans then imposed on themselves a rigorous system of physical training and institutional control aimed at maintaining their authority over a very large, servile population. By contrast, Athenian society in the sixth century BC developed increasingly open and democratic institutions resulting, by the fifth century, in the most radically democratic government the world has seen. This does not mean that the Athenians did not own slaves; like the Spartans, indeed like members of all ancient societies, free Athenians relied very heavily upon the economic contribution of forced labor. Radical democracy is based on the notional equality of all its free citizens, which may be perceived to be inconsistent with the aristocratic values exhibited by "the best" members of society. Athenian democracy therefore devised the practice of ostracism to remove from the city on a temporary basis any citizen who appeared to pose the risk of subverting democratic values and usurping power as a tyrant. The Athenian navy depended upon oarsmen drawn largely from the lower classes of citizen, whose interests were served by the extension of democratic values and the expansion of Athenian naval power. In the course of the fifth century BC, the naval alliance of which Athens had become the leader, the so-called Delian League, in effect turned into an Athenian empire. The chapter closes with a consideration of the dramatic works of the playwright Aeschylus, the earliest representative of the new genre of tragedy, which arose in Athens at the end of the sixth century and flourished in the fifth century BC.

The successful defense of Greece against invasion by non-Greeks was decisive, not only for determining the way in which Greek civilization was to develop throughout the rest of Greek history, but for the way in which the Greeks conceived of themselves and their past. In the *Iliad*, Homer had not represented the Trojans as being "foreigners": the combatants on both sides of the Trojan War spoke the same language, worshiped the same gods, and adhered to the same customs. By contrast, during the Persian Wars many Greeks encountered at close quarters the "barbarians" (as the Greeks called all people whose native language was not Greek) and found that there were significant differences between themselves and their attackers, who included not only Persians but also Phoenicians, Egyptians, Ethiopians, and other non-Greek subjects of the Persian king. Since the Greeks had defeated these "barbarians" in battle on both land and sea, it was almost inevitable that those

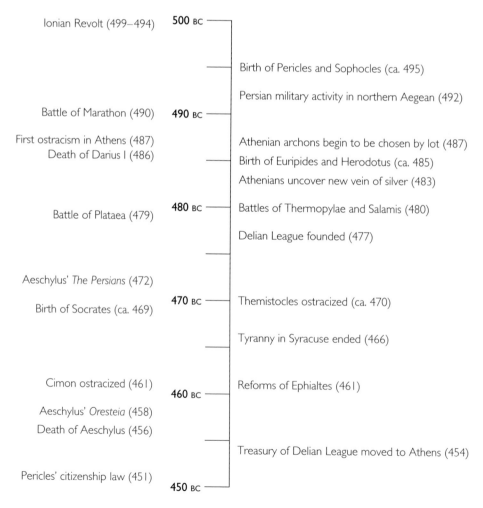

Ionian Revolt (499–494)	**500** BC
	Birth of Pericles and Sophocles (ca. 495)
	Persian military activity in northern Aegean (492)
Battle of Marathon (490) **490** BC	
First ostracism in Athens (487)	Athenian archons begin to be chosen by lot (487)
Death of Darius I (486)	Birth of Euripides and Herodotus (ca. 485)
	Athenians uncover new vein of silver (483)
Battle of Plataea (479) **480** BC	Battles of Thermopylae and Salamis (480)
	Delian League founded (477)
Aeschylus' *The Persians* (472)	
Birth of Socrates (ca. 469) **470** BC	Themistocles ostracized (ca. 470)
	Tyranny in Syracuse ended (466)
Cimon ostracized (461) **460** BC	Reforms of Ephialtes (461)
Aeschylus' *Oresteia* (458)	
Death of Aeschylus (456)	
	Treasury of Delian League moved to Athens (454)
Pericles' citizenship law (451) **450** BC	

Timeline 5   The early fifth century BC.

differences would prompt in them a certain feeling of superiority. In addition, through poetry and myth, the Greeks began to think of the legendary Trojan War in the light of their recent experience, imagining the defeated Trojans as barbarians who were earlier overcome by the superior civilization of the Greeks. This feeling of superiority to non-Greeks was, naturally, strongest on the part of the Greeks in those cities that had actually contributed to the resistance to the Persians, principally the cities of Athens and Sparta. It was these two cities that were to dominate the life of Greece for the next hundred years or more, and their development will serve as the focus for the present chapter.

A word needs to be said first about another polis, the city of Miletus, which occupied a prominent place in the previous chapter. Miletus had been utterly destroyed in 494 BC because of its role in the Ionian Revolt. After the wars ended, with freedom from Persian domination restored to the Greek cities of Asia Minor, it was possible for the Milesians to rebuild their home and to do so following a rational and uniform plan. The new city of Miletus was laid out according to a grid in which all the streets were either parallel or at right angles to one another (figure 36). This plan is generally associated with the figure of Hippodamus, a citizen of Miletus who is often considered the father of urban planning. It is not certain that Hippodamus was actually connected with the plan to rebuild Miletus. We know, however, that he was responsible for similar rectilinear plans for other Greek cities later in the fifth century BC, and we know that his planning proceeded on the basis of theoretical considerations that sought to create rational divisions both of the space of the city and of the city's population. In this respect, and in the comprehensiveness of his planning, he seems to have followed in the spirit of the Milesian philosophers of the previous century. The rationalizing tendency in Hippodamus' plan for Miletus is characteristically Greek, and his plan may in fact have had precedents elsewhere in Greece as early as the seventh or even late eighth century BC. For, during the period of colonization, many new Greek cities were laid out, some of them on what appear to have been quite a regular plan, but more limited in scope than the all-inclusive design of Miletus. The basis for these colonies was the equality of the size of the parcels of land, which were distributed among the colonists by lot, and the simplest way of ensuring equality was by using straight lines and right angles.

Now, it should be understood that insistence upon equality is not necessarily a "democratic" feature of these colonies or of Greek poleis in general (although this adherence to an ideal of equality was instrumental in the eventual creation of democracy in Greece). For, while it is true that all the colonists would have equal plots of land allotted to them and all would have the same social and political status, they would by virtue of their landholdings all have sufficient wealth to be of hoplite status. That is, their equality would have assured them of a position of leadership in the polis, which would have been organized in such a way that the relatively few landholders had control of the government while the majority (landless trades people, hired workers, slaves) had little if any share in the political process. This was the type of organization that was normal for poleis in the Archaic Period, the only real exceptions being those poleis in which political power was arrogated by a tyrant.

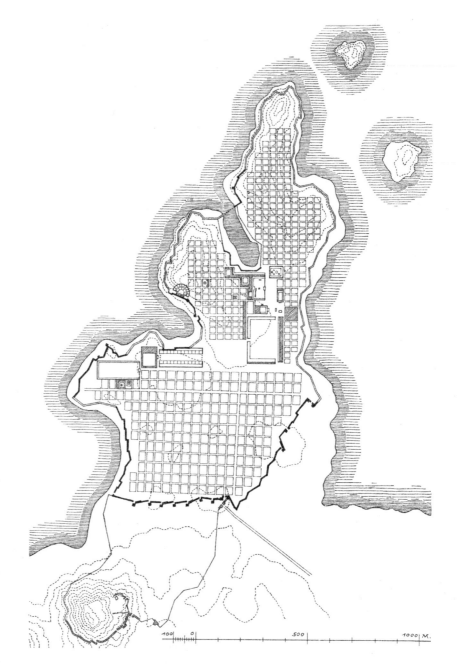

Figure 36 Town plan of Miletus, fifth century BC. Reproduced with the permission of Walter de Gruyter GmbH & Co. KG from A. von Gerkan, *Griechische Städteanlagen: Untersuchungen zur Entwicklung des Städtebaues im Altertum* (Berlin and Leipzig 1924), Tafel 6.

Because it was the normal type of organization, the Greeks had no name for it until something that appeared to be a distinct alternative came into being. That alternative was "democracy," which is a form of government that is not in fact different in kind but only in degree, as it expands the distribution of power to include some of those who were previously excluded. There were, of course, people who opposed this extension of political power to their supposed inferiors, and they chose to regard democracy as a fundamentally new and radically different type of organization. These people adhered tenaciously and sometimes forcefully to the older form of government, which came to be called "oligarchy," or "rule by the few," because political power continued to rest with the relatively few landowning citizens. The most prominent of the poleis that maintained an oligarchic form of government, and by far the most interesting, was Sparta.

The Development of Spartan Oligarchy

The success of the Greek army against the Persians at the battle of Plataea was due in large measure to the training and discipline of the Spartan hoplites under their commander Pausanias who, by virtue of his position at the head of the Spartan forces, was also the commander of the allied Greek army as a whole. This military pre-eminence was a product of the peculiar way in which Sparta had developed during the Archaic Period. Unfortunately, the details of this development are very obscure, but the general picture is reasonably clear. The leaders of Sparta were two kings, members of two Spartan families that considered themselves to be descended from two sons of the legendary hero Heracles. Kingship may seem to be incompatible with the equality of status characteristic of an oligarchy, but in fact the Spartan kings were not so much monarchs – after all, there were two of them at any one time – as they were military leaders whose position happened to be hereditary. The power of the kings was limited by the fact that they could be exiled or otherwise deprived of their position (and replaced by another member of the same family) and by the fact that they were only two members of what was in effect the governing body of Sparta, the *gerousia*, or council of elders. The *gerousia* consisted of 28 men over 60 years of age plus the two kings, who were, therefore, often the junior members of the council. It was the *gerousia*, and the *gerousia* alone, that had the authority to introduce measures to be voted upon by the assembly of Spartan citizens. The existence of such an assembly may give the impression that the Spartans had a democratic rather than an oligarchic government – democratic Athens, too, had a comparable assembly of all Athenian citizens – but the power of the assembly was virtually confined to ratifying decisions already reached by the *gerousia*.

What is more, the number of Spartan citizens represents only a small fraction of the total population of the territory governed by Sparta. The reason for this is that, during the eighth and seventh centuries BC, Spartan territory was gradually extended by conquest until, by the start of the sixth century, it comprised nearly half the area of the Peloponnese. During this time, Spartan citizenship was not conferred upon the inhabitants of the newly incorporated territories. Instead, the earliest victims of Spartan expansion, those who lived in the areas closest to Sparta, were given the status of dependent allies, while those who fell under Spartan authority at a later time became HELOTS, or slaves who were the property of the

HELOT   One of a group who had been collectively enslaved by, and was owned by, an alien state (especially Sparta), as opposed to the more common type of slave, who was privately owned by an individual.

Spartan state. When the historian Herodotus, writing within 50 years of the battle itself, records the figures for the Spartan forces at Plataea, he tells us that there were 5,000 Spartan hoplites, 5,000 hoplites from among the dependent allies, and 35,000 lightly armed helots. If these figures are approximately correct – and they are generally accepted by modern historians – they would seem to indicate that Spartan citizens made up less than 12 percent of the total male population of the territory ruled by Sparta and, since citizen status did not extend to women in ancient Greece, just over 5 percent of the adult population.

"Lycurgus is the man who established the laws that are followed by the Spartans and are responsible for their welfare. I have the highest regard for Lycurgus and I consider him wise in the extreme. For he made his homeland pre-eminent in prosperity not by imitating the other poleis but by pursuing a line of thinking that actually ran counter to the majority. To begin with the fundamentals, when it comes to childbearing, elsewhere girls who are brought up properly and are expected to become mothers are fed the plainest fare possible, with the very minimum of exposure to haute cuisine. They are either not allowed to have wine at all or it is given to them watered down. The rest of the Greeks think that girls should sit quietly in one place, like ordinary trades people, and work wool. How can girls brought up like this be expected to give birth to anything other than ordinary children? Lycurgus felt that the production of clothing could be left to slaves, of whom there is no shortage. Free women, he thought, had no higher calling than producing children, and so he required physical exercise for women no less than for men, and he established competitions for speed and strength among women, just like those for men, thinking that children are more robust if both their parents are able-bodied." (Xenophon, *The Spartan Way of Life* 1.2–4)

In order to maintain control over a population of which they were only a small minority, Spartan citizens developed a way of life and a system of training that were a source of fascination for other Greeks and have been a source of fascination ever since. To begin with, Spartan citizens were forbidden to engage in commerce or to pursue a trade; instead, they were supported by the labor of the helots, while commerce was in the hands of the dependent allies. This did not mean, however, that the Spartans were a "leisure class" who enjoyed a life of relaxation and pleasure. On the contrary, they devoted themselves to a rigorous physical and military training that enabled them to control, by force and intimidation, the non-citizen population. At birth, the children of citizens were inspected by representatives of the community to determine whether they were likely to be physically capable of completing the required training. Those who failed this first test had no further demands placed on them: they were simply set out in a ravine to die. Spartan boys who were found to be worthy of rearing were taken from their parents at the age of seven and trained with other boys in what the Spartans called "herds." The training was of a largely military nature, with the boys living in communal barracks and dining at a communal mess. At the age of 20 they could be admitted on a permanent basis to a communal mess, admission to which was a requirement for full citizen rights as an adult. Not until the age of 30 could they set up households on their own and live as part of a family. Even after that, the men were required to dine in the communal messes, the fare of which was notoriously austere and unappetizing. Spartan women were also subjected to rigorous physical training, in the expectation that they would as a result give birth to strong and healthy citizens. The aim of this training was to create uniformity among the Spartan citizens and, in fact, the Spartans were in the habit of referring to themselves as "the peers." For, in consequence of the equal distribution of conquered lands among the Spartans, all citizens were at least nominally landholders of equal status.

The Spartan fighting force was consequently remarkably disciplined and obedient to the dictates of the Spartan state. Spartan society was, as might be expected, quite conservative: innovation and foreign influence were firmly resisted, and Spartan citizens were uncomfortable about straying very far from their home territory, where they might be needed on short notice to react to disturbances or outright rebellion on the part of the helots. Another reason for the Spartans to be apprehensive of contact with the outside world is illustrated by the fate of Pausanias, the commander at Plataea. In the years immediately following the victory at Plataea it was necessary for the allied Greek forces to liberate from the Persians some of the Greek cities on the coast of Asia Minor. In the course of this campaign, exposure to the luxury and wealth of the east, along with a consciousness of his extraordinary success at Plataea, seems to have unhinged Pausanias' Spartan sensibilities. He began dining on exotic delicacies and dressing up in oriental finery. Pausanias even went so far as to suggest to Xerxes that he would be willing to help the Persians in a new attempt to conquer Greece, hoping that he would himself be given mastery of all Greece. When the Spartans learned of this, they recalled Pausanias from overseas to face trial at home, where he eventually died without causing further damage. This experience reinforced the Spartans' already firm reluctance to engage in operations in alien territory.

The Development of Democracy in Athens: Solon

The Athenian reaction to the successful outcome of the Persian Wars was very different, largely because of the very different character of Athenian society. By the time of the battle of Plataea, Athens had developed into a democracy that was very much interested in seeing its influence expand. In addition, the reluctance of the Spartans to assume a position of leadership in Greece after the departure of the Persians from mainland Greece encouraged the Athenians first to assume that position and then to attempt to impose their will on the Greek poleis in and around the Aegean Sea. We are much better informed about the development of Athenian society in the Archaic Period than we are about Sparta, and it will be instructive to outline that development as a means of understanding Athens' rise to power in the aftermath of the Persian Wars.

It is paradoxical that the basis of Sparta's oligarchic government lay in the supposed equality of Spartan citizens, whereas democracy in Athens arose in response to a crisis brought about by an uneven distribution of wealth. As we have seen, Sparta attained its eventual size by expansion, with members of a relatively small

"If some other man had held the whip-hand as I did, some greedy and devious man, he would not have restrained the rabble. If I had been willing to go along, now with the wishes of one side, now with what their opponents thought best, this polis would have seen the loss of many lives. For this reason I kept my guard up on every side; a wary wolf I was, surrounded by hounds." (Solon, fragment 36.20–7)

territory, the area in the immediate neighborhood of the town of Sparta, incorporating and dividing up the surrounding territories. Attica, or the territory of Athens, had by contrast attained unity by the consolidation, perhaps at the end of the Dark Age, of several scattered villages into a political entity with the urban center of Athens as its focus. The citizens, then, of this entity included subsistence farmers, craftsmen, merchants, and prosperous landowners. By the beginning of the sixth century BC, inequality in the distribution of wealth had reached such a point that many landowners had had to give up their rights to their own land in order to pay off debts and some had even been sold into slavery. The conflict that arose as a result of this situation was only resolved by the appointment of a respected member of a prominent Athenian family to mediate between the opposing forces and to formulate laws that would bring about stability. This man was Solon, and his appointment appears to have taken place in 594 BC. In addition to being a political figure and a lawgiver, Solon was also a poet of considerable distinction, and we are fortunate that a number of lengthy quotations from Solon's poems survive, some of which are concerned with his political and legislative reforms. He claims that he restrained the ambition of the wealthy as well as the immoderate demands of the poor, steering a middle course that ensured justice for all Athenians. Further, he repatriated many Athenians who had been sold abroad into slavery and who had been away from Athens for so long that they no longer spoke the Attic dialect, and he made it illegal for such debt slavery to occur in future.

The distinguishing feature of Solon's reforms was his restructuring of political power in Athens, which caused him to be regarded in antiquity as the founder of Athenian democracy. He divided the citizen population of Athens into four categories, distinguished by the quantity of produce that their land yielded. Ownership of land was therefore, as at Sparta, the basis for participation in government. But, while in Sparta all landholders were nominally of equal status, Solon's categories acknowledged the unequal distribution of wealth and were designed to apportion political power in accordance with wealth. This was the provision that would have been acceptable to the more affluent members of the polis. So, for example, only members of the highest property class were eligible to fill the most important state offices, including that of treasurer, while members of the lowest class were not eligible for any state office. Members of the lowest class, which included all those below hoplite status, were, however, eligible to participate in and vote in the assembly of all Athenian citizens. Further, since the categories created by Solon were based on wealth rather than birth, the possibility of upward (as well, of course, as downward) mobility was built into the system. Ownership of land was not a requirement for citizenship, as it was in Sparta and many other poleis, and the lowest class of citizens in Athens included many men whose status would otherwise have precluded any participation in state affairs. Other measures implemented by Solon that were acceptable to the less wealthy citizens involved the expansion of citizen rights with regard to the judicial system, including the right of appeal "to the people" of a decision made by an officer of the state. Of particular importance is the fact that Solon's reforms were made public in written form, and were thus available to all who could read (or had access to a person who was both literate and trustworthy).

Other Persons: Slavery and Democracy

All of these "democratic" reforms were concerned primarily with the citizen body of Athens. It should not be forgotten that there existed also a substantial body of non-citizens, including a large number of slaves. Slavery is a universal feature of life in ancient Greece (and among ancient societies generally), although the extent to which different poleis relied upon slavery, and the type of slavery found in different poleis, could vary considerably. In Sparta, as we have seen, the vast majority of slaves were owned not by individual citizens but by the Spartan state. There were also

> "A piece of property, then, is an instrument that enhances the quality of life, and we refer to the totality of these instruments as one's 'property' in general. A slave is a sort of animate piece of property and, as such, has precedence over other instruments. For if it were possible for each instrument to perform its own work on command or by its own prior understanding of its duties, managers would have no need of workers nor would masters have need of slaves; that is, if a loom could do weaving on its own or a plectrum could play the lyre unaided, like the legendary statues of Daedalus or the tripods of Hephaestus, which Homer says 'moved under their own power into the assembly of the gods.'" (Aristotle, *Politics* 1253b30–54a1)

state-owned slaves in Athens: for example, in the fifth century BC, law-enforcement authorities had at their disposal a squad of Scythian archers who could be used to keep public order and place citizens under arrest. But most Athenian slaves were the personal property of individual citizens. The modern term that is used to refer to the type of slavery found in ancient Athens (and in most other Greek poleis) is "chattel slavery." The origin of the English word "chattel" gives a good idea of the humiliating status to which Athenian slaves were subjected: it derives from a Latin word that is also the origin of the English words "cattle" and "capital." That is, Athenian slaves were the living property of their owners; they could be sold at will or they could be beaten and branded and forced to work for their owners like an ox. The difference, however, between a slave and an ox (apart from the fact that the former could generally fetch a higher price on the open market) was that, while any shortcomings in the latter might be attributed to physical defects, failure on the part of the former could be blamed on moral inferiority. For a slave was considered to be inherently inferior in character to his or her citizen owner. This belief in the "natural" superiority of the citizen to his slaves could, paradoxically, help promote "democratic" values by setting up a clear differentiation between slave and free citizen: just as slaves are more or less interchangeable, so citizens can imagine their very citizen-status as conferring on them a kind of equality with other citizens.

It is, in fact, in democratic Athens among the poleis of ancient Greece that chattel slavery was most extensively employed, not only for purely economic reasons but also as a means of marking the owner's status as a free citizen. Estimates vary considerably for the number of slaves in classical Athens, but it is safe to say that slaves outnumbered adult male citizens, and perhaps even outnumbered them by a wide margin. Slaves could be acquired as a result of warfare – that is, through the enslavement of the population of a defeated state – or they could be purchased from a dealer. Once a citizen owned slaves in sufficient numbers and of the right ages, he could more economically obtain additional slaves by breeding those already in his possession. Slaves were used for a great variety of tasks: as agricultural workers, in manufacture (with the profits accruing to the owner), to perform household duties, as workers in the silver mines, or for purposes of "entertainment," often including prostitution. All of this sounds thoroughly incompatible with a sophisticated, democratic society capable of the highest achievements in intellectual and artistic pursuits. We are, however, familiar with the similar dependence on chattel slavery among some very cultured citizens of the democratic United States before 1865. Indeed, the precedent set by the ancient Greeks and Romans was frequently offered as partial justification for the institution of slavery in the Southern states. A further justification was that those enslaved were "naturally" suited to servitude by virtue of belonging to a supposedly "inferior" race. Likewise, in ancient Athens, the great majority of slaves were non-Greeks, drawn from those barbarian nations that had been subjects of the Persian Empire and, hence, the "slaves" of the Persian king. It was, in fact, typical of most Greek poleis that their slaves were of barbarian origin. (In this regard, as in so many others, Sparta was unusual, with its large population of helots, consisting of the enslaved populations of Sparta's Greek neighbors.)

In the context of this slave-owning society, with its clear distinction between slave and free citizen and between Greek and barbarian, Solon's reforms succeeded in alleviating the hostility between rich and poor citizens, but nothing could be done to reduce the rivalry among the *aristoi*. As we saw in chapter 5, this rivalry often resulted in the rise to power of a tyrant, and Athens was no different from many Greek poleis in this regard. In 561 BC Peisistratus, a distant relative of Solon's, seized power and made himself tyrant of Athens. Although Peisistratus was driven out on more than one occasion by rival *aristoi*, he managed to return to power and he and, later, his son Hippias maintained the tyranny until 510 BC. Like most Greek tyrants, Peisistratus and Hippias sought support among "the people" in their conflicts with rival *aristoi*. This support was encouraged, as we saw in chapter 5, by the tyrants' promotion and expansion of popular festivals like the Panathenaea, which fostered a sense of community among all residents of the polis. In this way, the influence of "the people," which had been strengthened by the reforms of Solon, was further increased under the tyranny. In addition, the period of the tyranny was a time when expanding markets for Athenian pottery and olive oil (like the

Panathenaic amphoras and their contents) brought considerable prosperity to Athens, a prosperity that, as a result of Solon's reforms, gave a larger number of Athenians a greater stake in the government of the polis. The role of "the people" was extended even further after the end of Hippias' tyranny. The expulsion of Hippias, which was brought about by an alliance between a very prominent Athenian family and one of the kings of Sparta, opened Athens up to still further rivalry among the *aristoi* who hoped to attain the kind of power that Hippias had exercised. One of those rivals, a man named Cleisthenes, recognizing that the success of Peisistratus and Hippias lay in the support they received from "the people," courted and won popular support by proposing, in 508 BC, a series of reforms that made Athens into the most radically democratic state that we know of.

The Development of Democracy in Athens: Cleisthenes

We saw earlier that the new plan for the city of Miletus, following its destruction in 494 BC, created a geometrically regular structure on an irregular terrain. The reforms of Cleisthenes imposed a similar pattern, not on the land of Attica but on its citizen population. Following Cleisthenes' reforms, the fundamental division of the population was according to DEMES, a word whose basic meaning appears to have been something like "divisions." In the rural parts of Attica, the deme was a village or a town, while in the urban area of Athens the deme corresponded to what we would call a "neighborhood." There were 140 of these demes, which Cleisthenes distributed into 30 newly created entities, called TRITTYES, each consisting of from one or two large demes to about 10 smaller demes. Ten of these trittyes were located in and near the city of Athens, 10 along the coast, and 10 in the inland area away from the city. While the demes in each trittys were in many instances geographically contiguous, that was not always the case, and in some instances 40 or more kilometers might separate two demes belonging to the same trittys (map 11). The purpose of these trittyes seems to have been to arrange Athens in such a way as to create divisions that could represent a cross-section of the population. For one trittys from each of the three areas, city, coast, and inland, was combined into one of 10 newly created tribes (figure 37). Previously, the population of Attica had been divided among four ancestral tribes, the names of which are also found as the names of tribes in several Ionic poleis. The 10 new tribes were named after legendary Athenian heroes and membership in them was hereditary, giving the impression that all members of the tribe were descended from a common heroic ancestor. In fact, this new and arbitrary arrangement represented a significant break with the past and had the (undoubtedly intended) effect of reducing the influence of traditional family connections. What is perhaps most surprising is the ease with which the Athenians appear to have been willing to adopt this new organization. Cleisthenes must have counted on the readiness of the Athenians to reinvent their past, a readiness that, as we have seen, is characteristic of the Greeks generally.

DEME A local territorial district, either a village or a neighborhood of a larger urban area; also, by extension, the inhabitants of the district.

TRITTYS (PLURAL: **TRITTYES**) One of 30 units into which the population of Attica was divided by Cleisthenes in 508 BC, with one trittys from each of the three geographical divisions (city, coast, and inland) combining to constitute one of the 10 tribes created by Cleisthenes (figure 37 and map 11).

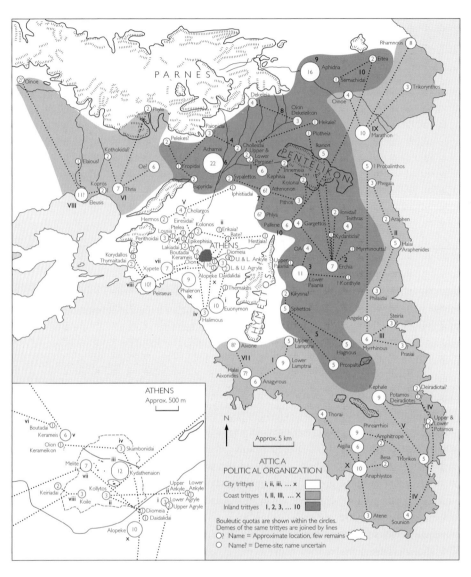

Map 11
Cleisthenes'
organization of
Attica according
to demes, trittyes,
and tribes. Map
reproduced from
J. S. Traill, *The
Political Organization
of Attica*, Hesperia
Supplement 14
(Princeton 1975),
map 2.

The division into 10 tribes served a partly military and partly administrative function. When Athens was at war, all soldiers from the same tribe stood together in battle and were commanded by a member of their own tribe; there were 10 generals, one elected annually from each tribe. Each of the 10 tribes also selected 50 of its own members each year to represent it in the Council of 500. This Council was itself a newly created body, replacing an earlier Council of 400, which had consisted of 100 members from each of the (now discontinued) ancestral tribes. The new Council of 500 set the agenda for the meetings of the assembly of all Athenians, so that all matters of public policy necessarily passed through it. Every deme was represented on the Council by a number of its members ranging from

Name of tribe	City trittyes	Coastal trittyes	Inland trittyes
1 Erechtheis	Euonymeis	?	Kephisieis
2 Aegeis	Kollyteis	Halaieis	Gargettioi
3 Pandionis	Kydathenaieis	Myrrhinousioi	Paianieis
4 Leontis	Skambonidai	Phrearrhioi	Diakrioi
5 Acamantis	Cholargeis/Kerameis	Thorikioi	Sphettioi
6 Oeneis	Lakiadai	Thriasioi	Pedieis
7 Cecropis	Meliteis	?	Phlyeis
8 Hippothontis	Peiraieis	Eleusinioi	Epakreis
9 Aeantis	Phalereis	Tetrapoleis	?
10 Antiochis	Alopekeis	Anaphlystioi	Palleneis

Figure 37   The arrangement of the 30 Cleisthenic trittyes, based on the table in J. S. Traill, *Demos and Trittys: Epigraphical and Topographical Studies in the Organization of Attica* (Toronto 1986), 110. (Not all of the names of trittyes are certain.)

one to 22, depending on the population of the deme. In this way, the government of the state was rooted at the level of the deme where, presumably, every citizen was familiar with all his fellow demesmen. This was the level of "the people." In fact, the Greek word for "the people," the word from which English "democracy" is derived, is precisely the word "deme," which can mean either "the people as a whole" or "the local division of the people." The structure through which the inhabitants of each deme participated in the government of the polis was both elaborate and arbitrary, giving each individual citizen a genuine sense of participation while ensuring that no one individual was in a position to exercise undue influence. The sense of familiarity that a citizen felt toward his fellow demesman, whom he saw and dealt with locally on a daily basis, was combined with a feeling of solidarity with his fellow tribesman, who might live at quite a distance in a very different environment, but by whose side he risked his life in battle and with whom he served in the Council deciding on matters of state.

Ostracism

There was one other institution that the Athenians attributed to Cleisthenes – whether correctly or not is matter for debate – that also had the effect of both promoting a sense of grassroots participation and of preventing any individual from attaining excessive power. This was the practice known as OSTRACISM, which takes its name from the Greek word *ostrakon* (plural *ostraka*), meaning "broken piece of pottery." As we have seen, ceramic vessels were in very common use in every period of ancient Greek civilization. Because of their fragile nature and because they are not readily biodegradable, fragments of these vessels are the most numerous, and the most long-lasting, components of ancient Greek trash. The Athenians discovered a way of

OSTRACISM The Athenian practice of holding an election, in which fragments of pottery (*ostraka*) were used as ballots (figure 38), to determine whether one prominent political figure should be removed from the polis for a 10-year period.

"For ostracism was not a punishment for wrongdoing. Rather, while it was ostensibly a means of abasing and curtailing oppressive pride and power, it was in reality a humane method of assuaging envy, which could direct its malicious desire to injure, not toward some irreparable harm, but toward a penalty consisting of a ten-year expulsion. But they ceased the practice of ostracism when some men began inflicting this punishment on low and lawless individuals. Last of all was Hyperbolus, who was said to have been banished for the following reason. Alcibiades and Nicias, the most powerful men in the state, were the leaders of rival factions. So, when the people were about to impose ostracism, and when it was clear that they were going to decree the banishment of one or the other of them, the two men called a conference, reconciled their respective factions and brought about the banishment of Hyperbolus. As a result of this, the people, upset because the institution of ostracism had been abused and debased, entirely gave up the practice and abolished it."
(Plutarch, *The Life of Aristeides* 7.2–3)

recycling these fragments by using them as ballots in an unusual form of popular self-expression. Once every year, the Athenian assembly decided whether or not an ostracism was to be held. If a majority voted in favor, an election of sorts was held in the agora later that year, in which each citizen had the right to cast a ballot by inscribing the name of any Athenian on an *ostrakon*. The person receiving the largest number of votes – but only if the total number of votes cast exceeded 6,000 – was given 10 days to leave Athenian territory, to which he was not allowed to return for a period of 10 years. At the end of that time he could resume his normal life and, if he wished, continue his involvement in political affairs. The effect of this procedure was to reduce political tensions in the city by temporarily removing a controversial figure from circulation; that is, not punishing him so severely that he and his supporters would be tempted to engage in desperate acts of vengeance.

"He was successful in subsidizing an entry in the competition for tragedies, a contest that already at that time was subject to contentious rivalry, and he erected a monument to his victory that bore the following inscription: 'Themistocles of Phearrhioi was the producer; Phrynichus was the author; Adeimantus was the archon.' At the same time, he made himself popular with the masses; he knew each and every citizen by name and he made himself available as someone who could act as an objective arbiter in disputes over contracts." (Plutarch, *The Life of Themistocles* 5.5–6)

The first time an ostracism was held was in 487 BC, and it was resorted to only about a dozen times before the practice fell into disuse shortly before 415 BC. Even so, large numbers of ballots were cast in the course of this relatively brief span of time and thousands of them have been recovered, particularly in the excavations of the agora that have been undertaken by the American School of Classical Studies in Athens. All the prominent political figures of fifth-century Athens are represented, in some cases on hundreds of *ostraka*. In some instances, it is possible to recognize the same hand at work in the production of large numbers of the inscriptions, so that it is clear that supporters of one candidate came to the ostracism prepared to distribute ballots already inscribed with the names of rival candidates. After all, not every Athenian citizen is likely to have been fully literate in the fifth century BC, and many, though they may have been able to read, might not have felt comfortable writing. As it is, the *ostraka* that have been found are riddled with misspellings, as is the case with the *ostrakon* illustrated in figure 38. Despite the problems with the spelling, the man

Figure 38
Ostrakon from
Athens, inscribed
"Themistocles (son)
of Neocles of (the
deme) Phrearrhioi,"
with the name and
the deme misspelled
("Themisthocles,"
"Phrerrhios"); width
10 cm, 480s or 470s
BC. American School
of Classical Studies
at Athens: Agora
Excavations, P 9950.

who scratched Themistocles' name on this *ostrakon* managed to identify his chosen candidate by using the full, official designation, giving name, father's name, and deme. Before the reforms of Cleisthenes, it was normal to refer to a citizen simply by using his name and his father's name, which would be sufficient to indicate the (aristocratic) family from which he came. Designation by deme was felt to be more "democratic," since it made reference to the local units of government that were so strongly emphasized in Cleisthenes' reforms. How, then, did the man who inscribed this *ostrakon* know to which of the 140 demes Themistocles belonged? It seems that Themistocles, who was himself an ostentatiously democratic politician, was in the habit of conspicuously using the new Cleisthenic designation, so that he was widely known, to supporters and enemies alike, as "Themistocles son of Neocles of the deme Phrearrhioi."

The Delian League

One of the effects of Cleisthenes' reforms was to encourage a sense of uniqueness among the Athenians. Since they were no longer members of the traditional tribes whose names they shared with other Ionian poleis, they began to consider themselves as having a special status among the Greeks. This feeling only increased following their military successes, first at Marathon and then at Salamis. It was easy for the Athenians to convince themselves that their success was due in large measure to their newly reformulated and radically democratic government and their recently reorganized military structure, especially since their victories had been won over an oriental monarchy that could easily be thought of as the antithesis of a direct democracy. The naval success at Salamis, in particular, was imagined as a "democratic" victory because the oarsmen in the Athenian fleet were men of less than hoplite status and, therefore, could make the best claim to represent "the people." For this reason, when the Spartans declined to continue their position of leadership of the allied Greek states after the embarrassing recall of Pausanias, the Athenians were confident that they could effectively assume that role.

Thus, in 477 BC, a new alliance was created, with no participation by the Spartans, under the leadership of Athens. The alliance consisted primarily of those poleis that felt most at risk of renewed attack by the Persians, namely the Greek cities along the coast of Asia Minor and on the Aegean islands. This was, accordingly, a defensive alliance intended for protection against Persian aggression, and each member of the alliance was required to furnish annually a number of manned warships depending on its size. In the event that any of the allies were not in a position to supply the required number of ships or crews, they were allowed to contribute an equivalent amount in cash, to be housed at the alliance's treasury, located on the small island of Delos. (For this reason, scholars today often refer to the alliance as the "Delian League," but its official designation was rather "the Athenians and their allies," and the command of the alliance's military forces on campaign was in the hands of the Athenians.) Increasingly, members of the alliance found it more convenient to contribute cash than ships with crews and, increasingly, the Athenians found themselves using these financial contributions to fund their own navy. For the Athenians were quite willing to build Athenian triremes and to pay Athenian crews at their allies' expense. As the Athenian navy grew, the number of these crew members necessarily increased, and they became an increasingly influential group of voters in the Athenian assembly. These sailors, then, had a vested interest in the continuance of the alliance, which provided them with steady employment.

The alliance was quite successful in neutralizing the Persian presence in the waters of the Aegean. In fact, the alliance was so successful that some of the allies began to wonder whether there was really a need for its continuing existence. In the 460s, first Naxos and then Thasos tried to discontinue their membership of the alliance, but they were forcibly prevented from doing so. By this point (if not, indeed, sooner) it began to appear to many Greeks that the "alliance" was in effect an Athenian protectorate or even empire, and the alliance's "contributions" in effect a form of tribute. It often happens that the victor in a war takes on some of the characteristics of the defeated foe, and Athens was seen to have assumed the role of the Persian king, who demanded and received tribute from his subjects. When the alliance's treasury was moved from Delos to Athens in 454 BC, there could be no more uncertainty regarding the nature of this alliance. The Athenians began to use the annual payment of the allies' contributions as part of a very public ceremony that demonstrated to themselves and their allies the authority that the city of Athens wielded and the prosperity that this alliance conferred upon its citizens. Every year the magnificent festival of the Dionysia opened with the 10 generals pouring libations to the god Dionysus and with a procession in which the financial contributions of the allies were brought into the theater, talent by talent, and placed on the stage to arouse the admiration of the assembled spectators (figure 39).

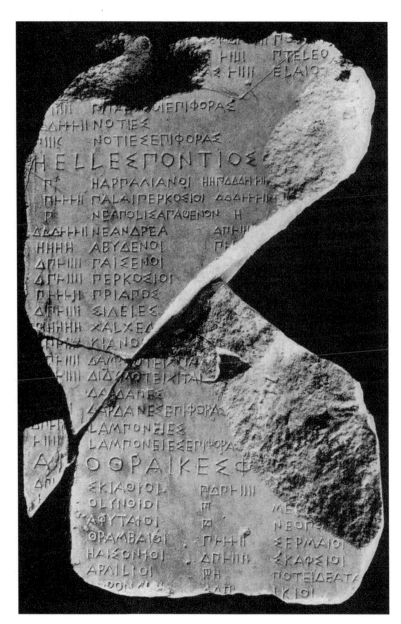

Figure 39
Fragments of an inscription on marble listing the allies of Athens and the sixtieth part of each city's monetary contribution that was dedicated to Athena; total width 38 cm, 440–439 BC. Epigraphical Museum of Athens, EM 5384 (*IG* I³ 272). Hellenic Ministry of Culture – Archaeological Receipts Fund.

The Dionysia and the Drama of Aeschylus

We saw earlier (p. 98) that the Athenian tyrant Peisistratus promoted and expanded the festival of the Panathenaea. During his tyranny, the festival of the Dionysia also attained much greater prominence. These became, in fact, the two

Figure 40 Detail of red-figure amphora by the Kleophrades Painter, showing Dionysus (left), holding a wine cup and a vine branch, with a MAENAD and a satyr; height of figured band 21.6 cm, ca. 490 BC. Munich, Staatliche Antikensammlungen und Glyptothek, Inv. 2344.

MAENAD A woman inspired to ritual frenzy by the god Dionysus, often represented in the wilds of the countryside or mountains (figure 40).

most lavish religious festivals of the Athenian polis, the former in honor of Athena, the latter in honor of the god Dionysus. Athena, the patron deity and protector of Athens, was a virgin goddess whose iconography (see figure 29) suggests her formidable character. In contrast to Athena, who is not normally depicted in the company of her worshippers, Dionysus is regularly shown on Attic vases surrounded by his devotees, with whom he associates freely and whom he joins in drinking wine (figure 40). Dionysus is, in fact, the god of wine. He is also the god of masks and of the drama, which was a central element of the festival of the Dionysia in sixth- and fifth-century Athens. What wine and acting on stage have in common is that they allow a person to set aside temporarily his or her ordinary, everyday identity, and so the worship of Dionysus is characterized by a momentary suspension of the roles that society imposes on individuals. Thus, in the drama, a male Athenian citizen can play the role of a woman or slave, or he can impersonate a mythical king or hero or even a god. Dionysus is, therefore, a fundamentally democratic divinity, and it is appropriate that his festival should have flourished in democratic Athens.

The drama is an Attic creation, developing just at the time when Athenian democracy was being born. The Greeks themselves attributed the invention of the drama to the Athenian Thespis, who lived in the second half of the sixth century, but about whom almost nothing is known. A good deal is known, however, about the Attic playwright Aeschylus, six of whose tragedies have survived and whose works represent the earliest examples of drama that we possess. Aeschylus was born around 525 BC and died in 456 BC. His creative life therefore spanned almost the whole of the first half of the fifth century. Aeschylus' earliest surviving tragedy – that is, the earliest work of dramatic literature available to us – is *The Persians*, first staged in

472 BC. It is in many ways quite an untypical Greek tragedy, but it is fascinating both for its historical significance and because of its literary accomplishment. The play is concerned with the Persian defeat at the battle of Salamis, which occurred only seven and a half years before *The Persians* was produced. Very many members of the original audience, therefore, had witnessed or even participated in the battle. Aeschylus' brother had fought and died at Marathon and he himself is likely to have fought both at Marathon and at Salamis. He was, then, an eyewitness to the event that *The Persians* celebrates.

The most remarkable feature, however, of Aeschylus' play is that it is not at all overtly celebratory. In fact, the play is set in Persia and has an entirely Persian cast: Xerxes, Xerxes' mother, the ghost of Xerxes' father Darius, a Persian messenger, and a chorus of Persian elders. Following the conventions of Attic drama, these characters were impersonated by a group of 14 male Athenian citizens: 12 members of the chorus, and two actors who divided the four remaining roles between them. Later in Aeschylus' life the convention was changed to allow a third actor, but fifth-century drama never exceeded that limit and never permitted the use of female performers. In other words, no more than two characters, in addition to the chorus, could appear before the audience at any one time. That does not mean that Aeschylus' play, or Attic tragedy in general, was in any way austere or unsophisticated. The costumes would have been quite elaborate and would have emphasized the oriental luxury of the Persian court. The drama was composed in verse of uncommon complexity and expressiveness, some of it recited and some of it sung to musical accompaniment. In addition, the chorus accompanied much of its sung contribution with intricately choreographed dance. Attic drama, then, is more closely akin to modern opera than to the plays of Henrik Ibsen or Tennessee Williams. Indeed, *The Persians* concludes with an extended and impassioned lamentation over the defeat at Salamis, sung by the chorus and the actor who played Xerxes and accompanied by the dance of the chorus. During the course of the play, no individual Greek is named by the Persian characters. The Greek victory, therefore, is presented as the result of a collective effort on the part of the Greeks, and especially the Athenians. In contrast, on the Persian side, responsibility for the defeat is firmly lodged with the individual Xerxes, whose earlier behavior is shown to have been reckless and arrogant, and therefore deserving of punishment by the gods. This will have been pleasing to the democratic Athenian audience, who are implicitly represented as the agents of the divine will.

Accordingly, the democratic Athenian audience rewarded Aeschylus by conferring first prize on *The Persians* and the other plays with which Aeschylus competed in 472 BC. For Attic tragedies were performed at the Dionysia as part of a competition with firm rules that date back to the second half of the sixth century. The competition took place in a theater built next to the sanctuary of Dionysus, on the south slope of the acropolis. In the time of Aeschylus, the seating in the theater consisted of wooden bleachers arranged in banks on three sides of the performance area (called the *orchestra* or "dance-floor"). Later, extensive stone seating was constructed, on a semi-circular plan, which accommodated more than 10,000 spectators (see figure 43). These were, then, performances that attracted a very large audience. They were part of an important religious festival and, like religious festivals generally in the ancient Greek world, the festival of the Dionysia was organized by and for the polis. The poets who hoped to compete in the tragic competition submitted their work to a public official called an *archon* who selected the three poets whose work would be granted public performance. This official served a one-year term of office to which he was elected by popular vote; after 487 BC, however, he was named to his one-year term by the still more democratic method of being chosen by lot. The poets who presented their work to him submitted not a single play but a group of four plays, consisting of three tragedies followed by a satyr play. A satyr play is a burlesque drama in which serious heroic characters are confronted by a chorus of satyrs, mythical creatures who are mostly human but who have equine appurtenances and bestial appetites (figure 40). During the course of the festival, the four plays by each of the three dramatists were performed and 10 judges, one from each tribe, voted to decide the victor in the competition. The prize, apparently, was a goat, as well as the honor of sacrificing the goat to Dionysus. (The Greek word *tragodia* means, in effect, "goat-song.")

We know the names of the two other tragedies and the satyr play that Aeschylus wrote to accompany *The Persians*, but the plays themselves have not survived. The titles indicate that they dealt, like almost all the other Attic tragedies and satyr plays that we know of, not with recent historical events (as in *The Persians*) but with the distant mythical past. There was, then, no apparent connection among the four plays that Aeschylus produced for the festival of 472 BC; they were, following the usual Athenian practice, four separate and unrelated dramas. Aeschylus was, however, a bold and brilliant innovator, and he did not always follow the usual Athenian practice. On a few occasions he treated the four plays as, rather, four stages of the same action, enabling him to pursue one theme more expansively. One of those occasions was in 458 BC. The satyr play that he produced in that year is lost, but the three tragedies survive. They are *Agamemnon*, *The Libation Bearers*, and *The Eumenides*, known collectively as *The Oresteia* because they dramatize the story of the family of Orestes. *The Oresteia*, which was produced only two years before Aeschylus' death, also won first prize in the tragic competition. It begins in the darkness of the mythical past and ends in the radiance of an Athens that is very much like that of Aeschylus' own day. Indeed, progression from darkness into the light, both literally and metaphorically, is one of the recurring images that enriches the language and the drama of *The Oresteia*.

Agamemnon opens at night, with a watchman hoping to catch sight of a beacon that will signal the successful end of the Trojan War. He has been stationed by Clytemestra, the wife of

"I struck him once and twice, and twice he bellowed. Then his limbs gave way, and when he was down I struck a bonus blow, dedicating the third stroke as payback to the redeemer, Zeus of the dead below. So he fell and spewed out his life. And as he spurted forth a ready stream of gore he spattered me with a Stygian spray of bloody rain. I welcomed it no less than the burgeoning seed revels in the glistening gift of showers sent by Zeus to sprout new life." (Aeschylus, *Agamemnon* 1384–92, Clytemestra speaking) the Greek commander Agamemnon, who plans to murder her husband on his return to Argos. She has been nursing her hatred of Agamemnon since he left for Troy 10 years previously because he had slaughtered their daughter Iphigeneia as a sacrificial victim in order to secure favorable winds for his fleet. In contrast to Xerxes in *The Persians*, whose arrival in disarray on stage is accompanied by lamentation, Agamemnon arrives in triumph, but when he enters his palace he is killed in sordid fashion by Clytemestra and her lover. In an outrageous parody of animal sacrifice, which is intended to secure prosperity and fertility, Clytemestra describes the murder of her husband in terms appropriate to the ritual slaughter of a sacrificial beast. This deed, in turn, requires retribution, which is effected in the second drama, *The Libation Bearers*. Orestes, the son of Agamemnon and Clytemestra, has now grown to maturity and he returns to his home from exile to avenge his father's murder, having received encouragement from the oracle of Apollo at Delphi. Orestes and his sister Electra are reunited and they carry out the murder of their mother and her lover. Justice, it would appear, has been served. But what kind of justice is it that requires matricide, itself a hideous crime? This is the question that is explored in the final tragedy, *The Eumenides*, which is set not in Agamemnon's kingdom but, initially, in Delphi and, finally, in Athens.

Orestes has been pursued by the Furies, divine daughters of Night who ruthlessly punish those who shed kindred blood. Aeschylus' powerful language and imagery impress on us the seeming inevitability of vengeance as something that is generated by violence as if by some natural process of procreation. Orestes has fled from the Furies and has taken refuge at the sanctuary of Apollo at Delphi. He is now at the center of a conflict between two groups of divinities, the daughters of Night, for whom relationship by blood overrides all other considerations, and the Olympian deities, whose social organization parallels that of the polis in that it is based on a hierarchy of power. Only the goddess Athena (who is herself one of the Olympian deities) can resolve the issue, and Orestes, Apollo, and the Furies all travel to Athens, of which Athena is the patron goddess. In a strikingly original departure from the traditional version of the myth, Aeschylus represents Athena as empanelling a jury of Athenian citizens to decide the matter. We will recall that there was another mythical occasion on which the gods relied upon a mortal decision to resolve a conflict among them, namely the judgment of Paris (see p. xiv). But that was merely a beauty contest and the judge, who allowed his decision to be influenced by bribery, met with disaster himself and brought about the total destruction of his own city. The issue in *The Eumenides*, however, is decided in an incorruptible court of law, which Athena establishes for the purpose of determining Orestes' guilt or innocence. This court, the court of the Areopagus, was located on a hill in Athens, only 500 meters, as the owl flies, from the theater in which Aeschylus' play was performed. Three years before the production of *The Oresteia*, the court of the Areopagus had been at the center of a further round of democratic reforms involving the Athenian judicial system. By constructing his drama as he has done, Aeschylus has bridged the distance between the mythical and the contemporary: he has provided his Athenian audience with mythical and divine sanction for their newly enacted reforms, and he has projected into the mythical past a resolution to a legendary conflict that could only have been brought about by the institutions created in democratic Athens.

Recommended for Further Reading

Cartledge, P. *The Spartans: An Epic History* (London 2002): a provocative and very readable portrait of the ancient Spartans, by the leading authority on Spartan history, written to accompany the Channel 4 and PBS series, *The Spartans*.

Csapo, E. and Slater, W. J. *The Context of Ancient Drama* (Ann Arbor 1995): a very full compilation of the available evidence, both textual and visual, for the texts, performance, and setting of ancient Greek and Roman drama.

Fisher, N. R. E. *Slavery in Classical Greece* (London 1993): a sound and succinct (120 pages) introduction to the complex issues surrounding slavery in Classical Greece.

Grene, D. and Lattimore, R. (eds.) *The Complete Greek Tragedies*, vol. 1: Aeschylus (Chicago 1959): excellent translations of all of Aeschylus' surviving plays, including Richmond Lattimore's powerful version of *The Oresteia* and Seth Benardete's translation of *The Persians*.

Rhodes, P. J. *A History of the Classical Greek World, 478–323 BC* (Malden, MA 2006): a masterful survey of Greek history from the end of the Persian Wars to the death of Alexander the Great.

Stockton, D. *The Classical Athenian Democracy* (Oxford and New York 1990): a clearly written and well-organized introduction to the development of democracy in Athens, with detailed descriptions of the workings of the various democratic institutions.

Taplin, O. *Greek Tragedy in Action* (Berkeley and Los Angeles 1978): a stimulating introduction to the Attic tragedies as works for the theater, rather than as texts to be read, with much attention paid to Aeschylus' *Oresteia*.

Whitby, M. (ed.) *Sparta* (New York 2002): a collection of essays and excerpts from larger works by prominent scholars, illustrating the variety of recent approaches taken in the controversies surrounding much of Spartan society.

HISTORY AND TRAGEDY IN THE FIFTH CENTURY

8

Chapter 8 concerns itself with two important fifth-century literary figures who lived and worked in Athens, the historian Herodotus and the tragic poet Sophocles, and closes with a consideration of the position of women on the tragic stage and in Athenian society. Herodotus composed the first serious work of historical investigation, his extended account of the Persian Wars. Herodotus is not merely concerned to record the events of the wars, but to understand the causes that underlie these events and, in general, to attempt to understand what causes wars to occur and what causes states to increase and decrease in power. In this regard, Herodotus reflects the influence of the Ionian philosophers, who were concerned to understand the underlying causes of natural phenomena and in whose milieu Herodotus spent his formative years. Prose literature, like that of Herodotus, depends upon relatively widespread literacy, and Greece in the time of Herodotus and his contemporary Sophocles was undergoing a transition from a largely oral to an increasingly literate society. The characters in Sophocles' dramas, however, seem to be drawn from an earlier, heroic age, like that depicted in the (orally composed) epics from which the Homeric poems arose. Indeed, many of Sophocles' main characters share the unyielding, heroic nature of Homer's Achilles, whose refusal to compromise is both admirable and disastrous. Even the female characters around whom some of Sophocles' tragedies revolve, like Antigone and Electra, are presented in strong, heroic terms. The chapter closes with a discussion of the way in which powerful female characters like those in Sophocles are reflective not of the realities of democratic Athenian life but of the need for male poets and their largely male audiences to come to terms with the limited roles women were permitted to play in contemporary society.

The spectacle that opened the annual festival of the Dionysia at Athens, including the procession and the conspicuous display of the financial contributions by Athens' allies (see p. 138), was intended not only for the benefit of the Athenians in the audience, but for the purpose of impressing visitors to Athens from other Greek poleis as well. For, by the middle of the fifth century BC, Athens had begun to attract substantial numbers of Greeks who came either to visit briefly or to take up residence in a city that was flourishing both economically and culturally. Representatives of the allied cities came of necessity, to pay their contributions into the treasury of the alliance, but many came voluntarily, either to take advantage of the financial opportunities that were now available or to participate in the vibrant intellectual life of democratic Athens. In this chapter, we will examine the intellectual contribution made by one of those visitors, Herodotus of Halicarnassus, whose history of the Persian Wars has justifiably conferred on him the title "Father of History." We will also discuss the work of an Athenian contemporary who was said to have been a friend of Herodotus, the tragic poet Sophocles.

Herodotus and the Invention of History

As we have seen, the outcome of the Persian Wars was unexpected. Even the responses of the Delphic oracle, which the Greeks considered to be the expression of divine wisdom, seemed to predict victory for the Persians, an outcome that appeared inevitable even to those endowed with merely human wisdom. Somehow, the surprising success of the Greeks had to be accounted for. In *The Persians*, Aeschylus represented the Persian defeat at Salamis as an instance of divine punishment occasioned by Xerxes' insolent disregard for propriety and due measure, or what the Greeks call HYBRIS. *The Persians* is a work of poetry, and it is a traditional theme of Greek poetry that the gods severely chastise mortals who exhibit hybris. Since the Persian Empire could be thought of as nothing more than an extension of the person of the Persian king, this type of explanation could be accepted as adequate, particularly in the context of a poetic and dramatic text. But the Greeks were well aware that not all political entities were absolute monarchies. How could the fate of states like democratic Athens or oligarchic Sparta be accommodated within a scheme that traditionally concentrated on individual, personal responsibility?

HYBRIS Wanton behavior aimed at the humiliation of another person for the sole purpose of asserting one's own actual or imagined superiority in status, power, wealth, and so on.

Some such question as this must have been what prompted Herodotus to embark on the composition of his massive and revolutionary history of the Persian Wars. Herodotus was born some time around 485 BC (that is, during the time of the Persian Wars) in the Greek city of Halicarnassus, on the southwest coast of Asia Minor. Halicarnassus is only about 60 kilometers, as the eagle flies, from Miletus, so that Herodotus was born into an intellectual milieu in which the ideas of the earliest philosophers were readily accessible and still fresh. Those philosophers had attempted to account for the workings of the universe by applying something resembling universal laws of nature. In particular, Anaximander had written about the compensatory "retribution" that natural entities suffer as a result of their encroachment upon the realm of other entities. For example, the hot and the cold prevail at different seasons, but in the course of a year they balance each other out and create an equilibrium as each pays an equal penalty to the other. Anaximander, in other words, had tried to account for natural phenomena using concepts, like "penalty," "retribution," and "justice," that are familiar from human interactions. What Herodotus did was to turn this around and to account for human interactions in the more "abstract" terms appropriate to natural phenomena. In doing so, Herodotus invented not only history, but the social sciences as well.

Like all innovative work, that of Herodotus is firmly based in a tradition, from which it takes its departure. In the case of Herodotus, the literary tradition of which he is a part is, perhaps surprisingly, that of Homeric epic. The *Iliad* is set during the Trojan War, a conflict between forces from opposite sides of the Aegean Sea, and is on a very large scale. In fact, Homer's *Iliad* is the longest literary work the Greeks of Herodotus' day were familiar with. Herodotus' history is even more ambitious, being some 64 percent longer than the *Iliad*, so in terms of size alone it demands comparison with the most illustrious work of Greek literature. Since Herodotus, too, is concerned to recount a war between European and Asiatic forces, comparison with Homer is inevitable and seems to have been courted by Herodotus himself. The *Iliad* begins, after a request of the Muse that she sing of the anger of Achilles and the quarrel with Agamemnon that provoked that anger, with Homer asking, and then answering, the question, "Which of the gods set these two men to oppose each other in conflict?" Homer's assumption is that any explanation is going to involve the gods and, indeed, the first sentence of the *Iliad* includes reference to the "fulfillment of Zeus' plan."

The opening sentence of Herodotus' history is very different. There is no invocation of the Muse and no reference to the gods; rather, Herodotus names himself and says that he will be especially concerned with "the cause of the conflict" between Greeks and barbarians. His analysis of the cause of the conflict proceeds, as Herodotus tells us, from his "investigations," the Greek word for which is *historia*. This word is used very early in Herodotus' first sentence; in fact, the only two words that precede it in the text are "Herodotus" and "Halicarnassus." The word *historia* was often used to refer to investigations into natural phenomena (a meaning that is preserved in the English expression "natural history") and Herodotus' use of the word is perhaps a further indication of his indebtedness to the Milesian philosophers, who were also natural scientists. Because of Herodotus' prominent use of it here, the Greek word *historia* became specialized and came to be used primarily to refer to what we usually mean today by "history." What we usually mean today by "history," however, is not merely an account of events in the past but an account that shows an awareness of the need to explain why and how those events took place. Herodotus' emphasis in his first sentence on "the cause of the conflict" displays this awareness, and his concentration on causes is reflected in the structure of his history. For it is only about halfway through his history, in the fifth of the nine books into which his work is traditionally divided, that Herodotus begins his account of the Ionian Revolt, the event that many historians today would regard as being the "cause" of the Persian Wars.

Herodotus is interested in investigating not only the cause of the Persian Wars but the nature of historical causation itself. He cannot, however, conduct this investigation directly, since the necessary concepts and theoretical terminology could not begin to develop until after Herodotus' pioneering work. Instead, his examination of the nature of causation is implicit in his method and needs to be extracted carefully from his easygoing and seemingly anecdotal manner. After his opening sentence, Herodotus spends two pages recounting what the Persian authorities have to say about the origins of the hostilities between the inhabitants of Europe and Asia. Herodotus dismisses what these authorities have to say, but not because

> "According to the Persians – but not the Greeks – that is how Io wound up in Egypt and that is what began the series of criminal acts. After that, they say, some Greeks landed at the Phoenician port of Tyre and abducted Europa, the king's daughter. (The Persians are not able to identify these Greeks, but I assume they were from Crete.) Well, now things were even, but then the Greeks are supposed to have become responsible for the second offense: they sailed as far as the Phasis river, to the city of Aea in Colchis, on board a warship and there, after they had taken care of the business that had brought them to that place, they abducted the king's daughter Medea. When the king of the Colchians sent a herald to Greece to seek recompense for the abduction and to demand the return of his daughter, the Greeks are alleged to have responded by saying that, since they hadn't paid them back for the abduction of Io of Argos, they weren't going to pay them back either." (Herodotus 1.2)

they are Persians – in fact, what Herodotus puts into their mouths is a collection of purely Greek stories – but because their account cannot be verified. Their account relates the abductions of various mythical women, among whom is Helen, whose abduction precipitated the Trojan War. Helen had been carried off from Greece by the Trojan Paris in retaliation for the Greeks' abduction of the Asiatic Medea, whose abduction in turn was a response to a still earlier pair of reciprocal intercontinental abductions. Although Herodotus discounts the connection between these mythical accounts and later "historical" events, he calls attention to these myths by placing them right at the start of his history. The reason he does this is that, while the stories themselves cannot be confirmed, they epitomize what is regarded as an acceptable type of explanation. No one is likely to doubt the importance of desire, and particularly sexual desire, as a motive in human behavior. Similarly, the urge to retaliate to aggression, to "even the count," is so common as to appear natural.

These stories introduce two fundamental themes of Herodotus' history, the themes of desire and retribution, as well as the framework through which these themes are to be explored, namely a narrative account, or "story." A story is coherent – that is, it "makes sense" – only if the storyteller and the audience share an understanding of what constitutes an acceptable causal connection. In the case of myths like that involving Helen's abduction and Menelaus' desire to recover his wife and punish her abductor, the motivation and causation are transparent and readily understandable. What Herodotus has done is to combine this type of narrative structure that is intelligible on the human level with the Milesian philosophers' search for abstract cosmic principles. After he has dismissed the accounts of the Persian authorities, he says that he will in the course of his history relate events connected both with powerful and insignificant states because, over time, those that are insignificant become powerful and vice versa. That is, just as the natural world exhibits evidence of encroachment and retribution on the part of conflicting elements, so states (or "poleis," as Herodotus in character-istically Greek fashion expresses it) have a natural tendency to expand at the expense of their neighbors, until such

> "When Cyrus heard this argument [that the Persians should migrate to a more fertile territory], he was not impressed by it. He told them to go ahead and do it, but he gave them a piece of advice, telling them to be prepared to stop being rulers and to start being ruled. For, he said, lux-uriant lands tend to breed luxury-loving men, since it is just not in the nature of things for the same region to produce both wonderful crops and good fighting men. The Persians saw the wisdom of what he said and took their leave, won over by the reasoning of Cyrus. And so they chose to live in a rugged land and be rulers rather than sow rich farmlands and serve others as slaves." (Herodotus 9.122.3–4, the clos-ing words of Herodotus' history)

time as they suffer retribution and are punished for their misdeeds. Herodotus illus-trates this process most notably with his very detailed narrative of the expansion of the Persian Empire, and he even seems to supply an account of the dynamics of this "natural tendency": the homeland of the Persians is rugged and harsh and, there-fore, of necessity breeds inhabitants who are accustomed to difficulty. When such people come in contact with neighbors whose lands are more fertile and prosper-ous, they are seduced as if by erotic desire to possess those lands. Because of their toughness, it is easy for them to conquer their neighbors' lands, but in the course of time they begin to lose their original tough character, softened by the luxuries that they have now acquired, and they in turn are at risk of conquest by others.

In order to show this process in continual operation, it is necessary for Herodotus to track its occurrence in more than one state. For this reason, he begins, not with the Persians but with the Lydians, whose expansion brought them into contact with their Persian neighbors, by whom they were con-quered. And in his account of the rise of the Persian Empire he describes how

> "As far as the climate and the seasons are concerned, these Ionians to whom the Panionium belongs, of all people that we know of, have established their poleis in what is in fact the finest location. For neither the lands to the north nor those to the south are similarly endowed, being afflicted either with the cold and the damp or with parching heat." (Herodotus, 1.142.1–2)

the Persians had earlier been subjects of the Medes, whom they overthrew. The climax, of course, of Herodotus' history is the lengthy account of the Persians' defeat at the hands of the Greeks. The causes of this defeat are manifold and complex, but the background and the theoretical framework that Herodotus has provided help to create a coherent story through which those causes can be understood. The land that the Greeks inhabit is not very productive, so that the Greeks are natur-ally tough and familiar with hardship. Further, the climate of Greece (which is located, according to Herodotus, at the center of a more or less circular earth; map 12) is temperate, so the energies of its inhabitants are sapped neither by excessive heat

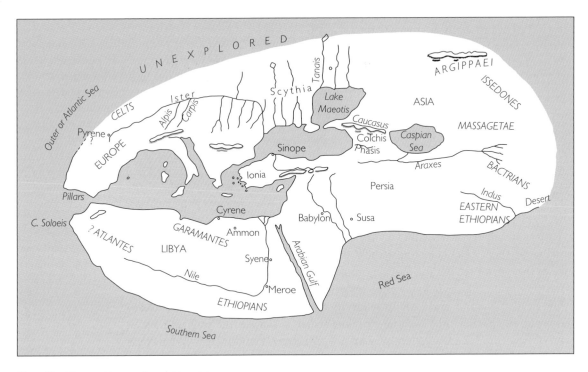

Map 12   The world according to Herodotus.

nor by excessive cold. By contrast, the Persians' long history of successful conquest has furnished them with luxuries that have made them soft, even effeminate. Their previous successes have made them masters of many peoples, on whose efforts they have come to rely. Herodotus gives a detailed description of the numerous nations whose soldiers, equipped in many instances with outlandish native weapons, make up the ungainly invasion force. Because of its heterogeneous nature, the Persian army lacks the uniformity and unity of purpose that characterize the Greek forces.

There is one additional factor that has not yet been mentioned, and that is the gods. It would seem that Herodotus is quite capable of accounting for historical causation without any recourse to the supernatural. But to ignore the gods is dangerous in the extreme, and Herodotus takes account of the agency of the divine alongside his more "scientific" understanding of the workings of historical causation. One of the results of success and prosperity is a self-confidence that is to some degree justifiable but that can lead to the kind of hybris for which Xerxes, according to Aeschylus' *The Persians*, was punished by the gods. In fact, this more traditional form of explanation, in terms of divine punishment for outrageous violation of accepted norms, has inevitably influenced and helped to shape Herodotus' more abstract thinking. The pattern that Herodotus has outlined, according to which nations expand and then, through overconfidence, inevitably overextend themselves and suffer retribution, is clearly related to the conventional piety, according to which individuals are liable to divine retribution for behavior inappropriate to mere mortals.

Instances of divine retribution are not uncommon in Herodotus' history, but Herodotus (like some investigators even today) seems to have had no difficulty allowing some events to be explained *both* by natural causes *and* by divine intervention. So, for example, before Xerxes' troops cross over into Europe, Herodotus puts into the mouth of one of Xerxes' advisers a lucid appraisal of the dangers that so large a force is likely to face: the land and the sea, he tells Xerxes, will become our enemies; there are not enough harbors in Greece to accommodate so large a fleet, leaving many vessels unprotected from the elements; and the land is too poor to supply provisions for an army of this vast size. Later, Herodotus records that on two occasions storms arose, of the sort that are quite common in the Aegean at just that time of year, wrecking several of the Persian ships. In one instance, Herodotus explicitly attributes the destruction to divine activity, intended "to make the Persian fleet equal in size to the Greek." In the other instance, he hints at divine agency by telling us that the winds that brought the storm came from the direction of the Hellespont, the strait that Xerxes had earlier whipped and insulted for causing the failure of his first attempt at bridging it. To Herodotus, there is no incompatibility between a "natural" and a divine explanation. The Greeks of the fifth century BC did not in fact have a concept that corresponds to our notion of "nature." When Xerxes bridges the Hellespont and cuts a canal through the peninsula at Mount Athos, he is violating what we might perhaps regard as the natural order of things, by making dry land to appear where formerly there was water and vice versa. For Herodotus, as for Aeschylus before him, these actions are those of a man who behaves as only a god is entitled to act. To punish him, therefore, rests with the gods, who take offense at this or, as Herodotus likes to put it, are jealous of their own prerogative.

For Herodotus, naturally, the gods are a universal force. But he recognizes that different peoples worship the gods in different ways and call them by different names. Indeed, he is well aware, probably as a result of his extensive travels, that in general the customs of one people differ considerably from those of other peoples. A surprisingly large proportion of Herodotus' narrative is taken up with a detailed description of the customs of the Persians, the Ethiopians, the Scythians, and a host of other nations. In addition, he provides us with accounts of the physical characteristics of several of these peoples and with details of the topography and climate of the lands that they inhabit. In fact, the entire second book of his nine-book work is given over to an extended treatment of the history and ethnography of Egypt and the Egyptians. In part, this fascination with foreign nations and their customs is a

> "You are aware that it is always at the largest buildings and the tallest trees that the god hurls his lightning-bolts. That is because the god has a tendency to deflate everything that is overgrown. And so, even a huge army can be wiped out by a small one. How can that be? Well, whenever the god, being indignant, inflicts panic or hurls a thunderbolt, it suffers a humiliating defeat. The god does not allow anyone but himself to feel self-important." (Herodotus, 7.10e, a Persian adviser warning Xerxes of the dangers of attacking Greece)

product of Herodotus' limitless curiosity and his passion for sharing with his reader the many curious bits of information that he has amassed. There is also a deeper, more programmatic reason for his inclusion of this type of material in a work of history. We have seen that Herodotus' primary concern is to understand the causes of historical events, and he recognizes that such things as the natural landscape and traditional patterns of behavior often determine the way events turn out. So, for example, Herodotus' narrative makes it clear that the failure of the Persian King Darius to annex the territory of the Scythians is largely a result of the topography of Scythia and the nomadic ways of its inhabitants, both of which are described at some length. Since the territory contains many rivers, there is no need for the Scythians to build fixed settlements near a reliable source of water and, since their land is flat, they have become accomplished horsemen and can easily outrun any attackers. Characteristically, however, Herodotus combines this naturalistic explanation for the Scythians' ability to frustrate Darius' invasion with suggestions that Darius has angered the gods with his presumptuous designs on Europe when he was already master of Asia.

Books and Readers

What Herodotus has done, then, is to attempt to reconcile, in one prose narrative of epic proportions, an historical account that applies the most advanced, "scientific" thinking and a more standard form of explanation, in terms of the traditional anthropomorphic gods, of a sort that is normally found in works of Greek poetry. The very fact that Herodotus writes in prose is itself a departure, and is an indication of the "analytical" character of his work. For the predominant means of literary expression before Herodotus' time was in verse, as in the heroic poetry of Homer or the more recently developed poetic genre of Attic tragedy. Prose had been used, but never on such a vast scale, by the early Ionian philosophers to communicate their scientific theories and occasionally by others for other purposes. It is only in the fifth century that we begin to see the development of prose as a frequent vehicle for literary and technical expression. One of the reasons for this is the increasing (but still relatively limited) level of literacy in Greece. Prior to this time, poetry, even if it existed in written form, was disseminated largely in performance rather than in writing: epic poems were recited either by the poets themselves or by professional performers known as "rhapsodes," lyric poetry was composed for performance by an individual or a chorus, and tragic poetry was intended for a mass audience in the theater. With increased literacy, it became more usual for works of literature to be read by individuals in private, rather than to be experienced in common with other members of the community.

   This, in turn, had an effect on the character of what was written, and we begin to see a division between poetry, which is more suited for public performance because its metrical form allows it to be more easily remembered, and prose, which can forgo the fancier trappings of verse, particularly when it is intended for a more limited and more solitary audience. Thus we hear of technical and theoretical treatises being written in prose in the middle of the fifth century BC – the treatises themselves have for the most part not survived – on such specialized subjects as medicine, music, architecture, city planning, and sculpture. The development of prose literature, however, was slow and gradual, and it should not be thought that there was a sharp distinction between largely "oral" poetry and largely "written" prose. Both poetry and prose were normally written down in the fifth century BC and both were, to a certain degree, "oral" as well. To begin with, reading a written text in ancient Greece, even if the reader was completely isolated from other people, was generally done out loud. Such graphic conventions as punctuation, division between words, accent marks, and the distinction between upper-case and lower-case letters had not yet been invented in the fifth century – and even much later were used only intermittently (see figure 24) – so that it was often necessary for the reader to "sound out" the words of a text in order to interpret it correctly. In addition, even works of prose could on occasion be performed as display pieces, and we are in fact told that Herodotus recited portions of his history in public. In any event, the essentially oral nature of Herodotus' work is apparent from its structure, which some readers today find difficult to follow, precisely because we are no longer accustomed to listening to large-scale oral narratives. Herodotus' narrative does not proceed in a straight chronological sequence but is interrupted by frequent and sometimes quite lengthy digressions. But Herodotus could count on the fact that his contemporary audience, whether they read the work to themselves or heard it recited, would be able to keep the sequence of events securely in their mind because their memory was developed by frequent exposure to oral performance.

It was necessary for them to do so, even if they were reading a text of Herodotus' history, because of the nature of ancient texts. We are accustomed today to reading books that adhere to a standard format, like the book you are reading now, with (numbered) pages, binding, and a spine, and often including such amenities as a title page, table of contents, and index. That format, known as a "codex," was not invented until after the time of Christ. Herodotus and his contemporaries read literary texts that were produced in the form of rolls, written so that each roll contained many columns of text (figure 41). There was no use in numbering the columns, since each hand-written copy of the same text would differ in the size of the writing, the width of the columns, the height of the roll, and so on. A long work like that of Herodotus would require several rolls, making cross-references nearly impossible: references to earlier or later points in the text would require that the ancient reader pay close attention and have an excellent memory. Those readers who have paid close attention to this chapter will have noticed that no title has been given for Herodotus' history. This is because ancient texts, which had no title pages, often had no specific title. The title that today is frequently given to Herodotus' work, *The History* or *The Histories*, is simply taken from Herodotus' opening words: "The investigations [*historia*] of Herodotus of Halicarnassus are herein disclosed . . ."

Figure 41 Attic red-figure hydria (water pitcher), by a painter of the Group of Polygnotus, showing the poet Sappho holding open and reading a roll; height of vase 40 cm, 440–430 BC. Athens, National Archaeological Museum, 1260.

Sophocles

As far as we can tell, Herodotus wrote only one, very long work. By contrast, composers of tragedies were required to write four plays for submission in the annual tragic competition in Athens. Aeschylus produced some 80 or 90 dramas, a few of which have been referred to by name in chapter 7. Tragedies and satyr plays needed to have titles, both because each playwright was expected to produce multiple dramatic works that needed to be distinguished from one another and because records were kept of the dramatic competitions, since they were official events sponsored by the state of Athens. The titles of Attic tragedies and satyr plays were generally simple and straightforward, consisting of the name of the most prominent character (like *Agamemnon*) or of the chorus (*The Eumenides*). Occasionally, a playwright would compose two or more plays of the same title, as the dramatist Sophocles did when he composed two plays entitled *Oedipus*. But these two plays were written some 20 or 30 years apart, for production at different festivals, so there was no need to differentiate them at the time of their original performance. Those two tragedies, however, are among the seven by Sophocles that have survived, and we refer to them, as they were referred to already in antiquity, as *Oedipus Tyrannus* (or *Oedipus the King*) and *Oedipus at Colonus*. These are only two of the well over one hundred dramas that Sophocles composed. One of the reasons Sophocles was so prolific is that he lived a long and successful life, being born in the middle of the first decade of the fifth century and dying in the middle of the last. His first entry into the tragic competition, in the days when Aeschylus was still at the peak of his creative powers, is said to have won first prize, and he went on to win first prize at the Dionysia on more occasions (18) than any other tragic poet.

Sophocles did not share Aeschylus' fondness for producing four plays connected in plot and theme. Instead, each of Sophocles' tragedies is self-contained and unrelated to the other dramas that he wrote for the same year's competition. (As it happens, three of Sophocles' surviving tragedies, the two *Oedipus* plays and *Antigone*, dramatize a sequence of events in the same family and the three plays are occasionally today produced in conjunction, but Sophocles wrote them for three festivals in widely separ-

> "His words to me were few, but he kept repeating, 'Woman, women gain glory by keeping their mouth shut!' Chastened, I held my tongue and he rushed outside, alone. What he did there I cannot tell, but he came back in, leading his captives: tethered oxen, herd-dogs, and wooly plunder. He beheaded some and he slit the throat of others, pulling their heads back, and then butchered the carcasses. Others still he kept in bondage, tormenting them as though they were men." (Sophocles, *Ajax* 292–300, Tecmessa describing Ajax's deranged behavior)

ated years.) Further, each of Sophocles' surviving tragedies concentrates on a single individual whose extraordinary strength of character and unwillingness to compromise isolates him or her from the remaining cast of characters. Typical of Sophocles' approach to tragic composition is his *Ajax*, which dates from the 450s or 440s BC and is perhaps his earliest surviving play. (Sophocles wrote another tragedy of the same title, about another man named Ajax, but since that play has not survived we can simply refer to the surviving play as *Ajax*, with no further qualification.) The play is set during the Trojan War, with characters that were familiar to the audience from the Homeric poems. Ajax, who appears frequently in the *Iliad*, was the most accomplished Greek warrior at Troy, with the exception of Achilles. Sophocles' play takes place at a point in the war after Achilles has been killed in battle. The magnificent armor that was made for Achilles by the god Hephaestus has been awarded, not to Ajax, but to Odysseus. Ajax is convinced that he deserved to receive the armor himself and that Odysseus had used underhanded means to influence the process by which the award was made, a process that, the play suggests, involved something resembling democratic balloting. Because of what he regards as a humiliating slight to his standing as the foremost Greek warrior, Ajax goes into a violent rage and attempts to kill Odysseus and the leaders of the Greek army, Agamemnon and Menelaus. But the goddess Athena has so unhinged Ajax's mind that, instead, he binds, tortures, and slaughters some of the army's livestock, thinking they are his human enemies.

"The other spirits of the dead and departed stood there sorrowfully, each one of them asking about friends and relatives. Only the spirit of Ajax, the son of Telamon, kept his distance in resentment at the victory that I won over him beside the ships, when judgment was rendered concerning the arms of Achilles. The revered mother of Achilles had offered them as a prize and the sons of the Trojans along with Pallas Athena decided the issue. How I wish I had not won such a prize! What a great man lies buried in the earth because of them!" (Homer, *Odyssey* 11.541–9, Odysseus describing his visit to the Underworld)

This is the background to the play, which opens with Ajax, who has now come to his senses, feeling still greater torment and humiliation, since his murderous intentions have been revealed without his having enjoyed at least the satisfaction of exacting vengeance. There is nothing left for Ajax but to do what everyone in Sophocles' audience knew he was going to do, commit suicide by falling on his sword (figure 42). In order to do so, Ajax requires solitude, something that is hard to find on the Greek tragic stage because of the almost constant presence of the chorus, which in this play consists of soldiers under Ajax's command. What Ajax needs to do, therefore, is to persuade the chorus and his concubine Tecmessa that he is going off by himself for some reason other than to kill himself. So he tells them that he is going down to the seashore, where he will cleanse himself of the defilement that he has incurred and where he will "lay to rest" the sword with which he has done such shameful deeds. He has now, he says, learned to be sensible; he has come to

Figure 42   Attic black-figure amphora by Exekias, showing Ajax preparing to commit suicide; height of vase 45.1 cm, ca. 530 BC. Boulogne-sur-mer, Le Château-Musée de Boulogne-sur-Mer, 558.

realize that all things are subject to change and that "an enemy ought to be hated only to the extent that he is likely some day to become a friend." Tecmessa and the chorus are persuaded that Ajax has been humbled by his experience and that he is willing to be reconciled with his former enemies, Odysseus, Agamemnon, and Menelaus. But every member of the audience who recalls the *Odyssey* – which is to say, every member of Sophocles' audience – knows that this is not the case. In a particularly memorable scene in the *Odyssey*, which was later to be memorably imitated by the Roman poet Virgil, Odysseus travels while alive to the Underworld, where he encounters some of his deceased companions from the Trojan War, including Ajax. Odysseus speaks gentle words to Ajax, praising his valor and urging that the two of them forget their former animosity. Ajax walks away without saying a word to Odysseus. Instead, he rejoins his companions in the land of the dead.

The audience, then, knows the meaning of Ajax's words, but the characters on stage to whom they are addressed, Tecmessa and the chorus of soldiers, take them to mean something else entirely. This technique, whereby the dramatist exploits the disparity between the audience's knowledge and that of the dramatic characters, is called "dramatic irony" and is particularly characteristic of Sophoclean tragedy. Having convinced the chorus and Tecmessa to stay behind, Ajax goes off and the scene changes, unusually for Attic tragedy. At an isolated location by the sea Ajax delivers a magnificent soliloquy, which he ends with another allusion to the Underworld scene in the *Odyssey*, saying that Ajax will speak no more to the living; his next words will be addressed to those in the land of the dead. Ajax then leaps upon the sword whose hilt he has buried in the sand. At this point, only three fifths of the play have taken place. The remainder of the play is taken up with the discovery of Ajax's body and a debate over whether Ajax should receive proper burial or, since he has proved to be a traitor to the army, should suffer the humiliation of being left unburied. Agamemnon and Menelaus, the authoritarian commanders of the army, are eager to humiliate Ajax, which they were unable to do while he lived because of his superior strength and value to the army. Odysseus, however, true to the character that he displays in the *Odyssey*, is more flexible, and he eventually persuades Agamemnon and Menelaus to allow Ajax's burial.

This last portion of the play highlights Ajax's greatness as well as his isolation. There is a conspicuous contrast between the powerful, unyielding hero, whose on-stage body is the focus of the dramatic action, and the lesser men who engage in a dispute, the techniques of which were familiar to Sophocles' audience from the debates in their contemporary, democratic assembly. Ajax is, in a sense, a throwback to the vanished days of the heroic past, familiar from Homer's epics. Indeed, Ajax bears a resemblance to Homer's Achilles: both men are bitterly enraged at Agamemnon because they feel slighted by their commander; both men endanger their fellow soldiers as a result of their rage; and the death of both men arises from the sequence of events set in motion by their furious response to Agamemnon's slight. Achilles' death does not form part of the action of the *Iliad* (although his imminent death is hinted at repeatedly), and Homer's epic poem ends with Achilles and Agamemnon reconciled. Ajax, on the other hand, can never be reconciled with a former enemy, and this uncompromising attitude makes him typical of Sophoclean heroes, who are at once admirable because of their steadfast adherence to principle and unwelcome members of a community because of their total self-reliance. In the case of Ajax, this self-reliance contributes significantly to his doom. In the course of the play, it is revealed that, in the past, Ajax had boasted that he was quite capable of winning glory on the battlefield without any assistance from the gods and, on another occasion, when the goddess Athena had stood by his side and urged him on, Ajax had told her to go and stand beside some lesser warrior who might actually need her help. This was what caused Athena to madden Ajax, so that he slaughtered livestock instead of attacking his enemies, thereby incurring humiliation beyond bearing.

Sophocles would have been quite capable of treating the tragedy of Ajax exclusively in terms of Ajax's character, without any recourse to the supernatural. But the gods are a traditional feature of Attic drama, which is performed at a festival in honor of the god Dionysus. The gods occasionally appear as characters in the drama, and in fact Athena appears briefly in the opening scene of Sophocles' *Ajax*. In another of Sophocles' tragedies, the *Electra*, the gods are conspicuously absent. *Electra* was produced many years after *Ajax*, toward the end of Sophocles' long career. It dramatizes the same events that formed the plot of Aeschylus' *The Libation Bearers*, namely the return of Orestes from exile, his reunion with his sister Electra, and his murder of Clytemestra and her lover. But, while the main character of Aeschylus' play was Agamemnon's son Orestes, Sophocles' play focuses, as its title indicates, on Orestes' sister. Although Electra is a woman and therefore, according to ancient Greek thinking, weaker than a man and less capable of independent action, she is a typical Sophoclean hero and has much in common with Sophocles' Ajax. She is isolated not only by circumstances but by deliberate choice. It has been some years since the murder of Agamemnon, and Electra has incurred the hatred of her mother by refusing to allow Clytemestra to forget the heinous nature of her crime in murdering her husband. In Aeschylus' treatment of the story, Clytemestra herself had sent the child Orestes away at the time of the murder, but in Sophocles' version it is Electra who saved her younger brother by sending him to another city, in the hopes that he will grow up to avenge their father's death. Electra now spends her time impatiently awaiting Orestes' return, disappointed that he apparently does not share her decisiveness and her eagerness for revenge.

Because she is a woman Electra cannot act alone. Her mother and her mother's lover have refused to allow Electra to marry for fear that she will bear male offspring who will grow up to avenge Agamemnon's murder. Electra's isolation is further emphasized by Sophocles, who has given her a sister,

"What could you possibly have been relying upon to arm yourself with such audacity and invite me to be your helper? Are you blind? You're a woman, not a man, and your strength is nothing compared to our enemies'. Upon them fortune smiles day after day but on us she turns her back and leaves us cold. How then could we contrive to overpower so potent a foe and hope to escape disaster? Take care that we not make a bad situation worse if someone so much as hears our words!" (Sophocles, *Electra* 995–1004, Chrysothemis trying to restrain Electra)

Chrysothemis, whose character contrasts conspicuously with Electra's. Unlike Electra, her sister is willing to accept the current situation, and she urges Electra to "yield" to Clytemestra and her lover. The one thing Electra cannot do is yield and, when a report is brought of the death of Orestes, Electra tries to persuade Chrysothemis to join her in taking matters into their own hands and exacting vengeance themselves, even though they are only women. Chrysothemis, while acknowledging the justice of what Electra proposes, is too weak to follow her sister's lead. Electra resolves, therefore, to act alone.

The report of Orestes' death, however, is a fabrication, as the audience knows but the characters on stage do not. By this point in his career Sophocles had thoroughly mastered the technique of dramatic irony and one of the most dramatically effective scenes in this play is the detailed description of a chariot race at the Pythian Games, in the course of which Orestes' chariot crashes and he is killed, his body so horribly mangled that "no friend or relative could recognize him." This scene has been brilliantly prepared by Sophocles, who earlier in the play brought a stealthy Orestes on stage, instructing one of his servants to deliver to the palace a false account of his death so that he can catch Clytemestra and her lover off guard. The scene in which the false report is conveyed also exploits another feature of Attic drama that Sophocles had been experimenting with since his earliest years as a dramatist. Near the beginning of Sophocles' career it had become permissible to add a third actor to the two that had sufficed for Aeschylus' *The Persians* and for other early dramas. This innovation (which some ancient sources ascribe, probably wrongly, to Sophocles himself) took place before the end of Aeschylus' lifetime, and Aeschylus took advantage of the opportunity, to a limited extent, in *The Oresteia*. Sophocles' use of the third actor in his early *Ajax* had likewise been limited, but in *Electra* full dramatic advantage is taken of having three speaking actors on stage at once. The account of Orestes' death is delivered in the hearing of both Electra and Clytemestra (as well as the chorus). We, the audience, are dynamically drawn into the action of the play, not so much by the content of the speech, which we know to be false (although it is a skillful and stirring narrative), but by the varying reactions that it elicits from the two women. For Electra, this is the crowning disaster in a life that has been filled with wretchedness; it means the end of the one hope that still remained for her, the hope of securing vengeance and, thereby, justice. Electra's reaction is contrasted directly with that of Clytemestra. Sophocles is too accomplished a dramatist to portray a mother who is overjoyed at news of her son's death, but he does make it clear that Clytemestra's response to the servant's report is a sense of relief and security: she can now sleep at night, knowing that she no longer needs to fear that Orestes will return and avenge her murder of Agamemnon.

The reactions of Electra and Clytemestra, different as they are from each other, are both misguided. In fact, Orestes has returned, unrecognized by friends and relatives, and by the end of the play he has brought relief to Electra and vengeance upon Clytemestra and her lover. Of course, the members of the audience were fully aware from the start how the action would be resolved: not only were they well prepared by Sophocles' skillful dramatic handling of the material, but the material was itself familiar from *The Oresteia* and from other literary and artistic representations of the story. Sophocles' originality lay in the way in which he adapted and reacted to the work of his predecessors, especially Aeschylus. The resolution in *The Oresteia* had involved the gods and the city of Athens, and the crisis on both the divine and the human levels could be settled only by subordinating the claims of the family to the civic organization of the state. But in Sophocles' *Electra* the family reasserts itself, in the form of Electra's unbending devotion to her father's memory and to her brother's justification in avenging Agamemnon's murder. As in *The Oresteia*, the gods seem to give their approval, but not in any direct manner, since they take no part in the action of the play; rather, the role of the gods is hinted at through Sophocles' subtle use of prayers offered by the characters. Just before Orestes' servant enters the scene to report Orestes' fictitious death, Clytemestra prays to Apollo that her enemies – she means her son Orestes – may fail in their plots to overthrow her. Her prayers, she thinks, are answered by the servant's account of Orestes' death, but she is mistaken. By contrast, just before Orestes enters the palace to carry out his vengeance on Clytemestra, Electra prays to Apollo that Orestes' actions may be successful. Her prayers are answered and the family of Agamemnon is restored.

Other Persons: Women and Athenian Democracy

In addition to Sophocles' Electra and Aeschylus' Clytemestra, fifth-century tragedy is populated with a number of extraordinary female characters, ranging from the model heroine of Euripides' *Alcestis*, who agrees to die so that her husband may live, to the same dramatist's Medea, who murders her own children to avenge herself on the children's father for abandoning her. This is all the more striking when we consider that these characters, like all characters in Attic tragedy, were played by male actors, that all the dramatists whose names are recorded were men, and that it is uncertain whether the audience for dramatic performances even included women. We may be inclined, then, to dismiss these representations as merely male fantasies or caricatures, and we may regret the absence of the voice of a "real" woman who can speak for the female population of ancient Greece. There are, of course, women's voices that are available to us, although they are far less numerous than their male counterparts: in addition to the Archaic poet Sappho, whom we have already considered, we find in later periods other women who wrote for publication as well as a number of women whose personal letters and other documents have survived by chance on papyri. It is questionable, however, whether any of these writers can be regarded as representative of ancient Greek women, just as it is questionable whether Hesiod or Theognis or Herodotus can be regarded as representative of ancient Greek men. For one thing, these three writers come from different periods and different parts of Greece. For another, they are thoughtful individuals with their own developed views. The same would naturally be the case with any women who expressed themselves in writing. Further, as we have seen in the case of Sparta, the way in which women functioned within their society varied from one polis to another.

Even if we confine ourselves to fifth-century Athens, we find that there can be no such thing as a typical woman or a representative woman's voice. For, just as what is expected of a woman differs from polis to polis, so it differs within a given polis depending on the social and economic milieu and even whether the setting is rural or urban. The one thing, however, that is expected of all women who belong to citizen families is that they maintain the family by giving birth, preferably to male offspring. Since the life expectancy of women was short, owing to the very dangers associated with childbirth, and since infant mortality rates were high, it was felt necessary for women – or, more accurately, girls – to be married shortly after men-arche, that is, when they were 13 or 14 years of age, so that they could get an early start on their childbearing responsibilities. Their marriage would be arranged for them by their family, as is the case in many parts of the world today, to a husband who was ordinarily around 30 years old, the age at which citizen men could be expected to participate fully in the political life of the community. Except during periods of prolonged and intense warfare, life expectancy for men was longer than that for women, so that this disparity in age had little effect on the couple's prospects of producing a viable male heir. The disparity in age, however, did affect the wife's prospects of developing independently as an individual. For her marriage consisted of her transfer at a very young age from the household of her adult father to that of her adult husband. It had been the father's responsibility to ensure that his daughter not be sexually active; it was now the husband's concern to ensure that her sexual activity be restricted to him, since his aim in procuring a wife was to provide him, not his next-door neighbor, with sons. To the extent possible, then, the husband would try to make sure that his bride was well supervised while he was away from the house, as he often was, whether attending to public matters or supervising the management of his landholdings. This was easier in the case of wealthy citizens with a large and trusted staff of slaves and servants than in the case of those households that could afford to maintain only a small number of slaves, and those of perhaps questionable character. In addition, it might be necessary for women from poorer families to work outside the house, selling goods in the agora or work-ing as a nurse or a midwife, or to leave the house for other purposes, such as going to the spring or fountain to fetch water.

Thus we find that, in fifth-century Athens, and presumably in most other Greek poleis, it was the mark of a woman from a family of upper-class citizens that she spent most of her time inside the house. Among her most frequent activities will have been the production of fabrics for use by the household by spinning wool, weaving, and embroidering. Because these activities took place largely out of sight of the male members of the family and because they involved the application of intricate and subtle skills, textiles came to have an ambivalent character in the eyes of Greek men. For all their beauty and value, textiles could have associations with deviousness, and there are a number of myths and stories in which fabrics are used by women for destructive means. In Aeschylus' *Agamemnon*, for instance,

Clytemestra first lures her husband into walking on precious fabrics as a way of exposing him to divine anger and then she snares him with woven garments before he is stabbed to death. In addition to spinning and weaving, a married woman's responsibilities will have included supervising other household chores and ensuring that the resources of the house not be expended in a wasteful manner. The Greek word that refers to this "household management" is *oikonomia*, the word from which English "economy" is derived, so that the role of the citizen wife is, in the most literal sense, an economic one. Even her role as mother is, strictly speaking, economic in nature, since her production of male heirs serves the purpose of providing a new family member to whom the father's property can be transferred. The role of the woman, then, like the role of her husband, is determined by what is in the best interests of the family. As we have seen, however, the role of the family within the Athenian polis had changed, or was still in the process of changing, as a result of the democratic reforms of the sixth and fifth centuries. The aim of several of those reforms had been to reduce the power of the main aristocratic families to influence public policy; political influence now was vested more widely and, supposedly, in a more egalitarian fashion in the collective body of adult male citizens. Another such measure was taken in the middle of the fifth century when the Athenian assembly voted in 451 BC to approve a proposal by Pericles to restrict citizenship to men both of whose parents came from citizen families. Previously, the male product of a marriage between a citizen father and a non-Athenian or even a non-Greek mother could enjoy the benefits of citizenship. Such marriages had often in the past been used by aristocratic families to solidify alliances with powerful families in other poleis, and there was always the danger that such connections could be exploited by someone who wished to establish himself as tyrant. Now, however, by exercising its control over who could become a citizen, the state made such marriages undesirable because any offspring would be barred from participation in political affairs.

In this way democracy had the effect of exaggerating and validating the separation of men and women into denizens of, respectively, the public space of the out of doors and the private space inside the house. At the same time, the Athenians were well aware, through their familiarity with the Homeric poems and with countless other tales and myths, that things had been different in an earlier time, that such women as the wives of Priam or Menelaus had had the opportunity to act in a much more public manner than was felt proper for a contemporary Athenian woman. In the *Odyssey*, for example, Homer represents Odysseus' wife Penelope as managing the absent Odysseus' estate on her own, during

"Hear me, you imperious suitors, you who have always been incessantly taking advantage of this house for your feasting and drinking, a house that belongs to a man who has long been absent, nor have you been able to make any excuse other than to say that you are eager to marry me and make me your wife. Suitors, it is time for action, since the prize is now here before you. I present to you the great bow of godlike Odysseus. I will go off with whatever man can most easily take the bow in his hands and string it, and then shoot an arrow through all twelve axes. I will leave behind this lovely house, the house where I was a bride, which is filled with the memories of a lifetime." (Homer, *Odyssey*, 21.68–78, Penelope speaking) which time she publicly interacts with and frustrates the wishes of several dozen suitors. Those women, of course, were married to kings and were the daughters of kings or even gods, categories of persons no longer represented on the citizenship rolls of democratic Athens. Kings and tyrants still existed in some Greek poleis and among most barbarian peoples – we have even encountered a barbarian queen as a naval commander at the battle of Salamis (p. 120) – but Athenians liked to think of themselves and their democratic ways as more sober and reasonable. Barbarian kings and queens, like Euripides' Medea or Xerxes' mother in Aeschylus' *The Persians*, or legendary figures from the distant past of Greece, could be represented as extreme in their emotional make-up, and so were appropriate characters with which to populate the tragic stage. In fact, the very exaggeration of their desires and impulses could make them at the same time both fascinating and reassuring for their fifth-century audience, since they represent extraordinary, and extraordinarily destructive, individuals of the sort that the Athenian democracy could imagine that it had succeeded in taming.

Recommended for Further Reading

Brulé, P. *Women of Ancient Greece*, English translation (Edinburgh 2003): a clearly written, sensible, and thorough survey of all aspects of women's life from the time of Homer through late antiquity.

Gould, J. *Herodotus* (New York 1989): the most thoughtful and insightful introduction to Herodotus as historian, as thinker, and as literary artist.

Herodotus. *The Histories*, translated by Robin Waterfield (Oxford and New York 1998): a readable and accurate translation, with Carolyn Dewald's exceptionally helpful and informative introduction and notes, plus excellent bibliography, timeline, glossaries, maps, and index.

Lewis, S. *The Athenian Woman: An Iconographic Handbook* (London and New York 2002): a well-illustrated and controversial study of all aspects of women's life in ancient Greece that asks us to challenge our usual assumptions about what the frequent representations of women on Attic vases can actually tell us.

Scodel, R. *Sophocles* (Boston 1984): a fine introduction to the dramatic achievement of Sophocles, in the Twayne "World Authors" series.

Sophocles. *The Complete Plays*, translated by C. R. Mueller and A. Krajewska-Wieczorek (Hanover, NH 2000): the least unsatisfactory of the many desperate attempts to convey Sophocles' rugged language in English.

Thomas, R. *Literacy and Orality in Ancient Greece* (Cambridge and New York 1992): an important discussion of the complex issue of the transition from a largely oral to an increasingly literate culture in ancient Greece.

THE PELOPONNESIAN WAR: A TALE OF THUCYDIDES

9

For Athens, the late fifth century BC was both the best of times and the worst of times. Athens was at the pinnacle of its intellectual and artistic creativity, but it was also involved in a prolonged and, ultimately, disastrous war with Sparta and its allies, the Peloponnesian War. This war served as the subject of perhaps the greatest historian of the ancient world, the Athenian Thucydides, who fought in the war himself and recorded its progress in great detail. But it is not the detailed description of events that makes Thucydides' work a landmark of historical investigation. Rather, it is the historian's conviction that intense, objective observation of human affairs can contribute to an increased ability to foresee the outcome of current events. In this respect, Thucydides was reflecting current trends in the science of medicine, of which Thucydides' contemporary Hippocrates is often considered to be the founder. A large number of medical treatises preserved under the names of Hippocrates and his followers are devoted to the detailed observation and description of the symptoms of diseases, in the expectation that the more we know about the progress of morbid conditions the more successful we will be in anticipating and averting an unpleasant outcome. At the same time as the Athenians were engaged in the war that provided Thucydides with his material, they were creating the most notable architectural monuments in their illustrious history. The buildings on the acropolis had been destroyed by the Persians when they occupied Athens in 480 BC. Now, in the second half of the fifth century, the revenues from the Delian League enabled the Athenians to rebuild their temples and other monuments on the acropolis on a magnificent scale. The Parthenon, in particular, is regarded as definitive of "the classical" in art, not only because of the elegance and refinement of its architectural proportions and detail, but because of the sculptural frieze, created under the direction of the Athenian artist Phidias, that decorated the building. The Parthenon frieze depicts a ritual procession of the sort that formed one of the central events in the religious life of contemporary Athenians. Finally, the chapter closes with a brief consideration of the nature of religious practice in Athens and in ancient Greece generally.

The influence of Herodotus, the "Father of History," began to be felt almost immediately, not only because the importance of his work was readily apparent but because events in the late fifth century BC created a need for continued historical analysis. We saw earlier (p. 138) that after the Persian Wars Sparta retreated from a position of leadership among the Greek poleis and Athens stepped in, creating an alliance that gradually became virtually a maritime empire. Many Greeks, including the Spartans, felt that the "allies" of the Athenians had in fact become the Athenians' subjects and that something needed to be done to "liberate" them. Sparta was clearly the only polis with the resources and prestige adequate to take the lead in limiting Athens' power, but the Spartans were notoriously slow to take action. Eventually, however, the war that for long seemed inevitable broke out, in 431 BC, between two coalitions of Greek poleis: Sparta and its allies, mostly located in the Peloponnese, and Athens and its allies, mostly located in and along the coast of the Aegean Sea (map 13).

The war, which continued with interruptions until 404 BC, is generally known as the "Peloponnesian War" because our primary source of information regarding the war is the detailed history written by the Athenian Thucydides, who was a contemporary of, and briefly a participant in, the conflict. Although Thucydides may have begun work on his history while Herodotus was still alive, his work could hardly be more different from that of the older historian. Indeed, the difference may well be deliberate, as Thucydides seems in many ways to be in competition with Herodotus and to be trying (although he never mentions Herodotus by name) to improve upon Herodotus' method of writing history. Whether it is an improvement is a matter for debate; what is beyond doubt is that Thucydides, by concentrating on strictly political and military history and ignoring the cultural and ethnographic details that often fascinated Herodotus, set a fashion that was to be followed by historians for centuries to come. In this chapter, we will look at the war between Athens and Sparta through Thucydides' eyes (the only way that event can be viewed), and we will compare Thucydides' methods with those of his contemporaries, the earliest Greek medical writers. We will also see how Athenian material prosperity before and during the war created an atmosphere in that city that encouraged the flourishing of the visual arts, as exemplified by the classical buildings on the Athenian acropolis.

Thucydides and the Writing of the Peloponnesian War

Just as the first two words of Herodotus' work were "Herodotus" and "Halicarnassus," so Thucydides begins with "Thucydides" and "Athenian": "Thucydides the Athenian wrote up the war between the Peloponnesians and the Athenians." He does not use the word *historia* here or anywhere else in his account. He does, however, emphasize the written character of his history and he tells us that he began work

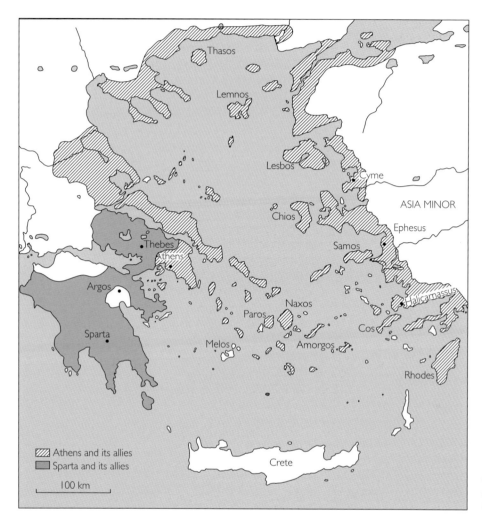

Map 13 Athenian and Spartan alliances at the start of the Peloponnesian War.

On the map: Thasos, Lemnos, Lesbos, Cyme, ASIA MINOR, Chios, Ephesus, Thebes, Athens, Samos, Argos, Halicarnassus, Naxos, Paros, Cos, Sparta, Melos, Amorgos, Rhodes, Crete

Athens and its allies
Sparta and its allies
100 km

on his narrative as soon as the war began, "in the expectation that it was going to be a major war and that it would be more deserving of renown than any previous war." Thucydides then spends the next few pages (or columns of text in its original format) telling us what led him at the start of the war to expect that it would eclipse previous wars by its magnitude. In the course of his explanation he mentions the Trojan War, the setting of Homer's epic poems, and the Persian Wars, the object of Herodotus' investigations, making clear his ambition to rival those two of his predecessors who had produced the works of literature that were greatest both in terms of repute and length. (As it happens, Thucydides' history is about 20 percent shorter than Herodotus'; if he had lived to complete it – his work breaks off in mid-sentence, with the events of the last six years of the war still to be related – Thucydides' history would surely have surpassed Herodotus' in size.) The Trojan War, according to Thucydides, fell far short of what could be expected of the war

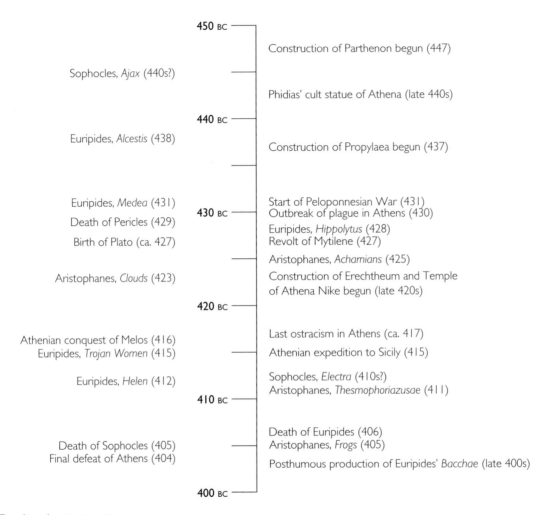

Timeline 6   The late fifth century BC.

between Athens and Sparta because of the size and might of the respective combatants: even if we ignore the likelihood that Homer, being a poet, engaged in exaggeration, the number of soldiers that he represents as having taken part in the Trojan War was much smaller than the number prepared to fight on either side in the coming conflict between Athens and Sparta. In the case of the Persian Wars, of course, Thucydides could not hope to be believed if he claimed that Athens, Sparta, and their various Greek allies were more numerous than the Greek and Persian forces that had participated in the Persian Wars, so he abandons his aim of explaining why he thought at the beginning of the war that the Peloponnesian War would surpass the Persian Wars. Instead, he hopes to get away with saying, in effect, that the Peloponnesian War *turned out to be* more prolonged and more destructive than the Persian Wars, "which were quickly resolved by two battles by sea and two by land."

Why has Thucydides begun his history with a prediction about the future course of the war, followed by a demonstration that the prediction was accurate (even if he has to equivocate a bit concerning the grounds for the prediction)? The answer to this question reveals Thucydides' special contribution to the understanding of history's value, namely its potential for use as an instrument of prognostication. By telling us at the very start about his forecast of the future magnitude of the war and about the success of that forecast, Thucydides enlists our confidence in him as a reliable historian and in history as a diagnostic tool. Herodotus had opened the way for this by examining events of the past to see how those events could be accounted for in terms

> "Consider also, if you follow the advice of Cleon, how much you shall offend likewise in this other point. For in all your cities the commonalty are now your friends, and either revolt not with the few, or if they be compelled to it by force, they presently turn enemies to them that caused the revolt: whereby when you go to war, you have the commons of the adverse city on your side. But if you shall destroy the commonalty of the Mytilenaeans, which did neither partake of the revolt, and as soon as they were armed presently delivered the city into your hands: you shall first do unjustly, to kill such as have done you service; and you shall effect a work besides, which the great men do everywhere most desire. For when they have made a city to revolt, they shall have the people presently on their side; you having foreshewn them by the example, that both the guilty and not guilty must undergo the same punishment." (Thucydides, translated by Thomas Hobbes, *The Peloponnesian War* 3.47.1–3, Diodotus opposing Cleon's view that all the Mytilenaean rebels should be executed)

of general or universal laws. The notion that understanding those laws might allow one to predict the future course of events was not exploited by Herodotus, but in Thucydides, although the notion is never made explicit, it pervades his account of the Peloponnesian War. For Thucydides constantly presents the words and thoughts of the participants in the war as they try to anticipate the course of events and try to persuade others to act in one way or another on the basis of their confident expectations. Then, by describing what in fact subsequently took place, Thucydides allows us to evaluate the success or failure of those predictions. The participants in the war often present their assessments of what is likely to happen by means of formal speeches that Thucydides features as a prominent element of his history. These speeches often take the form of a general's address to his troops or of contributions to a debate in a public assembly. In the latter case, the speeches frequently occur in pairs, in which one speaker expresses support for a policy or a course of action and another speaker opposes it, with each speaker generally providing reasons why he – all the speeches in Thucydides are delivered by men – is confident that events will turn out as he predicts. In this way it becomes relatively easy to see, in the light of Thucydides' description of subsequent events, which of the major players in the conflict had a good understanding of the situation at the time.

Among those whom Thucydides represents as being especially acute in his ability to forecast the future is the Athenian Pericles, three of whose speeches are presented in the opening books of Thucydides' history. Pericles was the leading figure in Athens at the time the Peloponnesian War began. He rose to prominence in the 450s as a champion of popular democracy by supporting the introduction of pay for service on Athenian juries. This measure had the effect of increasing participation in

"Nevertheless you must know, that of necessity war there will be; and the more willingly we embrace it, the less pressing we shall have our enemies; and that out of the greatest dangers, whether to cities or private men, arise the greatest honours. For our fathers, when they undertook the Medes, did from less beginnings, nay abandoning the little they had, by wisdom rather than fortune, by courage rather than strength, both repel the barbarian and advance this state to the height it now is at. Of whom we ought not now to come short, but rather to revenge us by all means upon our enemies; and do our best to deliver the state unimpaired by us to posterity." (Thucydides, translated by Thomas Hobbes, *The Peloponnesian War* 1.144.3–4, Pericles addressing the Athenians before the start of the war)

public affairs among those who needed to be paid for their time; that is, the less affluent Athenians. This group did not include Pericles himself, who belonged to one of the most prominent Athenian families and whose mother was the niece of the democratic reformer Cleisthenes. Pericles' wealth enabled him to serve in the highest public offices in Athens, which he did with some regularity. At this time, the mid-fifth century BC, most public offices at Athens were filled by a process of drawing names at random from among those eligible to serve, on the theory that, in a true democracy, any citizen can serve the public interest as well as any other. This process also ensured that no one individual could be repeatedly elected to public office merely as a reward for pandering to the electorate (the practice preferred by representative democracies today). But there was one office that was immune from selection by lot, and immune as well from the provision that restricted service in many areas of Athenian government to no more than once or twice in a lifetime. That was the office of general, which the Athenians thought required experience and expertise. Every year, 10 generals were chosen by popular election, one from each tribe, and there was no limit to the number of times an individual could be elected to serve in that capacity. While it was not unusual for a prominent citizen to serve as one of the 10 generals on one or two occasions – for example, the poet Sophocles was elected general in 441 BC – Pericles was elected every year or almost every year from 443 BC until his death in 429 BC. As general, he could speak with some authority in the assembly concerning military matters and matters of public policy generally. In addition, he was known to be an especially accomplished public speaker.

There is a heated debate among scholars today regarding the accuracy of Thucydides' reporting of the speeches that he includes in his history, so that it is unclear to what degree he is reproducing Pericles' actual words. Since Pericles' speeches were delivered in public, to an audience that included many of Thucydides' readers, it is reasonable to assume that the general content at least is fairly accurately represented in Thucydides' account. Nonetheless, Thucydides also reports verbatim many speeches at which he was not present, and it is clear that he uses all the speeches for dramatic effect in his own writing. This tends to support the view that, while Thucydides expresses the general content of the actual speaker's words, we must imagine that the specific structure and diction are Thucydides' own. Furthermore, Thucydides himself naturally controls the placement of the speeches in his narrative. For example, in the first book of his history, Thucydides recounts a speech that Pericles delivered in the Athenian assembly before hostilities between

Athens and Sparta actually broke out. In it, Pericles recommends that the Athenians vote in favor of going to war, gives an assessment of the likely progress of the war, and advises his fellow citizens regarding what they ought to do in order to be successful against the Spartans. At the same meeting of the assembly there were many other speakers who, Thucydides tells us, expressed very varied points of view. Pericles' speech, however, is the only one that is reported, partly no doubt because Thucydides wishes to hold it up as a model of clear and sensible thinking, and partly because subsequent events in Thucydides' account will be seen to confirm the accuracy of Pericles' assessment. Pericles predicts that the war will last longer than most people expect. He is confident that the Spartans, lacking in naval resources and experience, will be reluctant to challenge Athenian supremacy at sea, but instead will invade Attica with their superior land forces and destroy the Athenians' crops. But Pericles encourages the Athenians not to be disheartened by these invasions: as long as they maintain control of the seas they will be able to supply themselves from their overseas allies as they keep safe behind the walls that connect the city of Athens to its harbor. In fact, Pericles tells the Athenians that he has great confidence in Athens' prospects for success in the war "as long as you are willing to refrain from further acts of conquest while you are at war and from importing dangers of your own devising; for I am more afraid of our own lapses of judgment than of our enemies' schemes." All of Pericles' predictions will later be confirmed by Thucydides' narrative: the war lasted well beyond anyone's expectations; the Spartans did, indeed, invade Attica nearly every year during the course of the war, but the Athenians were able to supply themselves by sea; as long as the Athenians concentrated their efforts on the war they were in fact successful.

The Athenians' success suffered a disastrous setback precisely when they took it into their minds to expand the war in hopes of extending their control to include the territory of Sicily. This was in 415 BC, after Pericles had died and was no longer available to provide sensible advice. Thucydides makes explicit the contrast between Pericles and those who became the leaders of Athens after Pericles' death: whereas Pericles had only the best interests of the people at heart, those men were for the most part more interested in securing their own personal advancement, and so they threw their support behind whatever appeared to be attractive to the people. The campaign against Sicily was so attractive that Thucydides describes the eagerness of the Athenians using the word *eros*, the Greek word for sexual passion or lust. Both young and old were aroused by the prospect of conquest. In particular, the military and

> "Let not the speech of Nicias, tending only to laziness, and to the stirring of debate between the young men and the old, avert you from it: but with the same decency wherewith your ancestors, consulting young and old together, have brought our dominion to the present height, endeavour you likewise to enlarge the same. And think not that youth or age, one without the other, is of any effect, but that the simplest, the middle sort, and the exactest judgments tempered together, is it that doth the greatest good; and that a state as well as any other thing will, if it rest, wear out of itself; and all men's knowledge decay; whereas by the exercise of war experience will continually increase, and the city will get a habit of resisting the enemy, not with words, but action." (Thucydides, translated by Thomas Hobbes, *The Peloponnesian War* 6.18.6, Alcibiades supporting the expedition against Sicily)

the lower classes were convinced that the wealth of Sicily would provide the Athenian state with limitless funds to confer lifelong employment on all its citizens. According to Thucydides, only the general Nicias recognized that, as Pericles had warned more than 15 years earlier, expansion of the theater of operations was likely to lead to disaster. But Nicias lacked Pericles' charisma and his effectiveness as a public speaker. Those qualities were, however, possessed in abundance by another of the Athenian generals, Alcibiades, who hoped to enhance his political career by leading a successful and profitable attack on Sicily. Thucydides gives the speeches that both men delivered in the assembly, Nicias sensibly urging his fellow Athenians to abandon their ill-conceived plan to invade Sicily and Alcibiades depicting the Sicilian expedition as necessary to ensure Athenian security and hinting that it will prove to be the first step in Athens' eventual domination of all Greece.

Having heard what it wanted to hear from Alcibiades, the Athenian assembly voted to mobilize what Thucydides describes as "the most lavishly funded and most impressive military force deployed by a single Greek city up to that time." Thucydides further describes the magnificent spectacle of the fleet's departure and the unbounded confidence of the Athenian people who witnessed it. The contrast with the utter catastrophe that the expedition suffered two years later could not be greater. Herodotus would presumably have explained the Athenian defeat, at least partially, in terms of divine punishment for the Athenians' overconfidence. There is not the slightest hint of this in Thucydides' account, which presents the Athenian failure instead in terms of poor planning and indecisiveness, particularly on the part of Nicias. In fact, on one crucial occasion, that indecisiveness arose out of Nicias' conventional religious outlook: on August 27, 413 BC, when things were going very badly for the Athenian forces in Sicily and they decided to remove themselves to a more secure location, an eclipse of the full moon took place. Nicias, whom Thucydides characterizes as being "excessively superstitious," refused to order his troops to move until a period of 27 (= 3^3) days had elapsed, the period of time prescribed by the seers. As a result of this delay, the size and morale of the enemy forces were allowed to increase. The Athenians, finding themselves blockaded, were disastrously defeated in a naval battle and were forced to retreat into the interior of Sicily, where many of them, including Nicias, were killed and the remainder taken prisoner.

For Thucydides, then, success in political and military matters depends upon how well men are able to foresee the outcome of their own actions and those of others and how well they are able to convince others of the accuracy of their predictions. Pericles, for example, knew that it would be disastrous for the Athenians to expand the scope of the war; the mass of the Athenians did not know that, and so they embarked on an expedition to Sicily that resulted in the loss of tens of thousands of Athenian lives. What distinguishes men like Pericles from the masses and enables them to excel at predicting the future course of human events? First, extensive experience of the way in which humans behave under various circumstances and, second, a detachment that prevents them from allowing personal bias to color their assessment. (Pericles' aloofness was such as to earn him the nickname "The Olympian," as though he were one of the Olympian gods.) Naturally, experience of human behavior is best acquired directly, by observing events as they unfold and by noting the reactions that they provoke. Most people, however, are limited by personal circumstances and do not have the opportunity to observe as wide a variety of events as they might desire. This, then, is the value of a work like Thucydides' history. Thucydides was himself a general who held command during the early part of the war but, he tells us, because of his failure to hold a strategically important city against the Spartans in the winter of 424 BC, he was exiled (not ostracized) from Athens for 20 years. During that period of exile he had numerous opportunities to observe the events of the war from both sides of the action. Thucydides' account of these events is presented in a strictly chronological narrative divided into successive winters and summers, which helps give the impression that the war is recorded in the most detached and objective way possible. The aim is to give the reader the impression of having witnessed the events personally, thereby acquiring the experience necessary to be able to predict future occurrences that arise out of similar circumstances.

Diagnosis and Prognosis

Some things, of course, cannot be readily predicted, like the sudden appearance of a storm at sea that may affect the outcome of a naval engagement. Thucydides, unlike Herodotus, never suggests that events like these arise from anything but natural causes. One such event was the epidemic that began to afflict Athens in the summer of 430 BC, at the beginning of the second year of the war. The account that Thucydides gives of the disease and its disastrous effects on the Athenians is a model of clinical objectivity. Thucydides himself contracted the disease, but survived; tens of thousands of Athenians, including Pericles, died in the epidemic, whose effects were intensified by the overcrowding within the walls of the city as a result of the Spartan invasion of the Attic countryside. Thucydides does not attribute the disease to any divine visitation and, in fact, he refuses to speculate as to its causes, leaving that instead to the physicians and anyone else in a position to know. For his part, Thucydides will merely record in detail the symptoms, "from which, if the disease should ever recur, someone would best be able to recognize it, by combining observation with foreknowledge."

Observation and foreknowledge figured prominently in the medical literature that was beginning to be written just at the time Thucydides was alive and was to continue being written throughout antiquity. We possess today a large collection of medical treatises written in Greek that circulated in

"In Thasos Crito was walking normally when he was overcome by acute pain in the big toe. Immediately took to his bed, shivering, suffering from nausea, somewhat feverish. Toward nightfall became delirious. Day two: swelling of the entire foot, slight redness along with rigidity about the ankle, small black blisters, high fever, delirium. Passed rather frequent stools of a purely bilious nature. Died on the second day after the onset." (Hippocrates, *Epidemics* 1, patient no. 9) antiquity under the name of Hippocrates. The works in the collection were written over a period of some centuries, beginning at around the time of the Peloponnesian War, so that they are manifestly not the work of one person. There was a physician named Hippocrates, who was a contemporary of Thucydides, but it is impossible to tell which of the works in the collection are his, or even if any of them are by him. Hippocrates came from the island of Cos, just off the southwest coast of Asia Minor, where there was an important school of medicine and a major shrine dedicated to the healing god Asclepius. Hippocrates, like physicians generally in ancient Greece, was considered to be a "descendant of Asclepius," but the Hippocratic writings do not concern themselves with divine influences when discussing either the causes or the cures of diseases. One of the earliest medical treatises, almost certainly written by a contemporary of Thucydides, is entitled *On the Sacred Disease* and deals with epilepsy. The author of the treatise is concerned to show that this disease is caused not by some divine visitation (the belief that gave it the popular name "the sacred disease") but by environmental factors. This treatise and the others in the Hippocratic collection are written in the Ionic dialect and are clearly influenced by the early Ionian philosophers and natural scientists, who were similarly interested in discovering causes and who lived in the same general region of Greece as the authors of the medical treatises. While much of early Greek medical writing is taken up with theorizing about the causes of disease, some of the authors of the earliest treatises recognized as well the importance of case studies. So, for example, the earliest portions of the work called *Epidemics*, also dating from the late fifth century BC, consist largely of detailed clinical case histories that record the day-by-day symptoms of various individuals, in very much the same way Thucydides details the progress of the plague that struck Athens in 430 BC. (The title of the work does not refer to what we call "epidemic diseases," but means "visits to foreign cities"; ancient physicians traveled from city to city and the case histories in *Epidemics* are drawn from various locations along the coast of the northern Aegean.)

> "To the best of my ability and judgment I will employ procedures that are intended for the benefit of the sick. If asked I will not supply anyone with a drug that causes death, nor will I provide advice regarding such a matter. Likewise, I will not give a woman a drug to cause an abortion. I will maintain a pure and holy life and practice. I will not perform surgery, even on those suffering from the stone, but I will yield this practice to the specialists." (Hippocrates, *The Oath* 12–18)

The purpose of compiling medical case histories is to preserve a record in as objective a way as possible of the timing and the sequence of changes in the patient's status. This is necessary both in order to diagnose the disease and to give a well-founded prognosis. In addition, by noting variations among instances of the same disease, the physician can begin to determine how the progress of the disease is affected by treatment or by such factors as the patient's age, constitution, place of habitation, and so on. This seems to be Thucydides' purpose as well, not just in his description of the plague but in his history generally. By recording as accurately as possible the progress of the

Peloponnesian War, Thucydides makes it possible for future readers to compare the events of 431–404 BC with the progress of future conflicts, enabling his readers to foresee and perhaps even alter the course of events in their own time. It is the essence of a science to be able to predict successfully what will result from given circumstances, and it is in this sense that Thucydides' history is "scientific." This is the cause of a curious paradox that inevitably strikes Thucydides' readers: the inherently optimistic character of scientific thinking contrasts jarringly with the grim events to which it is applied in Thucydides' work. Thucydides chronicles not only the horrible destructiveness of the Peloponnesian War in terms of human and material loss, but also the deterioration in moral standards that accompanied the protracted and bitter conflict. Thucydides portrays a Greece that has abandoned human decency and is motivated by nothing but self-interest.

Nowhere is this more horrifyingly displayed than in the section known as the "Melian Dialogue," Thucydides' record of negotiations between the representatives of the Athenian army and of the people of Melos. Melos is an island in the Cyclades, of no particular strategic importance, that wished to remain neutral in the war. In 416 BC the Athenians attacked the island and gave the Melians the option of becoming members of the Athenian alliance either by choice or by force. To the Melians' objection that it is not right for the Athenians to use force on a sovereign people, the Athenians reply that the question of right or wrong is relevant only among those who have equal power. Since Athens is clearly vastly more powerful than Melos, the only means available to the Melians is to persuade the Athenians that it is not in the Athenians' interests to add Melos to their alliance. Since Melos was not a democracy, its representatives lacked the facility in debate for which the Athenians were famous and, in any event, it manifestly was in Athens' best interests to have as many allies as possible, so the Melians fail to persuade the Athenians to let them maintain their neutrality. Being confident that neither the gods nor the Spartans will allow the Athenians to conquer their island, the Melians choose not to join the Athenian alliance. Later that year, the Athenians conquered the island of Melos, killed all the men, sold all the women and children into slavery, and resettled the island with Athenian colonists.

A dozen years later, the Athenians, exhausted and desperate, surrendered to the Spartans, finally ending a war that had lasted almost a generation. The decisive defeat, in 404 BC, does not form part of Thucydides' account, which breaks

> "Life is short; science is vast; opportunity is fleeting; experimentation is risky; judgment is difficult." (Hippocrates, *Aphorisms*, 1.1)

off, unfinished, with the events of 411. Thucydides does recount the disastrous outcome of the Athenians' Sicilian campaign, and he does refer occasionally in passing to the final defeat of 404. It would have been easy, then, for Thucydides to present the Athenians' defeat as, in some sense, a punishment for their immoral dealings, or even as a visitation of divine judgment. He does not do that. Instead, he portrays Athens' downfall as an intellectual failure, as an inability on the part of its leaders to foresee accurately what needed to be done in order to secure the victory that the Athenians would undoubtedly otherwise have won. In what sense, though, is it legitimate to speak of Athens' defeat in the Peloponnesian War as a "downfall"? What Thucydides demonstrates, throughout his account of the war, is the remarkable resilience of the Athenian people, who repeatedly managed to absorb devastating setbacks and responded by renewing their efforts to continue the war. Even after the disastrous Sicilian campaign, which cost Athens an army and a navy, the Athenians regrouped and fought on for nearly 10 more years, winning some significant military victories against Sparta and its allies before finally surrendering in 404. And even then Athens did not lose its independence, although it was no longer in a position to extort financial contributions from its allies. In fact, the end of the Peloponnesian War no more represents the downfall of Athenian society than the end of the Second World War marks the downfall of German or Italian or Japanese society. Yet there has long been a tendency to regard the conclusion of the war as putting an end to a "Golden Age" of Greek, and particularly Athenian, culture. Thucydides' history is in part responsible for inspiring this tendency: its relentless realism and its insistence upon treating the events of the Peloponnesian War from the perspective of the pathologist have conditioned us to think of the war as a symptom of decay. War is, as we know all too well, an inevitable concomitant of human society, just as disease is of the human body. And, just as we sometimes dread a visit to the doctor, fearing that some morbid condition will be disclosed rather than trusting the doctor's capacity for minimizing the effects of any disease that might be found, so our attention is drawn more to the grimness of Thucydides' narrative than to its theoretical promise of enhancing our ability to predict future human actions.

The Invention of "the Classical"

In fact, many of the most glorious achievements of Greek, and particularly Athenian, culture were yet to come. The works of Greece's most influential philosophers, prose stylists, mathematicians, scientists, sculptors, and architects were created in the fourth and the following centuries. But the works that were created in the fifth century, between the beginning of the Persian Wars and the end of the Peloponnesian War, have always been felt to possess a special status, as embodying "the Classical," particularly in the visual arts. Nor has anything been seen to typify "the Classical" more comprehensively than the buildings that were added to the acropolis in Athens between the middle and the end of the fifth century BC (figure 43). When the Persians occupied Athens in 480 and again in 479 BC, they destroyed the temples and other buildings on the acropolis and threw down the many statues that had been dedicated there. Just before the battle of Plataea, the Greek forces that were prepared to resist the Persians swore an oath that, according to some sources, included the following clause: "I will in no manner rebuild any of the temples that have been burned and demolished by the barbarians, but I shall allow them to be left as a reminder to

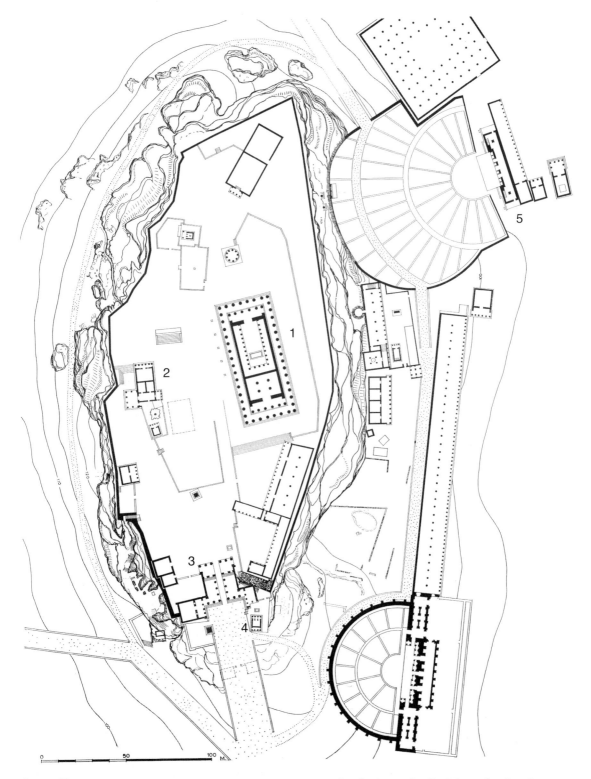

Figure 43 Plan of the acropolis in Athens in the second century AD (1 = Parthenon, 2 = Erechtheum, 3 = Propylaea, 4 = Temple of Athena Nike, 5 = Sanctuary and Theater of Dionysus). Reproduced from J. Travlos, *Pictorial Dictionary of Ancient Athens* (New York 1971), 71.

future generations of the barbarians' impiety." For the next 30 years, this provision of the oath seems to have been adhered to and the Athenians left the site of the acropolis in ruins. By 449 BC, however, circumstances seem to have allowed major rebuilding to take place and at that time, under the leadership of Pericles, the Athenians began construction of the first of several temples and other structures that were to transform the Athenian acropolis. This series of projects continued until shortly after the end of the Peloponnesian War and was financed to some degree by that portion of the allies' monetary contribution that was dedicated to the goddess Athena (see figure 39), in whose honor the buildings were constructed.

In a famous passage near the beginning of his history, Thucydides says that, if the land of the Spartans were abandoned and all that remained were the temples and the foundations of buildings, posterity would find it very difficult to believe that its power was such as to justify its reputation; on the other hand, if the same thing happened to Athens, people would imagine that its power was double what it actually was, judging from the observable aspect of the city. This is a very astute statement on Thucydides' part, and shows his recognition that some states place a high priority on magnificent public buildings while others do not. In the case of Athens, the tyrant Peisistratus had encouraged the development of public building projects along with the expansion of the festivals of the Dionysia and the Panathenaea. The acropolis was the focal point of both those festivals, since it was the site of the sanctuaries of Dionysus and Athena, in whose honor the festivals were held. The construction that began in 449 BC had little effect on the theater and the sanctuary of Dionysus on the side of the acropolis, concentrating instead on the surface of the acropolis, where the Persians had destroyed two large temples of Athena, one of which was still under construction at the time. The Athenians now began construction on a replacement for that temple. The replacement, which took 15 years to complete (from 447 to 432 BC), was the building known as the Parthenon, constructed of marble from Mount Pentelicus in Attica, about 20 kilometers from the acropolis.

At the time of its construction, the Parthenon was the largest building ever to have been erected in mainland Greece. Its importance, however, lies not in its size but in the sophistication of its design and in the refinement of its decoration. Like many Greek temples of the Archaic and Classical periods, the Parthenon consists of a rectangular inner building, usually referred to by the Latin word *cella*, surrounded by columns (figure 44). The plan of the building is based on simple geometric shapes and continues a two-century tradition of temples built to a similar plan. The architects of the Parthenon had learned from the products of that tradition that absolutely straight lines and perfectly uniform angles give an appearance that is mechanical and lacking in spontaneity. For this reason, the marble floor of the Parthenon was made with a very slight rise toward the middle, the columns were made to lean gently inward, and the tapering of the columns included a moderate swelling at the center (figure 45). The visual effect of these subtle deviations from rigid consistency is to give the structure a more pleasing, organic character and to allow it to "breathe." A similar effect is created in music by the sensitive use of phras-

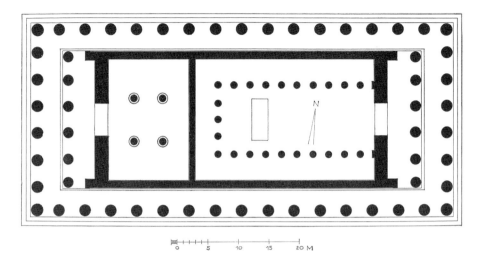

Figure 44 Plan, drawn by Gottfried Gruben, of the Parthenon in Athens; length 72.3 m, width 33.7 m, 447–432 BC. Reprinted with the permission of Himmer Verlag GmbH from G. Gruben, *Die Tempel der Griechen* (Munich 1966) p. 160, fig. 132.

Figure 45   The Parthenon as seen from the northwest. Alison Frantz Collection, American School of Classical Studies at Athens, AT 2.

ing and by slight deviations from strict rhythm to avoid machine-like uniformity. In addition, an organic feel was imparted to the Parthenon by the sculptured decoration that graced parts of the building. This type of decoration was a common feature of ancient Greek temples, but the quantity of the relief sculpture that the Parthenon contained and, as far as we can tell from what has survived, the skill with which it was executed set this building apart. Meager remains can be seen of the sculpture that originally filled the nearly square panels (called metopes) above

PEDIMENT The triangular area under the gabled roof, at either end of a Greek temple or similar structure (figure 45), often filled with RELIEF sculpture.

the spaces between the columns and the large triangular areas (the PEDIMENTS) just under the overhang of the roof at either end. These sculptures, carved in marble and originally painted, represented scenes from mythology. They are very badly preserved, owing to the effects of the elements to which they were for a long time exposed and as a result of defacement, neglect, and belligerence by later Christians and Moslems. (The Parthenon was converted, successively, into a church, a mosque, and an arsenal for the storage of gunpowder.)

The best preserved element of the Parthenon's sculptural decoration is the relief frieze that ran in a continuous sequence around the top of the four sides of the *cella*, about 10 meters above eye level. An unusual amount of attention has been paid over the past two hundred years to this frieze, almost half of which was removed to England between 1801 and 1805, where it is now displayed in the British Museum. Part of the reason for this attention, apart from the pressing ethical question of the appropriateness of these sculptures remaining outside Greece, is the nature of the scene depicted. Rather than portraying mythological scenes, like the reliefs in the pediments and metopes, the frieze appears to represent a procession moving toward the east end of the temple, the end at which one enters the main room of the *cella*. At the east end, the frieze depicts the twelve Olympian gods (figure 46), seated, flanking a scene in which some mortals are engaged in a ritual activity that cannot with certainty be identified. The ritual, witnessed by the gods, is clearly the object of the procession, which occupies the frieze on the other three sides of the *cella*. The participants in the procession appear to be contemporary Athenian citizens; that is, the very people who would see the frieze as they walked around the Parthenon toward its east end. Every year the citizens of Athens celebrated the festival of the Panathenaea, which included a procession through the streets of the city, culminating on the acropolis, at the altar of Athena, where animal victims were sacrificed in her honor (figure 47). The frieze, then, appears to represent either the procession associated with the Panathenaea or some other procession of the sort that fifth-century Athenians were accustomed to participating in themselves. The human figures on the frieze include men and women, old and young (figure 48), so that all Athenians could identify, and identify with, their own counterparts on the frieze. Or, rather, all Athenians could *aspire* to identify with the figures on the frieze: as in advertisements today on television or in glossy magazines, no unattractive or impoverished people are depicted. The frieze portrays an idealized image of the citizens of contemporary Athens, in the presence of the gods.

Worship in ancient Greece generally took place out of doors, in the form of sacrifices at an altar, not inside a temple. The purpose of a temple was to house dedications offered to the god or goddess as well as his or her cult image. In the case of the Parthenon, the cult image of the goddess Athena was particularly impressive. It was made of ivory and gold, costly materials appropriate for a goddess, and was created in the 440s by the Athenian sculptor Phidias. The statue, which stood some 10 meters in height, has not survived, but we know that it represented the goddess with a helmet and shield, holding in her right hand a small, winged female figure, the personification of Victory (NIKE). Athena was the patron and protector of the

NIKE The Greek word for "victory," often capitalized (Nike) to refer to Victory personified as a beautiful goddess, usually winged (figure 64).

Figure 46   Plaster cast, made ca. 1790 before the marble original suffered further damage, of the east frieze of the Parthenon, showing Poseidon, Apollo, and Artemis; height 106 cm, original (now in the Acropolis Museum, Athens) ca. 440–435 BC. Urbana, Spurlock Museum, University of Illinois at Urbana-Champaign (1911.03.0021).

city of Athens, and it was appropriate to attribute to her assistance the victory over the Persians who had invaded the city 40 years before. The figure of Nike in Athena's hand presumably alludes to this victory, which, in a sense, is also commemorated by the general rebuilding on the acropolis of which the Parthenon and Phidias' statue represent the first phase. In quick succession, during the remaining years of the fifth century, three other building projects were begun and completed on the acropolis, serving to complement the Parthenon and enhance its central significance. The first was the construction of an impressively dramatic entranceway to the acropolis, a structure known as the Propylaea (see figure 43), built in the years 437–432 BC, immediately before the outbreak of the Peloponnesian War. The Propylaea used the same Pentelic marble as the Parthenon and harmonized with it in design. Its Doric columns, of the same proportions as those of the Parthenon, marked the transition

Figure 47   Plaster cast of the south frieze of the Parthenon, showing sacrificial victim being led in procession; height 106 cm, original (now in the British Museum, London) ca. 440–435 BC. Urbana, Spurlock Museum, University of Illinois at Urbana-Champaign (1911.03.0010).

from the secular world outside to the sacred space of the acropolis. While the Propylaea marked that transition in unmistakable, monumental fashion, it invited the visitor with its side-wings, giving the impression of outstretched arms, and with a colonnade that provided welcome shade after the arduous climb to the summit of the acropolis.

The two other buildings on the acropolis whose construction followed shortly after completion of the Propylaea were two smaller temples, begun in the 420s BC, the Erechtheum and the Temple of Athena Nike. Unlike the basically Doric Parthenon and Propylaea, these buildings adopted the more delicate and elegant Ionic order. The Erechtheum is a remarkable and sophisticated structure that skillfully negotiates the complexities of the terrain on which it is built (figure 49). Each

Figure 48   Plaster cast of the east frieze of the Parthenon, showing girls and men (serving as marshals?) in procession; height 106 cm, original (now in the Musée du Louvre, Paris) ca. 440–435 BC. Urbana, Spurlock Museum, University of Illinois at Urbana-Champaign (1911.03.0017).

of its three wings lies on a different level and each has its own character, the most distinctive being the south porch, with its roof supported by statues of women ("caryatids") rather than by cylindrical columns. The Temple of Athena Nike, that is, of Athena in her capacity as bringer of victory, was likewise built in the 420s, while the Athenians were engaged in the Peloponnesian War. It is a very small building, only about eight by five meters, but it is dramatically positioned (figure 50): it stands on the bastion next to the Propylaea, so that it is hidden from sight on

Figure 49   The Erechtheum as seen from the west; width (north to south) 23.1 m, length (east to west) 26.9 m, ca. 421–405 BC. Photo: Hirmer Fotoarchiv (Archiv-Nr. 562.1024).

one's right as one mounts the entranceway toward the Propylaea, coming into view only when one is just about to enter sacred ground, and it overlooks the Bay of Salamis, the site of the Athenians' most glorious naval victory.

This temple, like all the fifth-century buildings on the acropolis, is the product of a remarkable sense of confidence and self-assurance: the Athenians had survived the Persian invasion and were now in possession of an empire of their own, whose revenues enabled them to advertise and celebrate their authority by constructing these buildings. The empire and the revenues came to an end during the lifetime of those who worked on the restoration of the acropolis, but the buildings themselves survived not, as Thucydides predicted, to deceive posterity about Athens' military power, but as a monument to the Athenians' cultural achievements, which have turned out to be more impressive and more influential than any accomplishments on the battlefield.

The influence exercised by the fifth-century buildings on the Athenian acropolis can be seen not only in the extensive artistic heritage that looks back upon these

Figure 50   The Temple of Athena Nike seen from the northwest; length (north to south) 8.2 m, width (east to west) 5.4 m, ca. 424–418 BC. Alison Frantz Collection, American School of Classical Studies at Athens, AT-64.

buildings and their decorations as defining moments in Western art and architecture, but also in the image that they convey of ancient Greek religion, an image that is distorted because it is incomplete. The acropolis is so familiar and so visible, seemingly frozen in time, that it is difficult to avoid the impression that it is *the* embodiment of ancient Greek religion. In fact, it is not even the embodiment of ancient *Athenian* religion, much less of *fifth-century* Athenian religion. Religious practices in ancient Greece differed from polis to polis and, even within a single polis, were subject to continual change and evolution. Unlike many religious traditions that we are familiar with today, which are often directed by a central authority and depend upon a written sacred text, Greek religion was multifarious and flexible. The standard Olympian gods were universally acknowledged and worshiped throughout the Greek world, but their roles might differ from one polis to another and one community might place greater emphasis than another community on the worship of a particular god. As its name shows, the city of Athens had a special connection with the goddess Athena and, while the Athenians did not neglect the worship of the remaining gods, they regarded it as especially important to venerate their patron deity. In return, the Athenians were convinced, Athena considered the city of Athens to be among her favorite cities and, consequently, she was particularly inclined to defend and protect it. The goddess Hera, for example, had a similar relationship with the inhabitants of Samos and Argos, and the goddess Artemis with those of Ephesus. Likewise, the names of the cities Poseidonia and Apollonia indicate their intimate connections with the gods Poseidon and Apollo, just as today the cities of São Paulo, San Francisco, and St. Petersburg proclaim their devotion to a particular divine patron.

We may wonder how it came about that one god rather than another was especially venerated in a given location. Often it is difficult or even impossible to tell, because the origins of such practices are lost in the haze of the Dark Age or the Mycenaean Period. The Greeks, too, wondered about the origins of their religious practices. The answer to the question, "How did it come about that Athena is the patron deity of Athens?" is a myth, to the effect that Athena and Poseidon both wished to take possession of so desirable a location as the Athenian acropolis and the ensuing dispute was adjudged in favor of Athena. That does not, of course, explain anything at all and, indeed, it raises more questions than it answers. But an important function of myth is simply to connect (or to appear to connect) the present with the past by means of a story. The story justifies itself merely by being (or appearing to be) coherent and it justifies current practice merely by connecting current practice with the past. For it is essential to the Greeks that religious practice be seen to reflect ancestral custom. This is such a strong feeling that innovations, of which there were many in the long history of Greek religion, were sometimes said to be "revivals" of long-neglected ancestral practice.

Innovation could take the form of new or altered rituals, the introduction of new divinities, or the elaboration, modification, or outright invention of stories about the gods in the form of myths. The worship of gods who had not previously been recognized in the community could be introduced from other parts of Greece, as worship of the Arcadian god Pan was introduced into Athens shortly after the Persian Wars, or from elsewhere, as was the case with the Semitic Adonis in the seventh century and, at a later time, the Egyptian Isis and the Persian Mithras. Subject to general acceptance by the populace, new gods could be welcomed into the polis provided that the existing rituals in honor

"While they were still in the city the generals dispatched a messenger to Sparta. This man was an Athenian named Philippides and his regular job was as a long-distance courier. According to Philippides himself in his report to the Athenians, when he was near Mount Parthenion, which rises up over Tegea, he was met by the god Pan. Pan called out to Philippides by name and told him to bring a message to the Athenians, asking them why they pay no attention to him, despite the fact that he is friendly toward the Athenians and had already proven to be of service to them in many ways and would continue to be in the future. The Athenians accepted this as the truth and, once their situation improved, they dedicated a temple to Pan at the foot of the acropolis and, as a result of what Philippides told them, they seek to propitiate him with annual sacrifices and torch-races." (Herodotus 6.105) of the older gods were not neglected. For the gods did not tolerate rejection or neglect. Just as they were thought to reward and protect those individuals and those cities that paid them respect, so they punished those that refused to worship them. For this reason, it could be dangerous to oppose the introduction of a new cult, but it was equally dangerous to slight a well-established divinity. The safest thing, therefore, was to be inclusive in one's worship of the gods, while not losing sight of the fact that some gods require, and deserve, a higher level of worship than others.

That worship could take a great variety of forms, again subject to the constant development of Greek ritual practice over the centuries. Those forms included prayer, the singing of hymns in honor of the gods, processions, the pouring of libations, and the ritual slaughter of animals as a form of sacrifice. The various forms of worship took place in a variety of contexts and a variety of locations. Thus, for example, animal sacrifice could be carried out by an individual as a thank offering for, say, the safe completion of a journey or by an army in hopes of securing divine favor in an impending battle. Or a sacrifice could be undertaken by an entire community in response to a specific directive from a seer or an oracle in order, say, to put an end to a drought or a plague. Or the sacrifice could be a required feature of a regularly recurring festival, like the annual Dionysia or Panathenaea in Athens. These, however, were only two of the many festivals to be found throughout the year in Athens. And, again, Athens was only one of very many Greek poleis, each with its own schedule of annual, biennial, quadrennial, and so on, festivals. Some of these festivals were joyful, some solemn, some exclusively for men, some exclusively for women, some for boys, some for girls. Thus, which god one worshiped at a particular time, and what form that worship took, depended upon such factors as one's age, status, and gender and which polis one lived in. Indeed, one of the important functions of Greek religious practice was to allow the individual, through his or her participation in various rituals, to define and come to terms with his or her place in the community. Thus, while the buildings on the Athenian acropolis appear to represent the religious expression of the Athenian community, they represent only one aspect – granted an impressive and enduring aspect – of that expression at only one time in Athens' history, and they can convey little, if anything, of what it meant to any given Athenian (or non-Athenian) who stood upon the acropolis and took part in individual or communal worship there.

_____ Recommended for Further Reading

Beard, M. *The Parthenon* (London 2002): an extraordinary and compulsively readable account, in the series "Wonders of the World," of the varied ways the Parthenon has been used, abused, and viewed from the time of Pericles to that of Shaquille O'Neal.

Hornblower, S. *Thucydides* (Baltimore 1987): the most sensible and penetrating introduction to the writing and thinking of Thucydides and to the intellectual context from which his history emerged.

Hurwit, J. M. *The Acropolis in the Age of Pericles* (Cambridge 2004): a detailed and comprehensive examination of the acropolis, its buildings, and dedications, including a CD-ROM with magnificent color images.

Jouanna, J. *Hippocrates*, English translation (Baltimore and London 1999): a comprehensive study of Hippocrates and his enormous influence, by the leading expert on the history of ancient medicine.

Lloyd, G. E. R. (ed.) *Hippocratic Writings* (Harmondsworth 1978): a selection of some of the most interesting and important Greek medical treatises in accurate translations, with an excellent introduction by Lloyd, the leading authority on ancient science.

Neils, J. *The Parthenon Frieze* (Cambridge 2001): an excellent account of the design, the iconography, and the influence of the Parthenon frieze, along with a sensible discussion of the ethical issues connected with its repatriation, illustrated with a CD-ROM that allows the entire frieze to be viewed as a continuum.

Strassler, R. B. (ed.) *The Landmark Thucydides* (New York 1996): the excellent Crawley translation, updated and printed in a brilliantly conceived layout, with numerous maps, helpful headers, and marginal notes, allowing Thucydides' narrative to be followed with ease.

STAGE AND LAW COURT IN LATE FIFTH-CENTURY ATHENS

10

Euripides

Aristophanes

Socrates

Three Athenian contemporaries are the subject of this chapter: the tragic dramatist Euripides, the comic poet Aristophanes, and the philosopher Socrates. The plays of Euripides were quite popular with Athenian audiences but, at the same time, they created considerable controversy. Euripidean characters are exceptionally articulate in their challenging of received notions and in their insistent demands that society and even the gods adhere to a rational pattern of behavior. But Euripides' tragedies are especially characterized by their striking dramatization of irrational behavior on the part of both humans and gods, and the incompatibility between reason and the apparently chaotic world in which his dramas unfold is a major source of the dramatic tension that gripped (and still grips) his audiences. The popularity and the controversial nature of Euripides' tragedies made him a natural target for parody in the comedies of his contemporary Aristophanes. Indeed, "Euripides" appears as a character in more than one of Aristophanes' plays; he is subjected to merciless ridicule along with other prominent Athenian intellectual and political figures. One of those prominent figures is the philosopher Socrates, who is the main object of abuse in Aristophanes' comedy *The Clouds*. In this play, Socrates is portrayed as a godless charlatan who uses his devious intelligence to swindle unsuspecting citizens. Aristophanes may not have believed that Socrates was in fact an atheist, but his portrayal of him as denying the existence of the traditional gods contributed to a prejudice among his fellow citizens that undoubtedly influenced the outcome of a trial that Socrates was subjected to. In 399 BC, for reasons that appear to have been at least partly political, Socrates was prosecuted for impiety. The jury of 501 Athenian citizens, convinced that Socrates was an enemy of their democratic values, voted to convict him and, on a separate vote, condemned him to death.

Throughout the second half of the fifth century BC the Athenians continued to celebrate the annual festival of the Dionysia by watching dramatic performances in the Theater of Dionysus on the slope of the acropolis while the new buildings on the surface of the acropolis were rising up behind them. Tragedies and satyr plays had formed part of the program of the Dionysia since the sixth century; beginning in 486 BC the program also included performance of comedies. The master of this dramatic form, and the only comic playwright of the fifth century whose works survive, was Aristophanes, a slightly younger contemporary of Thucydides. Unlike tragedy and the satyr play, which deal with the heroic past, Attic comedy is set in contemporary Athens and pillories with brutally merciless wit the prominent public figures of the day. We have 11 of the roughly 40 comedies that Aristophanes produced; those eleven date from 425 to 388 BC, and thus provide fascinating evidence of the preoccupations of the Athenians during and immediately after the Peloponnesian War.

Among the objects of Aristophanes' ridicule are the leaders of the democratic government of Athens, who could conveniently be blamed for any military reverses and for all inconveniences occasioned by the war, as well as the most notable intellectuals and literary artists of the time. These latter included two Athenians, the philosopher Socrates and the dramatist Euripides, both of whom Aristophanes represents as utter degenerates who are intent upon destroying the cultural and moral fabric of contemporary society. Aristophanes is a brilliant and hilarious parodist, and the success of his comedies has contributed, along with Thucydides' chronicle of contemporary political events, to the construction of the model that sees the "decline" of Greek culture as beginning to set in at just this time. In fact, Socrates and Euripides, about whom we have considerable evidence independent of Aristophanes' ridicule, are among the most important figures in the history of Western culture, and we should think of them (and Aristophanes himself) rather as restless pioneers in the attempt to comprehend the human experience.

Euripides

Of the three figures to be examined in this chapter, Euripides, Socrates, and Aristophanes, Euripides was the oldest, having been born around 485 BC. Throughout his career, Euripides was in competition with his older contemporary Sophocles; both men produced tragedies and satyr plays at the Dionysia in Athens until their deaths, a year apart, at the end of the fifth century. While Sophocles was remarkably successful with the judges, Euripides only rarely won first prize, in part perhaps because of the controversial and in many ways unsettling nature of his dramas. The tragedies of Aeschylus and Sophocles had been (and continue to be, whenever they are produced on stage) emotionally engaging in the extreme, dramatizing highly charged situations like the murder of near kin and devastating defeat in war. And

Figure 51
Terracotta figurine
of a masked tragic
actor portraying
Heracles; height
8 cm, ca. 250 BC.
Athens, American
School of Classical
Studies at Athens:
Agora Excavations,
T 862.

the emotional effects, as always in Attic drama, were intensified by the music and dance that accompanied portions of the drama. Euripides, too, presented on stage these same types of dramatic situations, even dramatizing on many occasions the very same mythical stories as the older playwrights, but the way in which he constructed his plays and, apparently, the kind of music that he began to employ had the effect of relocating the focus of dramatic effect from the stage to the heart of the audience. We have no access to the music and dance, and no way of comparing Euripides with his predecessors in that respect, but we are told that the music and the musicians used in Euripides' tragedies were characterized by an increased professionalism and by a greater capacity for conveying intense emotion (figure 51).

We have the texts of 17 of Euripides' tragedies and one satyr play. The representation on stage of intense emotion had always been a feature of Attic tragedy: the finale of Aeschylus' *The Persians*, for example, is a lengthy scene of extravagant lamentation, sung and danced by King Xerxes and the Persian chorus. Euripides, too, includes scenes in which the characters of the play react with violent emotion to the dramatic situation, but he often complicates the audience's emotions by causing the audience's perspective to shift during the course of the play. For example, Euripides' famous tragedy *Medea* dramatizes the story of the foreign-born Medea who was married to the Greek hero Jason. Medea had earlier used her intelligence and her knowledge of magic to help Jason on his quest to steal the Golden Fleece. In helping Jason, Medea had to abandon her home and her family, since her father was the king from whom the Golden Fleece was stolen. Now, when the play opens, Jason has decided to abandon his wife of several years and their children in order to marry the daughter of the king of Corinth, where the scene is set. Jason is a thoroughly unpleasant character whose only interest is in his own personal advancement, regardless of the harm he does even to members of his own family. The audience's sympathies, and the sympathies of the local Corinthian women who comprise the chorus, are entirely with Medea, alone and powerless, a woman in a foreign land who has done nothing to deserve the position in which she and her young children find themselves. In the course of the play, Medea decides to avenge herself – with some justification, we are bound to feel – on the husband who has cast her aside. We watch in horror as Medea's vengeance takes the form, first of killing the innocent princess to whom Jason is engaged, and then butchering her own children as a way of depriving Jason of the heirs that his ambition craves. Euripides has skillfully constructed his play so that the audience is carried along with Medea, sharing her anguish and, what is particularly troubling, fully understanding her desire for revenge, until the point is reached where the audience is shocked as much by its own responses as by the actions on the stage.

This pattern, in which the audience initially sympathizes with a character who, by the end of the play, has done things that no audience member would condone, can be seen in a number of Euripides' tragedies. In the *Bacchae*, composed at the very end of Euripides' life and only performed posthumously, the character in question is, remarkably, the god Dionysus himself. Dionysus is the son of Zeus and a mortal woman, a member of the ruling house of Thebes, but his divinity is denied by the current king of Thebes, the young and impetuous Pentheus. As a god, Dionysus is of course entitled to recognition and worship, particularly in the eyes of the audience at the dramatic competition held in Dionysus' honor, while Pentheus deserves punishment for his impious behavior. But the punishment takes a form that any sensible person would find revolting: Pentheus is lured by the god into dressing in women's clothes so he can observe the Dionysiac rites in the mountains, where he is savagely torn apart by the women of Thebes, including most prominently his own mother, whose minds have been unhinged by the god. The effect of all this is to call into question, not only the actions of the characters on stage, but the reactions of the audience as well, which is what makes Euripidean drama even today so unsettling and so "modern."

> "His mother was the first to fall upon him and serve as officiant of the bloodshed. He threw the headband off from his head, so that his poor mother might recognize him and spare him. Reaching out to touch her cheek he said, 'It is I, mother, Pentheus, your son! You bore me in the halls of Echion. Have pity on me, mother, and do not kill your own son! I have done wrong!' But she was foaming at the mouth and her eyes had a crazed look. She could not think straight, being in the grip of bacchic power, so she paid no attention to his words." (Euripides, *Bacchae* 1114–24, a messenger reporting Pentheus' last moments)

Plays by Euripides seemed modern to their original audiences as well, both because they often reflected the latest intellectual trends and because they challenged, sometimes quite directly, the works of older, more established dramatists. Like

Sophocles, Euripides too composed an *Electra*, dramatizing the same events Aeschylus had made the subject of his *The Libation Bearers*. (It is not known which version, that of Euripides or that of Sophocles, is the earlier, but both are certainly later than Aeschylus' play.) In *The Libation Bearers*, Electra discovers at Agamemnon's tomb a lock of hair left as an offering by someone whose footprints are visible. The hair and footprints match her own, but, since she knows that they are not her own, she reasons that they must be those of Orestes, who has apparently returned surreptitiously. In his own play, Euripides tweaks the older dramatist by having an elderly servant rush onto the stage to tell Electra excitedly that he has found a lock of hair and footprints at Agamemnon's tomb and to urge her to go and compare them with her own, hoping that they will turn out to be those of Orestes. Instead, Electra ridicules the old man for his naïveté, pointing out that men and women, even if they are sister and brother, have hair of different textures and feet of different sizes. (The hair and footprints, of course, turn out to be those of Orestes, who has in fact returned surreptitiously; Euripides thus manages to tweak his own audience, as well as Aeschylus and Aeschylus' audience.) *Electra* also illustrates, although not so clearly as *Medea* and *Bacchae*, the characteristic Euripidean shift in sympathy: Electra and Orestes reveal themselves to be considerably less "heroic" than their situation and their pedigree would lead us to expect, while their victims, Clytemestra and her lover, turn out not to be quite the odious villains that Electra portrays them as being. Orestes stabs Clytemestra's lover in the back after he had hospitably invited Orestes, not knowing his identity, to share in a sacrifice and feast; Clytemestra is lured to her death by a fictitious report that Electra has just given birth and she comes to perform the standard ritual of purification for her daughter and grandchild, displaying the maternal feelings that Electra had insistently claimed that she lacked.

The impact of Euripidean drama is produced not only by emotional but by intellectual means. A striking feature of Euripides' tragedies is the extent to which his characters are capable of articulating their state of mind and justifying their actions in well-organized and clearly expressed speeches. Athenian democracy encouraged the development of formal, public oratory and attracted from all over Greece skilled teachers of public speaking and argumentation. Euripides' audience was therefore accustomed to hearing closely argued debates both in the assembly and in the law courts. As we have seen (p. 169), these

"I have only gone on at such length about my own problems because of this competition in words that you initiated. With regard to your condemnation of me in the matter of my engagement to a royal bride, I propose to show, first, that in this particular I am exhibiting my inherently reasonable nature, next, that I am behaving prudently and, what is more, that I am acting as a great friend to you and to my children. Wait! Let me finish! When I came here from the land of Iolcus, with a massive freight of insuperable difficulties, what greater stroke of luck could I, an exile, have happened upon than to marry the daughter of a king? It was not a matter of my finding your bed displeasing and being smitten with a passion for a fresh mistress, which is what seems to have caused your annoyance, nor was I eager to engage in a competition to see who could produce the most children – I have no complaint with the children I have – rather I did this above all so that we could live a decent life and not have to live from hand to mouth." (Euripides, *Medea* 545–60, Jason justifying himself to Medea) practices are reflected in Thucydides' use of pairs of speeches in his history of the Peloponnesian War. Euripides, too, often presents the dramatic conflict in the form of a debate in which two characters deliver formal speeches, sometimes refuting the opposing argument point by point. In *Medea*, for example, there is an extraordinary scene in which Medea condemns Jason to his face, listing the benefits that she has conferred on him and convicting him of ingratitude and violation of his marriage oath. In a speech of almost exactly equal length, Jason responds, arguing that, so far from harming Medea he actually has her best interests at heart and, therefore, she should instead be grateful to him! This is a tactic that was familiar from the contemporary law courts, where the defendant sought to show that, not only was he innocent of the charges, but he was in fact a public benefactor deserving of rewards rather than punishment. In Jason's case, his assertions are so obviously outrageous that his very ability to express himself in so articulate a fashion increases the audience's disgust.

Aristophanes

The world of Euripidean drama is entirely new, its novelty only enhanced by contrast with the rigid dramatic form to whose traditional requirements Euripides strictly adheres. In formal terms, Euripides' tragedies are scarcely distinguishable from those of Aeschylus and Sophocles, but the characters he puts on the stage think and act more like contemporary Athenians than like the mythical figures whose names and situations they are given. For this reason, his tragedies intrigued their original audiences, and for this reason Euripides was an easy target for parody in comedies like those written by Aristophanes. Tragedy and comedy were closely related genres: they were presented competitively as part of the festival of the Dionysia; they were performed exclusively by male citizens wearing masks; they involved a pattern of spoken scenes broken by passages of singing and dancing; and they used many of the same metrical forms. Therefore, it was not unusual for comic playwrights to parody authors and works of the older genre. But Aristophanes ridicules the plots, the characters, and the language of Euripides far more frequently than he does those of any other tragic poet, and he even makes Euripides a character in some of his plays, including three of the plays that survive. In the earliest of Aristophanes' preserved comedies (*Acharnians*, produced in 425 BC), Euripides has only a small part. The hero of the play, an Athenian farmer of modest means who is fed up with the hardships imposed by the Peloponnesian War, has negotiated a personal peace treaty between himself and the Spartans. Since this is treasonable behavior, he needs to defend himself against a crowd of angry neighbors, so he goes to the house of the sophisticated and highly educated Euripides to borrow rags to wear in order to arouse sympathy when he makes his speech of defense. The rags in question are the costume in which the hero of Euripides' (lost) tragedy *Telephus* disguised himself in order to plead his case before his enemies. Euripides has many such costumes and

Aristophanes comically makes his character in *Acharnians* name all of them, the implication being that Euripides habitually parades his tragic heroes on stage in rags to make them appear less "heroic" and to enhance the drama's pathos.

Twenty years later, in 405 BC, Aristophanes made Euripides a major character in his comedy *The Frogs*. The playwright Euripides had recently died and, in Aristophanes' comedy, the god Dionysus is so distraught at the loss of his favorite tragic poet that he determines to go to the Underworld and bring Euripides back to the land of the living, so he can continue creating his passion-filled dramas. Dionysus, the patron of the drama, is himself an unstable and emotionally volatile character, making his particular fondness for Euripides perfectly understandable. When he gets to the Underworld (encountering on the way the chorus of frogs that gives the play its title), Dionysus discovers that Euripides is trying to oust Aeschylus, who died 50 years earlier, from his place of honor among the dead: in the Underworld, just as in the land of the living, the majority are corrupt and undiscriminating, so that Euripides has already attracted a large following. It is decided that a contest is to be held, with Dionysus as judge, to determine which of the two is the more worthy poet. The two characters, Aeschylus and Euripides, appear on stage to argue their case, or, rather, to revile one another. There follows a scene containing some of the most brilliant and hilarious literary parody ever composed. Aeschylus criticizes Euripides on both aesthetic and moral grounds: the younger poet has debased the lofty art of tragedy by trivializing its plots and by introducing depraved characters who shamelessly seek to justify their morally objectionable behavior with clever words. His plots often involve the depiction of erotic passion, which panders to the prurient interests of the masses and which is, Aeschylus contends, beneath the dignity of the tragic genre.

No one, however, panders more shamelessly to the prurient interests of his audience than Aristophanes himself, whose comedies are riddled with sex and with the ancient Greek equivalent of four-letter words (of which the Greek language possesses an impressive supply). These last are characteristic elements of fifth-century Attic comedy, and part of Aristophanes' criticism of Euripides seems to be inspired by the concern that Euripidean tragedy, with its interest in the erotic and its lowering of tragedy's heroic tone, is beginning to encroach upon the territory proper to comedy. In the event, it was comedy that would encroach, in the fourth century BC, upon tragedy, by incorporating numerous features of Euripidean plot, diction, and psychology, and transforming Attic comedy from the polemical and political drama of Aristophanes and his contemporaries into something much more genteel and cosmopolitan. But while Euripides was still active and producing plays at the Dionysia, Aristophanes could not resist capitalizing on the comic potential that Euripidean tragedy provided, and in 411 BC Aristophanes presented his funniest comedy, a play that is saturated with Euripidean parody. The play is entitled *Thesmophoriazusae*, or "Women Celebrating the Thesmophoria." The Thesmophoria was an annual festival held in honor of the goddess Demeter and celebrated exclusively by women. The rites of the Thesmophoria were secret and it was a serious violation of religious custom for a man to be present. This festival, therefore, will have provided one of the very few opportunities for a large number of Athenian women to converse without male interference. Greek men were already paranoid concerning women, as is clear from the many myths involving divine and mortal females who do unspeakable things to men; the prospect of large numbers of women isolated and protected by religious custom must have aroused wild imaginings on the part of Greek men.

"Ladies, having heard the previous speakers' denunciations, it is clear that we have every right to be filled with indignation toward Euripides, even to be thrown into a ferment of rage. I swear by the children I have borne that I too, unless I am out of my mind, hate that man. And yet we women need to be reasonable with one another. After all, we are alone here and what we say will not leave this place. Why do we keep blaming that man and feel resentment if all he did was reveal two or three of our faults when we are guilty of thousands? I can only speak for myself, but I know that I'm no angel. I've done plenty of bad things, but the worst was when I had only been married for three days and my husband was asleep beside me. Well, I had this friend – he was my first lover when I was seven – and his passion for me had gotten the better of him, so he came over and scratched at the door. I immediately knew who it was and I sneaked downstairs to meet him . . ." (Aristophanes, *Thesmophoriazusae* 466–82, the old man in disguise defends his relative Euripides)

When *Thesmophoriazusae* opens, Euripides has received secret information that the women of Athens are going to take advantage of their isolation at the Thesmophoria to plot against him and bring about his destruction. The reason for their hostility toward him is that his tragedies have brought discredit upon womankind by frequently portraying women as overcome by and readily yielding to lust. Euripides, as is clear from his inventive plots, is never at a loss for ingenious schemes, and he now persuades a relative of his, an old man, to disguise himself as a woman and defend him at the Thesmophoria. Euripides promises to rescue the old man if he should get into trouble. When the scene shifts to the Thesmophoria, the old man hears the women delivering speeches, much in the manner of the formal debates familiar from the plays of Euripides, condemning Euripides for persuading the men of Athens that their women are compulsive adulterers and uncontrollable guzzlers of wine. The women do not contend that Euripides has misrepresented their character; on the contrary, their complaint is that he understands all too well women's psychology and has alerted their husbands to the truth, making it more difficult for them to conceal their many vices. The old man, disguised as a woman, then proceeds to defend Euripides, the defense consisting of a detailed enumeration of the many vices indulged in by women that Euripides has *omitted* from his plays. That is, he claims that "we" women are far worse than Euripides makes "us" out to be. The women are outraged and, when they are informed that Euripides has sent a relative to spy on them, they turn upon the old man, who seizes an infant from a nursing mother and flees to an altar for safety. All this is an elaborate parody of a scene from Euripides' *Telephus*, the same scene, in fact, that Aristophanes had parodied in *Acharnians*, in which the disguised king, his identity having been discovered, takes refuge at an altar holding the infant Orestes. In *Thesmophoriazusae*, however, what the woman has been "nursing" is a wineskin, which she is more eager to save than if it had been her own child

Figure 52 Apulian red-figure bell-krater illustrating a scene from Aristophanes' *Thesmophoriazusae*; height of vase 18.5 cm, 370s BC. Würzburg, Martin von Wagner Museum der Universität Würzburg; photo: K. Oehrlein.

(figure 52). There follows an astonishingly inventive scene in which Euripides makes various attempts to save the old man, each attempt based upon a different tragedy in which Euripides the playwright had represented his hero rescuing a damsel in distress. Eventually an agreement is reached: the women consent to release the old man and Euripides promises that he will no longer revile them in his plays.

Aristophanes thus manages to subject to merciless ridicule not only Euripides but the entire female sex. We have already seen, in chapters 3 and 4, that poets like Hesiod and Semonides have little to say about women that is not defamatory. It seems clear that those poets were addressing themselves to a largely, if not exclusively, male audience. But what about Aristophanes? Was the audience at the festival of the Dionysia entirely or predominately male? The evidence, unfortunately, does not allow us to answer that question with any confidence. What is interesting is that, even if women regularly attended the theater, the exclusively male dramatic poets, addressing their audience through the lips of an exclusively male cast, seem to assume that the audience as a whole shares their view that women belong to a different category from themselves. Even so, that does not justify (nor could anything justify) the almost entirely negative tone that characterizes Aristophanes', and other Greek poets', treatment of women. While it is not possible to understand fully the attitude of ancient Greek men toward women (or of Greek women toward themselves), we can begin to make some sense of it in terms of a concept that pervades Greek thinking about status, namely the concept of constraint. So, for example, what distinguishes a free male citizen from a slave is that, unlike the latter, the former cannot legally be constrained by another person. If an Athenian citizen falls upon hard times and becomes impoverished, he can be thought of as being constrained by circumstances, but he cannot, after the reforms of Solon (p. 130), become the slave of another citizen. In the eyes of Greek men, women pose the danger of a particularly interesting and particularly insidious form of constraint.

Everyone is subject to the constraint of sexual desire. For a man to be affected by desire for a woman is, of course, perfectly natural, but it has the effect – unwelcome to a free Greek male – of allowing another person a measure of power over him. (The equally natural desire of a woman for a man was not so problematic, as it did not diminish a woman's status to be subject to the attractive power of a man.) In order to assert their control in the face of this troublesome situation, Athenian men, and men in ancient Greece generally, made sure that women's opportunities for exercising constraint were limited. This was particularly the case among the wealthier members of the class of citizens; the poor and the enslaved had less need to be concerned with preserving their status. As we saw in chapter 8, the tasks expected of a woman from a family of upper-class citizens kept her indoors much of the time, while her husband's days were spent largely outside, supervising agricultural work or participating in public life in the agora or the assembly. That is not to say that women were strictly secluded, but their opportunities for free movement outside the house were limited. Weddings and religious festivals, like the one that serves as the setting for Aristophanes' *Thesmophoriazusae*, provided occasions for female socialization, as did visits to relatives, but there was little in a woman's life to compare with the daily freedom of the adult male citizen to go where he liked and see whom he wished to see.

"What claim do you have even to count as a man? You allowed yourself to be robbed of your wife by a man from Phrygia, when you left her at home unattended and not properly secured, as though the wife you had in your house was chaste, rather than the biggest slut of all. A Spartan girl couldn't be chaste even if she wanted to be. They dash out of the house, wearing skimpy dresses and with thighs bare, to join the boys at the track and – what I find really intolerable – at the gym. Is there any reason to be surprised, then, that you Spartans can't train your wives to be chaste?" (Euripides, *Andromache* 591–601, Peleus addressing Menelaus)

There were, however, exceptions. The majority of the evidence that we have for women's life, like the majority of the evidence that we have for everyday life in general, comes from democratic Athens, a polis that seems to have imposed constraints on its female inhabitants to a greater extent than other Greek cities. Spartan women, for example, were more visible than their Athenian counterparts, both in the sense that they could appear in public more freely and in the sense that they could be seen participating in athletic activities wearing outfits that exposed even their shoulders and ankles, for which they were occasionally condemned by (male) Athenian writers (figure 53). Even in Athens not all women adhered, or could adhere, to the pattern suggested in the previous paragraph, a pattern that reflects the situation of an idealized, that is to say reasonably wealthy, woman of the citizen class. Many women must have been forced by their economic condition to earn money themselves. For example, one of the women in Aristophanes' comedy says that her husband was killed in the war, leaving her with five children to

Figure 53 Bronze figurine of a Spartan girl; height 11.4 cm, ca. 520–500 BC. London, British Museum, GR 1876.5–10.1 (Bronze 208); photo: HIP/Art Resource, NY.

support, which she did by selling myrtle wreaths in the market. (These wreaths were worn by participants in religious rituals, and the woman complains that her business is wilting because Euripides' tragedies have had the effect of persuading the Athenians that the gods do not exist.) The only opportunity for a woman to attain something approaching financial independence in Athens was by means of prostitution, a profession that was promoted by the Athenian men's habit of waiting until the age of 30 or so before marrying. Yet this "independence" too was limited. Prostitution was not generally a profession entered into by choice, but rather because of the constraints of poverty or other unavoidable circumstances. In any event, most prostitutes were either slaves or aliens, so that their status, even disregarding their gender, consigned them to a subordinate position in the polis.

Socrates

Much of the humor in Aristophanes' comedies, it is clear, is crude and ribald, but much of it, equally clearly, is quite sophisticated and requires of the audience an intimate familiarity with details of the wording of the dramas, by Euripides and by others, that Aristophanes parodies. Written texts of these dramas were exceedingly rare, so that the audience's familiarity was generally based on the single performance that was given at the Dionysia, in some cases many years previously: Euripides' *Telephus*, for example, was produced in 438 BC, yet Aristophanes was still using it to raise laughs over a quarter of a century later. This testifies to the importance of Euripidean drama in the lives of the Athenians at the time of the Peloponnesian War and to the ability of that audience to appreciate the intellectual finesse of Aristophanes' parodies. We today are able to appreciate Aristophanes' humor in some instances because we possess written copies of the works that he parodies and we can compare in leisurely fashion original and caricature side by side.

In several cases the originals are no longer extant – that is the case, for instance, with Euripides' *Telephus*, of which only fragments survive – and often the objects of Aristophanes' humor are not written texts but contemporary intellectuals, politicians, and other public figures whose personal quirks were such as to inspire comic satire. That was the case with Aristophanes' *The Clouds*, originally performed in 423 BC, whose main character is the colorful Athenian philosopher Socrates. Socrates was a brilliant and influential thinker, but he never committed his ideas to writing, so it is exceptionally difficult for us to assess the accuracy of Aristophanes' criticisms of him. In fact, *The Clouds* represents the earliest evidence (if "evidence" is the right word) for this extraordinary individual and is the only account we have that dates from Socrates' lifetime.

That lifetime lasted from about 470 BC until Socrates was executed in an Athenian prison in 399 BC. He was, then, a vigorous man in his late forties when his fellow citizens sat down to watch *The Clouds*. Only a few months previously he had fought as a hoplite in one of the early battles of the Peloponnesian War, his hoplite status indicating that he was at least moderately well-off financially. This accords with the presentation of Socrates in *The Clouds*, for in his comedy Aristophanes depicts him as a man of leisure who runs a sort of advanced research institute, with a number of dedicated disciples who have come to study under the direction of The Master. The subjects studied include linguistics, geometry, and the physical sciences, particularly astronomy and cosmology. When the audience first sees Socrates he is suspended high above the stage, investigating celestial phenomena from a position like that of a god. Socrates literally and figuratively looks down upon ordinary mortals, whose thoughts are weighed down by the Earth's moisture, while his own mind is clear and elevated.

The institute, which is given the comic name "The Reflectory," is presented almost as though it were a religious institution, in which the disciples receive a kind of secret initiation into its mysteries. These mysteries, however, have nothing to do with traditional Greek religion; in fact, Socrates and his fellow intellectuals have entirely explained away the Olympian gods and have replaced them with natural phenomena like air currents and the clouds that make up the play's chorus. These natural phenomena are the divinities that Socrates and his disciples now worship; Aristophanes represents Socrates

> SOCRATES: These Clouds here are the only divinities. Everything else is a crock.
> STREPSIADES: But what about Olympian Zeus? Come on! Surely he's a god?
> SOCRATES: What Zeus? Don't be an idiot. There's no such thing.
> STREPSIADES: Huh? Then who causes the rain? That's what I need to know most of all.
> SOCRATES: They do, of course. And I'll prove it to you. Come on! When have you ever seen it raining when there are no Clouds? If it were Zeus who caused the rain he ought to be able to do it on his own, on a clear day when the Clouds are on vacation. (Aristophanes, *The Clouds* 365–71)

explicitly as denying the existence of Zeus and the other Olympian gods. Similarly, in *Thesmophoriazusae*, as we have seen, one of the women accuses Euripides of making atheism fashionable, so that lack of respect for the traditional gods seems to have been a standard charge directed at the purveyors of new ideas at this time. This is potentially a very serious charge. Religion in ancient Greece is not exclusively a matter of personal belief or individual observance, but is a communal concern. If the entire community does not participate in the traditional ritual practices, the gods will feel slighted and may be justified in punishing the entire community. But Aristophanes is producing comedies, not accusations in a court of law, and there is no compelling reason to believe that Aristophanes sincerely regarded either Euripides or Socrates as guilty of impiety.

There is, however, additional evidence that Socrates held religious beliefs that were not shared by his contemporaries, and this evidence comes from sources that are quite sympathetic toward Socrates. The Athenians Plato and Xenophon, both of whom were devoted followers of Socrates and both of whom composed works that attempted to convey in writing the experience of conversing with Socrates in person, represent Socrates as mentioning an unnamed divine entity that communicated directly and uniquely with him. Both men are very careful to make it clear that Socrates did not neglect traditional ritual practices; indeed, both Plato and Xenophon go out of their way to claim that Socrates was the most upright and pious of men. *The Clouds* was produced at a time when the Athenians were involved in a major war and only a few years after their city had been ravaged by a devastating

"I suppose it must seem odd to you that I go around and give this kind of advice in private and get involved with people's personal lives but I can't bring myself to enter politics and get up in front of the people to tell them what I think is in the best interests of the polis. The reason for this, as I have often said in your hearing in a variety of settings, is my experience of a divine and supernatural entity, the very one that Meletus holds up to disrespectful ridicule in his indictment. This is something that began for me in childhood. It comes in the form of a voice which, whenever it comes to me, never prompts me to do something but always merely restrains me from doing what I am about to do. It is this which has opposed my entering politics, and I think this opposition has been a blessing. For you are well aware, my fellow Athenians, that if I had attempted at an early age to enter political life I would have ended my life at an early age, without having done any good either to you or to myself." (Plato, *The Apology of Socrates* 31c–d)

SOPHIST   One of a number of specialists in higher education who traveled through the Greek world, beginning in the fifth century BC, giving public displays of their expertise and offering instruction in a variety of subjects, particularly formal oratory.

HERM   A sculptural representation of a mortal or a divinity, usually the god Hermes (hence the name), in the form of a pillar surmounted by a head and furnished with genitals (figure 54).

epidemic, which some contemporaries undoubtedly attributed to divine disfavor. It is likely, therefore, that Aristophanes was simply reflecting a popular view, that the advanced thinkers of the day, like Socrates and Euripides, were engaged in a program of probing and questioning that was in danger of overturning traditional beliefs and values. Most of the advanced thinkers of the day were not Athenians, but many of them spent time in Athens and made a name for themselves, some of them as highly paid private teachers, whom we have come to call SOPHISTS. Aristophanes is not concerned to ridicule non-Athenians, except incidentally; the main targets of his humor are Athenian citizens, whom he can count on to be well known to his Athenian audience. So, it seems, Aristophanes has attributed to Socrates some views that Aristophanes may himself have known that Socrates did not hold but that were held by prominent non-Athenian sophists. The fact that Socrates was thought to have personal contact with some mysterious divine entity would have made it easy, particularly in the context of a farcical comedy, to pretend that Socrates had turned his back completely on the gods that the rest of the polis worshiped.

There were in fact, at the time of the Peloponnesian War, men who had turned, or who were thought to have turned, their back on the traditional gods. Around 415 BC, the Athenian assembly set a price on the head of Diagoras of Melos (often referred to in our sources as "Diagoras the Godless") because he allegedly ridiculed the mystery rites that were celebrated annually in the deme of Eleusis and because he tried to discourage people from having themselves initiated into the mysteries. At about the same time, shortly before the Athenian fleet was to set sail to attack Sicily, someone had gone through the streets of Athens in the middle of the night and had vandalized the many statues of Hermes (called HERMS) that stood outside houses and in public places. These herms took the form of a pillar surmounted with a head of Hermes and equipped with prominent male genitals (figure 54). Many people must have thought that this act of desecration of the images of a god was at least partly responsible for the Athenian defeat in Sicily. The atmosphere in Athens at the end of the fifth century was such that it was dangerous to raise questions concerning traditional religious forms. This, presumably, is why Protagoras, the leading sophist of the day and a man who spent a considerable amount of time in Athens, expressed himself as cautiously as he did in the opening of his (now lost) treatise *On the Gods*: "Concerning the gods, I am in a position to know neither whether

Figure 54 Interior of red-figure cup, attributed to the Triptolemus Painter, showing a man carrying a provocatively phallic sack past a herm; diameter of figured scene 15.5 cm, ca. 490 BC. Berlin, Antikensammlung, F 2298; copyright 2002 Bildarchiv Preussischer Kulturbesitz, Berlin; photo: Jutta Tietz-Glagow.

they exist or not nor what their character is; among the many factors that hinder knowledge are the inscrutability of the matter and the brevity of human existence." Protagoras claimed to be able to argue both sides of any issue with equal effectiveness and he was greatly admired for his rhetorical skill, which he was willing to teach to anyone in exchange for a substantial fee. He seems to have drawn the line, however, at arguing for and against the existence of the gods.

It is clear that, at the time *The Clouds* was produced, a number of radical and potentially subversive ideas were in the air, and Aristophanes seems blithely to have attributed the lot of them to the Athenian Socrates, who at one point in the play is referred to as "Socrates of Melos," as though he were indistinguishable from the godless Diagoras, the most notorious inhabitant of Melos. Aristophanes presents Socrates as being prepared, like Protagoras, to teach his disciples how to argue effectively for any position, even an outrageously immoral one: at one point a young pupil of Socrates seeks to persuade his father that he, the son, is justified in battering his father, having been shown how to use Zeus' mistreatment of his father as a precedent. This portrait of Socrates, as a godless and immoral sophist who taught the young men of Athens disrespect for tradition and for their elders, made an indelible impression on the Athenians and nearly a quarter of a century later, in 399 BC,

Socrates was successfully prosecuted before a popular court for impiety. The specific charges were that "Socrates is guilty of not recognizing the gods that the polis recognizes, importing instead other new divine entities; in addition, he is guilty of corrupting young men."

Obviously, charges like these are especially difficult to prove, and equally difficult to refute. But Athenian popular courts did not operate under the same rules of evidence or proof that we are accustomed to in a modern courtroom. In fact, it cannot be said that there were rules regarding these matters at all, nor was there a judge to enforce them if they had existed. The court before which Socrates was tried was presided over by one of the magistrates of the state whose annual appointment was determined by lot and the jury consisted of 501 Athenian citizens. A jury of this size was not at all unusual in Athens; the large number was intended to frustrate the expected attempts at bribery and to encourage the notion that the jury was genuinely representative of the citizen body. (In fact, since the pay for jury duty was less than what an able-bodied man could expect to earn from manual labor, the jurors tended to be poor, elderly, and, if we are to believe Aristophanes' satire of the legal system in his comedy *The Wasps*, notably ill tempered.) There was no arm of state government that was charged with prosecuting violations of law; rather, it was up to individual citizens to bring charges, and often individuals were inspired to bring charges from personal or political motives.

Almost nothing about the trial of Socrates apart from its outcome is free from controversy. We do not know what the real motives were that caused these charges to be brought, nor do we know what arguments were used on either side. Three Athenian citizens joined in the accusation of Socrates, two of whom are quite obscure but the third, Anytus, was a prominent political figure. He had been a general during the Peloponnesian War and was instrumental in the restoration of democracy in 403 BC. Following the Athenian surrender in 404, Sparta had allowed an oligarchic government to take power in Athens. This government consisted of 30 wealthy Athenian citizens who came to be known as The Thirty Tyrants because their brutal and rapacious regime resulted in the murder of hundreds of democratic leaders and the confiscation of their property. Anytus and several other supporters of the democracy went into exile during the "tyranny" of The Thirty. When they returned in 403 to overthrow the government of The Thirty and restore the democracy, there was bitter resentment of those who had been sympathetic toward The Thirty. In order to minimize the damage that this resentment might cause, an amnesty was enacted that prohibited the prosecution of Athenian citizens other than The Thirty for crimes committed before 403. This amnesty had the effect of encouraging a certain degree of creativity on the part of those who wished to indulge their resentment and to demonstrate the power of the newly restored democracy.

The accusation of Socrates may have been one of the many creative prosecutions that ensued. For some members of The Thirty and a number of their relatives and supporters had been among the young men who were known to have associated with Socrates. Of these, the most notorious was Critias, who was the most ruthless and despised member of The Thirty. Critias was also the author of tragedies and philosophical works. These works have not survived, but we do have a fascinating 40-line quotation from one of his dramas in which a character claims that "some devious and clever man" fabricated the idea of the gods in order to intimidate wrongdoers with the threat of divine punishment. Sentiments like this could easily be thought to derive from the corrupting influence of the godless man whom Aristophanes had portrayed in *The Clouds*. Another Athenian who was known to have associated in his youth with Socrates was Alcibiades. Alcibiades was not connected with The Thirty, but he had been accused of involvement in the vandalizing of the herms in 415, when he was one of the 10 Athenian generals. Rather than face prosecution, he had fled to the enemy and had joined the Spartan war effort against Athens. Socrates was, then, guilty of association with notorious enemies of the democratic state and this undoubtedly contributed to his prosecution and eventual condemnation.

What was it that attracted Critias, Alcibiades, and many other wealthy and talented young Athenians to Socrates? The fact of the matter is that we do not know. Nor, presumably, did the members of the jury. The jurors' ignorance encouraged them to imagine the worst and to condemn him. Our ignorance encourages the writing of countless books and articles on "the Socratic problem." The problem consists in the fact that the only direct evidence we have, apart from *The Clouds*, that derives from people who actually knew Socrates are the works of Plato and Xenophon, who were in their late twenties at the time of Socrates' trial. They belonged to the same upper class of Athenians from which most of Socrates' admirers were drawn; in fact, Plato was a relative of Critias as well as of Charmides, another member of The Thirty and an admirer of Socrates. After Socrates' trial and death both Plato and Xenophon wrote many works in which Socrates is a character. It is scarcely surprising that this Socrates bears little resemblance to the morally bankrupt character satirized in Aristophanes' comedy; frustratingly, Plato's Socrates and Xenophon's are very different from one another. What the two have in common can probably be taken as representing a reasonable portrait of the real Socrates. Unfortunately, it amounts to very little indeed and that little conflicts markedly with what we find in Aristophanes: the Socrates of Plato and Xenophon did not teach in any formal sense and certainly did not charge a fee for instruction. Instead, he spent his time for the most part in public places in the city eagerly engaging in conversation with anyone who shared his interests. Those interests were not at all connected with linguistics, geometry, and the physical sciences, but almost exclusively with questions of ethical behavior and moral character.

This is not very concrete and may be thought to be a description that could fit any number of Athenians. Clearly, there was much more to Socrates' character than this. Still, even this little can be seen to be politically subversive in the context of democratic Athens. The fact that Socrates did not engage in formal instruction and did not charge a fee set him apart from the sophists, who claimed to be able to teach virtually anything and who prided themselves on the size of their earnings. Only the very wealthiest citizens could afford the services of the sophists, and yet there is something inherently democratic about the sophists and their teaching. Democratic Athens operated on the assumption that public office could be filled by any citizen, as is clear from its use of a lottery for selecting most public officials, and the sophists accordingly advertised their services as guaranteed to confer on any citizen the ability to be an effective public speaker and to hold successfully a position of leadership. This is why the sophists spent so much of their time in democratic Athens rather than in oligarchic cities, even in quite wealthy oligarchic cities like Corinth. For an oligarchic government is based on the conviction that there is an inherent and inborn quality or set of qualities by virtue of which oligarchs are naturally suited to rule. This distinction is nicely articulated in a speech that Thucydides puts into the mouth of a Corinthian envoy trying to persuade the Spartans to go to war with Athens in 432 BC. The Corinthian acknowledges Athens' obvious military superiority at sea, but he insists that Sparta, Corinth, and their Peloponnesian allies can easily learn skill in naval warfare, whereas the Athenians can never attain by instruction the innate superiority that the Peloponnesians enjoy in character and in courage. By spending his time discussing ethical issues, Socrates must have seemed to his fellow citizens to consider himself an expert. But by declining to teach (and perhaps even rejecting the notion that such things can be taught at all) he must have seemed entirely too sympathetic to the oligarchic way of thinking, and the oligarchs, after all, had been "the enemy" in the recent war and had inflicted an appalling reign of terror on the city in the war's aftermath. All of this will have been confirmed in the minds of many jurors by the fact that Socrates' closest associates included several of those very oligarchs.

> "So, given the kind of man I am, what penalty do I deserve? A proper one, my fellow Athenians, if the assessment is truly to be made according to my merits, a proper sort of thing that would be suitable for me. So, what is suitable for a man of modest means whose role as a public benefactor requires leisure in order to serve as an inspiration to you? There is nothing more suitable, my fellow Athenians, than that a man like that should be fed at public expense at city hall, much more so than if one of your citizens has won a prize at the Olympic Games in the horse race or in the two- or four-horse chariot race. After all, he merely makes you think you are blessed whereas I confer true blessings on you. Also, he doesn't need to be given nourishment whereas I do."
> (Plato, *The Apology of Socrates* 36d)

The writings of both Plato and Xenophon include works that purport to record all or part of the speech that Socrates gave to the jury in his defense. (The Greek for "speech for the defense" is *apologia*, and so each of these works is called *The Apology of Socrates*.) These works bear scant resemblance to one another, but what little they have in common strongly suggests that Socrates' manner of speaking further antagonized the jury: Socrates expressed his conviction that he had done nothing wrong and, what must have considerably annoyed the jury, gave the impression that his personal sense of his own innocence mattered much more to him than the jury's verdict. He asserted that the divine entity that occasionally communicated with him made no effort to oppose the method of defense that he was using, thus suggesting that his apparent condescension toward the jurors had at least the tacit approval of the gods. Further, he recounted the story of one of his associates who had gone to Delphi to consult the oracle of Apollo and was told that there was no one either (according to Plato) wiser or (according to Xenophon) more free, more just, or more moderate in his ways than Socrates. Since juries in Athens thought of themselves as truly representative of the democratic citizenry of the polis, Socrates' superior attitude seemed to constitute convincing proof of his oligarchic frame of mind. The jury condemned Socrates by a vote, apparently, of 280 to 221. There were no fixed penalties in Attic law for trials of this nature; instead, the accuser and the condemned each proposed a penalty and the jury was required to choose between them. Socrates' accusers proposed the death penalty, while Socrates, after first claiming that he was in fact a public benefactor deserving of rewards rather than punishment, proposed a fine equivalent to about 13 kilos of silver, to be paid by his wealthy friends. The jury, no doubt thoroughly exasperated by this point, elected the death penalty by a vote of 360 to 141. That is, some of those who had earlier voted "not guilty" now voted in favor of putting Socrates to death. The voice of the democracy had spoken. But Plato, whose writings we will examine in the following chapter, was to have the last word.

Recommended for Further Reading

Conacher, D. J. *Euripidean Drama: Myth, Theme and Structure* (Toronto 1967): the best general introduction to Euripides, emphasizing the variety of his output and the complexity of his drama.

Dover, K. J. *Aristophanic Comedy* (Berkeley and Los Angeles 1972): an excellent introduction to all aspects of Aristophanes and his theater, by the leading Aristophanic scholar of the twentieth century.

Euripides. *Ten Plays*, a new translation by Paul Roche (New York 1998): a very reasonably priced volume containing over half of Euripides' surviving dramas in fresh, readable translations.

Henderson, J. (trans.) *Three Plays by Aristophanes: Staging Women* (London 1996): brilliant, uncensored, contemporary translations of *Thesmophoriazusae* and two other Aristophanic comedies that are particularly concerned with women's issues.

Kerferd, G. B. *The Sophistic Movement* (Cambridge 1981): a brief and very perceptive introduction to the sophists and their important place in the intellectual and social life of fifth-century Greece.

Reeve, C. D. C. (ed.) *The Trials of Socrates: Six Classic Texts* (Indianapolis and Cambridge 2002): excellent translations, with helpful notes, of Aristophanes' *The Clouds* and of works by Plato and Xenophon concerned with the trial, imprisonment, and execution of Socrates.

Sprague, R. K. (ed.) *The Older Sophists* (Columbia, SC 1972): a complete translation of the fragments and the surviving works of the fifth-century sophists.

Stone, I. F. *The Trial of Socrates* (Boston and Toronto 1988): a lively and provocative book, by a man who was neither classicist nor philosopher, which takes seriously the political background and which illustrates the passions that the figure of Socrates can still arouse.

THE TRANSFORMATION OF THE GREEK WORLD IN THE FOURTH CENTURY

11

The trial of Socrates had a profound effect on his most brilliant and creative follower, the Athenian Plato. Plato's philosophical outlook was inspired by Socrates' persistent investigation of basic ethical matters, but in the course of his career he made fundamental contributions to nearly every branch of philosophical inquiry. He did this, not by composing a series of philosophical treatises, but in the form of dialogues, most of which feature the figure of Socrates in fictional conversations with other intellectually committed contemporaries. The ideas presented and discussed, however, are largely those of Plato himself, which have been the subject of intense philosophical discussion ever since. Plato did not confine himself to committing his philosophy to writing; he also established at Athens a school, the Academy, which allowed him and his followers to engage in the pursuit of philosophy without the need for participating actively in the chaotic political affairs of fourth-century Greece. Those affairs were in the hands of political leaders and advisers who used their study of the art of rhetoric to become persuasive molders of public opinion. The most potent fourth-century orator was the Athenian Demosthenes, who repeatedly warned his fellow citizens of the menace to their freedom posed by the growing power of Macedon, under the leadership of King Philip II. Demosthenes' eloquence, however, was no match either for Philip's military might or for Athenian indolence and, by 338 BC, Philip effectively brought Athens and virtually all the other mainland poleis under the control of one leader for the first time in Greek history. On Philip's death two years later, his kingdom and control of the Greek poleis fell to his son, Alexander the Great, who sought to unify the Greeks by leading an invasion aimed at the conquest of the Persian Empire. As a result of the exceptional discipline and training of the Macedonian troops and, particularly, the brilliance of Alexander's military leadership, this invasion was entirely successful. By the time he died, apparently of natural causes at the age of 32, Alexander had made himself sole ruler of an empire that included Egypt, Greece, and all of Asia west of the Indus River valley. Alexander had not, however, left an heir to his throne, and his empire was immediately divided up among his generals.

Plato's Bright Ideas

Attic Oratory in the Fifth and Fourth Centuries

Philip II of Macedon and the Conquest of Greece

Alexander the Great and the Conquest of Asia

Throughout the Archaic and Classical periods, Greek civilization had developed within the context of the polis, with each polis following its own calendar of festivals, minting its own coins, choosing its own form of government, raising its own army, and so on. In many respects, that was to continue to be the case for centuries to come, at least for the majority of Greeks, who confined their activities to their native polis and thought of themselves first and foremost as Corinthians or as Argives or as Syracusans rather than as Greeks. But the Peloponnesian War had brought about a significant change of perspective that affected nearly all the cities in Greece. Athens had sought to create an alliance that would unify the Greek poleis. That alliance was successful in its primary aim of forestalling a possible further invasion by the Persians, but its result was that the Athenians began to run the affairs of their "allies" while the Spartans felt that they needed to "liberate" those poleis from Athenian domination. Eventually the Persians recognized that they could benefit from this situation, by helping to ensure that neither side in the Peloponnesian War became too dominant: they used funding, and even the mere promise of funding, in creative ways to prolong the war and to encourage disunity among the Greek poleis. Many poleis saw their form of government fluctuate between oligarchy and democracy depending on external circumstances, with Sparta promoting oligarchy among the poleis that it "liberated" and Athens promoting or even imposing democracy among its "allies." Even Athens itself briefly adopted an oligarchic government on two occasions, first in 411 BC and then, under the Thirty Tyrants, in 404. The war had polarized the Greek cities; the experience of Melos (p. 175) revealed the danger of attempting to remain neutral, and cities found that they had to align themselves with one side or the other to retain any hope of security. And the population of each polis was often polarized between the oligarchs, who favored alignment with Sparta, and the democrats, who naturally inclined toward Athens.

The fate of Socrates illustrates the effect that these tensions could have even on a citizen who had not committed himself to a life of political activity. Like other citizens of democratic Athens, Socrates had performed the civic functions expected of him, serving in the army and, on at least one occasion, being selected by lot to a one-year term on the Council of 500, but he did not seek to make a name for himself in the political sphere. In this regard, he was somewhat unusual, since political ambition was generally characteristic of men of his level of education and intellectual accomplishment. But in the changed circumstances that emerged from the Peloponnesian War, a number of intellectuals began to follow in Socrates' footsteps, forsaking the political life for the life of the mind, either because of the perils inherent in politics or because the affairs of the polis (which is what the word "politics" means) no longer seemed to be under the control of its citizens. One of those intellectuals who retreated from politics was the philosopher Plato, whose works we will consider in this chapter. By contrast, we will also examine the writings of some of his Athenian contemporaries who did not remove themselves from public view and who developed the art of oratory into a powerful instrument of literary expression. Finally, we will discuss the careers of King Philip II of Macedon and his son

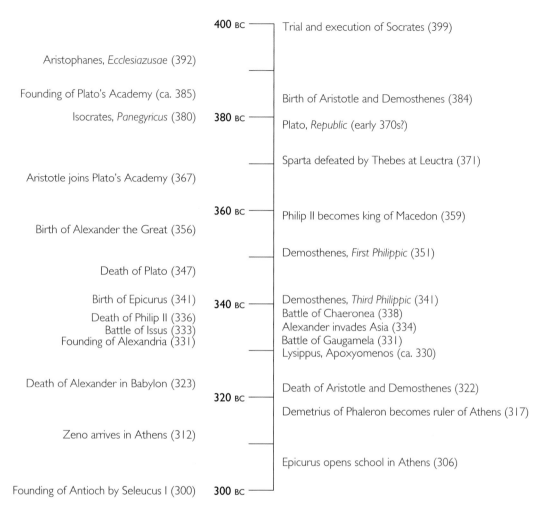

400 BC — Trial and execution of Socrates (399)

Aristophanes, *Ecclesiazusae* (392)

Founding of Plato's Academy (ca. 385)   Birth of Aristotle and Demosthenes (384)

Isocrates, *Panegyricus* (380)   380 BC — Plato, *Republic* (early 370s?)

Sparta defeated by Thebes at Leuctra (371)

Aristotle joins Plato's Academy (367)

360 BC — Philip II becomes king of Macedon (359)

Birth of Alexander the Great (356)

Demosthenes, *First Philippic* (351)

Death of Plato (347)

Birth of Epicurus (341)   340 BC — Demosthenes, *Third Philippic* (341)
Death of Philip II (336)   Battle of Chaeronea (338)
Battle of Issus (333)   Alexander invades Asia (334)
Founding of Alexandria (331)   Battle of Gaugamela (331)
Lysippus, *Apoxyomenos* (ca. 330)

Death of Alexander in Babylon (323)

320 BC — Death of Aristotle and Demosthenes (322)

Demetrius of Phaleron becomes ruler of Athens (317)

Zeno arrives in Athens (312)

Epicurus opens school in Athens (306)

Founding of Antioch by Seleucus I (300)   300 BC —

Timeline 7   The fourth century BC.

Alexander, who took advantage of the unstable situation in fourth-century Greece and changed entirely the world of the Greek polis.

Plato's Bright Ideas

As we saw in chapter 10, the problem of reconstructing the thinking of Socrates is a product of the fact that Socrates left no writings for us to read. The problem of reconstructing Plato's thinking is entirely different, but equally frustrating. Unlike Socrates, Plato produced a considerable number of written works, all of which survive today. They are among the most skillfully crafted and articulate pieces of prose

"You know, gentlemen, to have a fear of death is nothing other than to think one is intelligent when one is not, since it is equivalent to thinking that one knows what one does not in fact know. For no one knows whether death might actually be the greatest of all good things for a person, and yet people fear it as though they are quite certain that it is the greatest of evils. Is this not an instance of that reprehensible form of ignorance, thinking that one knows what one does not in fact know? This is perhaps another case of that disparity between me and most people; if I were to claim to be more intelligent than someone in some regard it would be just this, that since I do not have adequate knowledge about Hades I do not think that I have knowledge about it." (Plato, *The Apology of Socrates* 29a–b)

literature ever written in any language. The problem is posed by the form those writings take. With the exception of some letters which were supposedly written by Plato but whose authenticity is questionable, the works of Plato purport to convey in written form the words spoken by various people, none of whom is Plato himself. For the most part, they are in the form of dialogues, primarily involving Socrates engaged in fictional conversations with his contemporaries, which include both Athenians and prominent visitors to Athens. In other words, Plato never speaks in his own voice and never tells us what he knows. Nor are we entitled to assume that Plato has adopted Socrates as his mouthpiece and uses the words of Socrates to express his own thoughts, because Socrates makes it a point to claim that he has no special knowledge, and he generally confines himself to examining the ideas of his interlocutors, which he often shows to be inadequate. How can this "Socrates" be compatible with the man whom the Delphic oracle declared to be most wise? In the *Apology*, Plato's Socrates seeks to address this by saying that, when he heard the report of the oracle he immediately tried to prove the oracle wrong, by finding someone wiser than himself. So he sought out the experts in various fields, but his relentless interrogations revealed that, while these experts thought they knew something worthwhile they could not show that their "knowledge" was based on anything substantial. Socrates concluded from this that the wisdom the Delphic god had in mind was simply an understanding of one's own intellectual limitations, which Socrates possessed to a greater degree than anyone else.

SOCRATES: This knowledge of military matters that you have, does it come from your being an expert general or rhapsode?

ION: It doesn't seem to me to make any difference.

SOCRATES: How can you say that it doesn't make any difference? Do you mean that the rhapsode and the general possess one skill, or two?

ION: One, it seems to me.

SOCRATES: Then whoever is an expert rhapsode is in fact also an expert general?

ION: Absolutely, Socrates.

SOCRATES: By the same token, then, whoever is in fact an expert general is also an expert rhapsode.

ION: No, that doesn't seem to me to be the case.

SOCRATES: But it does seem to you to be the case that whoever is an expert rhapsode is also an expert general?

ION: Certainly.

SOCRATES: Well, you are the finest rhapsode in Greece, aren't you?

ION: By far, Socrates!

SOCRATES: So are you also the finest general in Greece, Ion?

ION: Be assured that I am, Socrates! And I learned it all from Homer. (Plato, *Ion* 540e–541b)

The question of what is known, or what can be known, is intimately related to the dialogue form that Plato adopted, under the influence, presumably, of his acquaintance with Socrates: Socrates had not written anything, apparently convinced that he knew nothing of permanent value; what Plato wrote, at least in his earliest works, has the permanent value of presenting "Socrates" questioning the experts and demonstrating that their expertise lacks a secure foundation. If this is how the historical Socrates spent his time, it is easy to see why he aroused such hostility. For the experts that he interrogated were the intellectual and political leaders whose advice was often sought, on the assumption that they had a firmer knowledge than most people of such concepts as justice, piety, and courage. But if the experts do not know, who does? And if the wisest man is the man who knows that he knows nothing, is there anything that can be known for sure? Socrates and Plato undoubtedly considered these questions, but we cannot know what answers, if any, they arrived at. In the case of Plato, however, there are at least some hints in his dialogues of what can be known for sure.

One of the areas of study that fascinated well-educated (and hence wealthy) Greeks in the time of Socrates and Plato was geometry. In *The Clouds*, Socrates is presented as drawing geometric figures with a pair of compasses (which he then uses to steal someone's clothes) and the school that Plato founded, the Academy, is supposed to have had the following inscribed over the entrance: "Let no one unversed in geometry enter here." Geometry had been a particular concern of the sixth-century philosopher Pythagoras of Samos, who influenced Socrates and Plato in a number of important ways. Pythagoras had taught the doctrine of the transmigration of souls, namely that the soul outlives the body and takes up residence in a succession of incarnations; he was also credited with the discovery of the "Pythagorean Theorem," although it was known to the Babylonians long before the time of Pythagoras. According to the theorem, the sum of the squares on the sides of a right triangle is equal to the square on the hypotenuse (figure 55). The appeal of a theorem like this is that it can be proved with absolute certainty, and the appeal of geometry in general is that it deals with what is eternally the case. In contrast to the messy world with which we come in contact every day, in which things are constantly changing and about which intelligent people are often in violent disagreement, the objects of geometric investigation enjoy a permanent, unchanging existence. What is more, the eternal truths about geometric figures like triangle $\alpha\beta\gamma$ (that $\alpha^2 + \beta^2 = \gamma^2$ or that its area = $\alpha\beta/2$) can be known and can be proved to be

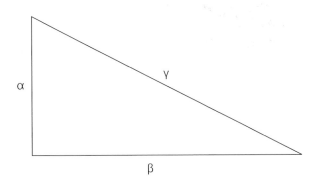

Figure 55
Right triangle
($\alpha^2 + \beta^2 = \gamma^2$).

the case without our ever having seen triangle αβγ. In fact, it is quite impossible for geometric figures to exist in the messy world with which we come in contact every day. And yet their existence cannot be doubted: how could we know with absolute certainty what we know about them if they did not exist?

Geometric figures are not available to the senses, but we do apprehend with the senses physical objects that approximate to geometric figures, like the triangular pediments of a temple or a hoplite's circular shield. This distinction, between a world of permanently unchanging entities about which we can have certain knowledge and the unstable, imperfect world of the senses which arouses unending debate, suggested to Plato the existence of a realm in which everything that we are familiar with from the world of the senses has a permanently unchanging correlate. To refer to these correlates Plato used the Greek word *idea*, meaning "shape, form, appearance," and this theory is often referred to as Plato's "Theory of Forms." While Plato's thinking about geometric figures may have inspired him to construct this theory, the Forms do not consist only of geometric shapes. Rather, there is an eternal, unchanging Form of everything, from sandals to triremes to sealing wax. We cannot perceive the Forms with our senses, just as we cannot perceive the hypotenuse of a right triangle. If the Forms can be apprehended at all, it is only through reason (the Greek for which is *logos*), just as it is by reason alone that we know what we know about right triangles. Reason, then, must have affinities with the realm of the Forms, rather than with the world of the senses. That is, reason must be everlasting, like the Forms themselves. But we humans are not everlasting, and yet we are endowed to a limited extent with reason. There must be, therefore, some part of us that is everlasting, in which reason can reside. That part, for Plato, is the soul, which according to the teaching of Pythagoras has an existence separate from and more enduring than that of the body.

The philosophy of Plato, it must be stressed, is never laid out in explicit terms, as it has been above, but must be reconstructed on the basis of the discussion in his dialogues, which rarely comes to conclusions that the interlocutors can agree upon. But that is part of the point of the dialogue form, which is an inheritance from the conversational method of Socrates and from Socrates' profession of his own ignorance. Philosophy is a process which, because of the inherent fallibility of human nature, cannot attain the certain knowledge that it seeks to attain. To read the dialogues of Plato is to accept an invitation to think and to question. That invitation has been repeatedly accepted, and Plato is generally regarded as the most influential thinker in history. His belief in the

"Well, since the soul is immortal and has been subject to frequent reincarnations, and since it has come in contact with all things, both here and in Hades, there is nothing that it has not learned. For this reason it is no wonder that it is capable of recalling what it knows about virtue and whatever else it has come to know on previous occasions. After all, since everything is connected and since the soul has learned everything, there is nothing to prevent a person, once he has recalled (or, in popular parlance, 'learned') one single thing, from recovering all the rest, as long as he meets the challenge resolutely and refuses to give up the quest. For the quest for knowledge is quite simply a matter of recollection." (Plato, *Meno* 81c–d, Socrates recounting what he has heard from certain unnamed priests and priestesses) separation between the body and the immortal soul, for example, was naturally appreciated by early Christian writers, and a number of the Church Fathers did everything in their power to reconcile the theology of the New Testament and the philosophy of Plato. But, as with the early Ionian philosophers, so with Plato, it is not so much his solutions to philosophical problems that are of greatest importance but the terms in which those problems are set out in his works. In recent years, philosophers, computer scientists, linguists, and neuroscientists have directed much of their energy toward many of the same questions that prompted Plato's Theory of Forms. What is the relationship between the mind and the body? What innate ability do we humans have that enables us to learn a language? How is it possible for us to generalize on the basis of limited experience? Plato's answer to these questions is that our soul attained knowledge of the Forms at a time when the soul was not tainted by contact with the body and with the world of the senses; for Plato, what we call "learning" is actually a laborious, progressive, and faint recollection of what we previously knew more securely. This view, of course, is not accepted by contemporary cognitive scientists, but the very fact that the field of cognitive science exists is proof that some of today's best minds are still wrestling with the problems posed by Plato in the fourth century BC.

Attic Oratory in the Fifth and Fourth Centuries

Plato's influence was exercised not only through his written works. In about 385 BC, Plato established in Athens an institute for higher learning in a public gymnasium dedicated to the hero Academus. The institute, called The Academy, continued in existence for nearly a millennium, until it was closed down in AD 529, along with other pagan institutions, by the Christian emperor Justinian. The Academy attracted philosophers from all over the Greek world – one of its earliest students was Aristotle, from Stagira in the northern Aegean – who investigated the philosophical questions raised by Plato. Not surprisingly, given Plato's conviction that the everyday world of the senses is of lesser importance than the world of the Forms, these investigations were carried out at a rather high level of abstraction. In his dialogues, Plato presents an unflattering image of the more practical type of instruction engaged in by the sophists, and his Academy sought to distance itself from the practices of those teachers of rhetoric. But the sophists attracted an impressive number of pupils willing to pay impressively high fees because the instruction that they offered was designed to enable their pupils to succeed in the world. For Athenians, that world was the everyday world of the democratic assembly and law courts, in which success awaited the man – for only male citizens were entitled to address the assembly or the jury – who was most skilled in persuading his fellow citizens. The unflattering image of rhetoric and its instructors has persisted (ironically, in part because of the stylistic sophistication and persuasiveness of Plato's dialogues) and today the word "sophistry" is used as a term of denigration.

But rhetoric can be, and has been, a serious intellectual pursuit. The formal study of oratory had only begun around the middle of the fifth century, but it immediately attracted the attention of many of the most brilliant and creative minds. These included not only the sophists but even Plato's pupil Aristotle, who in the middle of the fourth century BC wrote a treatise on rhetoric that includes important discussions of different types of argumentation, discussions that are closely related to Aristotle's groundbreaking development of formal logic. The fact that rhetoric had developed so rapidly and had become fully professionalized is testimony to the competitive nature of Greek civilization and to the pervasiveness of litigation, particularly in Athens. As we saw in chapter 10, it was up to the individual citizen to bring charges before the court, and it was required by Attic law that that individual, as well as the person against whom the charges were brought, address the court himself. For this reason, many Athenian citizens found it prudent to learn the skills that the sophists promised to teach. The alternative was to hire a professional to write a speech, which one could then memorize and deliver oneself. This had the effect of creating a demand for professional speechwriters and teachers of rhetoric, who came to Athens from all over the Greek world, and of encouraging the proliferation of speeches in written form. Copies of these written speeches could then be produced, either by the orator himself to advertise his skills or by others to serve as models. And copies continued to be made for educational purposes, since rhetoric formed the basis of higher education throughout antiquity. For this reason, we have today the texts of well over a hundred speeches delivered by Athenian orators in the late fifth and fourth centuries BC. Two of the most prominent of those orators were Isocrates and Demosthenes, who illustrate well the range of styles and outlooks among these men.

"It is disgraceful that, in the private sphere we see fit to use barbarians as slaves whereas, in the public sphere, we stand by and watch as so many of our allies are enslaved by them. It is disgraceful that, in the case of the men engaged in the Trojan War, the abduction of a single woman aroused such universal indignation on behalf of the wronged party that no one was willing to end the war until the city of the man who dared to commit this crime had been obliterated whereas, in our case, when the whole of Greece has been outraged, we have taken no unified action in retaliation, although we have it in our power to accomplish what we have every right to wish for. This is the only case where war trumps peace. It is more like a pilgrimage than a military campaign. Both those who crave war and those who want peace would come out winners, for it enables the latter to enjoy the fruits of their labor without any dangers and the former to make a fortune at the expense of strangers."
(Isocrates, *Panegyricus* 181–2)

Isocrates lived for almost a hundred years, from 436 BC until 338. He came from a wealthy Athenian family and studied under the leading sophists. In particular, Isocrates was a pupil of the Sicilian Gorgias, who had developed a dazzling, incantatory style of delivery which introduced some of the effects of poetry into spoken prose. Of Gorgias it has notoriously been said, "starting with the initial advantage of having nothing in particular to say, he was able to concentrate all his energies upon saying it." But this comment, made in the 1950s, before we had learned that the medium is the message, is a good illustration of the suspicion in which rhetoric has been held and seems to proceed from the assumption that whatever is cleverly expressed must be lacking in substance. In fact, Gorgias and his pupil Isocrates had important things to say, some of which indicated that they understood better than many of their contemporaries the direction in which Greek civilization was headed. Or, rather, they helped to establish the direction in which Greek civilization was headed, by reminding the Greeks of their glorious past, which Gorgias and Isocrates themselves creatively reconstructed, representing the Trojan War and the Persian Wars as instances of superior Greek culture triumphing over the hapless barbarians. At some time around the start of the fourth century, Gorgias delivered a speech, which has not survived, to the visitors who had come from all over Greece to celebrate the Olympic festival. In front of a suitably Panhellenic audience, Gorgias urged the Greeks to end their continual warring against each other and to unite against the Persians, who remained as a potential threat to the easternmost Greek poleis. Isocrates inherited this Panhellenic sentiment from his teacher and spent much of his long life trying to persuade his fellow Greeks to adopt a new way of thinking about themselves. For Isocrates, what was distinctive about the Greeks was their shared Hellenic culture, which could best be preserved by creating concord among all Greeks and by a program of education which Isocrates was prepared to implement. He opened a school in Athens whose aim was to teach the principles of oratory and moral uprightness as a means of effective and responsible political action. And he delivered a number of public oratorical displays designed to recruit various political figures as leaders in the unification of the Greeks. Some of these leaders were kings or tyrants on the fringes of the Greek world and included King Philip II of Macedon, who succeeded, as we will see, in imposing a sort of unity on the Greeks just at the end of Isocrates' lifetime.

Not everyone, however, shared Isocrates' vision of a united Greece or his favorable attitude toward Philip. While Isocrates was making speeches and writing letters, encouraging Philip to "lead the way in unifying the Greeks and attacking the barbarians," another Athenian orator, Demosthenes, was reviling Philip as an untrustworthy, power-hungry despot. Demosthenes (384–322 BC) was more than 50 years younger than Isocrates, but because of the latter's long life their careers overlapped for a quarter of a century. Like Isocrates, Demosthenes made a name for himself initially in the Attic law courts, composing speeches for various clients to use in their defense or (much more commonly) in their prosecution of others. In addition, he himself initiated successful litigation against two relatives who, as his guardians after his father died when he was a child, had squandered his inheritance. Demosthenes developed a forceful and vigorous style very different from the refined urbanity of Isocrates, and he earned a reputation as an aggressive and effective prosecutor. He did not share the idealism of Isocrates; rather, his practical experience in the law courts, as well as his treatment at the hands of his guardians, made him vigilant and suspicious of others' motives. So, when Philip and the Macedonians began interfering in the affairs of the Greek cities on the north coast of the Aegean, an area which was of economic and strategic importance to Athens, Demosthenes delivered a series of speeches in the assembly, beginning around

350 BC, in which he tried to arouse the Athenians to defend their interests and to forestall by military action the expanding power of the Macedonians. Among these speeches is a group called the *Philippic Orations*, or "speeches dealing with Philip," which are scathing denunciations of Philip's imperialist intentions. The title of these speeches has contributed the word "philippic," meaning "verbal tirade," to the English language.

These and the other speeches of Demosthenes are of interest not only for their historic importance and their literary merit, but because they provide us with a window into the workings of Athenian democracy in the fourth century BC. Like all Attic orators, Demosthenes came from a family whose considerable wealth enabled him to pursue the expensive and extensive training necessary to become proficient in public speaking. But the aim of the orator who addresses the assembly is to convince the mass of Athenian citizens to adopt this or that course of action, and his chances of success are greatly improved if he can first impress on his audience that he is a "man of the people." The same, of course, is true of modern representative democracies, in which the cost of campaigning for major public office often keeps the leadership in the hands of wealthy individuals, whose public addresses tend to adopt a folksy, down-to-earth tone. And, like many modern politicians, Demosthenes appealed to his audience's patriotism, their sense of uniqueness as, first, Athenians and, failing that, as Greeks. In his first *Philippic*, for example, Demosthenes reminds his fellow Athenians of how well organized and how lavish are their celebrations of the festivals of the Panathenaea and Dionysia, and he exhorts them to expend comparable effort and resources in eliminating the threat that Philip poses to them. Ten years later, after Philip's influence in the affairs of Greece had become more dominant and more alarming, Demosthenes in his third *Philippic* could represent the current state of affairs as having been caused by those who advised appeasement of Philip. The implication, of course, is that Demosthenes was right all along and so now the assembly, which Demosthenes rebukes as prone to being supine, should follow his sensible advice. This is the same technique we saw in Thucydides (p. 169), who assures his reader of his own competence as an analyst by revealing his successful prediction regarding the magnitude of the Peloponnesian War. Demosthenes further hammers home his point by emphasizing Philip's lack of those qualities that characterize a civilized, that is to say a Greek, head of state.

> "In all other cases you Athenians think that freedom of speech should be so widely available to everyone in the city that you even allow foreigners and slaves to share in it, and you can see any number of slaves here speaking their minds with greater freedom than free men in some other poleis. But when it comes to political deliberation, freedom of speech has been utterly banished. The result of this is that the assemblies are filled with nothing but self-indulgent flattery designed solely for the gratification of the listeners, while at the same time a clear and present danger threatens in the form of urgent affairs of state. Well, if that is what you are interested in hearing, I have nothing to say. But if you are willing to be given unvarnished advice, I stand ready to speak." (Demosthenes, *Third Philippic* 3–4)

Philip II of Macedon and the Conquest of Greece

While Isocrates encouraged Philip to lead the Greeks against the barbarians, according to Demosthenes Philip is himself a barbarian, and the only way to deal with people like that is by decisive military action, not negotiation. Demosthenes tries to rouse his Athenian audience to a frenzy of indignation by pointing out the absurdity of Philip's presiding over the Pythian Games, as he was invited to do by the Delphic authorities in 346 and again in 342 BC. For the Pythian Games were a Panhellenic festival, to be celebrated only by Greeks, as Demosthenes makes sure to point out. But the question of whether Philip, and the Macedonians in general, are Greeks or non-Greeks is by no means straightforward. Indeed, it is still today the cause of violent debate between the people of Greece and the people of the state admitted to membership in the United Nations in 1993 under the provisional name "The former Yugoslav Republic of Macedonia." There is no question that, in the fifth and fourth centuries BC, there were noticeable differences between the Greeks and the Macedonians: the latter did not live in a polis, they were ruled by a king, and their speech distinguished them from the Greeks. Unfortunately, the written remains from Macedon are so scanty that linguists today cannot agree whether Macedonian was a dialect of Greek or a separate language closely related to Greek. In fact, the terms "dialect" and "language" are themselves subject to controversy, and language was once defined by a speaker of Yiddish as "a dialect with an army and navy." In other words, the issue was (and is) an entirely political one. Demosthenes wished, for his own political purposes, to persuade the Athenian assembly that Philip was not Greek. On the other hand, Philip, like some of the earlier Macedonian kings, sought for political purposes to present himself as a Greek. By presiding over the Panhellenic Pythian Games, he was asserting his Greek identity, just as his ancestor, King Alexander I, had done early in the fifth century by entering the Olympic Games as a contestant. His right to compete was challenged on the grounds that he was not Greek, but Alexander somehow managed to "prove" to the Hellenodikai that he was descended from the Greek hero Heracles and he was permitted to compete. Those Macedonians, however, who were not members of the royal family seem not to have qualified as Greeks.

Subsequently, some of the Macedonian kings went out of their way to present their court as a fully Hellenized center of culture that patronized Greek artists and poets, including the Athenian Euripides, whose last years were spent at the Macedonian court. By the time Philip became king, in 359 BC, he was personally conversant with affairs in Greece, having earlier spent two years living in Thebes. While there, Philip learned a great deal about strategy and tactics, since Thebes was the leading military power in Greece at the time. The previous decades had seen Athens, Sparta, and Thebes, alone or in varying combinations, assert themselves militarily, and in 371 BC the Thebans soundly defeated the Spartans at the battle of Leuctra, establishing themselves as the dominant force in Greece. Philip put into practice what he had learned from his stay in Thebes when he ascended the

Macedonian throne. He reorganized the Macedonian army and fitted it out with a new type of equipment, imposing discipline on his troops and training them in a new style of warfare. The new equipment included a formidable spear more than 5 meters in length, and the new style of warfare involved a much more extensive and effective use of cavalry than Greek hoplites had been accustomed to facing. Philip was immediately successful in defending Macedonian territory against attacks by his neighbors to the north, and for the next 20 years his influence over the poleis in central Greece expanded until the last resistance to Macedonian power was eliminated in 338 BC. In that year, Philip and the Macedonians, along with a number of Greek allies, were victorious in the decisive battle of Chaeronea against the forces of Athens and Thebes. In the battle, the cavalry on the left wing of the Macedonian army was commanded by Philip's 18-year-old son Alexander.

Demosthenes had been right about Philip's ruthless character and his imperialist intentions. But the cities of Greece had exhausted themselves materially in a constant series of conflicts that had been going on since the time of the Peloponnesian War and they were no match for the energy of Philip or the professionalism of his troops. Those troops, however, needed to be kept busy now that there was no further need to campaign against the cities of Greece. Philip accordingly planned an attack on Persia, which was intended as retribution for Xerxes' invasion of mainland Greece 150 years before. But he did not live to carry out his planned expedition. In the summer of 336, Philip was murdered, shortly after his seventh (and only Macedonian) wife, Cleopatra, gave birth to a son. Philip's assassin was immediately executed, perhaps to prevent him from naming the person or persons who had put him up to it, and all those except Alexander who had a reasonable claim on the throne, including Cleopatra and her infant son, were quickly eliminated. Alexander, now 20 years old, became king of Macedon, succeeding his father Philip, whose ruthlessness he seems to have inherited.

Alexander the Great and the Conquest of Asia

Alexander's youth and the turmoil that followed in the wake of Philip's assassination encouraged Macedon's neighbors to the north and west to believe that the kingdom was vulnerable. Alexander acted with characteristic promptitude and decisiveness, securing the Macedonian borders and arousing the admiration and loyalty of his troops. Macedonian kings were expected to lead their army into battle: Philip had lost his right eye to an enemy missile while besieging a Greek city in 354 BC (figure 56) and Alexander was every bit as daring and fearless as his father. While Alexander was campaigning in the north, rumors of his death reached the cities of central Greece and, under the leadership of Thebes and with encouragement from Demosthenes, they set about "liberating" themselves from Macedonian control. But again Alexander was up to the task. Before the Greek cities could organize and put an effective army in the field, Alexander led his troops into Greece

Figure 56
Forensic waxwork reconstruction of the head of Philip II, based on the cremated skeleton of Philip found in 1977 at Vergina, Macedon (see J. Prag and R. Neave, *Making Faces Using Forensic and Archaeological Evidence*, London 1997). The Manchester Museum, The University of Manchester.

and captured Thebes. The residents who were not massacred were sold into slavery and the city was reduced to rubble. As if to show his respect for Greek culture, however, Alexander allowed the home of the fifth-century Theban poet Pindar to remain standing.

The rest of the Greek cities were intimidated, as Alexander had no doubt intended, and they readily acknowledged him as their leader. His intention now was to accomplish the invasion of Persia that Philip had planned. Preparations were made and, in the spring of 334, Alexander and his Macedonian army set out to cross the Hellespont into Asia. Alexander was 21 years old, but he only had 11 more years to live and he would never return to Macedon. In those 11 years, however, he brought under his personal control a larger fraction of the world's landmass and human population than any one man had ever ruled, and he changed forever the character of Greek civilization. But change in Greek civilization has always taken the form of reinventing the past, and Alexander was well aware of his position between the past and the future. On his father's side he traced his descent from Heracles;

on his mother's side from Achilles, the hero of the Trojan War. He was now embarking on a Herculean labor that involved the conquest of a wealthy Asiatic kingdom. And, indeed, the first town he visited after crossing over into Asia was Troy. This invasion, then, was the ultimate expression of the appropriation by the Macedonian royal family of Hellenic culture and identity. Alexander intended to become the new Achilles; all that was missing, as he is supposed to have lamented, was a Homer to sing of his accomplishments. Instead, he made sure that his accomplishments spoke for themselves.

The first military engagement was at the Granicus River, in northwestern Asia Minor (map 14). Alexander's victory there gave him control over most of Asia Minor, but he had defeated only the combined armies of a few of the Persian satraps. The Persian king, Darius III, still had enormous financial and military resources at his disposal, and he was in the process of mobilizing his forces in the Persian homeland. Alexander's army met Darius' at Issus in 333 BC, near what is now the Turkish city of Iskenderun, formerly Alexandretta, both forms of the name reflecting Alexander's abiding presence. The Macedonian forces were heavily outnumbered, but the battle took place on a narrow stretch of land between the sea and the mountains and the Persians were unable to outflank Alexander. The Macedonians were victorious and Darius fled, leaving his wife, his mother, and his children behind in camp. When Alexander's pursuit failed to capture Darius, Alexander marched his army south, along the eastern coast of the Mediterranean, capturing all the ports on the way and obviating the need for developing a navy. On his arrival in Egypt,

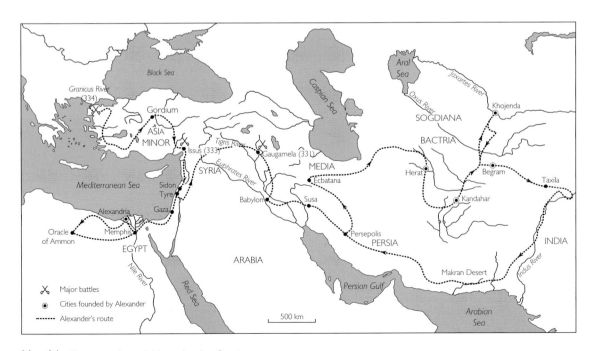

Map 14   The campaigns of Alexander the Great.

Figure 57
Obverse of silver coin minted by Alexander's successor Lysimachus, showing Alexander with ram's horns; diameter ca. 30 mm, 297–281 BC. Appleton, Ottilia Buerger Collection of Ancient and Byzantine Coins at Lawrence University, Inv. 91.046.

a country that had often revolted from Persian control, Alexander was welcomed as the country's liberator and new ruler. In 331 the city of Alexandria was founded, the first of a number of cities founded by and named after Alexander. While the new city was being built, Alexander took a small party of men into the desert to consult the oracle of the Egyptian god Ammon, a ram-headed deity whom the Greeks identified with Zeus. Alexander consulted the oracle in private and did not reveal what he was told, but from this point on he seems to have thought of himself as the son of Zeus and in his official portraiture he began to sprout ram's horns (figure 57). Alexander was already considered to be descended from Zeus through his remote ancestors Heracles and Achilles. But this was different, and the difference had to do in part with Alexander's status as ruler of Egypt. According to the Greek way of thinking, divine ancestry does not confer divinity, but Alexander as ruler of Egypt assumed the titles and attributes of the pharaoh. The pharaoh was considered to be not only the son of Ammon, but to be identified with that god and hence himself divine.

The divinity of Alexander the Great was to have important consequences: it set a precedent that was followed by his successors and it inspired Alexander with an even greater confidence in his personal invincibility. Without wasting any time he set out in pursuit of Darius, who was reorganizing his army near Babylon. This time, Darius was determined to meet the Macedonian army in a large, open plain. Alexander was willing to oblige and in October of 331 his troops

"Darius wrote a letter to Alexander which was delivered by his personal friends in which he asked him to accept ten thousand talents in exchange for the prisoners, granted him possession of all lands west of the Euphrates River, and offered to make him his friend and ally by letting him marry one of his daughters. When Alexander informed his Royal Companions of the offer, Parmenio said, 'If I were Alexander I would accept.' To which Alexander replied, 'By Zeus, so would I – if I were Parmenio.'" (Plutarch, *The Life of Alexander* 29.7–8) won a decisive victory at Gaugamela, near what is today Mosul in northern Iraq. He now had at his disposal the resources of the Persian Empire, and he rewarded his troops magnificently. For he would continue to need their services. Darius had still not been captured and the easternmost parts of the Persian Empire did not recognize Alexander as Darius' successor. Alexander pursued Darius, but before he could overtake him Darius was murdered by his satraps, who would not allow their king to fall into the hands of a usurper. Instead, one of Darius' satraps proclaimed himself king and for the next three years Alexander was occupied with reclaiming parts of what he had come to regard as his empire. This involved him and his troops in military operations in some of the most inhospitable terrain in all of Asia, in the territory of what is now Afghanistan, Uzbekistan, and Tajikistan. Once this region had been pacified and a number of new cities named Alexandria had been founded, including those now known as Herat and Kandahar, Alexander descended from the Hindu Kush into the Indus River valley with the intention of invading India. There seems to have been no limit to Alexander's energy or ambition. But there was a limit to what his army could withstand. After nearly a year of campaigning in the Punjab, Alexander's troops decided that they could go no further. It was the summer of 326 BC and some of his men had been away from home (which was now 4,000 kilometers away) for eight years.

Alexander was not a fool. He recognized that, despite his divinity and his extraordinary abilities, even he could not conquer India without an army, so he reluctantly gave in to his troops' request that they turn back. With the intention, apparently, of punishing his men for their refusal to continue to the east, Alexander led a large number of them back to Persia on a brutal march through the Makran Desert of Pakistan and Iran, where many of them died from heat and dehydration. Alexander finally returned to Babylon in the spring of 323 BC, where he began planning in earnest an invasion of Arabia for which preliminary arrangements had already been made. But he did not live to carry out those plans, or any plans for other conquests that he might have contemplated. On June 10, 323 he died, not yet having reached his thirty-third birthday. It is not clear what the cause of death was, but malaria is considered a likely candidate. In Macedonian fashion, Alexander had married more than once, but he did not have a living heir, although his Iranian wife Roxane was pregnant and would later give birth to a son, Alexander IV. Alexander had surrounded himself with a group of first-rate generals, each of whom thought that he, but not any of the others, had the requisite qualities to succeed Alexander. The quarrels that ensued rapidly caused the dissolution of Alexander's empire, which consisted, by the end of the fourth century, of three large and two smaller kingdoms, each ruled by a Macedonian who had served on Alexander's staff or by his successor. The history of the next century and a half is filled with a series of conflicts among these kingdoms. Each kingdom sought to expand its territory at the expense of the others, but these conflicts did little more than make the individual kingdoms vulnerable to encroachment from outside, and in the first century BC the last of these successor kingdoms became part of the expanding Roman Empire.

Recommended for Further Reading

Athenian Political Oratory: 16 Key Speeches, translated by D. D. Phillips (New York and London 2004): a good, representative selection of political oratory from the late fifth and fourth centuries BC in clear, accurate translations with helpful notes.

Bosworth, A. B. *Conquest and Empire: The Reign of Alexander the Great* (Cambridge 1988): a thorough and tough-minded attempt to reconstruct the reality that lies behind the romanticized and often idealistic ancient evidence for Alexander and his conquests.

Edwards, M. *The Attic Orators* (London 1994): an excellent brief (under 100 pages) introduction to the Attic orators and their work, with suggestions for further reading.

Lane Fox, R. *The Search for Alexander* (Boston and Toronto 1980): a fascinating and well-illustrated account of the career of Alexander the Great, by one of the leading authorities on Alexander, who is also the weekly gardening correspondent for *The Financial Times*.

Ober, J. *Mass and Elite in Democratic Athens: Rhetoric, Ideology, and the Power of the People* (Princeton 1989): an important study of the way in which elite Athenians of the fourth century negotiated through oratory their relationship with the mass of Athenian citizens, preceded by an excellent survey of the development of Athenian democracy.

Plato, *The Republic*, edited by G. R. F. Ferrari and translated by Tom Griffith (Cambridge 2000): Plato's masterpiece, embodying his developed thoughts on education, the arts, and the state, in an excellent translation with valuable notes and introduction.

Plato, *Symposium and Phaedrus*, translated by Tom Griffith (New York and Toronto 2000): two of Plato's most dazzling dialogues, in the very best translations available.

Szlezák, T. A. *Reading Plato*, English translation (London and New York 1999): the best brief introduction to Plato's thought and writing.

GREEK CULTURE IN THE HELLENISTIC PERIOD

12

The character of life and culture in the Greek world was profoundly affected by the life and campaigns of Alexander the Great. During the Archaic and Classical periods Greeks lived in more-or-less autonomous poleis. Now, during the Hellenistic Period (323 to 30 BC), those poleis fell under the rule of now one, now another of the Macedonian kingdoms that were created by the break-up of Alexander's empire and that engaged in almost constant warfare with one another. The rulers of these kingdoms followed Alexander's precedent in assuming divine status, and their cult had now to be added to that of the other gods worshiped by the polis. In most other respects, however, the day-to-day existence of the average citizen of one of the old Greek poleis was not significantly different from what it had been before the time of Alexander. But the career of Alexander the Great resulted in the establishment of many new centers of Greek culture throughout Asia and North Africa. Greek language and Greek culture were now the characteristic marks of a ruling class, and Hellenistic art and literature reflect this new prestige status and, at the same time, acknowledge the influence exerted by non-Greek cultures on the forms and methods of artistic expression. The very fact that Greek culture felt that it had to maintain itself in non-Greek contexts far from the mainland meant that traditional forms of expression were tenaciously adhered to, but the need to "say something new" within those forms led to a greater openness to the arcane and the exotic. So, in literature we find epic poems written in imitation of Homeric style and tragedies reminiscent of those of Euripides, but the subject of one might be an obscure local myth and the subject of another might be a story drawn from the Hebrew Bible. The visual artists of the Hellenistic period exhibit the same interest in experimentation within traditional forms that we see in Hellenistic literature. Indeed, Hellenistic art is often "literary," just as Hellenistic literature is often "pictorial." Artists of the fourth century and later are very much under the influence of Athenian tragedy and show a fondness for depicting extreme emotion in their subjects and arousing in their viewers complex and problematic emotions of the sort that Euripides exploited in his dramas. The poets and artists of the Hellenistic Period are among the most original and inventive in all of Greek culture; their sculptures were avidly collected by Roman patrons and their literary creations were the frequent subjects of imitation by the poets of Rome.

Political Life and the Polis

Hellenistic Literature

Hellenistic Art

The career of Alexander the Great produced rapid and momentous changes in the Greek world and, indeed, in the entire region that stretches from Italy in the west to India in the east. Changes of this magnitude generally prompt historians to see the changes as marking a new historical period, and it has become conventional to refer to the period from the death of Alexander in 323 BC to the end of the last independent Macedonian kingdom in 30 BC as the "Hellenistic Period." It is interesting to note, however, that the ancient Greeks themselves did not perceive a significant shift in their situation at the time of the death of Alexander. For, while the character of what we call the Hellenistic Period is noticeably different from that of the Classical Period that preceded it, many if not most of the differences were already beginning to make themselves felt in the fourth century, independently of the influence of Alexander's conquests. It might, in fact, make more sense to consider the end of the Peloponnesian War, rather than the death of Alexander, as marking the break between the Classical and the Hellenistic Periods. The changes brought about by the imposition of Macedonian rule, significant as those were, primarily concern government and the relationship between the people and the (now divine) ruler. In the realm of art, literature, and thought, however, the developments of the Hellenistic Period represent largely a continuation of what had begun before Alexander's death, and even, in many cases, before his birth. We will consider in this chapter the distinctive features of the Hellenistic Period and how those features emerged from the situation of the Greeks in the fifth and fourth centuries.

Political Life and the Polis

Even in the realm of government and politics, where the changes were more sudden and dramatic, the developments of the Hellenistic Period were not entirely new. The fundamental unit of Greek government throughout the Archaic and Classical periods was the polis, which is, indeed, one of the characteristic features of ancient Greek civilization. Already during the Peloponnesian War the integrity of the Greek polis was coming to be challenged. The Athenian "allies," for example, were not entirely free to determine their own policies and in some instances the Athenian judicial system had jurisdiction over the allies' internal affairs. Philip's imposition of Macedonian authority over the Greek poleis in the middle of the fourth century is in many ways a comparable infringement of the autonomy of the cities under his control. The Macedonian monarchies of the Hellenistic Period merely continued to exercise the kind of control that Philip had imposed. The kingdom that most directly affected mainland Greece was the Antigonid kingdom of Macedon, ruled by the descendants of Antigonus, one of Alexander's generals (map 15). The Greek cities in Asia Minor, however, fell at varying times under the influence of the Ptolemaic kingdom, whose court was at Alexandria in Egypt, and the Seleucid kingdom based in northern Syria. (Ptolemy and Seleucus had also been

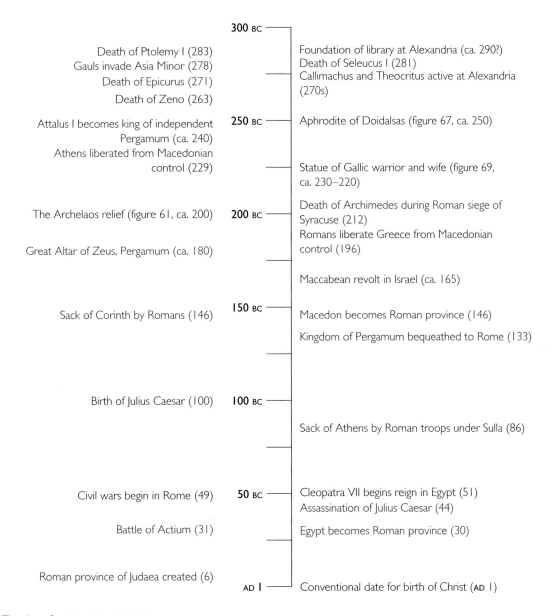

300 BC

Death of Ptolemy I (283)
Gauls invade Asia Minor (278)
Death of Epicurus (271)
Death of Zeno (263)

Foundation of library at Alexandria (ca. 290?)
Death of Seleucus I (281)
Callimachus and Theocritus active at Alexandria
(270s)

250 BC

Attalus I becomes king of independent
Pergamum (ca. 240)
Athens liberated from Macedonian
control (229)

Aphrodite of Doidalsas (figure 67, ca. 250)

Statue of Gallic warrior and wife (figure 69,
ca. 230–220)

The Archelaos relief (figure 61, ca. 200)

200 BC

Great Altar of Zeus, Pergamum (ca. 180)

Death of Archimedes during Roman siege of
Syracuse (212)
Romans liberate Greece from Macedonian
control (196)

Maccabean revolt in Israel (ca. 165)

Sack of Corinth by Romans (146)

150 BC

Macedon becomes Roman province (146)

Kingdom of Pergamum bequeathed to Rome (133)

Birth of Julius Caesar (100)

100 BC

Sack of Athens by Roman troops under Sulla (86)

Civil wars begin in Rome (49)

50 BC

Cleopatra VII begins reign in Egypt (51)
Assassination of Julius Caesar (44)

Battle of Actium (31)

Egypt becomes Roman province (30)

Roman province of Judaea created (6)

AD 1

Conventional date for birth of Christ (AD 1)

Timeline 8   The Hellenistic Period.

among Alexander's generals.) Each of these kingdoms had a different character and what would today be called a different "management style," depending partly upon the character of the individual king, but more importantly upon the history and the nature of the territory he governed.

The territory of the Antigonid kingdom of Macedon consisted of Macedon itself and, at various times, of different portions of mainland Greece. It was, therefore, the direct descendant of Philip's Macedonian kingdom, and its relationship with

Map 15 Hellenistic kingdoms in the early third century BC. Map based on A. Erskine (ed.), *A Companion to the Hellenistic World* (Oxford 2003), Figure 2.1, p. 20.

the Greek poleis was similar to what had been the relationship between Macedon and Greece in the mid-fourth century. That is, many of the Greek cities were nominally free and independent "allies" of the Macedonian king. Some managed to retain real independence from Macedonian power, like Sparta, which continued to pose as the "liberator" of the Greek poleis, engaging in periodic wars with cities that were allied with Macedon. And some of the cities that were "allies" of the Macedonian kingdom attempted occasionally to revolt from the alliance, with varying degrees of success. The military might of the region, however, lay largely in the hands of the Macedonian king and his professional army. The citizen armies and navies that had been a feature of the Greek polis in the Classical Period could no longer compete successfully with the well-financed mercenary forces of the Antigonid kingdom or of the other Hellenistic kingdoms. These armies, however, could also create a sense of security in the Greek poleis; provided that they were willing to tolerate Macedonian control, the citizens of the Greek poleis could go about their business without the fear that they might have to take up arms to defend their homeland. On the other hand, for those citizens who were drawn to the military life, the professional armies of the Hellenistic kings provided an almost constant source of employment and adventure.

For the most part, however, life within the cities of mainland Greece continued to be focused on the affairs of the polis, as it had been previously. This meant not only the administration of the city's political affairs but the cults of the polis as well. In Athens, for example, the festivals of the Panathenaea and the Dionysia, along with several other less important festivals, were celebrated annually. Every polis had its own cycle of similar religious festivals. These celebrations were conducted, as always, by and in the name of the polis, because ancient Greek religion was, for the most part, the religion of the polis. In the Classical Period, the cost of celebrating these festivals was borne by wealthy individual citizens, just as with many other expenses of the polis. So, for example, in a given year a prosperous Athenian citizen might be required to subsidize the cost of outfitting and training a chorus in the musical or dramatic competitions at the Dionysia, or he might defray the expense of maintaining a trireme and its crew for a year. The performance of a service of this nature to the polis was called a *leitourgia*, literally "public service," the origin of the English word "liturgy." Performing a liturgy was a financial burden, but it could have its advantages: the citizen who had performed the liturgy could claim to be, and might be recognized as, a public benefactor, thus enhancing his personal prestige and status, particularly if the liturgy was carried out with especial lavishness. During the Hellenistic Period, compulsory liturgies became less and less common, as the structure of public finance in the polis began to be influenced by the more centralized model of the monarchy. Individual citizens were still chosen to serve as organizers of festivals and contests, but the funding was now provided by the polis. Still, following the tradition of the earlier liturgies, and in imitation of the Macedonian rulers, who liked to advertise their lavish public benefactions, individual citizens often augmented the state funds with money of their own in order to make a name for themselves.

"There was another man whose obsequiousness surpassed that of Stratocles. He proposed a bill to the effect that, whenever Demetrius visited Athens, he should be accorded the same welcome as Demeter and Dionysus and that, further, whatever citizen provided the most lavish and costly reception should be granted at public expense a sum of money with which to make a dedicatory offering. Finally, the official designation of the month Mounychion became 'Demetrion' and of the last day of each month 'Demetrias,' and the name of the festival of the Dionysia was changed to 'Demetria.'" (Plutarch, *The Life of Demetrius* 12.1–2)

The character of the religion and the religious festivals of the polis remained essentially unchanged in the Hellenistic Period, with the exception of the introduction of the ruler cult, which was widespread in the Hellenistic kingdoms. All this meant in the Greek poleis, however, was the addition of another deity who might require worship, an altar, sacrifices, and so on. This was nothing new; the Greek poleis in the Classical Period were used to welcoming new divinities, as the Athenians had done with the Arcadian god Pan at the beginning of the fifth century and the Thracian goddess Bendis at the end. The difference, of course, was that the objects of the ruler cult could actually back up their claim to divinity with tangible and substantial benefactions. Demetrius I of Macedon, for example, liberated Athens from an oppressive ruler in 307 BC and restored to the Athenians their laws and their "traditional form of government." In gratitude, and in the expectation of further benefactions, the Athenians proclaimed Demetrius and his father Antigonus, the still living founder of the Antigonid kingdom, "savior gods" and appointed a priest to be in charge of the worship of these manifestly powerful divinities. In addition, a decree was passed that representations of Demetrius and Antigonus were to be included along with the representations of the Olympian gods that were traditionally woven into the robe that was presented to Athena every four years at the Panathenaea.

In the other Hellenistic kingdoms as well, the rulers were made the objects of cult, but, since those kingdoms included large non-Greek populations, the character of the cult and, indeed, the character of the kingship were necessarily different.

"What amazing power did Ptolemy the son of Lagus acquire from his ancestors! A power to accomplish any great deed that he set his mind to – a mind that could conceive what no other man's can imagine. Father Zeus made him equal in honor even to the blessed gods, and for him a golden throne is established in the halls of Zeus. Beside him is seated Alexander, the god with the intricate diadem, whose thoughts are friendly toward him but hostile toward the Persians. Facing them a seat made of solid adamant is set, the throne of Heracles the slayer of centaurs, where he feasts with the other Olympian gods. His joy is unbounded over the sons of his sons, for the son of Cronus has relieved their limbs of old age and they, his own descendants, are spoken of as immortal gods." (Theocritus, *Idyll* 17.13–25)

These rulers were following in the tradition of the Macedonian kings Philip and Alexander, who styled themselves as embodiments of Greek culture. Alexander had himself succeeded the rulers of the Persian Empire, and so his rule combined elements of Macedonian and Persian kingship, which his successors imitated in their own kingdoms. These kingdoms, then, imposed a Persian-influenced Macedonian governmental organization on regions that had their own traditions of government, in some cases traditions of very long standing. So, for example, the rulers of the Ptolemaic kingdom of Egypt established at

Figure 58   Detail of granodiorite statue of Queen Arsinoe II; height of statue 159.5 cm, ca. 270–246 BC. Shigaraki (Shiga Prefecture, Japan), Miho Museum.

Alexandria a court whose language was Greek and which became a leading center of Greek culture. The rulers were all directly descended from Alexander's general Ptolemy, were of pure Macedonian ancestry, spoke Greek as their native language, and bore names that advertised their Greek heritage, names like Ptolemy, Cleopatra, and Berenice (= "*nike*-bearing"). The Ptolemies were also the successors to the age-old dynasties of the Egyptian pharaohs, and had to represent themselves to their Egyptian subjects in appropriate fashion. Figure 58 shows Queen Arsinoe II, the wife (and full sister) of the Macedonian King Ptolemy II, as represented by an Egyptian sculptor in the style traditional for Egyptian queens. At the same time, the Ptolemies presented themselves to the Greek and Macedonian inhabitants of their kingdom as typical Macedonian monarchs: Figure 59 is a double portrait of Ptolemy II and Arsinoe II under the inscription, in Greek, "the siblings." Both Ptolemy and Arsinoe were nicknamed Philadelphus, or "sibling-loving," because of their marriage, a marriage which had a precedent in that of another pair of divine siblings, Zeus and Hera.

The effect of the creation of these Macedonian kingdoms was to spread Greek language, culture, and religion among many non-Greek regions as well as to expose Greeks and Macedonians to a great variety of non-Greek religions, cultures, and languages. Alexander had founded a number of new cities, often filling them with Macedonian and Greek settlers, and his successors continued the practice. Each of these cities was constructed so that it had the characteristic features of a Greek polis, such as a theater, a gymnasium, and an agora. The cities then became the centers of Greek culture and of trade, attracting additional settlers from Greece and

Figure 59
Obverse of gold coin minted by and showing in profile Ptolemy II and Arsinoe II; diameter ca. 30 mm, 260s BC. Appleton, Ottilia Buerger Collection of Ancient and Byzantine Coins at Lawrence University, Inv. 91.098.

Macedon as well as members of the indigenous population who wished to take advantage of the economic opportunities afforded by the city. In order to do this, however, they would usually have to become Hellenized and to learn the Greek language. There arose, then, in the Macedonian kingdoms a division between the cities and the countryside. In the latter, the inhabitants kept for the most part to their traditional customs and religions and spoke their native language, Demotic in Egypt, say, or Aramaic in Syria. In the cities, the language of commerce and administration was Greek. It will be remembered, however, that the Greek language was divided into a number of distinct dialects (p. 33). Which of these dialects was spoken in Egyptian Alexandria or in Kandahar? Because of the cultural and especially the literary prominence of Athens, the Macedonian kings had taken to using a form of the Attic dialect in order to project the image of a cultured Greek, and it was a version of the dialect of Athens that thus became a quasi-standardized form of Greek throughout the cities of the Macedonian kingdoms. This form of Greek is known as the Koine, or the "common (dialect)," and from it evolved the form of Greek spoken today.

Hellenistic Literature

Koine Greek also became the medium for prose literature throughout the Hellenistic Period and the period of the Roman Empire. Since Greek was now the lingua franca in the Macedonian kingdoms, works were written in Koine even by people whose ancestors were not Greek and who did not consider themselves Greek. There was, for example, in Egyptian Alexandria during the Hellenistic Period a very large population of Diaspora Jews, many of whom could not read the Hebrew of the Bible and for some of whom Greek may have been their native language. For their benefit, a translation of the Bible into Greek was made, beginning in the third century BC. This translation, known as the Septuagint, is the translation used by the authors of the books of the New Testament, and it is from the Septuagint that they quote, when they quote, as they often do, from the Old Testament. The Septuagint is still today the official text of the Old Testament used by the Greek Orthodox Church. A well-educated Greek of the Hellenistic Period, however, if he had encountered the Septuagint, would have regarded it as a curious and interesting text documenting the history of a barbarian nation, but as stylistically crude and lacking the rhetorical polish that distinguishes fine, literate Greek prose. Unfortunately, not a great deal of fine, literate Greek prose from the Hellenistic Period has survived. Instead, the surviving masterpieces of Greek literature from the period are in verse. Even so, what we have represents only a small fraction of what was produced in a particularly vital and inventive phase of Greek literature.

The transformation of the Greek world that had resulted from Alexander's campaigns and the division of his empire affected every aspect of Greek culture, not least Greek literature. Increased contact with non-Greek cultures and literatures had the effect of introducing "exotic" elements into Greek literature, but it also made Greek authors more acutely aware of the need to define and preserve the characteristically Greek elements of their literary heritage. This led to a need to "take stock," a need that was satisfied in part thanks to the patronage of Ptolemy I of Egypt. Near the grounds of his palace at Alexandria he established a library, associated with the Museum that he also founded. "Museum" is a Greek word that means "shrine dedicated to the Muses," the Muses being the divine patrons of all aspects of culture. The Museum at Alexandria was a research institute, fully funded by Ptolemy I and his successors, in which scholars could meet and live at royal expense while they discussed poetry, science, music, and other aspects of high culture. The resources of the library facilitated their research and, under royal patronage, the library at Alexandria grew to become a repository of Greek literature that aimed to collect the entire body of available Greek texts. The Ptolemies appointed a succession of brilliant scholars to serve as librarians, who organized and catalogued the library's holdings, making it possible to identify "gaps" in the collection. Gaps, of course, can occur only in what is considered to be a discrete entity, and so, for the first time the notion arose that the Greek literary tradition was closed, that there was a fundamental break between the present and the past. In addition, Alexandrian scholars saw themselves as literary critics; that is, as authorities in a position to evaluate and pass judgment on the literary creations of the past. Some of these scholars accordingly began to construct selective lists of "the best" authors in each of the various literary genres. In the eighteenth century, a Dutch classical scholar began to use the appropriately Greek word "canon," meaning "model" or "standard," to refer to these lists. While we do not know what word the ancient scholars themselves applied to them, the effect of these lists was to establish a selective body of earlier literature to be admired and emulated, thus rewriting the literary history of Greece in terms of the values of the Hellenistic Period. It is, thus, during the Hellenistic Period that Greek literature first becomes genuinely "literary," as it now regards literature as a collection of artifacts in the form of written texts rather than as an ongoing series of performances in the theater, the courtroom, or the symposium.

That is not to say that oral performance of literary works ceased in the Hellenistic Period. Old dramas continued to be performed and new ones continued to be written for the stage, and poets still recited their latest compositions to receptive audiences. The audience, however, was no longer the circumscribed community of the polis. Rather, literature was now intended for an educated class of Greeks and Hellenized non-Greeks, who lived in the cities, scattered over three continents, of the Macedonian kingdoms. In the fifth century, Euripides had composed his tragedies for an audience and cast of Athenian citizens. Now Euripides' works were performed as "classics" in Greek theaters built in places like Hamadan, Iran and Ai Khanoum, Afghanistan (figure 60). The dramatic works that were written in the Hellenistic Period have almost entirely perished. An intriguing exception is a 250-line fragment of a tragedy written by a Hellenistic Jew named Ezekiel who most likely lived in Alexandria. The tragedy, called *The Exodus*, dramatizes the Old Testament story and is written in a Greek that bravely tries to imitate the language, style, and meter of Aeschylus and Euripides. Other dramatists of the Hellenistic Period seem to have imitated the plots, as well as the diction, of fifth-century Attic tragedy, to judge from such titles that we know of as *Oedipus* and *Telephus*.

> GOD: What is this that you hold in your hands? Tell me now.
> MOSES: A staff to punish beasts and men.
> GOD: Cast it upon the ground and step back quickly. For it will become a frightful and awe-inspiring serpent.
> MOSES: There, it has been cast down. Lord, be merciful. Oh! How frightful, how prodigious! Have pity on me! I am terrified to look upon it and my limbs are shaking with fear.
> GOD: Be not afraid. Stretch out your hand and take it by the tail; it will be a staff again as it was before. (Ezekiel, *The Exodus* 120–8)

Imitation does not necessarily imply lack of originality or creativity. Certainly Euripides, the most original of all classical Greek poets, imitated and was influenced by Aeschylus, among others. The difference in the Hellenistic Period is that poets were now applying their creativity to imitation of predecessors who were felt to have inhabited a world that no longer existed. That no-longer-existent world of the past could

> They told me, Heraclitus, thou wert dead;
>   And then I thought, and tears thereon did shed,
> How oft we two talk'd down the sun; but thou,
>   Halicarnassian guest, art ashes now!
> Yet live thy nightingales of song. On those
>   Forgetfulness her hand shall ne'er impose.
>   (Callimachus, *Epigram* 2, translated
>   by Henry Nelson Coleridge)

only be recovered by study and research, and the poets of the Hellenistic Period were among the foremost scholars and literary historians who worked in institutions like the library at Alexandria. (One does not, after all, think it necessary to conduct "research" into a living tradition of which one feels a part.) This lends a scholarly, almost academic, tone to much of Hellenistic poetry. This is especially

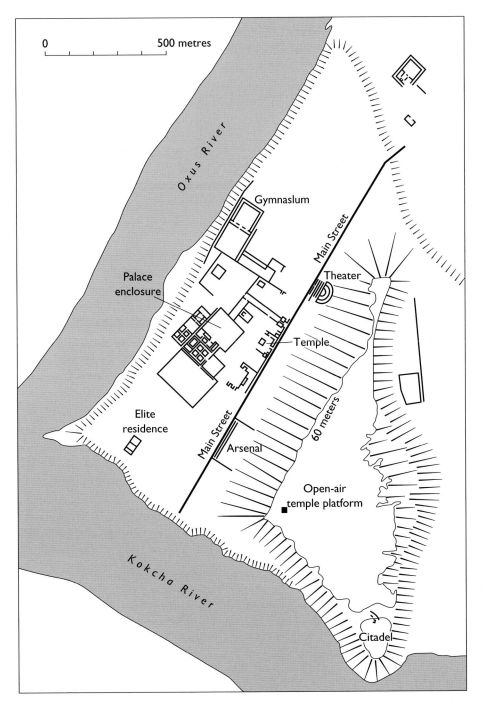

Figure 60 Plan
of Hellenistic city
located at what is
now Ai Khanoum,
Afghanistan.
Reproduced from
B. A. Sparkes (ed.),
Greek Civilization:
An Introduction
(Oxford 1998),
p. 85, figure 5.1.

apparent from the work of Callimachus, the most outstanding poet of the Hellenistic Period and also one of the most outstanding scholars. Most of his vast literary and scholarly output has been lost, but enough of his poetry survives to enable us to get a sense of his style and his literary aims. For Callimachus, as for all Greeks, poetry is virtually defined by the epics of Homer, whom the Greeks often referred to simply as The Poet. Callimachus and all the other Hellenistic poets undertook an exhaustive study, not only of the Homeric poems, but of the ways in which the Homeric poems had been imitated and emulated by the various lyric, dramatic, and elegiac poets who lived between the time of Homer and the Hellenistic Period. What emerged from this study was that, while it was not possible to compete directly with Homer, there were various ways of being "Homeric" without composing large-scale epic poems on heroic subjects. In fact, since direct comparison with Homer would always be to the later poet's disadvantage, the best way of asserting one's Homeric credentials was by creatively emulating one or two Homeric characteristics at a time, and doing it in a conspicuously unHomeric manner.

So, for example, Callimachus composed a poem entitled *Hecale*, of which only fragments survive but which can be reconstructed with some confidence. It is written in the same epic meter, the dactylic hexameter, and the same artificial dialect used in the poems of Homer and Hesiod. Likewise, it is concerned with the heroic past of Greek myth. But it does not focus on the heroic aspect of the myth and, in fact, it deals with a myth that is so obscure that almost no author before Callimachus had treated it. Hecale was an old woman living alone who welcomed into her cottage the Athenian hero Theseus when he was on his way to perform one of his heroic labors. Theseus returned to Hecale's cottage after he had completed his task, only to find that she had died. In gratitude for her hospitality, Theseus established a shrine in her honor and named an Attic deme after her. The contrast between the Homeric diction and the humble surroundings of Hecale's cottage are striking and quite characteristic of Hellenistic poetry. Also characteristic are the use of an arcane story, the interest in an elderly character, and the inclusion of a link between the present and the mythical past, in the form of the shrine and the deme. In keeping with the more modest subject matter, the scale of Callimachus' *Hecale* was considerably more restrained than that of the *Iliad* and the *Odyssey*: each of the Homeric poems consists of 24 books, while the *Hecale* was contained in a single book of perhaps 1,200 lines. This reduction in scale is also characteristic of the poetry of the Hellenistic period. Callimachus is famous for reportedly having said, "Big book equals big disaster," and certainly there is nothing in Hellenistic poetry that remotely approaches the size of the Homeric poems. It is not that lengthy compositions are inherently inferior – no one would deny that the Homeric epics are the greatest works of Greek poetry – but that the nature of poetic composition in the Hellenistic Period is incompatible with poetry on a very large scale. For the Hellenistic poet is expected to spend a great deal of time, first seeking out arcane subjects for poetic treatment (or arcane versions of more familiar subjects) and then laboriously refining the verse until it has been purged of anything that might strike a learned reader as common or ordinary. If a Hellenistic poet had produced a poem

Figure 61 Marble relief by Archelaos showing (bottom) Homer being crowned by Time and Humanity and receiving worship at a round altar; height 1.18 m, ca. 200 BC. London, British Museum, 2191.

the length of the *Odyssey*, either the poet must have lived well beyond the normal human life span or standards of quality control must have been unacceptably lax. The only possible explanation for the length as well as excellence of the *Iliad* and the *Odyssey* was that Homer was, if not divine, at least divinely inspired (figure 61).

The Hellenistic poet who came closest to challenging Homer directly was the epic poet Apollonius of Rhodes. Like Callimachus, Apollonius lived in the first half of the third century BC and, like Callimachus, he was associated with the library in Alexandria. His poetry is, accordingly, learned and refined, like that of his contemporary. The ambitious poem for which Apollonius is known is the (by Hellenistic standards) lengthy *Argonautica*, which recounts the heroic exploits of Jason and the crew of the Argo on their quest for the legendary Golden Fleece. The *Argonautica*, in four books, is about a third as long as the *Iliad* or the *Odyssey* and it imitates Homer's language and style quite closely. Despite its setting in the world of heroic myth, however, the *Argonautica* seems quite deliberately to undermine the heroic aspects of the story and to underline the distance between the epic past and the Hellenistic present. Apollonius expects his readers to be intimately familiar, not only with the Homeric poems but with the entire range of Greek poetry from the time of Homer to the third century, in particular with the works of the Attic dramatists. Part of the story of Jason had been memorably treated in Euripides' *Medea* (p. 192), and Apollonius counts on his readers to have that tragedy constantly in mind. For the *Argonautica* treats of those events that occurred before the dissolution of Jason and Medea's marriage, and the reader of the *Argonautica* cannot help but recall the sordid outcome of the story as dramatized by Euripides.

The *Argonautica* recounts, among other things, the beginning of the relationship between Jason and Medea. Jason and his fellow Argonauts have sailed to the remote easternmost shore of the Black Sea, in what is now the Republic of Georgia. The vicious king of the region, who possesses the Golden Fleece, imposes on Jason a seemingly impossible task before he will hand over the fleece to the young Greek hero. The stage is set for an ordeal that will put Jason's strength and courage to a test of heroic proportions. But Jason's ultimate success in the ordeal depends as much upon his sex appeal as on his fortitude. For Medea, the king's daughter, is smitten with uncontrollable passion at her first glimpse of Jason, and she has knowledge of magical means that make Jason invulnerable. The erotic had not been a conspicuous feature of earlier epic poetry, but the Hellenistic poets (and artists) were fascinated by the irresistible attraction of this irrational force. Aristophanes had criticized Euripides (p. 195) for trivializing tragedy by introducing the erotic element, but the influence of Euripides was so pervasive that the erotic became an essential feature of subsequent Greek poetry. In the *Argonautica*, Apollonius introduces Eros, the god of erotic passion, himself. It is Eros whom the goddesses Hera and Athena recruit to inspire Medea with love for Jason, so that the success of Jason's heroic quest lies in the hands of Eros, who, it turns out, is a mere child, a spoiled brat, the son of Aphrodite. Apollonius very perceptively conveys the parallelism of adult erotic passion and the uncontrollable cupidity of an overindulged child in his portrayal of this mighty deity. According to Albert Einstein, "God does not play dice," but it is precisely dice-playing that this god is engaged in when we first encounter him in the poem: he is playing at knucklebones with Ganymede, a boy who is the object of Zeus' erotic passion. Eros has won almost all of Ganymede's pieces, but he will not be happy until he has won them all, which he gleefully proceeds to do. Later, he has to be bribed to shoot one of his arrows into the marrow of Medea. The bribe is a toy, a brightly colored ball, the symbolism of which is made clear by Apollonius' description: the ball resembles the sphere of the earth, and we are left in no doubt that Apollonius wishes to suggest that the world is controlled by a mighty force that is utterly unstable, irrational, and unpredictable.

This vignette is matched by another, earlier in the poem, when Jason is on his way to meet another princess who, like Medea, immediately falls in love with him. Jason is wearing a magnificent cloak, made for him by the goddess Athena. Apollonius describes the figured scenes with which the cloak is decorated, one of which portrays Aphrodite, the goddess of sexual allure, wielding the great bronze shield of Ares, the god of war and Aphrodite's lover. As she does this her dress slips off her shoulder and she admires her lovely reflection in the curve of the gleaming shield. Again, the symbolism is readily apparent: the weapons of war, like their master, are mere playthings in the hands of the overmastering mistress of passion. This image embodies many of the characteristics of Apollonius' poetry, indeed of

Figure 62 Plaster impression of an engraved garnet gemstone set in gold ring, inscribed "created by Gelon," showing Aphrodite holding a shield and spear; 29 × 24 mm, late third century BC. Boston, Museum of Fine Arts, Francis Bartlett Donation, 21.1213; copyright 2002 Museum of Fine Arts, Boston.

Hellenistic poetry in general: a concern with the erotic and a rejection of the heroic, a recognition of the force of irrational impulses in human behavior, a delight in paradox, and a sensitivity to the pictorial. In fact, this scene is found in the visual arts of the period and can be taken as emblematic of Hellenistic art as well. Figure 62 is a plaster impression (because it reveals the details more readily than the stone itself) of a gemstone carved by an engraver who lived, like Apollonius, in the third century BC. The gem is set in a gold ring of a type that was popular in Ptolemaic Egypt, and it may be that the engraver, like Apollonius, also worked in Alexandria. It is not clear whether Apollonius' description was influenced by an already existing pictorial tradition or the artist of this gem was inspired by the *Argonautica*. What is clear, however, is that the cross-pollination of literature and the visual arts was more fruitful during the Hellenistic Period than at any other time in Greek history.

Hellenistic Art

We have already seen that Apollonius relates in detail the scenes depicted on Jason's cloak. This type of elaborate description of a work of art is very common in Hellenistic poetry. By the same token, Hellenistic art is often very "literary," in the sense that it alludes to or takes its inspiration from works of literature. Greek artists had always concerned themselves with the depiction of myth, but now they often depicted myth with reference to a version in a particular literary text. Just as Hellenistic poets grounded their verse in their laborious reading of the work of their predecessors, so their counterparts in the visual arts made themselves intimately familiar with the literature of the past. A particularly impressive example of this is the structure built at Pergamum in the first half of the second century BC to house the Great Altar of Zeus. Pergamum, a city on the west coast of Asia Minor, was the site of a small, independent Hellenistic kingdom whose founder controlled the treasury of one of Alexander's generals. The kings of Pergamum, known as the Attalid dynasty, sought to make Pergamum into a center of learning and culture comparable to what Athens had been in the fifth and fourth centuries. The Attalid kings established an impressive library in Pergamum, second only to that in Alexandria, and they built up the acropolis of the city in magnificent fashion with several imposing public buildings, including the Altar of Zeus. This structure was of an unusual design: the altar was set on a high platform and surrounded by a colonnade, which projected out on either side of the grand staircase leading up to the platform (figure 63). The platform was decorated with a large sculptured frieze, over 2 meters high and about 120 meters in length, depicting the mythical battle between the gods and the

Figure 63   Reconstruction of the west side of the Great Altar of Zeus; width 36.44 m, first half of second century BC. Berlin, Pergamum Museum; copyright 2002 Bildarchiv Preussischer Kulturbesitz, Berlin (Neg.-Nr. PM 6922).

giants. The artists responsible for the frieze designed it following an elaborate program that is carefully based on Hesiod's *Theogony*, in which the battle is described. In learned fashion, the approximately one hundred figures that appeared on the frieze were identified by inscriptions.

In addition to this frieze, a smaller frieze decorated the upper portion of the walls of the colonnade. It, too, displays its artists' extensive learning by depicting in great detail the life of the local hero Telephus. In order to construct this visual narrative, the artists needed to make use not only of well-known texts like Euripides' *Telephus* (p. 194), but also some very obscure epic accounts that modern scholars have had great difficulty identifying and reconstructing. The importance of the Telephus frieze, which is unfortunately very poorly preserved, lies in its careful narrative sequence. It is the earliest example of such continuous narrative in Greek art, following as it does a chronological sequence that can be "read," like a text, from left to right. The importance of the frieze showing the battle between the gods and the giants, however, lies in its flamboyant, restless style. Unlike the restrained and Classical frieze from the fifth-century Parthenon (p. 180), everything here is a swirl of motion and emotion. The action is violent and disordered and the entire surface of the frieze is filled with figures: gods and giants (some winged), wild beasts, and the serpents that take the place of some giants' legs. In contrast to the conventions of Classical art, there is here no hesitation to represent emotion outright, by showing its effects on the features of the participants (figure 64).

Characteristic of Hellenistic art is the artist's desire to engage the viewer more directly and with greater immediacy than had been the case in the Classical Period. The creators of the Altar of Zeus have accomplished this not only with the emotionally involving style of presentation, but by the very design of the altar and the frieze. For one thing, the frieze is much more conspicuous and more readily visible than, say, the frieze of the Parthenon: there is no roof above the frieze to cast a dark shadow over it and the frieze is only slightly above eye-level. Further, as one mounts the stairway, one finds oneself on the same level as the action. Indeed, some of the action of the frieze is taking place on the stairway, encroaching upon the very space occupied by the viewer (figure 65). This encroachment of the work of sculpture into the viewer's space was cultivated by Hellenistic artists as a means of engaging the viewer's attention and emotional involvement, but like many features of the Hellenistic Period we find its roots already in the fourth century. Unfortunately, the originals of most fourth-century sculptures have perished, but copies were made during the Roman period of many of the most famous works and some of these copies have survived. Roman copies can only give a general impression of what the original looked like, particularly since in many instances the originals were hollow-cast in bronze while the copies were carved in marble. Still, they provide valuable evidence of the statue's original pose, as well as evidence of the influence of Greek art in Rome and of the taste of Roman collectors. Figure 66 shows a Roman copy of a lost bronze original by Lysippus, a sculptor who held an important place in the period of transition between Classical and Hellenistic art and whom Alexander the Great appointed as his court sculptor. The statue is of a young

Figure 64   Part of the east frieze of the Great Altar of Zeus, showing Nike crowning Athena as she battles an unidentified giant, with Gaia (Earth, the mother of the giants) rising up to entreat her; height of frieze 2.3 m. Berlin, Pergamum Museum; copyright 2002 Bildarchiv Preussischer Kulturbesitz, Berlin (Neg.-Nr. PM 7328).

athlete using a scraper to remove sand, sweat, and olive oil from his body after exercising and was known in antiquity as the Apoxyomenos, or "The Man Using a Scraper." It was a famous statue that the emperor Tiberius himself appropriated for his palace in Rome in the first century after Christ. The sculpture does not depict a subject from the remote mythical past, but something that would have been a common, everyday sight for a Greek man who spent time (as most leisured Greek men did) in the gymnasium. The familiar character of the subject was further enhanced by the revolutionary pose of the statue, with its languorously outstretched arms abruptly dismantling the barrier between the viewer's space and that of the statue.

   In the Hellenistic Period, this intimacy between viewer and work of art was taken still further, into a realm that bordered on the perilous. Several Roman copies survive of a lost original from the middle of the third century BC depicting the goddess Aphrodite kneeling at her bath (figure 67). It was thought to be dangerous to

Figure 65 Part of the west frieze of the Great Altar of Zeus, showing the gods of the sea battling unidentified giants. Berlin, Pergamum Museum; copyright 2002 Bildarchiv Preussischer Kulturbesitz, Berlin (Neg.-Nr. PM 6923).

Figure 66 The Apoxyomenos by Lysippus: marble copy of bronze original (which needed no struts or braces); height of copy 2.05 m, original ca. 330 BC. Vatican Museums, Museo Pio Clementino, Gabinetto dell'Apoxyomenos, Inv. 1185; photo: Vatican Museums.

Figure 67 Marble copy of an original statue, attributed to Doidalsas, depicting Aphrodite at her bath; height of copy 98 cm, original ca. 250 BC. Paris, Musée du Louvre, MA 2240; copyright Erich Lessing/Art Resource, NY.

see a goddess in the nude, and a number of myths told of men who had been blinded or subjected to even worse punishment for accidentally seeing a naked goddess. But this sculpture not only reveals Aphrodite in the nude, it positively invites the viewer to inspect the goddess from every angle. For her twisting pose means that there is no "front" and "back" to this statue. There is no single, proper point from which to view the goddess and be done with it. This is sculpture that is fully in the round which, by its pose and by the sensuousness of its subject, quite literally moves the viewer.

It may seem to be obvious that any work of art is intended to move (in the sense of arouse the emotions of) the viewer, but in fact something new and important began with the art of the fourth century and the Hellenistic Period. The emotions aroused by the artists of the Classical Period had been admiration for the artist's ability to produce a convincing likeness and, in the case of representations of the gods, awe inspired by the majesty, power, and remoteness of the images (figure 68). In the art of the Hellenistic Period, however, we find a deliberate attempt to arouse more complex, even problematic emotions. This is analogous to what we saw earlier (p. 192) in literature, in the case of the emotions aroused by Euripidean tragedy. The drama, and particularly Euripidean drama, exercised a pervasive influence on later Greek literature, and it is legitimate to speak of the impact of the drama on the visual arts in the Hellenistic Period as well. For there is something dramatic, even theatrical, about much of Hellenistic art. This is quite obviously the case with the frieze on the Great Altar of Zeus in Pergamum, with its exaggerated gestures and the pathos evoked by some of the defeated giants.

Figure 68
Hollow-cast original bronze statue from the Classical Period, recovered in the 1920s from an ancient shipwreck, showing Zeus hurling a thunderbolt; height 2.09 m, ca. 460 BC. Athens, National Archaeological Museum, 15161.

The same is true of a series of sculptures, also from Pergamum, that decorated monuments erected by King Attalus I to commemorate his military victories in the 230s and 220s BC over the Gauls. The Gauls were a Celtic people who invaded and raided western Asia Minor in the early third century, settling in Galatia, the region named after them and familiar from Paul's epistle in the New Testament to its inhabitants. The sculptures, some of which survive in Roman copies, depicted the defeated Gallic warriors and their families, dead and dying. One work that has not survived, even in a copy, showed a pathetic tableau of a young Gallic child affectionately stroking its slain mother. A different set of emotions is evoked by a work that does survive in a Roman copy, a group showing a Gallic warrior and his wife (figure 69). Rather than allow himself and his family to be enslaved by the victorious Macedonians, the Gaul has stabbed his own wife and, with a look of defiance on his proud face, is plunging his sword into his chest. These are uncivilized barbarians, who do not live in poleis and who have none of the refinements of Greek culture. Still, their spirit is admirable and their passionate desire for freedom is something that Greeks can appreciate. It is this defiant spirit that the artist captures and

Figure 69   Marble copy of an original bronze statue of a Gallic warrior and his wife; height of copy 2.11 m, original ca. 230–220 BC. Rome, Museo Nazionale Romano, Palazzo Massimo alle Terme, 8608; copyright Scala/Art Resource, NY.

displays for his Greek viewer's admiration (along with the suggestion that "we" Greeks were successful in subduing this brave people). Within a hundred years of the creation of this sculpture, however, the Attalid kingdom of Pergamum would come to an end, its territory and wealth falling under the control of a much better organized and more civilized nation of barbarians, the Romans. In 133 BC, King Attalus III died; in his will he left his kingdom to the Roman people. One by one, all the Macedonian kingdoms became part of the Roman Empire, the last of them, the Ptolemaic kingdom of Egypt, becoming a Roman province in 30 BC. This did not mean the end of Greek civilization but, rather, the beginning of a new phase that lasted, remarkably, for nearly a millennium and a half, until the conquest by the Turks of the eastern half of the Roman Empire in AD 1453.

Recommended for Further Reading

Canfora, L. *The Vanished Library*, English translation (Berkeley 1989): a very readable and imaginative (but not fanciful) account of the library in Alexandria and the fascination it has had for posterity.

Fantuzzi, M. and Hunter, R. *Tradition and Innovation in Hellenistic Poetry* (Cambridge and New York 2004): an important and authoritative work by the scholars who are in the forefront of the study of Hellenistic literature.

Hellenistic Poetry: An Anthology, selected and translated by B. H. Fowler (Madison 1990): a generous selection (including the whole of Apollonius' *Argonautica*) of Hellenistic poetry in translations that are of consistently fine quality.

Irby-Massie, G. L. and Keyser, P. T. *Greek Science of the Hellenistic Era: A Sourcebook* (London and New York 2002): an excellent anthology of selections from the Golden Age of Greek science, with helpful introductions to the various sections (mathematics, astronomy, biology, etc.) and up-to-date bibliography.

Lloyd, G. E. R. *Greek Science after Aristotle* (London 1973): an excellent general survey of science, technology, and mathematics in the Hellenistic Period and the early Roman Empire, including important observations on the place of science in ancient Greek society.

Pollitt, J. J. *Art in the Hellenistic Age* (Cambridge 1986): a penetrating study of Hellenistic art and what makes it distinctive, a study that has important implications for the understanding of all aspects of Hellenistic culture.

Rihll, T. E. *Greek Science* (Oxford 1999): a brief and engaging survey that starts from the encouraging proposition that "not knowing much modern science can be an advantage" in "understanding what is going on in most Greek science."

Shipley, G. *The Greek World after Alexander, 323–30 BC* (London and New York 2000): a clear, detailed, and up-to-date survey of the history of the Hellenistic Period, including excellent general accounts of Hellenistic literature, science, philosophy, and religion.

AFTERWORD: LOOKING FORWARD

The conventional date for the end of the Hellenistic Period is 30 BC, the year in which Ptolemaic rule in Egypt came to an end and Egypt became a province of the Roman Empire. The end of the Ptolemaic kingdom, the last of the Hellenistic monarchies to fall to Rome, came as a result of the battle of Actium, a town on the west coast of mainland Greece, in the previous year. The last Ptolemaic ruler, the fascinating Queen Cleopatra VII, was among those who suffered defeat at Actium, but the battle was primarily a contest between two Roman leaders, Octavian (who later adopted the name Augustus) and Cleopatra's lover Marc Antony. This was the culmination of a series of civil wars that had for decades embroiled the Roman state, the effects of which were often felt directly in the cities and the countryside of Greece and other areas in the east that had formerly been controlled by the Hellenistic kingdoms. The city of Athens, for example, at various times in the first century BC found itself under the control of the Roman generals Sulla, Pompey, Julius Caesar, Brutus, and Marc Antony. Nor was the battle of Actium the only engagement between opposing forces in the Roman civil wars to take place on Greek soil.

By the time the Roman province of Achaia was created in 27 BC, the province that comprised most of mainland Greece and many of the Aegean islands, the Greeks had had ample opportunity to acquaint themselves with the Romans and to accept their seemingly inevitable role as rulers of the world. In addition, because of the political developments that had taken place during the Hellenistic Period, the cities of Greece had become accustomed to being part of a larger political entity. During the Hellenistic Period that entity had been one of a number of kingdoms ruled by Greek-speaking Macedonians, whom the Greeks were willing to acknowledge as being at least in some sense Greek. While these Macedonian kings possessed considerable

"Last of all he saw the souls who were returning to birth, being forcibly turned into all sorts of beasts, having their shapes changed by the shapers of animals, with blows of curious instruments. In some cases they hammered the whole of their parts together; in others they twisted them back, and some parts they planed off smooth, and got rid of them entirely, so that they might be fitted to other habits and modes of life. Among them he saw the soul of Nero in a bad state generally and pierced with red-hot nails. The smiths had in hand for it the form of Pindar's viper, in which it would be conceived and come to life by gnawing itself through its mother. Hereupon, he said, a great light suddenly shone forth, and a voice from the light was heard giving orders to change it into a milder type, and devise a creature that croaks round marshes and lakes; he had been already punished for his crimes, and now some favour was due to him from the Gods for having freed Greece, the most excellent nation of his subjects and the one dearest to the Gods." (Plutarch, *God's Slowness to Punish* 567e–68a, translated by G. R. S. Mead)

AD 1

Birth of Plutarch (ca. 45)

Nero tours Greece (67)

AD 100

Hadrian's wall across Britain begun (122)

Marcus Aurelius becomes emperor
of Rome (161)

AD 200

Roman citizenship granted to all free inhabitants
of the empire (212)

AD 300

Dedication of New Rome, later Constantinople (330)

Administrative division between Eastern
and Western Empires (364)

AD 400

Alaric and Goths plunder Greece (396)

Nonnus active (ca. 450–470)

Last Roman emperor in West deposed (476)

AD 500

Justinian I closes Academy in
Athens (529)

Paulus Silentiarius active (ca. 550)

AD 600

Arab conquest of Egypt (640)

Muhammad enters Medina (622)

AD 700

Iconoclastic movement bans representation of
divine form (726–843)

AD 800

Photius composes synopses of many
works of Greek literature (ca. 850)

AD 900

Palatine Anthology compiled (early tenth century)

AD 1000

The Passion of Christ composed
(eleventh or twelfth century)

AD 1100

Eustathius writes commentaries on Homeric
poems (late twelfth century)

Venetians sack Constantinople during
Fourth Crusade (1204)

AD 1200

AD 1300

Editing of Classical texts during "Palaeologan
Revival" (late thirteenth to early fourteenth
centuries)

Manuel Chrysoloras goes to Florence to
teach Greek (1397)

AD 1400

Birth of Lucas Cranach the Elder (1472)

Constantinople falls to Ottoman Turks (1453)

AD 1500

Timeline 9   The Roman Empire.

power and were, indeed, recipients of divine honors from their Greek subjects, they were clearly fallible, particularly when confronted with the relentless might of their Roman conquerors. The Romans were able to bring to the cities of Greece what the Hellenistic monarchs could never achieve, namely peace and a general sense of security. Thus, the Roman emperor was felt to be even more deserving of divine honors than the Antigonid or Ptolemaic rulers because he ruled over a vastly more extensive territory and because he was nearly invisible. Like Olympian Zeus, the emperor in Rome appeared very infrequently to his worshipers in Greece. In the first century after Christ, Nero visited Greece, and in the second century Hadrian did the same, on more than one occasion. But these were unusual emperors, who were unusually fond of Greek culture, and their special attention to their Greek subjects was warmly appreciated. For the most part, however, the Greeks came in contact with their Roman rulers in the form of the itinerant provincial governor (or proconsul), who was appointed by the Roman senate for a one-year term of office, and his staff. Roman administration naturally brought with it an obligation to pay taxes to the central government, but it was an obligation felt by only a small percentage of the population and, in any event, it was worth paying the price for the security that Roman rule both promised and delivered.

Now, under the control of Latin-speaking Roman administrators, the Greeks once again needed to redefine themselves in an awareness of their lack of political power, but confident of their cultural superiority to their Roman masters. The Romans, too, were well aware of the merits of Greek civilization, and a number of educated Romans either went to Greece to study oratory and philosophy or imported Greek experts to teach those subjects in Rome. It was, thus, necessary for the Romans to come to terms with Greek culture and for the Greeks to come to terms with Roman authority. This process of accommodation gives Greek civilization during the Roman period its own particular flavor and makes it a fascinating subject of study. The term "Greek" was now, however, coming to have more a cultural than a geographical or genealogical significance. Greek culture during the time of the Roman Empire was becoming a "heritage," rather like what it has become today: a possession to be appropriated by Greeks and non-Greeks alike. This broadening out of Greek culture to embrace people who were not Greek by birth had begun with Alexander's conquests and the founding by him and his successors of Greek cities in Egypt and throughout Asia. This process continued during the Hellenistic Period, when Greek culture became a mark of prestige and power in the Macedonian kingdoms. When those kingdoms were absorbed into the Roman Empire, the appeal of Greek culture spread over a still greater geographical range, including even the westernmost parts of the empire. This meant that those who thought of themselves as "Greeks" in the stricter sense felt an even greater responsibility as, in a sense, the caretakers of this increasingly venerable heritage. That responsibility was felt most strongly in connection with literary expression, which depends, naturally, upon a secure command of the Greek language and a refined sense of style and idiom.

Later Greek Literature: Poetry

Greek literature during the period of the Roman Empire thus displayed a remarkable continuity with the past. Literary forms that had developed in the Archaic and Classical Periods continued to be pursued, and the results are nearly indistinguishable in formal terms from their predecessors of hundreds of years earlier. The epic was always considered to be the highest form of literary creation, and we saw (p. 238) that the most ambitious poets of the Hellenistic Period sought to continue the tradition of Homeric poetry, usually on a smaller scale. The same was the case later as well. A poet who went by the name of Musaeus, for example, about whom we know nothing at all but who seems to have lived in the fifth or sixth century after Christ, composed an elegant miniature epic that told the tragic love story of Hero and Leander. Everything about this poem is steeped in the distant past: the focus on the erotic recalls the poetry of the Hellenistic Period, the language, style, and meter are thoroughly Homeric, and even the poet's pen name is appropriated from a legendary poet who is supposed to have lived at a time still earlier than that of Homer.

Not all epic poets of the time, however, exercised the restraint that Musaeus displayed in limiting his poem to fewer than four hundred lines. A third-century poet from the Greek city of Smyrna, with the Roman name of Quintus, wrote an epic poem in 14 books that picks up the story of the Trojan War just at the point at which the *Iliad* ends, continuing the story to the fall of Troy and the departure of the Greek heroes for home. Even more ambitious was the fifth-century poet Nonnus, from the Greek city Panopolis in Egypt, who composed an exuberant epic in 48 books (the combined length of the *Iliad* and the *Odyssey*!) entitled *Dionysiaca*, concerned with the birth and fabulous adventures of the god Dionysus. What is perhaps most remarkable about this poem is that its author was apparently Christian. At any rate, the only other work of his that survives is a recasting in verse of the Gospel according to John, composed in the same meter (dactylic hexameter) and observing the same Homeric language as his massive epic about the pagan god of wine.

What we have, then, in the *Dionysiaca* is a very elaborate literary creation that tries to give the impression of ignoring everything that had happened in the more than one thousand years since the time of Homer, including the career of Alexander the Great, the incorporation of Greece into the Roman Empire, and the advent of Christianity. In fact, Nonnus' subject matter, which includes an extensive account of Dionysus' campaigns in India, is unimaginable without Alexander's conquests, and Nonnus' style is heavily influenced by Homer's Hellenistic successors. Nevertheless, Nonnus and, it would seem, his audience wished to pretend that the

> My name – my country – what are they to thee?
>   What, whether base or proud my pedigree?
> Perhaps I far surpassed all other men;
>   Perhaps I fell below them all; what then?
> Suffice it, stranger! that thou seest a tomb!
>   Thou know'st its use; it hides – no matter whom.
>   (Paulus Silentiarius, *The Greek Anthology*
>   7.307, translated by William Cowper)

poetry written in fifth-century Egypt was indistinguishable in important respects from that composed in Archaic Greece. The same is true in the case of another poetic genre that persisted from the Archaic Period to the time of Nonnus and beyond, namely the epigram. Originally "epigram" simply referred to anything inscribed, most commonly a text either in prose or verse on a marker for a grave. Already in the Classical Period poets had written epigrams, almost exclusively in elegiac meter, that were not necessarily composed for inscription on a tombstone. In some cases, these were not even seriously intended, but were rather *jeux d'esprit* with playful or satirical intent. Before long, epigrams came to be written that had no funerary connection, dealing instead with poets and the poetic craft, with the visual arts and, increasingly, with erotic matters.

The epigram was especially cultivated during the Hellenistic Period, which valued refinement and brevity, and Hellenistic poets began to collect in anthologies epigrams of their predecessors and contemporaries. The practice of composing and collecting epigrams continued for a thousand years, and we are exceptionally fortunate that two substantial manuscripts have survived, one from the tenth century and one from the fourteenth, between them preserving over 4,000 epigrams dating from the Archaic Period down to the tenth century after Christ. The collective contents of these manuscripts are known as *The Greek Anthology*, and they attest to the extraordinary vitality and continuity of Greek literature. Every aspect of life, and death, is explored in this kaleidoscopic treasury of literary gems. In some cases, the same theme is treated again and again by successive poets, each trying to improve on the refinement and concision of previous generations of poets. The language and style of the epigrams are still essentially those of the Archaic Period, whether the author of the poem is a Spanish-born Roman emperor or a Christian bishop and saint from Cappadocia. These epigrams exercised an enormous influence on English and European poetry of the modern period: Shakespeare, Johnson, Herrick, and Dryden, among many others, either translated or adapted poems from *The Greek Anthology* in their own work.

> This wretched life of ours is Fortune's ball;
>   Twixt wealth and poverty she bandies all.
> These, cast to earth, up to the skies rebound;
>   Those, toss'd to heaven, come tumbling to the ground.
>   (Palladas, *The Greek Anthology* 10.80,
>   translated by Goldwin Smith)

> Soon fades the rose; once past the fragrant hour,
> The loiterer finds a bramble for a flow'r.
>   (Anonymous, *The Greek Anthology* 11.53,
>   translated by Samuel Johnson)

Later Greek Literature: Oratory

Greek literary expression during the Roman Empire did not confine itself to poetry. Authors writing in prose were very active and prolific in the areas of history, oratory, philosophy, and medicine, and a great deal of their literary output has survived. Modern sensibilities do not incline us to regard oratory as a particularly elevated branch of literature, or even as a form of literature at all. But to the ancient Greeks (and Romans), the orator was a literary artist who engaged in a sort of high-risk public performance that could result in great rewards, in terms of political success and prestige, or equally great humiliation. The orator put his person on public display and invited his character and his command of the Greek language to be appraised. For this reason, oratory always held an important place in establishing standards of expression and formed a vital part of Greek education. The great impetus for the development of public oratory had come in democratic Athens in the fifth and fourth centuries BC, where citizens trained by the sophists hoped to sway the assembly and shape public policy. After the end of the Classical Period, however, public policy in Athens and elsewhere was shaped by Macedonian kings and, later, by Roman emperors and by the proconsuls and procurators who administered the provinces of the Roman Empire. It might be expected that, under these conditions, the need for skill in public speaking would evaporate. But verbal proficiency had for so long virtually defined Greek culture that new outlets for its display were developed and Greek oratory experienced a renewed efflorescence in the first three centuries after Christ. Indeed, these changed circumstances presented a challenge to highly educated Greeks to use their rhetorical skill as a means of repossessing the past, thereby reshaping the past for their own purposes and asserting publicly their own control over it. Having had centuries of practice in reinventing their past, the Greeks rose to the challenge to do so once again.

The Greek orators of the early Roman Empire are generally spoken of as belonging to a "Second Sophistic," rivaling in verbal accomplishment the sophists of the fifth and fourth centuries BC. Indeed, some of the speeches they delivered were intended to represent what an historical character of the fifth or fourth century BC might have said if he had undergone the kind of rhetorical training that the orators of the Second Sophistic were prepared to impart to their pupils. That is, these sophists would compose and declaim display pieces, often to large and appreciative audiences of enthusiastic connoisseurs, that purported to be, say, the funeral oration over the Athenian dead at Marathon in 490 BC, or a speech urging the Athenian assembly in 415 BC to vote to send reinforcements to the embattled troops in Sicily. If this sounds as though the Greeks were now hopelessly mired in the past, trying to relive the "glory days" of the Classical Period, that is to a certain degree true. But it is equally true that the Greeks of the Classical Period had done exactly the same thing themselves, trying to relive the "glory days" of a still earlier age. So, for example, among the surviving works of the fifth-century sophist Gorgias (p. 216) is a speech ostensibly delivered by the mythical figure Palamedes, defending himself against charges brought by Odysseus of engaging in treasonous dealings with the enemy during the Trojan War. Another of Gorgias' surviving orations is a speech in praise of Helen, who is otherwise universally reviled for having caused the Trojan War by indulging her lust for her husband's guest, Paris.

We find the practitioners of the Second Sophistic and their successors producing the same kinds of rhetorical displays in the cities of the Roman Empire hundreds of years after the age of Gorgias and the earlier sophists. These displays took the form of impersonation either of historical figures from the Classical Period or of mythical characters (for example, a fourth-century speech in which Orestes justifies his murder of his mother). But these were not the only ways in which Greek orators of the Roman period displayed their skills. There was a constant need for their services in providing impressive speeches for the many public ceremonial occasions that arose, like funeral orations for members of the emperor's household or speeches welcoming Roman officials on state visits. Also, since many aspects of the life of the polis continued unchanged under Roman rule, orators were in demand as they had been for centuries for such local performances as a speech commemorating the dedication of a temple or praising a home-town athlete who had won a prize at the Panhellenic Games. The implied continuity between the Classical past and the Roman present is the key to the success of this new breed of sophists: by persuading themselves and their audiences that they were in no way different from their Classical forebears, they made it possible for them and their contemporaries to imagine that nothing had changed, that the Greeks were just as much in control of their own circumstances as they were in the age of Pericles. The popularity and the articulateness of these orators encouraged the Roman authorities to put them to use as spokesmen for official policy, particularly in the eastern half of the empire. For, as a result of its historical development, the Roman Empire was divided along "cultural" lines into two distinct halves, with the dividing-line running north and south somewhere between Greece and Italy: in the western half of the empire the Latin language and Roman culture had been adopted by peoples whom the Romans regarded as less civilized than themselves, whereas Greek language and culture were established in the eastern half long before the Romans assumed authority.

A Greek Writing about Romans and a Roman Writing in Greek

During the Hellenistic Period, the most noticeable split in the Greek world was between the cities, which were the centers of Hellenism, and the less urbanized areas, which preserved the language and culture of the indigenous populations. These indigenous languages and cultures could be treated with condescension or even ignored by the Greeks and by those who sought the prestige that Greek culture was thought to confer. Now, however, there were two cultures that could claim equal status and prestige, the culture of Rome in the west and that of Greece in the east. Anyone who wished to be taken seriously as an intellectual and anyone who wished to be well informed with regard to the latest developments in the world of ideas needed to be conversant with both cultures.

We can see this most clearly, perhaps, in the lives and writings of two very different men, one Greek and one Roman. Plutarch, who lived from about AD 45 until about AD 120, spent most of his life in the small town in central Greece where he was born. Marcus Aurelius (AD 121–180) was born in Rome at about the time of Plutarch's death and became the ruler of the Roman Empire before he reached the age of 40. Both men received the best education available in rhetoric and philosophy, Plutarch primarily at Plato's Academy in Athens and Marcus in Rome. Plutarch devoted his life to literature and philosophy, writing numerous works, most of which survive, on a great variety of subjects; Marcus' duties as Roman emperor prevented him from writing and studying as much as he would have liked, but he left behind one important work, written not in Latin but in Greek. The background and outlook of Plutarch and Marcus were clearly quite different, but they shared a deep and abiding commitment to the literary, intellectual, and cultural heritage of the Greek past.

> Chaeronean Plutarch, to thy deathless praise
>   Does martial Rome this grateful statue raise,
> Because both Greece and she thy fame have shared
>   (Their heroes written, and their lives compared).
> But thou thyself couldst never write thy own;
>   Their lives have parallels, but thine has none.
>   (Agathias, *The Greek Anthology* 16.331,
>   translated by John Dryden)

Although there survive today nearly a hundred works by Plutarch, mostly essays and dialogues of a moral, philosophical, or antiquarian nature that are collectively referred to by the title "Moralia," or "Ethical Treatises," Plutarch's reputation rests primarily upon another surviving collection of works, his "Parallel Lives," a series of paired biographies of prominent figures – all males, naturally – from the Greek and Roman past. Each pair of biographies concludes with a comparison (although for some pairs the comparison has not survived), detailing the good and bad points of each man's character and assessing the relative merits of each figure, one Greek and one Roman. So, for example, Demosthenes is paired with his Roman counterpart Cicero, and Alexander the Great is paired with Julius Caesar. It should be noted that there is no longer any hesitation on the part of the Greeks of the Roman period about including Alexander and other Macedonian rulers among the great figures of "Greek" history. Plutarch makes it quite clear, however, that "history" is not his primary concern. While his biographies are about the men who directed the course of Greek and Roman history, his focus is on the character, rather than on the accomplishments, of these men. In other words, the "Parallel Lives" no less than the "Moralia" are ethical treatises. Plutarch has treated his subjects in pairs so that he can explore the ways in which similar personalities react to different circumstances and the ways in which similar circumstances are responded to by different personalities. The fact that one member of each pair is Greek and one is Roman serves to convey the universality of ethical categories and to illustrate the fact that neither the Greeks nor the Romans have a monopoly on virtue. For what is most striking about Plutarch's comparisons is the degree to which he seeks to be fair and humane in his assessment. In one pair, the Greek holds a slight edge over the Roman in virtue; in another, the Roman is marginally more admirable. In still another pair, the balance is quite even, with the Greek surpassing the Roman in some respects and falling short in others. What is missing, in fact, from Plutarch's biographies is an historical sensitivity to the differences between, say, Athens in the fifth century and Rome in the first century BC. Everyone from the mythical Greek hero Theseus to Caesar's assassin Brutus is evaluated according to the same set of ethical values, namely the values of a Greek gentleman of the first century after Christ.

Plutarch's ethical values had been molded by his period of study in Athens, at the Academy founded over four hundred years previously by Plato. The Academy had naturally evolved considerably since the time of its founding and, at the time when Plutarch studied there, it taught a rather eclectic version of Platonic philosophy that incorporated some doctrines from other schools of philosophy. These included the school founded by Plato's pupil Aristotle and another school, housed in a STOA, or portico, in Athens. This school, known for this reason as the Stoic school, had been founded in about 300 BC by a Greek from Cyprus named Zeno and became the most influential school of philosophy in the Roman Empire. Fundamental to Stoicism is that its teachings enable the true Stoic to live in harmony with the world by distinguishing through reason between those things that are within the individual's control and those that are not. What are manifestly within the individual's control are his or her thoughts, behavior, and reactions to external events.

STOA A long colonnaded hall, sometimes capitalized (Stoa) to refer to the Stoic school of philosophy, whose founder taught in the Stoa Poikile in Athens.

Thus it is possible for the wise and virtuous Stoic to be in complete control of him or herself regardless of external circumstances. This is one of the prime reasons for the appeal of Stoicism to the ancient Greeks and Romans, both of whom regarded it as humiliating in the extreme to be under the control of someone or something else. The Stoic slave is as free as the emperor of Rome. In fact, a slave and a Roman emperor are the authors of the two most substantial surviving works of Stoic philosophy. Epictetus, a contemporary of Plutarch, was a Greek slave in Rome whose Stoic teaching and writings greatly influenced several prominent Greeks and Romans of the second century after Christ, includ-

"Men are disturbed not by things, but by the views which they take of things. Thus death is nothing terrible, else it would have appeared so to Socrates. But the terror consists in our notion of death, that it is terrible. When, therefore, we are hindered, or disturbed, or grieved, let us never impute it to others, but to ourselves; that is, to our own views. It is the action of an uninstructed person to reproach others for his own misfortunes; of one entering upon instruction, to reproach himself; and of one perfectly instructed, to reproach neither others nor himself." (Epictetus, *The Manual* 5, translated by Thomas Wentworth Higginson)

ing Marcus Aurelius. In his youth, Marcus enthusiastically pursued the study of Stoic philosophy, which provided him throughout his life with spiritual and intellectual guidance. It was apparently toward the end of his life that he began writing the work that is today known as the *Meditations*. This work seems not to have been intended for publication, and in fact the Greek title of the work means something like "Memos to himself." It is, accordingly, a very personal, introspective, ruminative series of reflections intended to inspire and console its author and keep his mind focused on his duty as emperor, as Roman citizen, as family man, as philosopher, and as human being. Although the *Meditations* were written, literally, "to himself,"

Figure 70 Marble statue of Marcus Aurelius from Alexandria in Egypt; height 1.84 m, ca. AD 200. London, British Museum, 1906.

they were not written in Marcus' native language, but in Greek. The same is true of the books of the New Testament, but they were written in Greek in order to communicate as widely as possible with the multi-ethnic population of the eastern Roman Empire. Marcus wrote in Greek because that was the language of the philosophical tradition of which he felt himself to be a part (figure 70).

East is East and West is Not

Well-born and well-educated men like Marcus Aurelius and Plutarch, because of their learning and their wealth, were able to bridge the gap between the two halves of the Roman Empire: the Roman Marcus wrote in Greek and was a devotee of Greek philosophy, while the Greek Plutarch lectured in Rome and had many friends among the elite of the empire's capital. But the division between the Latin west and the Greek east could not be so easily ignored by the mass of the empire's population. Despite the fact that only a generation after Marcus' death, in AD 212, Roman citizenship was extended to every free inhabitant of the empire, there continued to be a fundamental cultural split between the two halves of the empire. This split widened a century later, when the emperor Constantine (ca. AD 273–337) established a new capital for the empire in the Greek city of Byzantium. This city, the

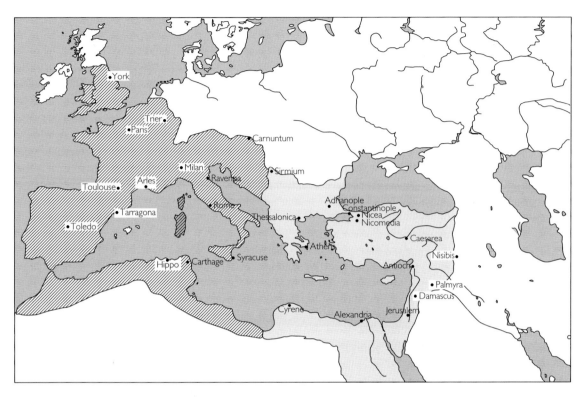

Map 16 The divided Roman Empire, ca. AD 400.

"New Rome," came to be called Constantinople, or "the polis of Constantine," and rapidly became the leading city of the east and the most important center of Greek culture. In the second half of the fourth century, the division of the empire was formally recognized with the creation of a new administrative structure (map 16). From then on there were concurrently two Roman emperors, one governing the Latin-speaking western empire from his capital in Rome and one governing the Greek-speaking eastern empire (now generally referred to as the "Byzantine" empire) from Constantinople.

In addition to establishing Constantinople as his capital, Constantine altered the character of the Roman Empire in another way, by his adoption of Christianity and his development of Constantinople as a Christian city. With only one exception, all subsequent Roman emperors were Christian, and eventually paganism was purged from the empire by the use of either conversion or persecution. Persecution of pagans was by no means either systematic or universal; rather, it occurred in isolated outbreaks at various times in various locations within the empire. A particularly violent clash occurred between pagans and Christians, for example, in Alexandria in the late fourth century. Hostility was especially directed at pagan philosophers and their schools. This was because it was only in the philosophical schools that anything resembling a "doctrine," corresponding to the teachings of

"After this he issued in rapid succession a series of universal laws and directives, forbidding sacrifice to idols, consultation of oracles, erection of statues of the gods, initiation into mystery rites, and the defilement of the cities by the butchery of gladiatorial combats. Another law was handed down concerning the inhabitants of Egypt and, in particular, of Alexandria, who had the custom of using eunuchs to serve in the worship of the river that runs through their territory; the law provided for the elimination of this whole effeminate tribe and ensured that those afflicted with this abomination would not be seen anywhere. And, while the superstitious pagans assumed that the river would no longer give them the benefits of its familiar flooding, quite the opposite of what they expected happened, as God in effect ratified the emperor's law. For those who were polluting their cities with their vice ceased to exist, while the river, as if to cleanse the land, flooded as never before, inundating all the fields with its fructifying stream, thereby instructing the ignorant that sinful men must abandon their ways and all must acknowledge that only the Giver of All Good is responsible for their prosperity." (Eusebius, *The Life of Constantine* 4.25)

the church, could be imagined to exist. Temples of the gods were places where worshipers interacted with the divinity by making offerings or performing sacrifices; priests and priestesses served to facilitate those interactions, not to propagate the faith. That is not to say that pagan temples and their contents were spared. Cult statues were frequent targets of Christian zeal, particularly given the biblical injunctions against the worship of idols. Many works of classical Greek and Roman sculpture that survive today bear the marks of defacement, presumably at the hands of the faithful. Indeed, the fervid opposition to idolatry eventually reached the point where some Christians condemned even the representation of Christ. In the eighth century, perhaps influenced by Islamic practice, a movement arose in the Byzantine Empire that succeeded in condemning the creation of images representing Christ or the saints. For a period of about a century, under the influence of this "iconoclastic" movement, religious images were removed from the patriarchal basilica of Hagia Sophia in Constantinople and from other churches in the empire.

By the middle of the ninth century, however, iconoclasm fell out of favor with the family of the Byzantine emperor, and the veneration of the holy icons was restored, an event that is commemorated still in the Orthodox Church by the annual celebration of the "Triumph of Orthodoxy." Like other churches throughout the empire, Hagia Sophia was once again decorated with magnificent depictions of Christ, the Virgin, and the various saints, but many of these representations were later vandalized or covered over, first by the Crusaders from the West at the start of the thirteenth century and finally by the Turks, who transformed the basilica into a mosque, in the middle of the fifteenth century. We noted earlier (p. 180) that the pagan Parthenon in Athens was similarly converted into a Christian church and then an Islamic mosque. In both cases these transformations helped to ensure the preservation, although in an altered state, of these irreplaceable monuments. It was not only buildings that were preserved in this way as the relics of Greek civilization fell into the hands, first of Christian then of Muslim conquerors. The most spectacular example of this is the Archimedes Palimpsest, whose sale at auction in 1998 and subsequent intensive examination have been widely covered in the media. A palimpsest is a text that is reused, by erasing or covering over an earlier script and then writing a new script over it. In the case of the Archimedes

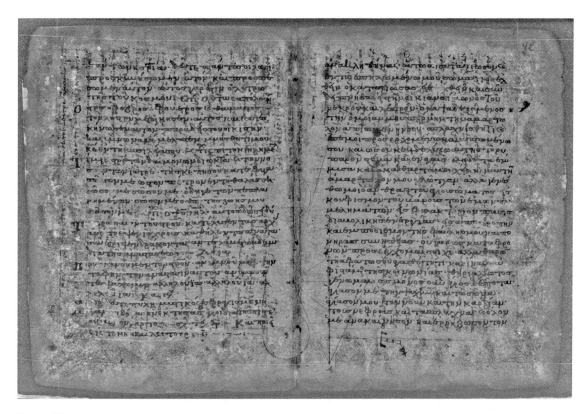

Figure 71   A Greek prayer book with its thirteenth-century text written at right angles over the tenth-century text and diagrams of a work of Archimedes, as revealed by advanced imaging techniques; copyright The Owner of the Archimedes Palimpsest.

Palimpsest, the older text was a collection of treatises by the third-century BC mathematical genius Archimedes of Syracuse, copied and illustrated with diagrams in the tenth century after Christ. The writing was done on parchment, also known as "vellum," that is, animal skin treated and prepared for use as a writing material. (The English word "parchment" is derived from the name of the city of Pergamum, famous for its library.) In subsequent centuries, interest in the rather abstruse and difficult writings of Archimedes faded, and the pages of these works were washed and reused around AD 1200 for the writing of a collection of devotional texts. Fortunately, it is now becoming possible, using multispectral imaging, to read the text of Archimedes that has been hidden from sight for nearly a thousand years (figure 71).

Christianity did not eliminate all traces of the pagan heritage, nor did it wish to. The Byzantine Empire, which lasted until Constantinople was captured by Ottoman Turks in 1453, was based upon a civilization that still preserved elements that could be traced with some pride to the early first millennium BC. The language of the Byzantine court and the Orthodox Church were still essentially the

"You are the brimstone that God rained down into the midst of Sodom and Gomorrah, Admah and Zeboim and Segor. You are the brimstone that served God's purposes; in the same way serve the purposes of me, _____, in regard to Ms _____. Do not allow her to get any rest or sleep until she comes to me and performs the secret rites of love sacred to Aphrodite." (From a collection of do-it-yourself magical spells contained on a Greek papyrus, *P. Osl.* 1, written in the fourth century after Christ)

language of Hellenistic Athens, and the rhetorical training of bishops and courtiers continued to be based upon techniques illustrated from Classical texts, which continued to be copied and read. A particularly interesting example of the recycling of Classical literature is the eleventh- or twelfth-century drama in verse entitled *The Passion of Christ*. This work is a "cento," or a patchwork quilt, made up entirely of elements pieced together from other works, about a third of it consisting of lines taken from fifth-century tragedy, mostly from Euripides. The anonymous author of this cento was taking to an extreme the practice of adapting the text of Greek tragedy for Christian purposes, a practice that is attested already in about AD 200. At that time, the Christian convert Clement of Alexandria wrote a work in which he put into the mouth of Christ some lines that Euripides had written to be spoken by the god Dionysus in his tragedy the *Bacchae*. The iconography of the new religion also was heavily indebted to the conventions that had been established by the pagan artists of Greece and Rome. For example, early Christian artists would portray Christ in the pose of a bearded philosopher transmitting his wisdom to his followers (figure 72; compare figure 70). Or works of art intended for a specifically Christian context might include representations of Orpheus (figure 73), who like Christ was credited with bringing the dead back to life, or the oriental sun god Sol Invictus (figure 74), whose commemorative festival day, December 25, was appropriated for use as Christ's birthday.

SARCOPHAGUS Literally "flesh-eating," a stone coffin, often embellished with sculptures or bearing inscriptions (figures 72 and 73).

Figure 72   Fragmentary marble SARCOPHAGUS, showing Christ (center) transmitting the law to Peter; 0.74 × 2.05 m, late fourth century AD. Rome, Museum of the Catacomb of St. Sebastian; photo: Pontificia Commissione di Archeologia Sacra.

Figure 73   Marble sarcophagus, with an inscription indicating that it was used as the last resting place for a Christian man, showing Orpheus playing the lyre; 0.59 × 2.17 m, middle of the third century AD. Ostia Antica, Museum, Inv. 1202; photo: Archivio Fotografico della Soprintendenza per i beni archeologici di Ostia.

Figure 74   Fresco in the Catacomb of Saints Peter and Marcellinus in Rome, showing the sun god Sol (center) driving his chariot through the heaven; early fourth century AD. Photo: Pontificia Commissione di Archeologia Sacra.

Even Christianity could not hold the two halves of the empire together, and a division opened up between the church in Rome and the church in Constantinople. Each church claimed (and claims) to be the true and legitimate bearer of the faith, just as the emperor in Rome and the emperor in Constantinople each claimed to be the true successor to Augustus, the founder of the Roman Empire. The emperor in Constantinople, however, was able to make that claim for nearly a millennium longer than his Western counterpart, for the empire based in Rome came to an end in the second half of the fifth century, when Germanic barbarians removed the emperor of Rome and ruled Italy in his place. Nearly a thousand years later, remnants of Greek culture were reintroduced to the West, when a number of scholars from Constantinople emigrated to Italy, bringing with them their books and their knowledge of the Greek language and contributing to the "revival of learn-ing" in thirteenth- and fourteenth-century Europe. One of the products of this revival was Lucas Cranach's painting of the judgment of Paris, with which we began (figure 1). In the East, however, there was no Renaissance, or re(dis)covery of Classical civilization. There was no need. Classical Greek civilization had never been lost or forgotten. Rather, it had been in the process of continual transformation, which is, indeed, the chief function of human culture, to allow a civilization to define itself in terms of continuity with the past at the same time as the past is being reconfigured to accommodate a changing present.

Recommended for Further Reading

Bowersock, G. W. *Hellenism in Late Antiquity* (Ann Arbor 1990): the publication of a wonderful series of lectures concerned with the survival of pagan Greek culture in the eastern part of the Christian Roman Empire.

Brown, P. *The World of Late Antiquity from Marcus Aurelius to Muhammad* (London 1971): the best general introduction to the late antique world, brilliantly written and well illustrated.

Cameron, A. *The Mediterranean World in Late Antiquity* AD 395–600 (London and New York 1993): a reliable guide to the history, society, and culture of the Roman Empire during the confused and confusing period from the division of the empire down to the time of Pope Gregory the Great.

Elsner, J. *Imperial Rome and Christian Triumph: The Art of the Roman Empire* AD 100–450 (Oxford and New York 1998): a dazzlingly illustrated account of Greek, Roman, and Christian art and how it functioned in the social and cultural life of the Roman Empire.

Jay, P. (ed.) *The Greek Anthology and Other Ancient Greek Epigrams: A Selection in Modern Verse Translations* (New York 1973): a very full selection of representative epigrams from the seventh century BC to the tenth century after Christ, in trans-lations by poets like Stephen Spender, Kenneth Rexroth, Ezra Pound, Christopher Logue, Tony Harrison, and Fleur Adcock.

Marcus Aurelius, *Meditations* (New York 2002): a meticulous and elegant transla-tion, by Gregory Hays, that was briefly a bestseller in Washington, DC (until, appar-ently, readers discovered that Marcus advocated the practice of virtue).

Mathews, T. F. *The Clash of Gods: A Reinterpretation of Early Christian Art* (Princeton 1993): an illuminating examination of the several ways in which the figure of Christ was depicted, between AD 250 and 550, under the influence of non-Christian iconography.

Netz, R. and Noel, W. *The Archimedes Codex: Revealing the Secrets of the World's Greatest Palimpsest* (London 2007): the astonishing story of the recovery of Archimedes' text, told by the director of the Archimedes Palimpsest Project and a brilliant historian of cognitive practices who is also a published poet.

Plutarch, *Greek Lives* (Oxford 1998) and Plutarch, *Roman Lives* (Oxford 1999): excellent translations by Robin Waterfield of many of the most interesting of Plutarch's Lives, with fine introductions and notes (but unfortunately omitting Plutarch's crucial comparisons).

Reardon, B. P. (ed.) *Collected Ancient Greek Novels* (Berkeley 1989): excellent, readable translations of the most accessible Greek writings that date from the first four centuries of the Roman Empire.

This book has been dedicated
to the memory of
Michael Ventris
July 12, 1922–September 6, 1956
and
Dennis Brain
May 17, 1921–September 1, 1957
who shared a destiny
and a destination

GLOSSARY

acropolis Literally "the highest point of the city," a rocky eminence sometimes used as the site of a citadel during Mycenaean times and later serving as the religious focal point of the polis from the Archaic Period onward; often used specifically to refer to the acropolis of Athens (figure 43).

aegis A divine attribute, usually worn by Athena on her chest (figure 64), represented as a Gorgon's head surrounded by scales or a fringe, which confers special powers on the wearer.

agora A centrally located open area of a polis where people could gather for political functions or for social and commercial purposes.

amphora A large, two-handled jar for storage of wine, olive oil or other liquids (figures 15, 16, 29–31, 33, and 42).

aristoi Literally "the best (men)," used to refer to the members of the leading landowning families of a polis and serving as the first element of the words "aristocrat" and "aristocracy."

aulos An oboe-like reed instrument, used as an accompaniment for sacrificial ritual, certain athletic activities, ELEGIAC poetry, and the advance of HOPLITES into battle (figures 25 and 26).

barbarian The term used by the Greeks to refer to any non-Greek, whose unintelligible speech was thought to resemble the nonsense syllables "bar-bar" from which the word was derived.

basileus (plural basileis) Originally the Mycenaean title referring to a man who held a position in the palace under the king, perhaps meaning something like "count" or "duke," a meaning that continued into the time of Homer and Hesiod; later used to refer to a foreign monarch, a Spartan king, or a Greek TYRANT.

dactylic hexameter A metrical form in which each line of verse is made up of six (Greek *hex*) dactyls (a unit consisting of one long syllable followed by one or two further syllables), a meter appropriate to epic poetry, prophecies given by the Delphic oracle, and other poetry of a serious or philosophical character (for example, the poems of Hesiod).

deme   A local territorial district, either a village or a neighborhood of a larger urban area; also, by extension, the inhabitants of the district.

elegiac   Referring to a metrical form consisting of couplets, the first line of which is a DACTYLIC HEXAMETER and the second is a shorter variant of the hexameter, used for funerary epigrams and for other small-scale poems, often composed for performance in the SYMPOSIUM.

epithet   An adjective or descriptive phrase indicating some quality or attribute which the speaker or writer regards as characteristic of the person or thing described, for example, "swift-footed" in the expression "swift-footed Achilles."

fresco   Painting in watercolor on a wall or ceiling whose mortar or plaster is still fresh and moist, so that the colors sink in and become more durable (figures 7 and 74).

frieze   A horizontal band of decoration, usually either painted or sculpted in RELIEF (figures 46–8 and 63–5).

Hellenodikai   Literally "assayers of Greeks," the title of the judges or umpires who were responsible for the organization and operation of the Olympic Games.

helot   One of a group who had been collectively enslaved by, and was owned by, an alien state (especially Sparta), as opposed to the more common type of slave, who was privately owned by an individual.

herm   A sculptural representation of a mortal or a divinity, usually the god Hermes (hence the name), in the form of a pillar surmounted by a head and furnished with genitals (figure 54).

hoplite   A heavily armed foot soldier, equipped with helmet, shield, spear, and body armor covering his torso and shins (figures 25 and 33).

hybris   Wanton behavior aimed at the humiliation of another person for the sole purpose of asserting one's own actual or imagined superiority in status, power, wealth, and so on.

iambic   Referring to a metrical form that was considered to approximate to the rhythm of ordinary speech, generally used in the Archaic Period for invective and satire, but later also used for epigram and other serious purposes, including the dialogue of drama.

intaglio   A figure or design carved into the flat surface of metal, stone, or other hard material, as opposed to carving in RELIEF.

kore (plural: **korai**)   An Archaic statue of a clothed young woman in a standing pose (figure 23).

kouros (plural: **kouroi**)   An Archaic statue of a naked young man in a standing pose (figure 22).

krater   A large, deep bowl for mixing wine with water (figure 52).

maenad   A woman inspired to ritual frenzy by the god Dionysus, often represented in the wilds of the countryside or mountains (figure 40).

nike   The Greek word for "victory," often capitalized (Nike) to refer to Victory personified as a beautiful goddess, usually winged (figure 64).

oligarchy   Literally "rule by the few," it denotes a type of government that, unlike democracy, excludes the majority of citizens from participation, generally restricting political power to a small number of wealthier citizens.

ostracism   The Athenian practice of holding an election, in which fragments of pottery (*ostraka*) were used as ballots (figure 38), to determine whether one prominent political figure should be removed from the polis for a 10-year period.

Panhellenic   Literally "referring to all (*pan-*) the Greeks (*Hellenes*)," often used in connection with the Panhellenic Festivals and Games, which were open to all Greeks and only to Greeks, or with reference to Panhellenism, the idea that what distinguishes Greeks from BARBARIANS outweighs what divides Greeks from one another.

papyrus   A marsh plant native to Egypt; also, the sheets used as a writing surface made by laying thin strips of the stem of the papyrus plant side by side, with another layer of similar strips crossing them, and usually a third layer again parallel to the first, the whole being then soaked in water, pressed together, and dried (figure 24).

pediment   The triangular area under the gabled roof, at either end of a Greek temple or similar structure (figure 45), often filled with RELIEF sculpture.

phalanx   A formation of heavily armed infantrymen (HOPLITES) drawn up in close order and carrying spears and overlapping shields (figure 25).

relief   Sculpture created in such a way that the figures project toward the viewer from a flat background (figure 46), as on most modern coins, in contrast to carving in INTAGLIO.

sarcophagus Literally "flesh-eating," a stone coffin, often embellished with sculptures or bearing inscriptions (figures 72 and 73).

satrap The title used to refer to the governor of a formal territorial subdivision (satrapy) of the Persian Empire.

satyr An imaginary creature appearing for the most part like a man but with some animal features (the tail, ears, or legs of a goat or a horse), who inhabits the wilds and has limitless appetites for wine and sex (figure 40).

sophist One of a number of specialists in higher education who traveled through the Greek world, beginning in the fifth century BC, giving public displays of their expertise and offering instruction in a variety of subjects, particularly formal oratory.

stele An upright stone slab, often carved in RELIEF and/or painted for use as a grave marker (figure 11).

stoa A long colonnaded hall, sometimes capitalized (Stoa) to refer to the Stoic school of philosophy, whose founder taught in the Stoa Poikile in Athens.

symposium Literally a "drinking together," a ritualized gathering of privileged males who, after dining together, drank wine mixed with water and entertained themselves with poetry, music, games, and sexual activity (figure 26).

terracotta Lightly fired, unglazed ceramic clay used for decorative tiles, architectural decorations, statuary, vases, and so on (figure 51).

tripod A pot or cauldron resting on three legs, often presented as a prize or as a votive offering (figure 18).

trireme The standard warship of the Greeks during the Classical Period, which used sail for long passages but was rowed into battle by oarsmen arranged in three rows, one above the other (figure 35).

trittys (plural: **trittyes**) One of 30 units into which the population of Attica was divided by Cleisthenes in 508 BC, with one trittys from each of the three geographical divisions (city, coast, and inland) combining to constitute one of the 10 tribes created by Cleisthenes (figure 37 and map 11).

tyrant One of a number of usurpers who, beginning in the middle of the seventh century BC, seized autocratic power in a polis and established (or attempted to establish) a hereditary monarchy.

INDEX

Note: page numbers in italic denote illustrations, maps, or boxed text